Management for Profession

The Springer series *Management for Professionals* comprises high-level business and management books for executives. The authors are experienced business professionals and renowned professors who combine scientific background, best practice, and entrepreneurial vision to provide powerful insights into how to achieve business excellence.

More information about this series at http://www.springer.com/series/10101

Daniel R. A. Schallmo • Joseph Tidd
Editors

Digitalization

Approaches, Case Studies, and Tools
for Strategy, Transformation and
Implementation

 Springer

Editors
Daniel R. A. Schallmo
Neu-Ulm University of Applied Sciences
Neu-Ulm, Germany

Joseph Tidd
SPRU
University of Sussex
Brighton, UK

ISSN 2192-8096   ISSN 2192-810X   (electronic)
Management for Professionals
ISBN 978-3-030-69382-4   ISBN 978-3-030-69380-0   (eBook)
https://doi.org/10.1007/978-3-030-69380-0

This Springer imprint is published by the registered company Springer Nature Switzerland AG.
The registered company address is: Gewerbestrasse 11, 6330 Cham, Switzerland

Editorial Board

Preface

Digitalization affects all sectors of society, particularly economies. At the same time, digitalization opens new networking possibilities and enables cooperation between different actors, who, for example, exchange data and, thus, initiate processes. In this context, digitalization has several aspects, e.g., measurement of digital maturity, digital strategy, digital transformation, and digital implementation.

This special issue delivers empirical and conceptual papers and studies that tackle the challenges and opportunities presented by digitalization. We have arranged the contributions in five parts: Digital Drivers, Digital Maturity, Digital Strategy, Digital Transformation, and Digital Implementation.

Digital Drivers and Digital Maturity addresses the question of what drivers exist for digitalization and how such drivers can be identified and evaluated. It also clarifies what digital maturity is and how it can be evaluated. Included contributions are (1) "Unchartered Territories—Treat your innovation as a disaster," a literature review and conceptual framework; (2) "Future-oriented technology analysis—A classification framework" based on a systematic literature review; (3) "Digital technologies for circular business models in the building industry, classification of conceptual framework," which includes a case study analysis; (4) "The impact of the novel coronavirus outbreak on the development of digital economy in commodity countries," a literature review and comparative analysis; (5) "Digital maturity models—A systematic literature review"; (6) "An approach for a digital maturity model for SMEs based on their requirements" based on a systematic literature review and action research; and (7) "Developing strategies for digital transformation in SMEs with maturity models."

Based on digital drivers and the digital maturity of a company, digital strategy development is an integral part of a company's activities. Although many companies have recognized the need for a digital strategy, developing that strategy in a structured way and integrating individual digitization efforts into a strategic concept still presents challenges. Companies often lack clarity regarding which direction to take with respect to their digital strategy and which general principles and options to apply.

A digital strategy is the strategic form of a company's digitization intentions. The short- and mid-term objectives are to create new or maintain competitive advantages.

Within the digital strategy, digital technologies and methods are applied to products, services, processes, and business models. To develop a digital strategy, the company and its environment have to be analyzed as a basis for several future scenarios. The digital strategy consists of a vison, mission, strategic objectives, strategic success factors, values, and measures. It also includes the design of ecosystems and networks.

Part digital strategies includes the following contributions: (1) "Same but different—An exploration of alternative business model disruptions across German industries" based on a qualitative analysis, keyword analysis, and literature review; (2) "Productivity paradox in digital innovation for SMEs—A participatory inquiry" based on action research; (3) "Five topics for which industry needs innovation managers—A job advertisement analysis," which includes a qualitative examination of job advertisements in Germany; (4) "Connecting the corporate brain: How digital platforms accelerate digital transformation and cultural change," which includes survey data of listed companies' corporate incubators; and (5) "Development process for smart service strategies problem structuring to enable innovation in business IT projects" based on case study research.

The digital transformation of business models is conducted on a tactical level. This digital transformation concerns itself with individual business model elements, the entire business model, value chains, and the networking of different actors into a value network. It serves to define the digital strategy more clearly within business models. It is based on an approach with a sequence of tasks and decisions that are logically and temporally related to each other.

In this part, we address the following contributions: (1) "Systematic review of the literature on SME digitalization—Multi-sided pressure on existing SMEs"; (2) "Identifying barriers for digital transformation in public sector," which includes a case study as a basis for a constructivist grounded approach and a qualitative research method; (3) "Crisis-driven digital transformation—Examining the online university triggered by COVID-19" with an explorative case study; (4) "Selecting, combining, and cultivating digital deep-tech ecosystems," applying an explorative early stage action research process; and (5) "The pro-poor digitalization canvas— Shaping innovation towards SDGs 1 & 10" based on focus groups, expert interviews, and literature review.

Within the digital implementation, the digital strategy is implemented, and the digital transformation of business model is supported. In general, the following areas are relevant for digital implementation: Organization (e.g., definition of structures and responsibilities, establishment of departments, and the definition of processes); technical implementation (e.g., use of sensors, creation of databases, and networking of components), skills (e.g., IT know-how, use of collaboration tools, development of leadership and collaboration skills, and acquisition of methods), and culture (e.g., cultural anchoring in the company, sensitization of employees, and communication within the company).

This part includes the following contributions: (1) "Digital needs diversity— Innovation and digital leadership from a female managers' perspective" based on a literature review and semi-structured interviews; (2) "Developing creative leaders learner's reflections on methodology and pedagogy," which includes a literature review and experiential learning cycle theory with empirical study in qualitative design; (3) "An integrated approach to digital implementation—TOSC-model and DPSEC-circle" based on a literature review and the development of their own approach; (4) "Challenges, lessons and methods for developing values-based intrapreneurial culture" with several case studies; (5) "A practitioner-oriented toolkit to foster sustainable product innovation" with a case study survey examining a set of 196 consumer product innovations; (6) "Success factors when implementing innovation teams" based on interviews and the observation of real life innovation teams; and (7) "Fly the flag—How to innovate management practices for the best in the world" based on the design thinking approach.

We hope that this special issue stimulates an intensive discussion among scientists, lecturers, and students from the fields of digitalization, digital strategy, digital transformation, and digital implementation and that the contents are used in research and teaching. Our aim is that practitioners from the areas of management, strategic planning, and business development can apply the insights to successfully practice digitalization and, thus, take advantage of its potential within their business model or an industry.

The editors would also like to thank the team of Springer and everyone who was involved in the typesetting and design. In particular, we would like to thank Mr. Prashanth Mahagaonkar and Ms. Ramya Prakash from Springer and our research assistant at the University of Applied Sciences Neu-Ulm, Mr. Daniel Hasler, for their valuable input and their willingness to be at our side with advice and action at any time.

On behalf of all authors, we wish the readers of the compilation a great deal of knowledge and success in their work on digitalization.

Neu-Ulm, Germany   Daniel R. A. Schallmo
Sussex, UK   Joe Tidd
December 2020

Contents

Part I

Digital Drivers

Unchartered Territories: Treat Your Innovation as a Disaster

Mattia Vettorello, Boris Eisenbart, and Charlie Ranscombe

1   Introduction

The complexity of today's society is exponentially growing and requires firms to generate new processes to approach and deliver innovation. Organizations have to transform how they conduct business venturing and produce innovation toward a more adaptable and anticipatory practice (Landoni et al. 2016). In addition to this, organizations should become more futures literate in order to deal with complex dynamics (UNESCO n.d.). In such situations, there are uncertainties around risk evaluation, possible consequences, and long-term implications of decision-making (Lipshitz and Strauss 1997; Brunsson 1985; Kahneman et al. 1982; Corbin 1980). Scholars define two classifications for uncertainty: the first relates to whether or not the longed-for outcome will materialize. The second classification, also known as *ambiguity*, regards the lack of information regarding the probabilities of a desired outcome to occur (Liu and Colman 2009; Frisch and Baron 1988; Curely et al. 1986; Ellsberg 1961). Such decision instances where outcomes are uncertain and there is ambiguity of probabilities are commonly classified as *extreme uncertainties* (Diebold et al. 2010) The lack of information and extreme uncertainty are inhibitors of effective choice (Shane 2009; Teece 2007; Camerer and Weber 1992; Tversky and Kahneman 1974; Sherman 1974) and can cause bias in decisions (Dobelli 2013; Baron 1998; Kahneman and Tversky 1979, 1981; Tversky and Kahneman 1974). Similarly, the *analysis paralysis* bias, which is known for obstructing people to make a clear decision due to the many uncertainties (The Economist 2020; Snowden and Boone 2007) or the *confirmation bias*, which is the tendency to base decisions on previous experience that resulted in success (Dobelli 2013; Tversky and Kahneman 1974). These can also be described as the *framing bias, forecast illusion,* and *availability heuristic.* In order to overcome the lack of information and these biases,

M. Vettorello (✉) · B. Eisenbart · C. Ranscombe
Swinburne University of Technology, Hawthorn, VIC, Australia
e-mail: mvettorello@swin.edu.au

© The Author(s), under exclusive license to Springer Nature Switzerland AG 2021   3
D. R. A. Schallmo, J. Tidd (eds.), *Digitalization*, Management for Professionals,
https://doi.org/10.1007/978-3-030-69380-0_1

crisis-driven innovation demands new organizational capabilities such as the ability to think in a future-oriented manner, to be comfortable with uncertainties, to scan for weak signals, to make sense of the future, and to deaverage the organization portfolio (See also Reeves et al. 2020; Vettorello et al. 2019; Dong et al. 2016). Larsen et al. (2020) describe future thinking as the ability to generate assumptions about the future and to observe extreme uncertainties as opportunities to discover, rather than constraints or barriers to overcome.

In response to environments of rapid and unexpected change, organizations then have to shift their practices to manage innovation and focus on developing these new dynamic capabilities to support decision-making, which are a viable competitive advantage in the long term (See also Teece 2011; Xu et al. 2007; Assink 2006; Verganti 2003; Eisenhardt and Martin 2000; Pesendorfer 1995; Dumas and Mintzberg 1991). For this, inspiration may come from Disaster Management (DM) because of its nature to deal with unforeseen occurrences and decision-making under extreme uncertainty. Interestingly, Tighe (2019) presents analogies between IM and instances of emergency (i.e., situation of high-risk and uncertainty) (See also Ardeshir and Jahangiri 2018; Neale and Weir 2015; Walker et al. 2013; Bell 2002). These are summarized as:

- Involve multidisciplinary experts
- Deal with emergencies and system
- Deal with people
- Have phases
- Deal with extreme uncertainty

By exploring the DM literature, we have observed that foresight theory and hypothesizing scenarios have been used effectively for many years in supporting strategic decision-making during operation management in disastrous events (Kauffman 1994). Whether prior to or during a disastrous event, this entails characteristics such as readiness in case something suddenly changes (for example, wind carries chemical and chances direction), time-to-action (for example, acting quickly and sharply because "plans/consequences" have already been hypothesized), opportunity and weak-signals scan (e.g., scanning a particular environment/cause to generate anticipatory actions) (Ardeshir and Jahangiri 2018; Neale and Weir 2015; Walker et al. 2013; Bell 2002). Thus, by researching future thinking/abductive reasoning and contingency planning in DM and their correlation with innovation processes, this chapter seeks to add insight to the IM literature by proposing an approach to operationalize capabilities such as future thinking, being comfortable with uncertainties, weak signals scanning and sense-making of those. We propose the *Future-Led Innovation (FLI)* framework as a tool for reasoning. The proposed framework aims to stimulate future thinking and hypothesizing, contingency mapping, alertness to changes, and call-to-action to shape future-ready innovations. By doing so, organizations can drive innovation in a more deliberate and target-oriented manner in situations characterized by extreme uncertainty—as is the case in DM. The main contribution of FLI is in hypothesizing and contingency mapping. These entail the generation of future scenarios and abducting innovation roadmaps (thinking for contingency) to connect the present to the future (Vettorello et al. 2020). This in turn gives richer hypotheses and can guide strategic decision-making in situations of extreme uncertainty, high risks, and eventually reduce the analysis paralysis bias (See also Kleinsmann et al. 2017; Cross 2011; Dorst 2011; Brown 2009; Kelly 2005). Scholars such as Dong et al. (2015, 2016) and Kolko (2010) suggest that abductive reasoning and the action of thinking about "what might be" (rather than "what is") increases the likelihood of innovation in high-risk and high-performance scenarios. The reason being this is proactive thinking that requires hypothesizing preferable future-states and consequently orient actions to design toward it. By doing this, undesired consequences and external factors must be taken into consideration in outlining innovation strategic trajectories as elements to avoid in achieving that very vision. Inayatullah (2008) also indicates companies that look into alternative futures can plan for adjustments as uncertainties unfold. On this note and strictly related to DM, Kunz et al. (2014) advise that investing in preparedness capabilities—being ready, planning for, and knowing what to do in case something changes—results in lead time reduction of up to 67%. This means conscious actions are taken faster and more accurately. Transferring this to innovation and IM could mean that by being ready for unforeseen events—for example, new entrants, new technologies, or political change—organizations and innovation managers can evaluate the scenario at hand more easily and create flexibility by representations or proximity of alternatives. This would thus contribute to increasing dynamic capability.

The remainder of this chapter presents the procedural thinking behind DM as a source of inspiration. Learnings on how to manage a crisis are mapped to IM to improve dynamic capability to tackle complexity, unforeseen events, increase preparedness, and leverage flexibility that are significant elements of IM. In other words, it is recommended to roadmap innovation by hypothesizing scenarios and consequences in order to increase preparedness and enhance performance. Section 2 highlights the learning from DM with a focus on the effectiveness of developing strategic innovation roadmaps. Starting from the comparison between DM and IM, Sect. 3 provides a reason why future thinking is an important innovation capability to seize opportunity and tolerate uncertainty. Then, Sect. 4 focuses on the definition of abductive reasoning and connects DM into IM, thus presenting the proposed future-oriented approach and the argument for the positive impact of thinking about "what might be" during decision-making. Conclusions and further work are presented in Sect. 5.

2 Disaster Management: A Source of Inspiration for Innovation

Nowadays, we are observing a drastic change all over the globe (i.e., large-scale migration, nonstop urbanization, climate change, and pandemic) which results in a higher degree of danger, unknown consequences, and uncontrollability influencing the economy and humanity. In the context of innovation, extreme uncertainties rise significantly for organizations as the society has dramatically change work- and lifestyle, and therefore needs (Harari 2020). As we investigate DM, we observe similarities with IM in the need of managing uncertainties:

- Both DM and IM entail aspects of being prepared for the unknown future, which is likely to rely on or at least benefit from foresight techniques (Tighe 2019; Ardeshir and Jahangiri 2018).
- And both must address risks associated with that possible scenarios and probabilities of knowns/unknown consequences to occur (Lipshitz and Strauss 1997; Brunsson 1985; Kahneman et al. 1982; Corbin 1980).

Parallels of Anticipatory Practice

We built our analysis on extent literature that focuses on the application of foresight methods, frameworks and tools to DM (Jahangiri et al. 2017; Turoff et al. 2013, 2015; Watson et al. 2015; Lopez-Silva et al. 2015; McAllum and Egerton 2014; Aubrecht et al. 2013; Birkmann et al. 2013; Constantinides 2013; FEMA 2013; Beddington and McLean 2012; Prochazkova et al. 2012; Hellmuth et al. 2011; Scawthorn et al. 2006). In DM, whether in an instance of prevention from or in a situation of recovering from a disastrous event, possible damages are likely to be anticipated and dramatic consequences are reduced or fully mitigated. Pinkowski (2008, p. xxi) succinctly summarizes the benefit of future thinking in DM:

> Even if we cannot control all of the causes of disasters, we can prepare and respond based on the present state of development in the science of disaster management.

In order to prepare a response to unfolding circumstances, scenario planning is used by DM teams to quickly generate immediate alternative futures while taking into consideration as many cause–effects as possible (Turoff et al. 2013, 2015; FEMA 2013; Birkmann et al. 2013). This requires to rapidly formulate mental contingent scenarios that inform decision-making in high-stake and highly uncertain situations. As a witnessed example, during the COVID-19, suddenly unexpected behaviors have happened causing significant consequences—i.e., evacuating "red zone" causing a quicker spread of the virus or simply hoarding essential goods. These "unforeseen" circumstances could have been thought a priori, the DM teams could have proactively taken actions and adjust them as uncertainties unfold. In IM, foresight is intended to give richer information about "what an idea might be" and influence decision-making. For example, Firm A is pursuing an innovative idea. While still in the development phase, a competitor, Firm B, launches a product that fulfills the same need ending in occupying that market. Yet, because Firm A has already hypothesized different futures, they can quickly realign the innovation trajectory of that very idea. This analogy permits to determine how in both situations initially we work on one aspect, healthcare crisis, and business opportunity, respectively, but then changes of circumstances require adapting direction and adjustment of strategy.

The use of future thinking and anticipatory practices, therefore, influences decision-making as successful ideas are unlikely to not be dropped out. This refers to what Mounarath et al. (2011) call Type-I Error. In such decision situations, projects are rejected based on an underestimation of their potential success and not pushed forward to the next phase. Underestimating is also affected by the lack of analytical information, which halts decision-maker in paralysis. However, these ideas contain many potentials and are likely to yield successful business opportunities. With respect to anticipatory practice, as early as 1995, Martin (1995) lists four elements of anticipation and realignment that are of interest in this context of crisis-driven innovation: pre-foresight, foresight, post-foresight (consequent assessment), and implementation evaluation. He highlights different stages of foresight. As certainties come to light and there is a need to strategically readjusting the before taken trajectory. Simply put, developing contingency models aid strategic realignment and time-to-action due to representativeness or proximity of alternatives. As parallels related to the need for future thinking and contingency planning are drawn between DM and IM, we now focus on integrating these into IM dynamic capabilities.

3   Strategic Foresight as a Dynamic Capability in Crisis-Driven Innovation

Teece and Pisano define dynamic capabilities as (1994, p. 538):

> The term "dynamic" refers to the shifting character of the environment; certain strategic responses are required when time-to-market and timing is critical, the pace of innovation accelerating, and the nature of future competition and markets difficult to determine. The term "capabilities" emphasises the key role of strategic management in appropriately adapting, integrating and reconfiguring internal and external organisational skills, resources, and functional competences toward changing environment.

From this definition and related literature, it is possible to infer that dynamic capabilities required an ability at the individual and the organization level to deal well with the exposure to exogenous change, uncertainty, and unforeseen events. As described above, we read how future thinking is a significant capability to have in DM. It supports navigating uncertainty and unknown in decision-making instances. Drawing from DM parallels, Table 1 highlights in bold the "dimension" considered fundamental to foster innovation and embrace proactiveness, uncertainty, and risks. It is noted however that future thinking and contingency mapping lack mentions in the list.

Assink (2006) and Francis and Bessant (2005) define innovation capabilities to be an aptitude or a driving force to explore new ideas, to understand and calculate risks of investment. Furthermore, uncertainties should be seen as opportunities rather than not considering them or becoming inhibited by them (Larsen et al. 2020; Fayolle

Table 1 Innovation dynamic capabilities

Level	Characteristic	Dimension
Individual	Personality	*Tolerance of ambiguity*; *Self-confidence*; *Openness to experience*; *Unconventionality*; Originality; Rule governed (negative relation); Authoritarianism (negative relation); *Independence*; *Proactivity*
	Motivation	Intrinsic (vs. extrinsic); *Determination to succeed*; Personal initiative
	Cognitive ability	*Above average general intellect*; Task-specific knowledge; Divergent thinking style; Ideational fluency
	Job characteristics	*Autonomy*; Span of control; Job demands; Previous job dissatisfaction; *Support for innovation*; Mentor guidance; Appropriate training
	Mood states	Negative moods
Team	Structure	Minority influence; Cohesiveness; Longevity
	Climate	Participation; *Vision*; *Norms for innovation*; Conflict; *Constructive controversy*
	Membership	Heterogeneity; Education level
	Processes	*Reflexivity*; Minority dissent; Integration skills; *Decision-making style*
	Leadership style	Democratic style; Participative style; *Openness to idea proposals*; Leader–member exchange; Expected evaluation
Organization	Structure	Specialization; Centralization (negative relation); Formalization (negative relation); *Complexity*; Stratification (negative relation)
	Strategy	*"Prospector" type*
	Size	Number of employees; Market share (negative relation)
	Resources	Annual turnover; Slack resources
	Culture	Support for experimentation; *Tolerance of idea failure*; *Risk-taking norms*

Source: Adopted from Anderson et al. (2004)

et al. 2014). As the world becomes more complex and interconnected (Chesbrough 2003; Rothwell 1992), Hunt (2019, p. 127) states:

> To design in the context of complex system one must be attuned to the perverse and unintended consequences that might emerge. It is not a question of taming or solving the unknowns but modelling how they may play out and anticipating widely divergent futures. Designing to solve complex system is impossible. But that doesn't mean we shouldn't strive to model heuristically their tendencies, potentialities and misbehaviours.

In IM, organizations have to adapt to and explore the changing environment through technological, geopolitical, organizational, and strategic lenses (Helfat et al. 2007). In support of this, Tighe (2019) suggests the need to conduct an analysis of drivers—usually developed from STEEPLE: Social, Technological, Economic, Environmental (natural), Political, Legal, and Ethical factors—to inform the scenario planning. Noticeably, there are several instances that can enable innovation, and having solid dynamic capabilities is likely to support firms to improve the innovation process. This is highly analogous to the DM literature where people are encouraged to look at uncertainties, unknowns, and risks, and hypothesize alternative scenarios. In other words, people in DM have to be comfortable with ambiguity and not knowing likely or unlikely consequences. This is further supported by Eisenhardt and Martin (2000) who add to the above definition the importance of preparedness. The ability to be ready if an unexpected occurrence happens. Additionally, Flyvbjerg et al. (2009) state that in IM culture there is a lack of incentives to seek out uncertainties and risks. People strive for certainty. While in DM looking for uncertainty is essential to generate possible consequential scenarios upon which strategic decisions are made. Interestingly, *tolerance for ambiguity* is discussed in IM literature as the most pertinent to drive innovation (Barron and Harrington 1981, see Table 1) as well as in DM. Eisenhardt and Martin (2000), and Teece (2007) take a strong position toward the benefit that dynamic capabilities bring to an organization that has the knowledge and resources to handle them. Future thinking can be supportive in situations of uncertainty, complexity, and decision-making. In very high-velocity markets, recognizing changes has become very challenging and arduous due to the non-linearity or unpredictability of uncertainty. Different studies (i.e., Dong et al. 2016; Wally and Baum 1994; Judge and Miller 1991; Eisenhardt 1989) show that creating multiple alternatives—which are also supported by real-time information—results in an increase of successful strategic decision-making in high-velocity market and extreme uncertainty. In this discourse, we focus on the individual level to introduce the cognitive aspect of abductive reasoning. This is centered on the ability to think diversely and generate alternatives in situations of extreme uncertainty and possibly harsh consequences. In order words, future thinking helps mapping changes and working around them in order to influence the hypothesized future (Bishop and Hines 2012). The next section elaborates on this combining with the learnings from DM literature and dynamic capability suggesting FLI framework to drive innovation in times of great uncertainties.

4   Introducing the Future-Led Innovation Framework

So far, we have explored the DM literature and the effectiveness of hypothesizing alternative scenarios to support making decisions on where and how to plan/act for emergencies. We have also looked at the definition and classifications of dynamic capabilities. Noticing that foresight is not mentioned as a dynamic capability in IM, we now want to close that gap and operationalize this thinking. We focus on how to transfer *abductive reasoning* which is known as per inference and hypothesis (Kolko 2010) to the dynamic capabilities to drive innovation and support decision-making. Reasoning is an individual skill that helps individuals make sense of the surroundings by observing and validating assumptions (Walton 1990). Guenther et al. (2017, p. 392) states:

Fig. 1 Abductive reasoning (adapted from Dorst 2011)

> Abductive reasoning relies on mental capabilities that are also inherent to creativity [...]
> Both creativity and abductive reasoning aim to produce something novel for the future,
> i.e. something that does not exist yet in the market place in a similar form or proliferation.

Abductive reasoning, therefore, can actively support the generation of hypotheses and make sense of complex situations, the result of which is a better consideration and preparedness of alternatives future chain of actions (Vettorello et al. 2019; Voros 2017; Hiltunen 2010; Alstyne 2010). Following on Inayatullah's (2008) statement that embracing alternative thinking is beneficial to a discovery action, van der Duin and den Hartigh (2009) suggest that future thinking should be knowingly integrated in the design innovation process. Hence, an individual decides a most conforming and meaningful solution until new evidence is brought to discussion which consequently increases certainty (Dong et al. 2016). Maher and Poon (1996) inform how important it is to utilize gained evidence to adapt the trajectory throughout the design journey. This is also featuring in DM as evaluation and decision on the next actions to take are based on high stake and high uncertainty (Ardeshir and Jahangiri 2018). It is literally an explorative process where a certain comfort dealing with uncertainty and risk is required (Vettorello et al. 2019: Maher et al. 1996). Dorst (2011) supports sharing with the community that a *value* is the source of alternative generation and it is used as a guide/metric to make decisions (See also Dong et al. 2015). Dorst (2011) continues to suggest that organizations have to seek innovative approaches to resolve the algorithm (see Fig. 1).

The intricacy of this argumentation is that there is not a clear answer to what to create and this complexity is very related to designerly way of thinking (Roozenburg and Eekels 1995; Roozenburg 1993). In abductive reasoning, a hypothesis is generated to describe the process as per achieving the end-value, which does not exist yet (Vettorello et al. 2019). It is a desired state (i.e., in a disaster the end-value is to minimize and reduce to null the adverse event; in innovation, it is to generate novel solutions that solve [humanity] needs and give competitive advantage). In this scenario, the context in which the outcome is formed and the vehicles to accomplish it are "obscure" (Dorst 2011). For Roozenburg (1993), innovative abduction (abductive reasoning) is the most and only appropriate way of reasoning in design. Kolko (2010) in unison with Dorst (2011) and Dong et al. (2015) state that abductive reasoning allows for the generation of new knowledge through dealing with uncertainty and unknowns. And likely to induction—the result is known or at least expected, however the mechanisms to achieve that outcome are unknown to the individual—the aspired value may not be reached even though the premises were true. There is a clear link that in IM and DM there is a need to deal with uncertainty and generate hypotheses considering the current scenarios and exogenous elements

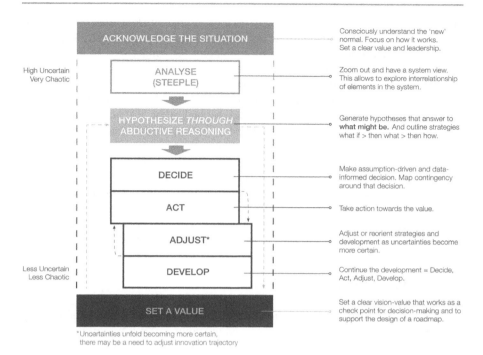

Fig. 2 Future-led innovation framework

that could positively or negatively affect the decision and create undesired consequences. The creation of possible trajectories indeed can help innovation managers to prepare them and the business for what might be. This anticipatory exercise to develop trajectories becomes an asset that is likely to increase adaptability, tolerance for ambiguity, and preparedness. Foresight is used in disaster management to identify possible future risks and generate likely consequences, which are often ignored in IM (Ardeshir and Jahangiri 2018; Flyvbjerg et al. 2009). IM is lacking in this type of contingent thinking (Reeves et al. 2016) and there are no strict incentives in the extent literature to include it (Flyvbjerg et al. 2009) as opposed to DM where by looking at undesirable consequences there is a higher chance to anticipate harsh consequences and increase the number of lives saved. As a result, what we call to be the *Future-Led Innovation* framework (FLI, see Fig. 2) is likely to support innovation managers reasoning through the design process in decision-making under extreme uncertainty. The FLI is a framework to facilitate the generation of alternatives (as emphasized by Dong et al. 2015, 2016; Kolko 2010). It allows flexibility as uncertainties unfold as the idea is moved forward in the developing process and builds for trajectory change when ideas do not work out as planned.

The FLI framework is suggested to design for innovation (as emphasized by Dong et al. 2015; Dorst 2011; Kolko 2010; Roozenburg 1993), scan the broader system (as emphasized by Tighe 2019; Eisenhardt and Martin 2000), generate hypotheses of new product development (as emphasized by Dong et al. 2015, 2016; Kolko 2010), increase adaptability (as emphasized by Kuosa 2016; Pinkowski 2008), and incentivize the tolerance for ambiguity (as emphasized by Barron and Harrington 1981), decisions are therefore based on short- and long-term strategy. It also asks and infers the development of a culture of innovation (see also Anderson et al. 2004). The innovation manager should analyze the ideas and mentally hypothesize in terms of what these ideas could be and what the consequences and interactions within the eco-system could be as an innovation chain reaction. This will inform possible future actions, the strategy to pursue, or indeed flexibly adapt the strategy. In addition, as a way to reduce the "time-to-action," this mental generation could be transferred in written form. Foresight then will enter the dynamic capability list because it is meant to increase agility, at the individual and at organizational level, enhancing future thinking, in turn inviting individuals to embrace uncertainty and seek for them in order to generate competitive advantage. Finally, we contend that this could further reduce analysis paralysis.

5 Discussion and Conclusion

In this chapter, we bring forward the impact of future thinking on decision-making under extreme uncertainties, high-stakes, and unknowns. DM is a source of inspiration for contributing to the IM literature where we combine knowledge of the former in the latter. The review highlights analogies between DM and IM hypothesizing how DM might support readiness in fast-paced environment and strategic decision-making. The FLI framework expands on current literature by integrating current IM knowledge and practices (i.e., Dong et al. 2015, 2016; Dorst 2011; Kolko 2010; Assink 2006; Barron and Harrington 1981) with new contributions as per abductive reasoning and continency mapping. Our aim was to explore a discipline that deals with crisis, emergency, and fast-changing circumstances. As societal complexity rises, it is no longer enough to focus on an individual innovation opportunity, but now it is necessary to manage the whole portfolio (Kahneman and Lovallo 1993). The ultimate desired dynamic state for an organization is to manage complexity, processes, and agility (Keim 2011). The framework is offered to any organization wishing to innovate, but more specifically to innovation managers. The FLI framework is thus more likely to guide to more accurate decisions around new ideas and take into account risks, unknowns, and uncertainty, to ultimately foster innovation. Biases can be mitigated and uncertainty can be reduced by hypothesizing future states and abducting pathways to reach said states. Specifically, *analysis paralysis* and *confirmation bias*. Organizations and managers should firstly acknowledge the situation which allows help evaluation and alertness of the context. It should be noted that this chapter is limited to crisis-related topics and that the suggested framework is based on a literature review. Future research, therefore, is targeted to substantiate this analogy by bringing more evidence from DM experts, evaluate the FLI framework, and test its effectiveness as a way to better inform innovation managers in the process of decision-making. We thusly offer as a conclusion that future thinking steps in the FLI framework should enter the dynamic capability list as a means to support design and decision-making processes.

References

Alstyne, G. V. (2010). How we learned to pluralize the future: Foresight scenarios as design thinking. In *Creating desired futures: How design thinking innovates business* (pp. 69–92). https://doi.org/10.1515/9783034611398.69.

Anderson, N., Dreu, C. K. W. D., & Nijstad, B. A. (2004). The routinization of innovation research: A constructively critical review of the state-of-the-science. *Journal of Organisational Behaviour, 25*(2), 147–173. https://doi.org/10.1002/job.236.

Ardeshir, S. M., & Jahangiri, K. (2018). Towards a customized foresight model on "disaster risk management" in developing countries. *Foresight: The Journal of Futures Studies, Strategic Thinking and Policy, 20*(5), 467–487.

Assink, M. (2006). Inhibitors of disruptive innovation capability: A conceptual model. *European Journal of Innovation Management, 9*, 215–233.

Aubrecht, C., Dilek, O., Klerx, J., & Freire, S. (2013). Future-oriented activities as a concept for improved disaster risk management. *Disaster Advances, 6*(12), 1–10.

Baron, R. A. (1998). Cognitive mechanisms in entrepreneurship: Why and when entrepreneurs think differently than other people. *Journal of Business Venturing, 13*(4), 275–294. https://doi.org/10.1016/S0883-9026(97)00031-1.

Barron, F., & Harrington, D. M. (1981). Creativity, intelligence, and personality. *Annual Review of Psychology, 32*(1), 439–476.

Beddington, J., & McLean, A. (2012). *Reducing risks of future disasters priorities for decision makers*. London: Government Office for Science.

Bell, W. (2002). What do we mean by futures studies? In *New thinking for a new millennium* (pp. 17–39). New York: Routledge.

Birkmann, J., Cutter, S. L., Rothman, D. S., Welle, T., Garschagen, M., Ruijven, B., & Cardona, O. D. (2013). Scenarios for vulnerability: Opportunities and constraints in the context of climate change and disaster risk. *Climatic Change, 1*, 1–16.

Bishop, P. C., & Hines, A. (2012). *Teaching about the future*. New York: Palgrave Macmillan.

Brown, T. (2009). *Change by design: How design thinking transforms organisations and inspires innovation*. New York: HarperCollins.

Brunsson, N. (1985). *The irrational organization*. Chichester: Wiley.

Camerer, C., & Weber, M. (1992). Recent developments in modeling preferences: Uncertainty and ambiguity. *Journal of Risk and Uncertainty, 5*(4), 325–370.

Chesbrough, H. W. (2003). *Open innovation: The new imperative for creating and profiting from technology*. Boston: Harvard Business School Press.

Constantinides, P. (2013). The failure of foresight in crisis management: A secondary analysis of the Mari disaster. *Technological Forecasting and Social Change, 80*(9), 1657–1673.

Corbin, R. M. (1980). Decisions that might not get made. In T. Wallsten (Ed.), *Cognitive processes in choice and decision behavior* (pp. 47–67). Hillsdale, NJ: Erlbaum.

Cross, N. (2011). *Design thinking: Understanding how designers think and work*. Oxford: Berg Publishers.

Curley, S. P., Yates, J. F., & Abrams, R. A. (1986). Psychological sources of ambiguity avoidance. *Organizational Behavior and Human Decision Processes, 38*(2), 230–256.

Diebold, F. X., Doherty, N. A., & Herring, R. J. (2010). *The known, the unknown, and the unknowable in financial risk management measurement and theory advancing practice*. Princeton, NJ: Princeton University Press.

Dobelli, R. (2013). *The art of thinking clearly*. New York: HarperCollins.

Dong, A., Garbuio, M., & Lovallo, D. (2016). Generative sensing in design evaluation. *Design Studies, 45*, 68–91. https://doi.org/10.1016/j.destud.2016.01.003.

Dong, A., Lovallo, D., & Mounarath, R. (2015). The effect of abductive reasoning on concept selection decisions. *Design Studies, 37*, 37–58.

Dorst, K. (2011). The core of 'design thinking' and its application. *Design Studies, 32*(6), 521–532. https://doi.org/10.1016/j.destud.2011.07.006.

Dumas, A., & Mintzberg, H. (1991). Managing the form, function, and fit of design. *Design Management Journal (Former Series), 2*(3), 26–31.

Eisenhardt, K. M. (1989). Making fast decisions in high velocity environments. *Academy of Management Journal, 32*(3), 543–576.

Eisenhardt, K. M., & Martin, J. A. (2000). Dynamic capabilities: What are they? *Strategic Management Journal, 21*(10–11), 1105–1121.

Ellsberg, D. (1961). Risk, ambiguity, and the savage axioms. *The Quarterly Journal of Economics, 75*(4), 643–669. https://doi.org/10.2307/1884324.

Fayolle, A., Liñán, F., & Moriano, J. A. (2014). Beyond entrepreneurial intentions: Values and motivations in entrepreneurship. *International Entrepreneurship and Management Journal, 10* (4), 679–689. https://doi.org/10.1007/s11365-014-0306-7.

FEMA. (2013). Toward more resilient futures: Putting foresight into practice. *Highlights from the Strategic Foresight Initiative.*

Flyvbjerg, B., Garbuio, M., & Lovallo, D. (2009). Delusion and deception in large infrastructure projects: Two models for explaining and preventing executive disaster. *California Management Review, 51*(2), 170–193.

Francis, D., & Bessant, J. (2005). Targeting innovation and implications for capability development. *Technovation, 25*(3), 171–183. https://doi.org/10.1016/j.technovation.2004.03.004.

Frisch, D., & Baron, J. (1988). Ambiguity and rationality. *Journal of Behavioral Decision Making, 1*(3), 149–157. https://doi.org/10.1002/bdm.3960010303.

Guenther, A., Eisenbart, B., & Dong, A. (2017). *Creativity as a way to innovate successfully.* Proceedings of the 21st International Conference on Engineering Design (ICED17), Vancouver, Canada, August 21–25.

Harari, Y. (2020). Yuval Noah Harari: The world after coronavirus. *Financial Times.* Accessed April 19, 2020, from https://www.ft.com/content/19d90308-6858-11ea-a3c9-1fe6fedcca75

Helfat, C. E., Finkelstein, S., Mitchell, W., Peteraf, M., & Teece, D. (2007). *Dynamic capabilities: Understanding strategic change in organizations.* New York: Wiley.

Hellmuth, M. E., Mason, S., Vaughan, C., Aalst, M. V., & Choularton, R. (2011). *A better climate for disaster risk management.* New York: International Research Institute for Climate and Society.

Hiltunen, E. (2010). *Weak signals in organizational futures learning.* Dissertation, Aalto University School of Economics, Helsinki.

Hunt, J. (2019). Anticipating future system states. *Journal of Futures Studies, 23*(3), 119–128.

Inayatullah, S. (2008). Six pillars: Futures thinking for transforming. *Foresight, 10*(1), 4–21.

Jahangiri, K., Eivazi, M. R., & Sayah Mofazali, A. (2017). The role of foresight in avoiding systematic failure of natural disaster risk management. *International Journal of Disaster Risk Reduction.* https://doi.org/10.1016/j.ijdrr.2017.01.008.

Judge, W. O., & Miller, A. (1991). Antecedents and outcomes of decision speed in different environmental contexts. *Academy of Management Journal, 34*, 449–463.

Kahneman, D., & Lovallo, D. (1993). Timid choices and bold forecasts: A cognitive perspective on risk taking. *Management Science, 39*(1), 17–31.

Kahneman, D., Slovic, S. P., & Tversky, A. (1982). *Judgment under uncertainty: Heuristics and biases.* Cambridge: Cambridge University Press.

Kahneman, D., & Tversky, A. (1979). Prospect theory: An analysis of decision under risk. *Econometrica, 47*(2), 263–291. https://doi.org/10.2307/1914185.

Kahneman, D., & Tversky, A. (1981). The framing of decisions and the psychology of choice. *Science, 211*(4481), 453–458. https://doi.org/10.1126/science.7455683.

Kauffman, S. A. (1994). *The origins of order: Self-organization and selection in evolution.* New York: Oxford University Press.

Keim, B. (2011). The startling science of a starling murmuration. *Wired.* Accessed October 19, 2019, from https://www.wired.com/2011/11/starling-flock/

Kelley, T. (2005). *The ten faces of innovation.* New York: Random House.

Kleinsmann, M., Valkenburg, R., & Sluijs, J. (2017). Capturing the value of design thinking in different innovation practices. *International Journal of Design, 11*(2).

Kolko, J. (2010). Abductive thinking and sensemaking: The Drivers of Design synthesis. *Design Issues, 26*(1), 15–28.

Kunz, N., Reiner, G., & Gold, S. (2014). Investing in disaster management capabilities versus pre-positioning inventory: A new approach to disaster preparedness. *International Journal of Production Economics, 157*(C), 261–272. https://doi.org/10.1016/j.ijpe.2013.11.002.

Kuosa, T. (2016). *The evolution of strategic foresight: Navigating public policy making.* New York: Routledge.

Landoni, P., Dell'Era, C., Ferraloro, G., Peradotto, M., Karlsson, H., & Verganti, R. (2016). Design contribution to the competitive performance of SMEs: The role of design innovation capabilities. *Creativity and Innovation Management, 25*(4), 484–499. https://doi.org/10.1111/caim.12165.

Larsen, N., Mortensen, J. K., & Miller, R. (2020). *What is 'futures literacy' and why is it important?* Copenhagen Institute for Futures Studies. Accessed from https://medium.com/copenhagen-institute-for-futures-studies/what-is-futures-literacy-and-why-is-it-important-a27f24b983d8

Lipshitz, R., & Strauss, O. (1997). Coping with uncertainty: A naturalistic decision-making analysis. *Organizational Behavior and Human Decision Processes, 69*(2), 149–163. https://doi.org/10.1006/obhd.1997.2679.

Liu, H. H., & Colman, A. M. (2009). Ambiguity aversion in the long run: Repeated decisions under risk and uncertainty. *Journal of Economic Psychology, 30*(3), 277–284. https://doi.org/10.1016/j.joep.2009.02.001.

Lopez-Silva, J., Banuls, V. A., & Turoff, M. (2015). *Scenario-based approach for risks analysis in critical infrastructures.* Paper presented at the Proceedings of the ISCRAM 2015 Conference, Kristiansand, May 24–27.

Maher, M. L., & Poon, J. (1996). Modeling design exploration as co-evolution. *Computer-Aided Civil and Infrastructure Engineering, 11*(3), 195–209. https://doi.org/10.1111/j.1467-8667.1996.tb00323.x.

Maher, M. L., Poon, J., & Boulanger, S. (1996). Formalising design exploration as co-evolution. In *Advances in formal design methods for CAD.* New York: Springer.

Martin, B. R. (1995). Foresight in science and technology. *Technology Analysis & Strategic Management, 7*(2), 139–168.

McAllum, M., & Egerton, L. (2014). *Strategic foresight and emergency management.* Paper Presented at the Strategic Foresight Social Media & Emergency Management Conference, Austria.

Mounarath, R., Lovallo, D., & Dong, A. (2011). Choosing innovation: How reasoning affects decision errors. In S. J. Culley, B. J. Hicks, T. C. McAloone, T. J. Howard, & P. Badke-Schaub (Eds.), *Proceedings of the 18th International Conference on Engineering Design (ICED 11), Lyngby/Copenhagen, Denmark, August 15–19* (pp. 54–63).

Neale, T., & Weir, J. K. (2015). Navigating scientific uncertainty in wildfire and flood risk mitigation: A qualitative review. *International Journal of Disaster Risk Reduction, 13*, 255–265.

Pesendorfer, W. (1995). Design innovation and fashion cycles. *The American Economic Review*, 771–792.

Pinkowski, J. (2008). *Disaster management handbook.* Boca Raton: CRC Press.

Prochazkova, D., Munne, R., Ahokas, J., & Drapalik, M. (2012). *Disaster management in the EU – present, and future: Challenges for research.* Accessed from Czech Technical University in Prague (CVUT), www.focusproject.eu

Reeves, M., Levin, S., & Ueda, D. (2016). The biology of corporate survival. *Harvard Business Review, 94*(1), 46–55.

Reeves, M., Fæste, L., Whitaker, K., & Abraham, M. (2020). *Reaction, rebound, recession, and reimagination.* BCG Henderson Institute. Accessed from https://www.bcg.com/publications/2020/covid-19-reaction-rebound-recession-reimagination.aspx

Roozenburg, N. F. (1993). On the pattern of reasoning in innovative design. *Design Studies, 14*(1), 4–18. https://doi.org/10.1016/S0142-694X(05)80002-X.

Roozenburg, N. F., & Eekels, J. (1995). *Product design: Fundamentals and methods.* Chichester: Wiley.

Rothwell, R. (1992). Successful industrial innovation: Critical success factors for the 1990s. *R&D Management, 22*(3), 221–239.

Scawthorn, C., Flores, P., Blais, N., Seligson, H., Tate, E., Chang, S., & Jones, C. (2006). HAZUSMH flood loss estimation methodology. Damage and loss assessment. *Natural Hazards Review, 7*(2), 72–81.

Shane, S. (2009). Why encouraging more people to become entrepreneurs is bad public policy. *Small Business Economics, 33*(2), 141–149.

Sherman, R. (1974). The psychological difference between ambiguity and risk. *The Quarterly Journal of Economics*, 166–169.

Snowden, D. J., & Boone, M. (2007). A leader's framework for decision making. *Harvard Business Review.* Accessed from https://hbr.org/2007/11/a-leaders-framework-for-decision-making

Teece, D. J. (2007). Explicating dynamic capabilities: The nature and microfoundations of (sustainable) enterprise performance. *Strategic Management Journal, 28*(13), 1319–1350. https://doi.org/10.1002/smj.640.

Teece, D. J. (2011). *Dynamic capabilities and strategic management.* New York: Oxford University Press.

Teece, D. J., & Pisano, G. (1994). The dynamic capabilities of firms: An introduction. *Industrial and Corporate Change, 3*(3), 537–556. https://doi.org/10.1093/icc/3.3.537-a.

The Economist. (2020, April 25). *The pandemic is liberating firms to experiment with radical new ideas.* Creative Disruption, Business. Accessed from https://www.economist.com/business/2020/04/25/the-pandemic-is-liberating-firms-to-experiment-with-radical-new-ideas

Tighe, S. (2019). *Rethinking Strategy: How to anticipate the future, slow down change, and improve decision making.* Richmond: Wiley.

Turoff, M., Banuls, V. A., Hiltz, S. R., & Plotnick, L. (2013). *A cross impact scenario model of organizational behavior in emergencies.* Paper presented at the 10th International ISCRAM Conference, Baden-Baden.

Turoff, M., Banuls, V. A., Plotnick, L., Hiltz, S. R., & de la Huerga, M. R. (2015). *Collaborative evolution of a dynamic scenario model for the interaction of critical infrastructures.* Paper presented at the Proceedings of the ISCRAM 2015 Conference, Kristiansand, May 24.

Tversky, A., & Kahneman, D. (1974). Judgment under Uncertainty: Heuristics and Biases. *Science, 185*(4157), 1124–1131. https://doi.org/10.1126/science.185.4157.1124.

UNESCO. (n.d.). *Futures literacy.* UNESCO. Accessed April 28, 2020, from https://en.unesco.org/themes/futures-literacy

Van der Duin, P. A., & den Hartigh, E. (2009). Keeping the balance: Exploring the link of futures research with innovation and strategy processes. *Technology Analysis & Strategic Management, 21*(3), 333–351.

Verganti, R. (2003). Design as brokering of languages. The role of designers in the innovation strategy of Italian firms. *Design Management Journal, Summer 2003*, 34–42.

Vettorello, M., Eisenbart, B., & Ranscombe, C. (2019). Toward better design-related decision making: A proposal of an advanced OODA loop. In *Proceedings of the Design Society: International Conference on Engineering Design* (Vol. 1, Issue 1, pp. 2387–2396). Cambridge University Press. https://doi.org/10.1017/dsi.2019.245.

Vettorello, M., Eisenbart, B., & Ranscombe, C. (2020). Paradoxical tension: Balancing contextual ambidexterity. In *Proceedings of the Design Society: 16th International Design Conference DESIGN 2020*. Cambridge University Press.

Voros, J. (2017). Big history and anticipation: Using big history as a framework for global foresight. In R. Poli (Ed.), *Handbook of anticipation: Theoretical and applied aspects of the use of future in decision making* (p. 40). Springer International.

Walker, W. E., Lempert, R. J., & Kwakkel, J. H. (2013). *Deep uncertainty encyclopedia of operations research and management science* (pp. 395–402). New York: Springer.

Wally, S., & Baum, J. R. (1994). Personal and structural determinants of the pace of strategic decision making. *Academy of Management Journal, 37*(4), 932–956. https://doi.org/10.2307/256605.

Walton, D. (1990). What is reasoning? What is an argument? *The Journal of Philosophy, 87*(8), 399–419. https://doi.org/10.2307/2026735.

Watson, H., Hagen, K., & Ritchey, T. (2015). *Experiencing GMA as a means of developing a conceptual model of the problem space involving understanding cascading effects of crises.* Paper Presented in the Short Paper – Researching Crisis: Methodologies-Proceedings of the ISCRAM 2015 Conference, Kristiansand, May 24–27.

Xu, Q., Chen, J., Xie, Z., Liu, J., Zheng, G., & Wang, Y. (2007). Total innovation management: A novel paradigm of innovation management in the 21st century. *The Journal of Technology Transfer, 32*, 9–25.

Mattia Vettorello is an innovation consultant with experience in co-designing actionable and adaptable new growth strategies. Mattia uses an integrated methodology – strategic foresight, design thinking and system theory – to explore innovative solutions that deliver positive impact to most people and planet. The focus of his scholarly activities is innovation management, entrepreneurship and futures literacy. Mattia current research focus on enabling and integrating anticipatory thinking in complex behavioral strategies to support strategic decision-making at early stage innovation management. Mattia holds a post graduate degree on strategy and innovation from Swinburne University of Technology, Melbourne, Australia, where he is competing his doctoral degree.

Boris Eisenbart is an Associate Professor and course director for Swinburne's product design engineering program. Boris obtained his Ph.D. in Engineering Design and Management focusing on interdisciplinary system design from the University of Luxembourg while receiving advisory supervision at the Technical University of Denmark. His research focuses on modeling and managing complex product development processes and behavioral strategies in decision-making for innovation management.

Charlie Ranscombe is a researcher and senior lecturer in Industrial Design and Product Design Engineering at Swinburne University of Technology (Melbourne, Australia). His experience is both as a practicing Industrial designer design researcher. His research is interdisciplinary in the domains of design practice and new product development with an emphasis on product esthetics and user experience. His current focus is on digital design tools and the way they influence design outcomes, offer new design opportunities and their integration into design education.

Future-Oriented Technology Analysis: A Classification Framework

Valeria Maria Urbano, Marika Arena, and Giovanni Azzone

1   Introduction

"We live at a time of technological change that is unprecedented in its pace, scope and depth of impact." This is the opening of the Technology and Innovation Report presented in 2018 at the United Nations Conference on Trade and Development. According to this report, the speed of technological development is expected to grow even more in the next decades driven by the opportunities provided by digital platforms and by the combination of different technologies (United Nations 2018). The same view emerges also from Butler (2016) who claims that technological change is accelerating at unprecedented speed following an exponential trend. In this context, anticipating future technologies and assessing their impacts became crucial for both business and governmental entities. The former can exploit the possibility of spotting new technologies as an important source of competitive advantage. The latter can leverage practices related to the analysis of future technologies to reduce uncertainties and to rapidly adapt to technological change.

Although first studies related to practices that aim at anticipating future technologies date back to the second half of the twentieth century, before 2004 no systematic approach was adopted to develop the field as a whole (Madnick and Cisl 2014). Different forms of process dedicated to the analysis of future technologies were, indeed, developed as individual topics, probably as a result of the fact that the different tools and approaches were developed in diverse contexts by different communities of practitioners (Eerola and Miles 2011).

Setting an important milestone, in 2004 Alan Porter and the Technology Futures Analysis Methods Working Group (TFAMWG) provided for the first time a framework regarding the different coexisting forms used to analyze future technologies

V. M. Urbano (✉) · M. Arena · G. Azzone
Department of Management, Economics and Industrial Engineering, Politecnico di Milano, Milan, Italy
e-mail: valeriamaria.urbano@polimi.it

© The Author(s), under exclusive license to Springer Nature Switzerland AG 2021
D. R. A. Schallmo, J. Tidd (eds.), *Digitalization*, Management for Professionals,
https://doi.org/10.1007/978-3-030-69380-0_2

and their consequences and gave a name to the field: Technology-oriented Future Analysis (TFA) (Porter et al. 2004). Used henceforth as an umbrella term and widely recognized by literature, the FTA concept framed by Porter comprises a number of overlapping forms and processes: Technology Forecasting, Technology Foresight, Technology Assessment, Technology Intelligence, and Technology Roadmapping. Defining these practices as "systematic processes to produce judgments about emerging technology characteristics, development pathways, and potential impacts of a technology in the future," the authors affirmed the need of developing the field as a whole.

The concern of the scientific community toward the FTA concept increased throughout the years and the processes covered by the field are widely shared across scholars. However, the different aspects characterizing approaches and practices that can be adopted are still object of analysis and discussion. In this respect, it is important to underline that some authors used some of the terms interchangeably (for instance, Technology Foresight and Technology Forecasting are in some cases used synonymously), while some others shed light on the aspects that differentiate one process from another (Cuhls 2003; Keenan et al. 2003). This makes the characterization of the different practices belonging to the FTA field even more complicated.

Furthermore, several authors focused on the investigation of a single FTA process dealing with both theoretical aspects and empirical research (Lichtenthaler 2004; Azzone and Manzini 2008; Boe-Lillegraven and Monterde 2015). Little attention has been given to the comparative analysis between two or more FTA processes highlighting similarities and divergences as an outcome of their research studies. What is therefore clear is that the literature lacks a comprehensive and exhaustive classification of the FTA processes.

First and foremost, starting from the FTA processes framed by the TFAMWG, this study explores in detail each FTA process in order to detect the main aspects that enable the characterization of the processes. In this specific case, this meant to determine the dimensions to be applied to perform a classification, hence building a classification framework. Secondly, through a systematic literature review, this study positions the FTA processes in order to classify the different forms of practices. Thirdly, the main interactions between the FTA processes are investigated in order to detect overlapping and divergence points. The research study addresses therefore three main research questions:

- What are the main attributes that enable the classification of the FTA processes?
- How are the FTA processes classified according to these aspects?
- Are there overlapping and/or divergence points between the processes pertaining to the FTA field?

The remainder of this chapter consists of four sections. Following the introduction, the second section provides an overview of the framework designed to classify the different FTA processes. In the third section, the overall approach to the research is explained. In the fourth section, the FTA processes are positioned according to the selected dimensions, and the main overlapping/divergence points are highlighted in order to build an overall framework. Finally, in the last section, the main results are reported and discussed.

2   Framework Design

In order to support the classification of the FTA processes, a framework defining the conceptual dimensions that characterize the different processes was designed. Five different dimensions were identified: objective, initiating entity, stakeholders involved, methodological approach, and time horizon (Fig. 1). It is worth highlighting that factors that are not distinctive, thus not allowing the differentiation process, were not taken into consideration. For instance, the scope of the process is not included in the framework since it can range from one specific technology to the entire set of technologies that may have an impact on the economic base of a nation (Madnick and Cisl 2014).

FTA processes involve the finding, deployment, usage, and even creation of knowledge supporting diverse innovation systems (Eerola and Miles 2011). However, differentiating the processes according to the diverse objective of the knowledge management process embedded in the different FTA practices enable a first

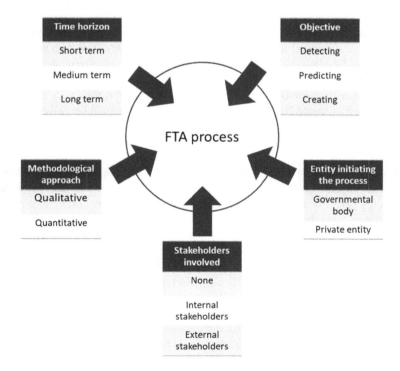

Fig. 1 Classification framework dimensions

crucial classification. The objective of the process is often the result of the different underlying assumption practitioners made when implementing FTA processes. This framework proposes a classification based on three main objectives, namely the detection, the prediction, and the creation of future technologies.

Starting from the purpose of detection, a subset of FTA processes is based on the concept of technological trends and on the possibility of reducing the probability of failure due to technological discontinuities (Lichtenthaler 2004). In these cases, FTA processes can provide opportunities for the early identification of critical technological advances by the monitoring of emerging technologies (Nosella et al. 2008). Hence, the aim is to observe the environment, analyze technology trends, and report the information related to technological development that are in progress in the present scenario. Moving to the prediction-oriented FTA processes, the main underlying assumption is the existence of a probable future that is linked in a deterministic way to the present and the past (Martin 2010). Extending the scope of the process, this entails that not only it is possible to identify emerging technologies, but, on the basis of available information, there is also the chance to predict technological development in order to study changes in technologies (Halicka 2016). Also, in this case, information on existing and emerging technologies is crucial to have a clue on the technological future scenario, but they are exploited as a starting point for forecasting exercises. Lastly, a subset of FTA processes goes beyond the mere identification or prediction of future technologies. The basic assumption behind this class of processes is that future is something that can be created rather than just predicted (Bañuls and Salmeron 2008) and that it is possible to shape the future according to the societal need (Martin and Johnston 1999). This hypothesis gives rise to vision-building FTA processes (UNIDO 2003), emphasizing the role of decision makers.

What further characterizes the different FTA processes is the entity that initiates the process which could be a business entity or a governmental body (Madnick and Cisl 2014). The ultimate purpose of the FTA processes accordingly varies, from better competing in the market to strengthening of the national system of innovation and policymaking.

FTA processes differ also in the number and typology of stakeholders involved during the implementation of the process. The FTA exercises can be, indeed, individually performed or it can engage a number of actors either internal or external to the organizations. In the latter case, this might mean involving experts of different industrial fields, academicians, and government representatives (Saritas et al. 2007). A further relevant classification, already pointed out by literature, concerns the methodological approaches adopted during the FTA processes which can leverage qualitative tools, quantitative tools, or a mix of both (Haegeman et al. 2013). Lastly, FTA processes can be classified according to the time horizon which can range from 1 year (short term) to 30 years (long term) (UNIDO 2003).

It is evident that the classification dimensions are not independent. Taking into consideration, for instance, methodological approach (qualitative/quantitative) and stakeholders involved (individual/participatory), as most of the qualitative approaches are experts opinion based, the qualitative approach often implies a participatory exercise. A further interrelationship that can be observed through the analysis of the dimensions is the one between the objective and the time horizon. When identifying future technologies practitioners generally adopt a short-term perspective, while when trying to create future technologies they often look beyond short-term future.

3   Methodology

In order to position the Future-oriented Technology Analysis processes in the classification framework, a systematic literature review was set up. Initially, leveraging on the Scopus database, the keywords used for conducting the literature review were selected on the basis of the FTA framework developed by Porter et al. (2004). Hence, the terms "FTA," "Technology Foresight," "Technology Forecasting," "Technology Roadmapping," "Technology Intelligence," and "Technology Assessment" were used as a baseline for the literature review.

The analysis of the literature revealed that more recently, two other concepts found space in the FTA field: Technology Scouting and Technology Monitoring (Rohrbeck 2007; Nosella et al. 2008). For the sake of completeness, the two keywords were, therefore, added for reviewing the existing literature.

Furthermore, the analysis of studies related to the Technology Assessment process led to the exclusion of the concept from the analysis. According to the literature, a significant overlapping between the Technology Assessment process and the Forecasting exercise exists (Braun 1998; Coates et al. 2001) as the assessment of new technologies inevitably implies a forecasting of the technology under scrutiny and the related alternative, complementary, and rival technologies. The assessment process may, indeed, entail a preliminary phase where development paths of technologies are described and this can be done through a range of techniques. Nevertheless, the main focus of Technology Assessment is to assess the impact of a technology; hence, the purpose of the Assessment exercise cannot be classified as identifying, nor predicting, or creating future technologies. Therefore, for the scope of this study, the keyword "Technology Assessment" was excluded.

Analyzing search results (Fig. 2) some patterns related to the relevance of the different FTA concepts can be detected. Indeed, analyzing the number of research articles containing the above-mentioned keyword in the title, abstract and keywords in the database "Scopus," it is possible to examine the evolution of the relevance of the topic.

The positive trend that can be detected from the analysis of each of the concepts under scrutiny emphasizes the importance of the role of the analysis of future technological developments in today's context. The ever-growing importance of the core concepts of this study is consistent with the fast-changing scenario, especially with regards to technology. Giving a quick glance at the comparison of the different concepts it emerged that similar increasing paths characterize the FTA processes and that the majority of the processes became the subject of research studies starting from the 1990s. Exceptions are the articles related to Technology

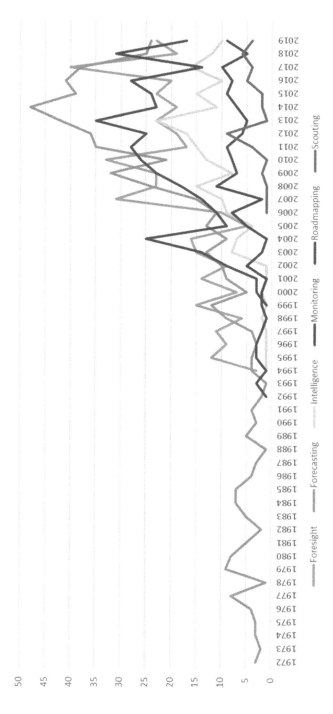

Fig. 2 Number of research articles in the Scopus database

Forecasting and Technology Scouting processes respectively published from the 1970s to 2000s.

As the topic has been widely discussed in existing literature, sources have been selected according to the criterion of relevance. As a result, 300 papers were reviewed. Integrating findings and perspectives from previous research studies, the FTA processes were positioned in the designed classification framework. Is it worth highlighting that the classification does not claim to be exhaustive as there may be exceptions that do not match with the classification. The goal of the framework is, indeed, to provide the predominant positioning of each FTA process in the light of the selected dimensions.

4   Positioning FTA Processes

Technology Foresight

The starting point of foresight is the idea that many futures are possible, and that today's decisions can influence, shape, and create the future. Therefore, the main assumption behind the technology foresight is that the future is something created, not simply predicted and controlled. This proactive attitude toward the future makes the technology foresight a fundamental element of the management of technology and innovation which represents an area with substantial uncertainties in technical progress, political developments, and social concerns (Grupp and Linstone 1999; Jørgensen et al. 2009; Martin 1995).

Literature often refers to technology foresight as a government-sponsored activity, introducing national foresight cases developed by different countries (Martin and Johnston 1999; Keenan 2003; Miles 2010; Proskuryakova and Filippov 2015; Saritas et al. 2007; Thomas 2003). Grupp and Linstone (1999) defined the foresight process as a political question that governments use to shape political tactics on innovation-related topics. Furthermore, the purpose of the technology foresight process is not only one of the identifying future technology developments but the understanding of their interactions with the society and the environment (Porter et al. 2004). When exploring the different possible scenarios, the process is not confined to the description of the future potential options, but it moves one step further to deepen and discuss the implications in social and economic terms. Technology Foresight is, therefore, no longer merely technology driven, but need and value driven (Reger 2003).

Technology foresight programs bring together social stakeholders (Canongia et al. 2004), experts of different industrial fields, academicians, and government representatives (Saritas et al. 2007). Since the purpose of the foresight practices is to shape and create the future, it is not enough to involve only experts of different domains. In this regard, it is fundamental to engage decisions-makers that could play an important role in the creation of future technological scenarios.

The first approaches of foresight practices in European countries added to the proactive attitude the participatory element and the process orientation in order to describe the "fully fledged" Technology Foresight Process. The word "fully fledged" has been added to demarcate the long-term orientation of the process (Miles 2010).

Regarding the methodological approach, literature provides diverse points of view. Some authors reported both qualitative and quantitative approaches as the main methods for conducting Technology Foresight (Saritas et al. 2014; Lisin et al. 2017). However, Saritas et al. (2014) claim that quantitative methods found application only in the most recent Foresight exercise and that qualitative methods are still the most popular methods compared to quantitative ones. This second perspective is shared by the majority of authors (Cuhls 2003; Jin et al. 2017) reporting that techniques such as expert panels, Brainstorming, Delphi, and Scenarios were considered to be the most popular among Foresight practitioners. Among them, the most popular used in large-scale analysis is the Delphi method (adopted in The Netherlands, Germany, France, Australia, the UK, and Austria) (Jin et al. 2017).

Technology Forecasting

Part of the literature considers Technology Forecasting as a collective term for a set of FTA processes, namely Technology Intelligence, Technology Foresight, and Technology Roadmapping (Grimshaw 1991; Zhu and Porter 2002). What is especially interesting is the analogy between Technology Foresight and Technology Forecasting that is still reported by authors using the two terms interchangeably (Itoh and Kano 2019). Nevertheless, the distinction between Forecasting and Foresight was formalized in the 1980s and supported by a considerable body of literature. According to Martin (2010), the FTA exercise introduced in Japan represented a substantial shift toward a new approach that led to the coinage of a new term: Technology Foresight. First and foremost, the two processes were built upon contrasting hypotheses. While the technology foresight assumes that the future can be created according to societal needs, the Forecasting process supposes the existence of one probable future that is linked to the present and the past. The purpose of the Forecasting is indeed to predict the development path of a given technology, generally illustrated as an S-shape curve by Forecasting practitioners (Chang et al. 2009). Furthermore, since the research questions of the Forecasting process have to be defined in advance (Cuhls 2003), technology monitoring has become a crucial activity to be implemented in the early stages of the Technology Forecasting process, enabling the identification of the initial parameters as well as the relevance of the forecasting process on a given technology.

Martin (2010) reported a number of elements of Technology Foresight that were inconsistent with those aspects characterizing the process of Forecasting (Table 1).

Furthermore, according to the author, by bringing together different stakeholders, the Foresight process facilitates the communication between them and forces them to periodically concentrate on the longer-term future. This enables the coordination of the R&D activities, the creation of a common consensus, and a feeling of commitment to the outcome of foresight.

Table 1 Main differences between Technology Forecasting and Technology Foresight

Forecasting	Foresight
Carried out by few forecasting experts	Involving thousands of scientists, industrialists, government officials, and others
Science and technology push	Considering demand side of future economic and social needs
Top-down	Top-down and bottom-up

Source: Martin (2010)

Fig. 3 Interaction between Technology Forecasting and Technology Foresight

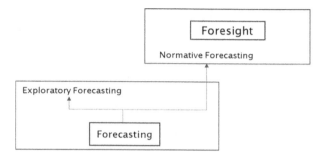

The characterization reported by literature highlights the nonparticipatory aspect and the short-term perspective as distinguishing elements of Technology Forecasting practices. Forecasting exercises are undertaken by both private entities and governmental bodies (Upadhyay and Fujii 2016). Concerning the methodological approach, Technology Forecasting generally leverages quantitative approaches mainly based on trend extrapolation (Wu et al. 2019). Patent analysis represents the most popular tool (Lee et al. 2012) as patents contain significant information on emerging technologies (Uhm et al. 2017).

A second considerable part of literature extends the concept of Technology Forecasting diving it into major classes: exploratory and normative forecasting (Boon and Park 2005). The former projects present and past data toward the future using quantitative approaches such as trend extrapolation, environment scanning, and bibliometric analysis. On the contrary, the latter is characterized by a goal-oriented approach. The normative type of forecasting defines desirable futures and generates the path that leads to the desired state by means of qualitative tools such as Delphi, TRIZ, and Scenarios (Yoon and Park 2007). The overlapping between the normative type of forecasting and the Technology Foresight is evident and requires the formulation of a unique definition of the Technology Forecasting process.

Consistently with the thesis formulated by the first group of authors representing the bulk of literature, in this chapter, the term Technology Forecasting will refer to the exploratory type of Forecasting as opposed to the Technology Foresight concept (Fig. 3).

Technology Roadmapping

Despite the concept is quite widespread in literature, the Technology Roadmapping struggles to find an academic systematization (Lee et al. 2007), probably as a result of the flexibility in terms of both purpose and format characterizing it (Phaal 2004).

Several authors refer to Technology Roadmapping as a technique used in the FTA field rather than a process. Suitable for different situations, this tool enables the exploration of relationships between future technologies, markets, and products (Phaal 2004). According to Garcia and Bray (1997), the outcome of the roadmapping activity can be (1) the consensus about a set of technologies required to satisfy a certain need, (2) a forecast of a technology development path, or (3) a framework to support the planning and coordination. This classification allows glimpses of (1) Technology Foresight, (2) Technology Forecasting, and (3) Planning process, hence shedding light on the extent of the area covered by the Technology Roadmapping.

The same author reports two types of technology roadmaps: product technology roadmap and emerging technology roadmap. While the former is driven by product or process needs, the latter aims at forecasting the development of an emerging technology. Once again, the analogy with Technology Foresight and Technology Forecasting is evident. The popularity of the roadmapping technique in the foresight area is emphasized by several authors which agree on the communicative strength of the tool (Hussain et al. 2017).

The flexibility of the roadmap exercises provides opportunities for not only corporations and industries but also for national entities for R&D planning supporting policy formulation (Zhang et al. 2016) and enables the adaptation of time horizon to the specific need (Phaal 2004).

To what concern methodological approach, although quantitative methods are increasingly applied to computation (Daim et al. 2018), they are outweighed by qualitative technology roadmapping methodologies, which remain the mainstream of current technology roadmapping activities and especially real-world applications (Zhang et al. 2016). Given the relevance of the normative component in this tool (Saritas and Aylen 2010), qualitative methods such as expert and researchers interviews, Delphi, scenario planning, discussion, seminars, and workshops, still play a fundamental role in technology roadmapping's creation and implementation (Madnick and Cisl 2014; Zhang et al. 2016). The typology and number of stakeholders involved depend on the context in which the roadmap is developed (corporate Roadmapping, Industry Roadmapping or national Roadmapping) (Garcia and Bray 1997), varying from stakeholders internal to the organizations to external stakeholder such as academic researchers, industrial stakeholders, and government officials (Madnick and Cisl 2014; Zhang et al. 2016).

Technology Intelligence

The concept of technology intelligence—sometimes referred to as Competitive Technology Intelligence in the literature—is related to the observation of technological trends in business contexts. Contrary to Technology Foresight, the term intelligence, indeed, suggests a direct link between actions and thought (Coates et al. 2001) implying its use within the private sector.

The academic world agrees that the core task of the Technology Intelligence process is the systematic capture and delivery of information related to new technologies (Kerr and Phaal 2018). Aiming at identifying new technologies, technology intelligence is not merely a gathering of information process, but it involves the analysis and transformation of information into actionable knowledge (Rodríguez-Salvador et al. 2017).

The ultimate purpose of the Technology Intelligence process is the identification of both technological opportunities and threats (Ashton and Stacey 1995; Kerr and Phaal 2018; Lichtenthaler 2003; Yoon et al. 2015). Firstly, the innovation opportunities arising from the Technology Intelligence practice could be related to the introduction of new products, processes, or collaboration as a result of change in the technological environment (Yoon 2008). Secondly, turning to the threat's identification, companies may use Technology Intelligence with the purpose of mitigating the risk coming from technology evolution. Indeed, by developing timely awareness of potential technological threats, companies can prevent market share reduction in existing or planned product lines (Ashton and Stacey 1995), that would undermine the future growth and survival of the business (Yoon et al. 2015).

Literature emphasize the relevance of patent intelligence as a result of the increasing number of patents registered by companies (Park et al. 2013; Yoon et al. 2015). On this matter, two main quantitative approaches can be distinguished: the bibliographic and the content-based approach.

The time horizon of the Intelligence process ranges from short to long term, depending on the organizational structure of the company and of the R&D activities (Lichtenthaler 2003). Moreover, when the Intelligence exercise is integrated with the company planning process, the activity is performed involving a number of internal stakeholders, hence resulting in a shift in the organizational understanding from "Intelligence of the Organization" to "Organizational Intelligence" (Lichtenthaler 2003).

Technology Scouting

The scouting process involves both the research of technology acquisition channels and the support to the process of innovation effort (Akinwale 2018). In this regard, the scouting process plays a crucial role in fostering innovation. Besides gathering ideas, information, and knowledge, the Technology Scouting exercise creates insight or awareness on significant technology trends that can be exploited by companies (Parida et al. 2012). Hence, the systematic observation of technologies enables the identification of opportunities and threats at an early stage of technology development (Akinwale 2018; Rohrbeck 2010; Parida et al. 2012).

A further remarkable aspect is the participatory nature of the process (Akinwale 2018; Rohrbeck 2010). The Technology Scouting process implies the participation of external actors to cope with the limited R&D resources and innovation skills required to carry out the scouting process (Akinwale 2018).

What emerged from the literature review is the connection of the Technology Scouting to the Technology Scanning. Some authors defined the latter as a method of Technology scouting which "investigate innovations new to the industry or outside the traditional industry practices" (Pöyhönen et al. 2017). Other authors refer to Scanning as part of the Technology Scouting process. Indeed, they described technology Scouting as an internal search or scanning function which aims at identifying technological trends (Akinwale 2018; Parida et al. 2012).

Technology Monitoring

Although widely discussed in the literature, the concept of Technology Monitoring struggles to find its definition. The description provided by the authors brings out elements of Technology Monitoring that recall the concept of Technology Intelligence and Technology Forecasting.

The main purpose of the Technology Monitoring process is to identify and evaluate critical technological advances that can have an impact on a company's competitive position (Nosella et al. 2008). This definition makes the overlapping with the Technology Intelligence process clear. Indeed, several authors refer to Monitoring as a phase of the Technology Intelligence process, following a scanning phase. Firstly, the technology scanning phase aims at exploring the external environment with no specific focus. In a second stage, the identified technologies are observed and tracked through the technology monitoring, hence with a more limited focus (Ruff 2004; Schuh et al. 2014) (Fig. 4). As in the case of Technology Intelligence activities, the Technology Monitoring process is generally carried out with the adoption of quantitative techniques such as bibliometric analysis performed on patents, the best source of technology information (Joung and Kim 2017).

Other authors defined the process of Technology Monitoring as a method supporting the Forecasting exercise. Two interactions between the two were identified: one in a preliminary phase of forecasting (exploring) and one on the final sept of the process (focusing). On one hand, continuous monitoring exercises provide input for the forecasting process (Roper et al. 2011). Taking as reference the

Fig. 4 Interaction between Technology Intelligence, Monitoring, and Scanning

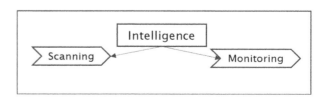

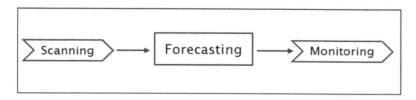

Fig. 5 Interaction between Technology Forecasting, Monitoring, and Scanning

Table 2 Summary of the FTA positioning in the classification framework

FTA process	Objective	Entity initiating the process	Stakeholders involved	Methodological approach	Time horizon
Foresight	Creating	Governmental bodies	External stakeholders	Qualitative	Long term
Forecasting	Predicting	Private entities and governmental bodies	None	Quantitative	Short term
Roadmapping	Creating/ predicting	Private entities and governmental bodies	Internal and/or external stakeholders	Qualitative	Short– medium– long
Intelligence	Detecting	Private entities	Internal stakeholders	Quantitative	Short– medium– long
Scouting	Detecting	Private entities	External stakeholders	N.A.	N.A.
Monitoring	Detecting	N.A.	N.A.	Quantitative	N.A.

distinction between Scanning and Monitoring highlighted by Ruff (2004), this phase, despite being named as monitoring by the literature, can be considered as a scanning phase. On the other hand, monitoring is activated following the forecasting in order to watch for changes that would alter the situation (Reger 2001). Technology Scanning can be therefore considered as a preliminary phase of forecasting while Technology Monitoring is a follow-up activity of forecasting (Fig. 5).

In conclusion, Table 2 shows the positioning of the FTA concepts according to the selected dimensions.

The understanding of FTA processes has allowed to draw a comparison between different FTA processes. This analysis triggered the generation of an overall conceptual framework, to provide a detailed snapshot of the overall literature position regarding the FTA (Fig. 6). In the first place, the conceptual model formulated classifies the different FTA processes according to their objective: Detecting, Predicting, and Creating future technologies. Secondly, the framework was formulated in order to highlight the main interactions between the processes that

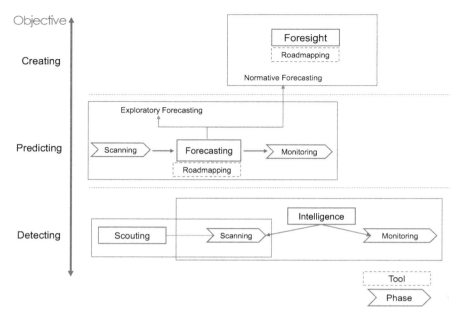

Fig. 6 Summary of the interactions between the different FTA processes

emerged from the analysis of the literature, hence shedding light on the overlapping forms and on the divergences.

5   Discussion and Conclusions

This research designed an FTA classification framework by providing five different dimensions that enable the characterization of the FTA forms. Providing a method to classify the FTA processes, the framework is built on five different dimensions: Objective, Entity initiating the process, Stakeholders involved, Methodological approach, and Time horizon. The proposed framework was then used to position the different FTA practices according to the predominant position found in the literature. What emerged is that the Technology Foresight process differs from the others for its purpose which consists in the creation of the technological future scenario. The process emphasizes the importance of today's action for the development of new technologies and accordingly, the importance of involving decision-makers in the process. The process of Technology Forecasting is, instead, built on the idea that there is a link between the future and the past. The main purpose of the Forecasting practice is therefore to predict the development path of future technologies on the basis of present and past information. The Technology Intelligence, Technology Scouting, and Technology monitoring processes do not claim to create nor to predict the future. These practices are designed to early identify critical emergent technologies. Furthermore, the analysis performed on the basis of the literature review was used in order to understand what are the main overlapping and divergence points between the processes investigated. The classification provided together with the comparison of the FTA processes triggered the generation of a second framework. In the first place, the conceptual model formulated classifies the different FTA processes according to their objective. Secondly, the framework was formulated in order to highlight the main interactions between the processes that emerged from the analysis of the literature, hence shedding light on the most relevant overlapping points and on the divergences.

To what concern the contribution that the framework adds to current theory, it is worth highlighting that existing literature proposes a comparison between a few of the FTA processes introduced by TFAMWG and that most of the previous studies analyze one single process belonging to the FTA field. What makes the results of this research study relevant to the IM community is that focusing not only on the individual processes but embracing the whole set of existing practices that aim at understanding future technologies, this study zooms out to a broader perspective in order to provide a more general framework. First of all, this broader perspective provides the basis for the integration of different techniques and methodologies. Secondly, the framework provides a means for understanding FTA practices implemented at a business or national level.

Furthermore, describing the FTA processes on the basis of the predominant position of literature led to the formulation of unique definitions that clarify the ambiguity of terminology that characterize the field.

While providing a tool to characterize the practices dedicated to the analysis of future technologies, this chapter has some practical implications as well. Since the FTA processes are classified according to three different objectives, the results of the research study reveal how to initiate or reorganize the practices implemented by companies or institutions and which methodologies/tools should be put in practice in order to reach the target set. In addition to providing the entire spectrum of potential processes that could be put in place in order to analyze future technologies, the framework reveals to companies and institutions further unexplored opportunities that could result from the implementation of these practices. Future research could investigate the relationships between the different classification dimensions identified. Moreover, the different FTA practices implemented in the business and/or institutional scenarios could be investigated in order to understand whether the results of the processes are consistent with the targets identified in the framework.

References

Akinwale, Y. O. (2018). Empirical analysis of inbound open innovation and small and medium-sized enterprises' performance: Evidence from oil and gas industry. *South African Journal of Economic and Management Sciences, 21*(1), a1608. https://doi.org/10.4102/sajems.v21i1.1608.

Ashton, W. B., & Stacey, G. S. (1995). Technical Intelligence in business: Understanding technology threats and opportunities. *International Journal of Technology Management, 10*(1), 79–104.

Azzone, G., & Manzini, R. (2008). Quick and dirty technology assessment: The case of an Italian Research Centre. *Technological Forecasting and Social Change, 75*(8), 1324–1338. https://doi.org/10.1016/j.techfore.2007.10.004.

Bañuls, V. A., & Salmeron, J. L. (2008). Foresighting key areas in the Information Technology industry. *Technovation, 28*(3), 103–111. https://doi.org/10.1016/j.technovation.2007.05.006.

Boe-Lillegraven, S., & Monterde, S. (2015). Exploring the cognitive value of technology foresight: The case of the Cisco Technology Radar. *Technological Forecasting and Social Change, 101*, 62–82. https://doi.org/10.1016/j.techfore.2014.07.014.

Boon, B., & Park, Y. (2005). A systematic approach for identifying technology opportunities: Keyword-based morphology analysis. *Technological Forecasting and Social Change, 72*(2), 145–160. https://doi.org/10.1016/j.techfore.2004.08.011.

Braun, E. (1998). Technology in context.

Butler, D. (2016). Tomorrow's world: Technological change is accelerating today at an unprecedented speed and could create a world we can barely begin to imagine. *Nature, 530*(7591), 398+.

Canongia, C., Antunes, A., & Pereira, M. D. N. F. (2004). Technological foresight – The use of biotechnology in the development of new drugs against breast cancer. *Technovation, 24*(4), 299–309. https://doi.org/10.1016/j.technovation.2003.10.001.

Chang, S. B., Lai, K. K., & Chang, S. M. (2009). Exploring technology diffusion and classification of business methods: Using the patent citation network. *Technological Forecasting and Social Change, 76*(1), 107–117. https://doi.org/10.1016/j.techfore.2008.03.014.

Coates, V., Farooque, M., Klavans, R., Lapid, K., Linstone, H. A., Pistorius, C., & Porter, A. L. (2001). On the future of technological forecasting. *Technological Forecasting and Social Change, 67*(1), 1–17. https://doi.org/10.1016/S0040-1625(00)00122-0.

Cuhls, K. (2003). From forecasting to foresight processes – New participative foresight activities in Germany. *Journal of Forecasting, 22*(2), 93–111. https://doi.org/10.1002/for.848.

Daim, T. U., et al. (2018). Strategic roadmapping of robotics technologies for the power industry: A multicriteria technology assessment. *Technological Forecasting and Social Change, 131*(June), 49–66. https://doi.org/10.1016/j.techfore.2017.06.006.

Eerola, A., & Miles, I. (2011). Methods and tools contributing to FTA: A knowledge-based perspective. *Futures, 43*(3), 265–278. https://doi.org/10.1016/j.futures.2010.11.005.

Garcia, M. L., & Bray, O. H. (1997). Fundamentals of technology roadmapping. *Distribution, 4205* (April), 34. https://doi.org/10.1109/LPT.2009.2020494.

Grupp, H., & Linstone, H. A. (1999). National technology foresight activities around the globe: Resurrection and new paradigms. *Technological Forecasting and Social Change, 60*(1), 85–94. https://doi.org/10.1016/S0040-1625(98)00039-0.

Grimshaw, D. (1991). Forecasting and management of technology. *The Journal of Strategic Information Systems, 1*(1), 47. https://doi.org/10.1016/0963-8687(91)90009-8.

Haegeman, K., et al. (2013). Quantitative and qualitative approaches in Future-oriented Technology Analysis (FTA): From combination to integration? *Technological Forecasting and Social Change, 80*(3), 386–397. https://doi.org/10.1016/j.techfore.2012.10.002.

Halicka, K. (2016). Innovative classification of methods of the Future-oriented Technology Analysis. *Technological and Economic Development of Economy, 22*(4), 574–597. https://doi.org/10.3846/20294913.2016.1197164.

Hussain, M., Tapinos, E., & Knight, L. (2017). Scenario-driven roadmapping for technology foresight. *Technological Forecasting and Social Change, 124*(July), 160–177. https://doi.org/10.1016/j.techfore.2017.05.005.

Itoh, S., & Kano, S. (2019). Technology forecasting for medical devices guidance formulation: A case study in Japan. *Therapeutic Innovation & Regulatory Science, 53*(4), 481–489. https://doi.org/10.1177/2168479018793370.

Jin, Y., et al. (2017). Selection and evaluation of priority domains in global energy internet standard development based on technology foresight. *IOP Conference Series: Materials Science and Engineering, 199*(1). https://doi.org/10.1088/1757-899X/199/1/012100.

Jørgensen, M. S., Jørgensen, U., & Clausen, C. (2009). The social shaping approach to technology foresight. *Futures, 41*(2), 80–86. https://doi.org/10.1016/j.futures.2008.07.038.

Joung, J., & Kim, K. (2017). Technological Forecasting & Social Change Monitoring emerging technologies for technology planning using technical keyword based analysis from patent data. *Technological Forecasting & Social Change, 114*, 281–292. https://doi.org/10.1016/j.techfore.2016.08.020.

Keenan, M. (2003). Identifying emerging generic technologies at the national level: The UK experience. *Journal of Forecasting, 22*, 129–160. https://doi.org/10.1002/for.849.

Keenan, M., Miles, I., & Koi-Ova, J. (2003, January). *Handbook of knowledge society foresight*. http://www.eurofound.eu.int/transversal/foresight.htm

Kerr, C., & Phaal, R. (2018). Directing the technology intelligence activity: An 'information needs' template for initiating the search. *Technological Forecasting and Social Change, 134*(February 2017), 265–276. https://doi.org/10.1016/j.techfore.2018.06.033.

Lee, S. et al. (2007) Technology roadmapping for R & D planning: The case of the Korean parts and materials industry, 27, pp. 433–445. doi:https://doi.org/10.1016/j.technovation.2007.02.011.

Lee, C., et al. (2012). A stochastic patent citation analysis approach to assessing future technological impacts. *Technological Forecasting and Social Change, 79*(1), 16–29. https://doi.org/10.1016/j.techfore.2011.06.009.

Lichtenthaler, E. (2003). Third generation management of technology intelligence processes. *R and D Management, 33*(4), 361–375. https://doi.org/10.1111/1467-9310.00304.

Lichtenthaler, E. (2004). Technological change and the technology intelligence process: A case study. *Journal of Engineering and Technology Management – JET-M, 21*(4), 331–348. https://doi.org/10.1016/j.jengtecman.2004.09.003.

Lisin, E., et al. (2017). Analysis of competitiveness: Energy sector and the electricity market in Russia. *Economic Research-Ekonomska Istrazivanja, 30*(1), 1820–1828. https://doi.org/10.1080/1331677X.2017.1392887.

Madnick, S., & Cisl, W. P. (2014). Technological forecasting – A review technological forecasting – A review Ayse Kaya Firat Wei Lee Woon Massachusetts Institute of Technology, May 2012.

Martin, B. R. (1995). Foresight in science and technology. *Technology Analysis & Strategic Management, 7*(2), 139–168. https://doi.org/10.1080/09537329508524202.

Martin, B. R. (2010). The origins of the concept of "foresight" in science and technology: An insider's perspective. *Technological Forecasting and Social Change, 77*(9), 1438–1447. https://doi.org/10.1016/j.techfore.2010.06.009.

Martin, B. R., & Johnston, R. (1999). Technology foresight for wiring up the national innovation system: Experiences in Britain, Australia, and New Zealand. *Technological Forecasting and Social Change, 60*(1), 37–54. https://doi.org/10.1016/S0040-1625(98)00022-5.

Miles, I. (2010). The development of technology foresight: A review. *Technological Forecasting and Social Change, 77*(9), 1448–1456. https://doi.org/10.1016/j.techfore.2010.07.016.

Nosella, A., Petroni, G., & Salandra, R. (2008). Technological change and technology monitoring process: Evidence from four Italian case studies. *Journal of Engineering and Technology Management – JET-M, 25*(4), 321–337. https://doi.org/10.1016/j.jengtecman.2008.10.001.

Parida, V., Westerberg, M., & Frishammar, J. (2012). Inbound open innovation activities in high-tech SMEs: The impact on innovation performance. *Journal of Small Business Management, 50*, 283–309. https://doi.org/10.1111/j.1540-627X.2012.00354.x.

Park, H., Kim, K., Choi, S., & Yoon, J. (2013). A patent intelligence system for strategic technology planning. *Expert Systems with Applications, 40*(7), 2373–2390.

Phaal, R. (2004). Technology roadmapping – A planning framework for evolution and revolution. *Technological Forecasting and Social Change, 71*(1–2), 5–26. https://doi.org/10.1016/S0040-1625(03)00072-6.

Porter, A. L., et al. (2004). Technology futures analysis: Toward integration of the field and new methods. *Technological Forecasting and Social Change, 71*(3), 287–303. https://doi.org/10.1016/j.techfore.2003.11.004.

Pöyhönen, P., Sivunen, M., & Kajander, J. (2017). Developing a project delivery system for construction project – a case study. *Procedia Engineering, 196*(June), 520–526. https://doi.org/10.1016/j.proeng.2017.07.233.

Proskuryakova, L., & Filippov, S. (2015). Energy technology foresight 2030 in Russia: An outlook for safer and more efficient energy future. *Energy Procedia, 75*, 2798–2806. https://doi.org/10.1016/j.egypro.2015.07.550.

Reger, G. (2001). Technology foresight in companies: From an indicator to a network and process perspective. *Technology Analysis and Strategic Management, 13*(4), 533–553. https://doi.org/10.1080/09537320127286.

Reger, G. (2003). Technology foresight in companies: From an indicator to a network and process perspective. *Technology Analysis & Strategic Management, 13*(4), 533–553. https://doi.org/10.1080/09537320127286.

Rodríguez-Salvador, M., Rio-Belver, R. M., & Garechana-Anacabe, G. (2017). Scientometric and patentometric analyses to determine the knowledge landscape in innovative technologies: The case of 3D bioprinting. *PLoS One, 12*(6), e0180375. https://doi.org/10.1371/journal.pone.0180375.

Rohrbeck, R. (2007, January). *Technology Scouting – A case study on the Deutsche Telekom Laboratories René Rohrbeck* (pp. 1–14).

Rohrbeck, R. (2010). Harnessing a network of experts for competitive advantage: Technology scouting in the ICT industry. *R and D Management, 40*(2), 169–180. https://doi.org/10.1111/j.1467-9310.2010.00601.x.

Roper, A. T., Cunningham, S. W., Porter, A. L., Mason, T. W., Rossini, F. A., & Banks, J. (2011). *Forecasting and management of technology* (2nd ed.). Hoboken, NJ: Wiley-Interscience. ISBN: 0470440902(hb), 1283175851(eb), 9780470440902(hb), 9781283175852(eb).

Ruff, F. (2004). *Paper 4: Society and technology foresight in the context of a multinational company* (pp. 44–70).

Saritas, O., & Aylen, J. (2010). Using scenarios for roadmapping: The case of clean production. *Technological Forecasting and Social Change, 77*(7), 1061–1075. https://doi.org/10.1016/j.techfore.2010.03.003.

Saritas, O., Burmaoglu, S., & Tabak, A. (2014, November). *The evolution of the use of foresight methods: A bibliometric analysis of global research output for cutting edge FTA approaches* (pp. 27–28). 5th International Conference on Future-Oriented Technology Analysis (FTA) – Engage today to shape tomorrow Brussels, 27–28 November.

Saritas, O., Taymaz, E., & Tumer, T. (2007). Vision 2023: Turkey's national Technology Foresight Program: A contextualist analysis and discussion. *Technological Forecasting and Social Change, 74*(8), 1374–1393. https://doi.org/10.1016/j.techfore.2006.07.005.

Schuh, G., et al. (2014). Concept for determining the focus of technology monitoring activities. *International Journal of Social, Education, Economics and Management Engineering, 8*(10), 3185–3192.

Thomas, D. (2003). Twelve lessons from 'Key Technologies 2005': The French technology foresight exercise. *Journal of Forecasting, 22*(2), 161–177. ST-Twelve lessons from 'Key Techno. http://ejournals.ebsco.com/direct.asp?ArticleID=PPMHN8GTB2VJ1D4RBEEC.

Uhm, D., Ryu, J. B., & Jun, S. (2017). An interval estimation method of patent keyword data for sustainable technology forecasting. *Sustainability (Switzerland), 9*(11). https://doi.org/10.3390/su9112025.

UNIDO. (2003). *Technology foresight for organizers.*

United Nations. (2018). *Technology and innovation report – Harnessing frontier technologies for sustainable development.* https://doi.org/10.1007/978-1-4471-6699-3_9.

Upadhyay, R., & Fujii, A. (2016). Semantic knowledge extraction from research documents. In *Proceedings of the 2016 Federated Conference on Computer Science and Information Systems, FedCSIS 2016* (Vol. 8, pp. 439–445). https://doi.org/10.15439/2016F221.

Wu, H. et al. (2019). *Deep technology tracing for high-tech companies*, (Icdm) (pp. 1396–1401). https://doi.org/10.1109/ICDM.2019.00180.

Yoon, B. (2008). On the development of a technology intelligence tool for identifying technology opportunity. *Expert Systems with Applications, 35*(1–2), 124–135. https://doi.org/10.1016/j.eswa.2007.06.022.

Yoon, B., & Park, Y. (2007). Development of new technology forecasting algorithm: Hybrid approach for morphology analysis and conjoint analysis of patent information. *IEEE Transactions on Engineering Management, 54*(3), 588–599. https://doi.org/10.1109/TEM.2007.900796.

Yoon, J., Ko, N., Kim, J., Lee, J. M., Coh, B. Y., & Song, I. (2015). A function-based knowledge base for technology intelligence. *Industrial Engineering and Management Systems, 14*(1), 73–87. https://doi.org/10.7232/iems.2015.14.1.073.

Zhang, Y., et al. (2016). Technology roadmapping for competitive technical intelligence. *Technological Forecasting and Social Change, 110*(November), 175–186. https://doi.org/10.1016/j.techfore.2015.11.029.

Zhu, D., & Porter, A. L. (2002). Automated extraction and visualization of information for technological intelligence and forecasting. *Technological Forecasting and Social Change, 69*(5), 495–506. https://doi.org/10.1016/S0040-1625(01)00157-3.

Valeria Maria Urbano is a Ph.D. candidate in Data analytics and Decision Science at the Department of Management, Economics, and Industrial Engineering at Politecnico di Milano. She obtained her Master of Science in Management Engineering at Politecnico di Milano in 2019 with a dissertation on Future-Oriented Technology Analysis. Her main research interests are technology and innovation strategy and data sharing processes between organizations.

Marika Arena, Ph.D. is a Full Professor of Accounting Finance and Control at Politecnico di Milano. She is the Director of the Master of Science in Management Engineering and she is part of the Board of the Ph.D. in Management Engineering. She is the author of over 100 papers published in national and international journals and conference proceedings and book chapters.

Giovanni Azzone graduated with his Master of Science, cum laude, in Management Engineering at Politecnico di Milano, in 1986. Since 1994 he is a Full professor of Business Economics and Organization at Politecnico di Milano, where he served as Rector from 2010 to 2016. He is President of Arexpo SpA—the public-owned company in charge of developing the 1-million-square-meters area where the 2015 world exhibition took place—and member of the Board of Poste Italiane SpA—the 33-billion-euros turnover National mail delivery company.

The Role of Digital Technologies in Business Model Transition Toward Circular Economy in the Building Industry

Davide Chiaroni, Matteo Orlandi, and Andrea Urbinati

1 Introduction

Circular business model has recently emerged as a new research field in the Circular Economy research to call scholars and practitioners in strategic and innovation management research streams for analyzing the transition of companies from a linear to a circular model (Geissdoerfer et al. 2017; Lewandowski 2016).

Among the several managerial practices that companies can put in place to allow this transition, the adoption of digital technologies, such as Big Data and Analytics (BDA), Internet of Things (IoT), and Cyber-Physical Systems (CPSs), is becoming of paramount importance (Papadopoulos et al. 2017a, b). However, the role that these technologies can play both in terms of functionalities and circular value targets, such as energy efficiency, product lifecycle extension, etc. (MacArthur and Waughray 2016; Bressanelli et al. 2018), which can be reached because of their adoption, is still largely unexplored.

Starting from this premise, this chapter is aimed to depict how digital technologies can be adopted by companies to support the shift from a linear to a circular business model. In particular, this study presents a set of digital technologies that can effectively improve the circular practices in the built environment and shows, through the analysis of exemplary projects in which a leader company operating in the building industry was involved, how digital technologies can be

D. Chiaroni
School of Management, Politecnico di Milano, Milan, MI, Italy
e-mail: davide.chiaroni@polimi.it

M. Orlandi
Arup Italia, Milan, MI, Italy
e-mail: Matteo.Orlandi@arup.com

A. Urbinati (✉)
School of Industrial Engineering, LIUC Università Cattaneo, Castellanza, VA, Italy
e-mail: aurbinati@liuc.it

© The Author(s), under exclusive license to Springer Nature Switzerland AG 2021
D. R. A. Schallmo, J. Tidd (eds.), *Digitalization*, Management for Professionals,
https://doi.org/10.1007/978-3-030-69380-0_3

used to support the business model transition of companies toward Circular Economy.

We focused on case studies of projects in the building industry as this industry is particularly interesting to analyze both in terms of Circular Economy and digital technologies adoption. First, "buildings accounted for 32% of total global final energy use in 2010. Moreover, the building industry consumes 40% of the materials entering the global economy, while only an estimated 20–30% of these materials are recycled or reused at the end of life of a building" (Leising et al. 2018, p. 977). Second, the building sector is rather unexplored from the point of view of digital technologies adoption, although a few emerging studies have shown their potential in this industry (Elmualim et al. 2018).

The chapter is structured as follows. After the Introduction, Sect. 2 presents the current state of research about the role of digital technologies in the Circular Economy. Section 3 presents the rationale of the methodology and the case study analysis. Finally, Sect. 4 presents and discusses the results, whereas Sect. 5 summarizes the conclusions, also depicting the limitations and avenues for future research.

2   State-of-the-Art

Circular Economy has undoubtedly become an interesting topic over the last years both in academia and among practitioners and companies, with the goal to overcome the linear, open, models of production and resource consumption (Kirchherr et al. 2017; Ghisellini et al. 2016), which rely on the "take, make, dispose" paradigm. The Circular Economy approach aims to minimize the utilization of input raw material, enhance as much as possible the product lifetime, exploiting the maximum value from it, and when reached the end of life, repurpose, reuse, and/or recycling spare parts and raw materials in order to decrease the total demand of input material (Stahel 2016; Potting et al. 2017).

Circular business model has recently emerged as a new research field in the Circular Economy literature to analyze the transition of companies from a linear to a circular business model (Ranta et al. 2018). In particular, studies in this direction are aimed to deepen the managerial practices that companies can implement at the business model level, and among three major dimensions of a company's business model, namely value creation, value transfer, and value capture, to design their own circular business model (Urbinati et al. 2017; Ünal et al. 2019). The value creation dimension involves a set of (1) activities, such as modularization, standardization, design for products' disassembly, design for products' recycling, and (2) resources' usage, such as natural, recyclable, durable, easy-to-separate materials, which are necessary for establishing a circular value proposition (Moreno et al. 2016). The value transfer dimension concerns how companies interact with customers to share and promote explicitly the circular value proposition (Linder and Williander 2017; Shao and Ünal 2019). The value capture dimension, finally, involves a set of mechanisms, such as pay-as-a-service, to properly gather the circular value generated and to convert it into revenue streams, cost savings, and value preservation of resources (Geissdoerfer et al. 2017; Jiao and Evans 2017).

Among the several managerial practices that companies can adopt to allow this transition, it is interesting to investigate the use of digital technologies to support the design of the above three dimensions of companies' business model (Centobelli et al. 2020). In particular, several digital technologies have proliferated in recent years to support companies in improving the performance of their products and services, production processes, and in redesigning their organizational structures (Del Vecchio et al. 2018). These technologies may represent promising levers to foster the transition toward Circular Economy (Bressanelli et al. 2019).

A recent theoretical contribution in the intersection between Circular Economy and digital technologies has proposed a five-categories classification of main technologies that can contribute to reach Circular Economy targets (Rosa et al. 2020):

- *Cyber-Physical Systems (CPSs):* CPSs are an integration of hardware and software components; computers and integrated networks monitor and control physical processes, generally through feedback systems, in which physical processes influence calculations and vice versa (Lee et al. 2015).
- *Internet of Things (IoTs):* IoTs is a set of technologies that allows the interaction and cooperation between devices, things, or objects, using modern wireless telecommunications, such as radio frequency identification (RFID), but also sensors, tags, actuators, and cell phones (Nasiri et al. 2017).
- *Big Data and Analytics (BDAs):* BDAs represent the application of advanced data analysis techniques for the management, processing, and storage of large data sets (Urbinati et al. 2019; Soroka et al. 2017).
- *Additive Manufacturing (AM):* AM consists of a suite of technologies that allows producing a growing range of products through the layering or 3D printing of materials (Mandolla et al. 2019; Dutta et al. 2001).
- *Simulation Systems (SSs):* SSs are decision support tools based on a wide range of mathematical programming techniques that allow achieving objectives related to both Circular Economy and digitalization, such as the modeling of material flows in recycling processes or the regeneration of products or urban areas (Akanbi et al. 2018; Lieder et al. 2017).

Table 1 summarizes the main functionalities of the above categories of digital technologies for a Circular Economy transition.

For example, the AM is clearly related to the recycling of products and materials and allows an innovative way to reintroduce them on the market—as in the case of the SEB Group, a French multinational world leader in the production of small appliances, which has undertaken a spare parts 3D molding project to facilitate assistance and repair processes (Perona et al. 2018). CPSs can support the development of innovative services, in particular for maintenance applications—as in the case of the Hera Group, one of the major Italian multiutilities, which through this technology collects data from the water recovery process to generate knowledge and

Table 1 Digital technologies for a Circular Economy transition (adapted from Rosa et al. 2020)

Digital technologies	Functionalities
Cyber-Physical Systems (CPSs)	• Improving the management of the life cycle of products (Caggiano 2018; Gómez et al. 2018) • Developing new services, especially in monitoring and maintenance activities (Herterich et al. 2015)
Internet of Things (IoTs)	• Pursuing new waste management strategies, creating collaboration along the supply chain (Esmaeilian et al. 2018; Romero and Molina 2012; Romero and Noran 2017) • Creating intelligent industrial environments or dynamic feedback control systems (Hatzivasilis et al. 2018; Reuter 2016) • Developing new services, especially in monitoring and maintenance activities and optimizing Supply Chain Management (SCM) performances (Alcayaga and Hansen 2017; Jun 2009; French et al. 2017)
Big Data and Analytics (BDAs)	• Developing automated approaches aimed at evaluating new pathways for secondary materials or discovering potential industrial symbiosis (Davis et al. 2017; Jose and Ramakrishna 2018; Song et al. 2017) • Developing open-source tools, procedures, and services for the promotion of reuse or cloud platforms of services for the collection, analysis, and data storage (Franquesa et al. 2016; Franquesa and Navarro 2018; Lindström et al. 2018) • Supporting the assessment of innovative business models through integrative frameworks or the collection and management of data along the life cycle of products or the implementation of smart production actions (Jabbour et al. 2019; Li et al. 2015; Kusiak 2018) • Improving product disassembly planning, considering both the recycling problems during their design, and evaluating the cost reduction through their redesign (Marconi et al. 2019; Lin 2018; Ge and Jackson 2014)
Additive Manufacturing (AM)	• Supporting the management of the life cycle of products and processes, the so-called Life Cycle Assessment (LCA), as well as the digitalization of manufacturing processes (Isaksson et al. 2018; Jensen and Remmen 2017; Dutta et al. 2001; Unruh 2018) • Optimizing recycling processes, redesigning, and reusing products and their components, using recycled and bio-based materials (Clemon and Zohdi 2018; Lahrour and Brissaud 2018; Nascimento et al. 2019)
Simulation Systems (SSs)	• Optimizing Supply Chain Management (SCM) performances, allowing, among other things, to model material flows in the recycling processes and consequently to calculate performance indices of recycling (Schäfers and Walther 2017; Van Schaik and Reuter 2016) • Supporting the regeneration of products (Kuik et al. 2016; Wang and Wang 2019)

implement interventions (Luksch 2018). Finally, BDA and IoT can allow reaching circular value targets in several ways, such as the digitalization of circular managerial practices (e.g., maintenance, reuse/redistribute, refurbish/remanufacture, etc.), the life cycle management, the development of smart services, and a more effective management of the supply chain—as in the case of Rolls-Royce, which through the "Power-by-the-Hour" program has implemented the IoT to monitor the engine performance data in real time and to process automatically such data collected through the BDAs (Perona et al. 2018).

However, the role that these technologies can play both in terms of functionalities and circular value targets, such as energy efficiency, product lifecycle extension, etc. (MacArthur and Waughray 2016; Bressanelli et al. 2018), which can be reached because of their adoption, is still unexplored. Moreover, the role these technologies can play to support the design of value creation, transfer, and capture dimensions of companies' business model, and thus, the transition of companies from a linear to a circular business model deserves further investigation. Although the presence of a few interesting examples, further empirical analysis is needed to analyze the role of digital technologies in a business model transition of companies toward a Circular Economy (Chiaroni et al. 2020).

Accordingly, the aim of the chapter is to answer the following research question: *"How can digital technologies be adopted by companies operating in the building industry to support the transition of their business model toward Circular Economy?"*

3 Methodology

Using a Case Study Analysis

The chapter leverages an empirical analysis of projects in which a leader company operating in the building industry was involved to gain a better understanding of the role of digital technologies to support the design of a circular business model. The choice of a case study analysis is favored when addressing complex organizational and managerial issues through a qualitative-oriented approach (Yin 2003). In addition, case studies across longitudinal information sources are suited to answer "how" questions, as in our case, and to investigate a phenomenon in its whole complexity and to obtain initial insights on the phenomenon under investigation adopting an inductive approach in the interpretive tradition (Siggelkow 2007). In addition, case studies avoid the weaknesses inherent in retrospective reconstruction, and the associated reinterpretation errors, by real-time data collection. Although the identification of the case study has followed theoretical and convenience sampling criteria (Voss et al. 2002), its selection was made due to its high involvement in Circular Economy activities, especially driven by digital technologies adoption, and thus it fits with the above research question.

For the collection of the information, we established a semi-structured interview protocol with open-ended questions, which we used to make the interviewees with the key respondents of the company. We append the interview protocol in the Appendix (Table 5). Data were collected during March–April 2020. Key informants of our case study belong to the Technology Team of the Italian business unit of the selected company, which deals with technologies for enhancing a Circular Economy transition of the company and its clients. The team is guided by a Team Leader, who is responsible for all the team's activities. The first round of interviews was followed by a second and, in some cases, a third round, to consolidate information collected and to crosscheck relevant data and clarify important issues. In some cases, interviews were also followed up by emails with questions of clarification. Once permission had been granted, all the interviews were recorded and were later transcribed by the co-authors of the paper, enabling the inclusion of additional notes, comments, and ideas.

Interview data were coded using an iterative process that attempted to capture all the relevant information. A within-case analysis was conducted (Weber 1990) and, again, a cross-information analysis to identify and corroborate the recurrent pattern of useful information. All the information gathered from the key informants was triangulated with secondary sources of information to avoid post-hoc rationalizations (Yin 2003). For the purpose of enhancing data triangulation, in particular (Eisenhardt and Graebner 2007), various documents or archival records regarding the company (such as annual reports or internal firm-specific documentation related to processes and outcomes) were used (Amankwah-Amoah 2016). Finally, to support the reliability and validity of the whole collected and analyzed information, the Technology Team Leader was responsible for revising the manuscript and given his contribution to refine and enrich the empirical investigation was definitely involved as third co-author of the present research.

We continuously compared the results of the empirical evidence with the information deriving from the scientific research to refine, enrich, and modify the theoretical setting. To describe the case, we adopted a narrative approach in the form of a "narrative report" (Langley 1999), as follows.

Presentation of the Company and the Industry

The Company[1]

The company chosen as a case study is Arup, a multinational firm of designers, planners, engineers, architects, consultants, and technical specialists, working across every aspect of the built environment, from buildings to infrastructures, committed to shaping the digital built environment. Born in 1946 in London, over time the company "has pushed the boundaries of what design and engineering can achieve", with the vision that a more collaborative and open-minded approach to engineering would lead to work of greater quality and enduring relevance. Arup continues to be recognized for bravely imaginative solutions to the world's most challenging projects. The company "has always nurtured pioneers and original thinkers, and for decades those creative and ambitious have come to the company to do their best work." "From concert halls that led to new definitions of acoustic engineering, to its

---

[1]The information included in this section about the company profile was taken, unless otherwise specified, from Arup website: https://www.arup.com/.

long history of developing the digital tools the building industry relies upon, that of the company is a story of relentless innovation." Globally, Arup has annual revenues accounting for approximately £1.71 billion with more than 15,000 staff members and almost 7000 customers served across the world (year 2019). Employees are also "independent by nature, with the confidence to take on some of the world's most challenging projects." In addition, in 2016 the company started a strategic partnership with the Ellen MacArthur Foundation, the pioneer international organization for developing Circular Economy. Arup is present with several business units in America, Australia, East Asia, Middle East, and Europe, including Italy. The Italian business unit, named Arup Italia, was established in the year 2000 in response to an ever-increasing demand for specialist consultancy and the number of complex projects being developed.

The Industry[2]

The building industry is the world's largest consumer of raw materials. It represents 50% of world steel production and consumes over 3 billion tons of raw materials (WEF 2016). The demand for the building resources is also increasing by global demographic and lifestyle changes, and many of them are becoming scarcer and more difficult to extract. For example, natural resources are currently consumed at twice the speed with which they are produced. By 2050, this speed rate could be three times (Arup 2016). In addition, the growth of the world population and, especially, of its middle class (which will expand from 2 to 5 billion by 2030) is putting unprecedented pressure on natural resources (Pezzini 2012). Competition for resources and supply disruptions are already contributing to volatile materials prices, creating short-term uncertainty, and increasing overall costs. Stricter global environmental regulations to protect fragile ecosystems are also making it more difficult and expensive to extract and use certain resources. The built environment is under increasing pressure to minimize its impact. A Circular Economy approach could help the sector to reduce its environmental footprint, avoiding rising costs, delays, and other consequences of volatile commodity markets. Given the potential to save £60 billion of primary resources by 2030 in the European Union (EU) (Ellen MacArthur Foundation and McKinsey Center for Business and Environment 2015), there are clear advantages in adopting Circular Economy practices across the EU sector. This would involve remodeling the way projects are purchased, designed, built, managed, and reused. A recent study from Arup (2016) has highlighted how the Circular Economy approach can be applied in the built environment. For example: efficient and circular building performance (e.g., net zero energy strategies) reduce negative externalities, consumption of primary resources and waste, and help safeguarding, restoring, and increasing the resilience of ecosystems;

---

[2]The information included in this section about the industry in which the company operates was taken, unless otherwise specified, from Arup (2016) Report: "The Circular Economy in the Built Environment", available at: https://www.arup.com/perspectives/publications/research/section/circular-economy-in-the-built-environment.

sharing of spaces and infrastructure (e.g., peer-to-peer sharing, and co-living) allows for optimizing asset use; modular buildings may optimize also the efficiency and resource consumption in the production phase; remanufacturing, recovering, and recycling loops allow for closing the materials and components flows that take place in both the biological and technical cycles, creating new uses for materials.

Digitalization Initiatives[3]

The role of digital technologies across the built environment is enormous. As underlined by Will Cavendish, Global Digital Services Leader at Arup, *"digital technologies are transforming every aspect of the built environment. We help clients take advantage of this new, connected world."* Indeed, digital technologies allow organizations "to make informed decisions about the design, management, and performance of their assets, helping them to be more sustainable and resilient to change." Among the several solutions, the built environment can especially benefit from the exploitation of a digital twin, i.e., "a digital representation of a real-world entity—a building, a bridge, a rail network, even an entire city—aimed at making that entity safer, more efficient, and more resilient to change." Digital twins are also undergoing a period of rapid innovation. Arup, for example, uses the digital twin for predicting traffic patterns, energy usage, building stresses, develop predictive maintenance, assess fire risk and other resource and risk profiles. In this perspective, the Digital Transformation Plan of the company is based on four main work streams: Data, Automation, Services, and Products. Along these workstreams, six main digital services can be identified: (1) Building Information Modeling (BIM), (2) Data insights and analytics, (3) Geographic Information Systems (GISs), (4) Information and Communication Technology (ICT) infrastructure design, (5) Software products, and (6) Visualization. In particular, (1) BIM represents "the bedrock of intelligent assets, embedding data in every aspect of a smarter built environment. It consists of an advanced design process that brings to life the interactions between designers and between each design element." As pointed out by Volker Buscher, Chief Data Officer, *"digital tools like data-driven analysis are already helping us improve how assets are designed and constructed. We can enhance the experience of the people who interact with them and analyze how these assets will perform in future";* (2) data insights and analytics are aimed to "provide important insights, create a single point of truth on project performance, answer key commercial questions, and help organizations to predict and react to future trends"; (3) in addition, the company leverages the Geographic Information Systems (GISs) technology to visualize, manage, analyze, and collate data based on geo-referenced locations. The services range from web-based mapping tools to 3D models, often incorporating BIM. GIS solutions "make it simpler and quicker to manage assets geographically, to identify opportunities, reduce risk, and adapt to better face the future"; (4) moreover, ICT infrastructure and integrated technology

---

[3]The information included in this section about the digitalization initiatives of the company was taken, unless otherwise specified, from Arup website: https://www.arup.com/.

designs support buildings and businesses to operate effectively. The company's "consultants combine technology expertise with built environment knowledge to design network and ICT infrastructure solutions, which ensure operations are never compromised and reach their full potential"; (5) the company also began developing its own software suites more than 40 years ago in response to the building environment evolving challenges. Today, the company's software house brings relevant, flexible, tools to organizations and leads the field in structural, geotechnical, crowd simulation, and document management solutions; (6) finally, the company combines "design data from across all disciplines to create robust representations for architects, engineers, developers, planners, and governments. Multidisciplinary visualizations bring future projects to life, aiding decision-making, and engagement. These benefit any stage of a project—feasibility, early design, planning, consultation, detailed design, or marketing."

4   Results and Discussion[4]

The intersection between digital technologies and Circular Economy becomes tangible in a large variety of consultancy and projects where Arup is involved. We had the chance to access data and discuss exemplary projects, involving different usage of digital technologies.

Interestingly the company focused one of its major development on Simulation Systems (SSs). The goal of the company was to build a digital twin that could be used for supporting decisions at different levels and at different stages of development of the project and operation of the building. The SS of Arup is named Neuron and its main characteristics are reported in Table 2.

The tool Neuron is a clear example of how far digital models of buildings can go and where data analytics and Artificial Intelligence & Machine Learning (AI/ML) techniques are used to perform advanced analysis, collect real-time data, and autonomously predict the user profiles of the building, the energy and water consumptions and then set maintenance scenarios. These outcomes are fundamental for clients and facility management teams to make informed decisions about achieving the most efficient use of resources and save energy costs. Maintenance activities and replacement of components can be scheduled according to business models based on a circular approach. For example, lighting fixtures may follow a product-as-a-service scheme, where the provider will guarantee a performance rather than selling a product; other components might require a replacement at a point of their lifetime that can be set when they still have a value on the secondary market or can be reused for other purposes, thus generating an opportunity for cost savings or additional revenues.

---

[4]The information included in the Results and Discussion was elaborated from the combination of interviews and Arup website: https://www.arup.com/.

Table 2 The Neuron tool of Arup

Tool	Description
Neuron	Neuron is an integrated "BIM + IoT + Analytics" "platform for smart buildings, characterized by a cloud-based centralized management console that provides a foundation to connect disparate building systems and equipment, making them easily accessible and facilitating operation and maintenance. Neuron is named as a reflection of the human neuron network, just like our own neurons, the IoT sensor network enabled with analytics capabilities is deployed in the building environment, enabling prompt and adaptive response to dynamic environments. Therefore, the platform takes the concept of smart buildings to a new level and changes the way buildings are designed, constructed, managed, operated, and maintained. It does not only help buildings achieve energy savings, but also create a better indoor environment that focuses on the health and wellbeing of the occupants. Neuron has already been applied to several pilot projects. For example, in Hong Kong, Neuron is in use in One Taikoo Place, a brand-new triple Grade A 48-story office tower developed by Swire Properties, which is now the first AI and data-driven smart building in the city." A Project Manager of Swire Properties commented: *"By implementing Neuron, One Taikoo Place now becomes Hong Kong's first AI-enabled smart building. It is definitely another milestone for our continuous endeavour in data-driven building operation and asset management."* "Neuron was also implemented in the iconic Water Cube in Beijing with substantial improvement in its operation. For example, through energy usage optimization and predictive maintenance, an energy saving of up to 25% has been realized. In addition, with air pollution being a major concern for Beijing, a network of IoT sensors deployed in the venue continuously monitor the indoor air quality and collect data to help optimize building system operations."

To have an effective SS like Neuron, however, the company had to build several layers of related digital technologies, namely Cyber-Physical Systems (CPSs), Internet of Things (IoTs), and Big Data and Analytics (BDAs). Therefore, Neuron consolidates and links data from disparate equipment and devices and turn them into customized insights for energy and building system optimization through interactive and responsive dashboards. Accordingly, the adoption of digital technologies is fundamental to support the decision-making process toward the adoption of specific circular managerial practices and to increase the awareness of all the stakeholders. In particular, the adoption of live dashboards, shared on cloud platforms, can be also used to identify projects' ambitions, needs, and actions to be implemented in the design process. Since the early stages, a shared view of the workstreams and the areas of actions is essential for a holistic definition of project deliveries. Decision-making or framework definition dashboards can be developed at different levels of detail. On the one hand, they can be focused on Circular Economy only, thus identifying sub-workstream areas (e.g., technical, energy, economy, and social). On the other hand, they can be adopted at a broader level, where Circular Economy is one of the project drivers in a wider sustainability strategy. Both the two configuration frameworks of the dashboard require the end client to define initial aims and then all the stakeholders and the design team to be called in and provide proposals to populate the dashboard. It is initially evaluated through quantitative and qualitative Key Performances Indicators (KPIs); finally, through a series of buy-in sessions, the managerial actions to be implemented in the next stage of work are defined.

In addition to the focus on SSs, the company started exploring the usage of Additive Manufacturing (AM). Additive Manufacturing (AM) has been applied in several exemplary projects of Arup to enable a circular transition: (1) the 3D Housing 05 in Milan, (2) the MX3D bridge in Amsterdam, (3) the Daedalus Pavilion, and (4) the Cloud Pergola at the Biennale in Venice, are all projects where the digitalization of the design, manufacturing, and construction processes was the key to empower an approach based on the principles of Circular Economy. Table 3 summarizes the key aspects of each project.

Also in this case, the use of Big Data and Analytics (BDAs), empowered by Artificial Intelligence (AI), particularly on robotics and image recognition techniques, have allowed for the manufacturing of building and components capable to use the minimum amount of materials required, thus minimizing waste and pushing for the development of innovative and sustainable materials mix.

The overall results of the empirical analysis were finally mapped onto the dimensions of a company's business model, which have been particularly addressed by the analyzed digitalization projects, i.e., the value creation and value transfer dimensions (Table 4).

In particular, Additive Manufacturing (AM) was necessary to support the digitalization of the design, manufacturing, and construction processes of modular buildings. It is worth highlighting that Big Data and Analytics (BDAs), also empowered by Artificial Intelligence (AI), were useful to Additive Manufacturing (AM) for the manufacturing of buildings and components.

On the other hand, the value transfer dimension was especially enabled by Simulation Systems (SSs), which have required to build several layers of related digital technologies, namely Cyber-Physical Systems (CPSs), Internet of Things (IoTs), and Big Data and Analytics (BDAs), for exploiting the most of their effectiveness. In addition, although it is true that SSs require a direct involvement of customers, the company is still in the transition phase and we do not have yet available information and tools for deepening the business model dimension of value capture.

5   Conclusions

The chapter was aimed to depict how digital technologies can be adopted by companies to support the transition of their business model toward Circular Economy. The main outcome of the study is twofold. On the one hand, the chapter takes stock of the main research in the intersection between Circular Economy and digital technologies, by highlighting a set of relevant digital technologies, as well as their main functionalities, which allows to improve the circularity of business models. The chapter, moreover, sheds light on the different contributions of digital technologies to the value creation, transfer, and capture, in the building industry, pointing out that the transition toward Circular Economy requires a long journey and therefore is still far from being achieved. On the other hand, the findings of the empirical analysis allow managers and practitioners to reflect on the potentialities

Table 3 The role of AM in exemplary Arup projects

Project	Description
3D Housing 05 in Milan	3D Housing 05 is the first house printed on site with 3D technology in Europe, conceived and designed by the CLS Architetti together with Italcementi, Arup, and Cybe. Arup developed the engineering of the house by exploiting the most advanced analysis techniques. Italcementi took part in this new challenge by providing know-how, solutions, and performances resulting from the research activities carried out in most recent years in its i.lab, a research and innovation center. It is a house of about 100 square meters, with a living area, sleeping area, kitchen, bathroom, which is built in 2/3 weeks with a 3D printer. The house is sustainable, it can be dismantled and rebuilt elsewhere as you wish, enlarged, and having the possibility to build it in a very short time, it costs less than a traditional home. Besides, there is almost no waste produced during construction, as the engineering and control system allows for a precision of printing, which ensures that every centimeter of material is properly used.
MX3D bridge in Amsterdam	The first stainless steel bridge in the world was built thanks to the use of technologies inspired by the operation of traditional 3D printers. Over 4500 kg of material, four robots, and more than 1100 km of filaments were needed to create the structure in a span of about 6 months. The design was designed by the Joris Laarman Lab. The length of the bridge is 12.5 m, while the total width is 6.3 m. MX3D used three-dimensional printing to create the skeleton, while the robotic units took care of adding the layers to complete the structure and the finishes. The project managers conducted the necessary tests to certify their resistance to stress before everything can be laid. The first load tests carried out by passing around 30 people at the same time returned a positive result. These are the words of the team: *"It was a bit like being in a science-fiction story, it's different from everything else. Usually we work in the shipyards, where everything is geometrically perfect, while this bridge does not have a single straight line."* Arup collaborated in the initiative for the engineering design phase, Heijmans providing their expertise in the construction process, and AcelorMittal for the selection of materials. Once the test rock has passed, the bridge was laid in Amsterdam.
Daedalus Pavilion	Dedalus Pavilion is a "3D printed architectural installation built by robots, as part of NVIDIA's GPU Technology Conference in Amsterdam. Ai Build teamed up with Arup engineers for this project to showcase how the future of construction can be transformed by robotics and the use of AI techniques to optimize printing and the use of materials. Daedalus Pavilion measures 5 m wide × 5 m deep × 4.5 m high, and it consists of 48 pieces that are 3D printed using an industrial robot provided by Kuka. All pieces were 3D printed within 3 weeks, using 160 kg of biodegradable filament material supplied by Formfutura, a Dutch manufacturer. Ai Build made use of NVIDIA GPUs for running a combination of computer vision and deep learning algorithms to increase the speed and accuracy of large-scale 3D printing." NVIDIA's Deep Learning Start-up Business Manager for Northern Europe said:

(continued)

Table 3 (continued)

Project	Description
	"We're tremendously excited to premiere "Daedalus Pavilion" at our first GTC in Europe. This collaboration between Ai Build and Arup is a strikingly tangible taste of how even established industries like construction will be transformed by artificial intelligence." The Chartered Structural Engineer and the Structural Design Engineer of Arup also commented on their collaboration with Ai Build: *"The Daedalus Pavilion has been an incredible opportunity for Arup to collaborate with a promising start-up, Ai Build. Our structural engineering expertise, combined with the latest large-scale 3D printing technology, have enabled us to create an elegant and structurally efficient form with an optimized distribution of material."*
Cloud Pergola at the Biennale in Venice	It is a suggestive representation of a physical cloud that was shaped and elaborated digitally on the computer. The author is an architect, designer, innovator. The structure, born on the inspiration of structures co-designed with artificial intelligence tools, was entrusted, for 3D printing, to Ai Build, a London-based company specialized in robotics and AI, which proceeded to transform the author's concepts into reality, printing them in 3D, and sending them to Venice in blocks that were then assembled on site. In this project, Arup was a structural consultant. The structure is one of the largest 3D printed in Europe, one that measures 3.3 m in height and covers an area of 57 square meters. The CEO of Ai Build commented: *"This project is a look at what architecture is evolving with advances in technology. Traditionally architects were accustomed to designing under the constraints of standard manufacturing methods. Now we are giving designers the opportunity to produce almost anything with robots. This new paradigm in manufacturing is opening the possibility of producing very complex projects that are driven by innovative data and aesthetics. Cloud Pergola is the perfect example of a robust and light structure, with unprecedented aesthetic qualities, made possible by designers, engineers, and technology specialists who work synergistically."*

Table 4 Empirical findings mapped onto the dimensions of a company's business model

	Arup projects	
Business model dimensions	Modular buildings	Neuron
Value creation	Big Data and Analytics (BDAs) and Artificial Intelligence (AI)	
	Additive Manufacturing (AM)	Internet of Things (IoTs)
		Cyber-Physical Systems (CPSs)
Value transfer		Simulation Systems (SSs)

offered by the digital technologies to improve the effectiveness of circular initiatives in companies' business model operating in the building industry.

The transition toward Circular Economy is nowadays increasingly important, and although an increasing number of studies dedicated to this topic has proliferated, only a few, more recent, contributions have tried to deepen the relationship between digital technologies and Circular Economy. In other words, research still needs more theoretical and practical effort into the analysis of how companies design a circular business model while adopting digital technologies.

The present chapter offers an important contribution to the current scientific debate that crosses the themes of Circular Economy and digital technologies from a strategic perspective, posing the attention to how digital technologies can be adopted by companies to support the shift from a linear to a circular business model, especially in the building industry. Practitioners and managers with roles of responsibility in strategic and innovation departments of companies can benefit from our research, as it shows how digital technologies can increase the degree of circularity of companies' business model operating in the building industry, being more sustainable while profitable.

However, although we have leveraged a case study analysis of exemplary projects in which a leader company operating in the building industry is involved, our analysis has several limitations that claim for further studies. For example, studies are needed to deepen the analysis of the role of digital technologies in a circular business model, even beyond the boundaries of a single firm. Indeed, digital technologies can support the interactions of the several actors operating in the supply chain and enable a more effective exchange of information across the supply chain itself. This is of particular interest in the building industry as well. Therefore, the role that digital technologies can play within the circular supply chain management can be a particularly interesting point of study. Moreover, our results and conclusions are so far hard to statistically generalize or transfer across different companies and industries. Furthermore, a higher number of companies operating in the same sector of activity or in different industries could be involved, and more projects could be investigated, in order to enrich our findings and extend the knowledge into the building industry and other contexts, thus claiming for more studies to come in the field of Circular Economy.

Appendix

Table 5 Interview protocol

Company background
1. Types of firm
(a) Target market
(b) Size and performances
(c) Competences
(d) Portfolio of products and services
2. Structure and reference context
(a) Organizational structure
(b) Competitive arena
(c) Supply chain and supply chain relationship
Circular economy and digital technologies
1. How important is the Circular Economy for your company and your business?
2. In which projects, and how, do you apply the Circular Economy approach?
3. What is the role of digital technologies in your company?
4. What role have digital technologies played in your main projects?
5. Do you use any kind of online platform to manage and enhance customer relationships?
6. Do you use any kind of online platform to manage and enhance relationships with suppliers or partners?
7. Do you propose any digital technology for supporting the closing of material flows?
8. Do you implement any digital technology to monitor products over their lifecycle?
Impact of the digital technologies on circularity
1. Which lessons can be learned from the implementation of digital technologies in the view of Circular Economy?
2. How has digital technology changed the way employees work?
3. Which departments have been more affected by the change?
4. How have your clients reacted in the light of the digital technologies' adoption?
Problems of the use of design for circularity
1. Which problems and challenges have been faced in the implementation of digital technologies in support of the Circular Economy transition?
2. What are the main barriers that can be encountered for the digital technologies' adoption?

References

Akanbi, L. A., Oyedele, L. O., Akinade, O. O., Ajayi, A. O., Delgado, M. D., Bilal, M., & Bello, S. A. (2018). Salvaging building materials in a circular economy: A BIM-based whole-life performance estimator. *Resources, Conservation and Recycling, 129*, 175–186.

Alcayaga, A., & Hansen, E. G. (2017). Smart-circular systems: A service business model perspective. In *Research in Design Series, PLATE 2017 Conference Proceedings* (Vol. 9, pp. 10–13).

Amankwah-Amoah, J. (2016). Global business and emerging economies: Towards a new perspective on the effects of e-waste. *Technological Forecasting and Social Change, 105*, 20–26.

Arup. (2016). *The circular economy in the built environment*. Retrieved from https://www.arup.com/perspectives/publications/research/section/circular-economy-in-the-built-environment

Bressanelli, G., Adrodegari, F., Perona, M., & Saccani, N. (2018). Exploring how usage-focused business models enable circular economy through digital technologies. *Sustainability, 10*(3), 639.

Bressanelli, G., Perona, M., & Saccani, N. (2019). Assessing the impacts of Circular Economy: A framework and an application to the washing machine industry. *International Journal of Management and Decision Making, 18*, 282–308.

Caggiano, A. (2018). Cloud-based manufacturing process monitoring for smart diagnosis services. *International Journal of Computer Integrated Manufacturing, 31*(7), 612–623.

Centobelli, P., Cerchione, R., Chiaroni, D., Del Vecchio, P., & Urbinati, A. (2020). Designing business models in circular economy: A systematic literature review and research agenda. *Business Strategy and the Environment*. forthcoming.

Chiaroni, D., Del Vecchio, P., Peck, D., Urbinati, A., & Vrontis, D. (2020). Digital technologies in the business model transition towards a circular economy. *Resources, Conservation and Recycling*, 105286, in press.

Clemon, L. M., & Zohdi, T. I. (2018). On the tolerable limits of granulated recycled material additives to maintain structural integrity. *Construction and Building Materials, 167*, 846–852.

Davis, C. B., Aid, G., & Zhu, B. (2017). Secondary resources in the bio-based economy: A computer assisted survey of value pathways in academic literature. *Waste and Biomass Valorization, 8*(7), 2229–2246.

Del Vecchio, P., Di Minin, A., Petruzzelli, A. M., Panniello, U., & Pirri, S. (2018). Big data for open innovation in SMEs and large corporations: Trends, opportunities, and challenges. *Creativity and Innovation Management, 27*(1), 6–22.

Dutta, D., Prinz, F. B., Rosen, D., & Weiss, L. (2001). Layered manufacturing: Current status and future trends. *Journal of Computing and Information Science in Engineering, 1*(1), 60–71.

Esmaeilian, B., Wang, B., Lewis, K., Duarte, F., Ratti, C., & Behdad, S. (2018). The future of waste management in smart and sustainable cities: A review and concept paper. *Waste Management, 81*, 177–195.

Eisenhardt, K. M., & Graebner, M. E. (2007). Theory building from cases: Opportunities and challenges. *Academy of Management Journal, 50*(1), 25–32.

Ellen MacArthur Foundation, & McKinsey Center for Business and Environment. (2015). *Growth within: A circular economy vision for a competitive Europe*. Ellen MacArthur Foundation.

Elmualim, A., Mostafa, S., Chileshe, N., & Rameezdeen, R. (2018). Construction and the circular economy: Smart and industrialised prefabrication. In *Unmaking waste in production and consumption: Towards the circular economy* (pp. 323–336). Emerald Publishing Limited.

Franquesa, D., & Navarro, L. (2018). Devices as a commons: Limits to premature recycling. In *Proceedings of the 2018 Workshop on Computing within Limits* (p. 8). ACM.

Franquesa, D., Navarro, L., & Bustamante, X. (2016). A circular commons for digital devices: Tools and services in ereuse.org. In *Proceedings of the Second Workshop on Computing within Limits* (p. 3). ACM.

French, R., Benakis, M., & Marin-Reyes, H. (2017, October). Intelligent sensing for robotic re-manufacturing in aerospace—An industry 4.0 design based prototype. In *2017 IEEE International Symposium on Robotics and Intelligent Sensors (IRIS)* (pp. 272–277). IEEE.

Ge, X., & Jackson, J. (2014). The big data application strategy for cost reduction in automotive industry. *SAE International Journal of Commercial Vehicles, 7*(2014-01-2410), 588–598.

Geissdoerfer, M., Savaget, P., Bocken, N. M., & Hultink, E. J. (2017). The Circular Economy–A new sustainability paradigm? *Journal of Cleaner Production, 143*, 757–768.

Ghisellini, P., Cialani, C., & Ulgiati, S. (2016). A review on circular economy: The expected transition to a balanced interplay of environmental and economic systems. *Journal of Cleaner Production, 114*, 11–32.

Gómez, A. M. M., González, F. A., & Bárcena, M. M. (2018). Smart eco-industrial parks: A circular economy implementation based on industrial metabolism. *Resources, Conservation and Recycling, 135*, 58–69.

Hatzivasilis, G., Fysarakis, K., Soultatos, O., Askoxylakis, I., Papaefstathiou, I., & Demetriou, G. (2018). The industrial internet of things as an enabler for a circular economy Hy-LP: A Novel IIoT protocol, evaluated on a wind park's SDN/NFV-enabled 5G industrial network. *Computer Communications, 119*, 127–137.

Herterich, M. M., Uebernickel, F., & Brenner, W. (2015). The impact of cyber-physical systems on industrial services in manufacturing. *Procedia Cirp, 30*, 323–328.

Isaksson, O., Hallstedt, S. I., & Rönnbäck, A. Ö. (2018). Digitalisation, sustainability and servitisation: Consequences on product development capabilities in manufacturing firms. In *International Design Conference-Norddesign–Linköping*.

Jabbour, C. J. C., de Sousa Jabbour, A. B. L., Sarkis, J., & Godinho Filho, M. (2019). Unlocking the circular economy through new business models based on large-scale data: An integrative framework and research agenda. *Technological Forecasting and Social Change, 144*, 546–552.

Jensen, J. P., & Remmen, A. (2017). Enabling circular economy through product stewardship. *Procedia Manufacturing, 8*, 377–384.

Jiao, N., & Evans, S. (2017). Business models for sustainability: The case of repurposing a second-life for electric vehicle batteries. In *International conference on sustainable design and manufacturing* (pp. 537–545). Cham: Springer.

Jose, R., & Ramakrishna, S. (2018). Materials 4.0: Materials big data enabled materials discovery. *Applied Materials Today, 10*, 127–132.

Jun, X. (2009). Model of cluster green supply chain performance evaluation based on circular economy. In *2009 Second International Conference On Intelligent Computation Technology and Automation* (Vol. 3, pp. 941–944). IEEE.

Kirchherr, J., Reike, D., & Hekkert, M. (2017). Conceptualizing the circular economy: An analysis of 114 definitions. *Resources, Conservation & Recycling, 127*, 221–232.

Kuik, S. S., Kaihara, T., & Fujii, N. (2016). Product recovery configuration decisions for achieving sustainable manufacturing. *Procedia CIRP, 41*, 258–263.

Kusiak, A. (2018). Smart manufacturing. *International Journal of Production Research, 56*(1–2), 508–517.

Lahrour, Y., & Brissaud, D. (2018). A technical assessment of product/component re-manufacturability for additive remanufacturing. *Procedia CIRP, 69*, 142–147.

Langley, A. (1999). Strategies for theorizing from process data. *Academy of Management review, 24*(4), 691–710.

Lee, J., Bagheri, B., & Kao, H. A. (2015). A cyber-physical systems architecture for industry 4.0-based manufacturing systems. *Manufacturing Letters, 3*, 18–23.

Leising, E., Quist, J., & Bocken, N. (2018). Circular economy in the building sector: Three cases and a collaboration tool. *Journal of Cleaner Production, 176*, 976–989.

Lewandowski, M. (2016). Designing the business models for circular economy—Towards the conceptual framework. *Sustainability, 8*(1), 43.

Li, J., Tao, F., Cheng, Y., & Zhao, L. (2015). Big data in product lifecycle management. *The International Journal of Advanced Manufacturing Technology, 81*(1–4), 667–684.

Lieder, M., Asif, F. M., Rashid, A., Mihelič, A., & Kotnik, S. (2017). Towards circular economy implementation in manufacturing systems using a multi-method simulation approach to link design and business strategy. *The International Journal of Advanced Manufacturing Technology, 93*(5–8), 1953–1970.

Lin, K. Y. (2018). User experience-based product design for smart production to empower industry 4.0 in the glass recycling circular economy. *Computers & Industrial Engineering, 125*, 729–738.

Linder, M., & Williander, M. (2017). Circular business model innovation: inherent uncertainties. *Business Strategy and the Environment, 26*(2), 182–196.

Lindström, J., Hermanson, A., Blomstedt, F., & Kyösti, P. (2018). A multi-usable cloud service platform: A case study on improved development pace and efficiency. *Applied Sciences, 8*(2), 316.

Luksch, A. (2018). *Gruppo Hera: la multiutility dell'energia innova scommettendo sulla "Circular Smart City"*. Retrieved from https://www.economyup.it/innovazione/gruppo-hera-per-innovare-la-multiutility-dellenergia-scommette-sulla-circular-smart-city/

MacArthur, D. E., & Waughray, D. (2016). *Intelligent assets. Unlocking the circular economy potential*. Cowes: Ellen MacArthur Foundation.

Mandolla, C., Petruzzelli, A. M., Percoco, G., & Urbinati, A. (2019). Building a digital twin for additive manufacturing through the exploitation of blockchain: A case analysis of the aircraft industry. *Computers in Industry, 109*, 134–152.

Moreno, M., De los Rios, C., Rowe, Z., & Charnley, F. (2016). A conceptual framework for circular design. *Sustainability, 8*(9), 937.

Marconi, M., Germani, M., Mandolini, M., & Favi, C. (2019). Applying data mining technique to disassembly sequence planning: A method to assess effective disassembly time of industrial products. *International Journal of Production Research, 57*(2), 599–623.

Nascimento, D. L. M., Alencastro, V., Quelhas, O. L. G., Caiado, R. G. G., Garza-Reyes, J. A., Rocha-Lona, L., & Tortorella, G. (2019). Exploring Industry 4.0 technologies to enable circular economy practices in a manufacturing context: A business model proposal. *Journal of Manufacturing Technology Management, 30*(3), 607–627.

Nasiri, M., Tura, N., & Ojanen, V. (2017). Developing Disruptive Innovations for Sustainability: A Review on Impact of Internet of Things (IOT). In *2017 Portland International Conference on Management of Engineering and Technology (PICMET)* (pp. 1–10). IEEE.

Papadopoulos, T., Gunasekaran, A., Dubey, R., Altay, N., Childe, S. J., & Fosso Wamba, S. (2017a). The role of Big Data in explaining disaster resilience in supply chains for sustainability. *Journal of Cleaner Production, 142*, 1108–1118.

Papadopoulos, T., Gunasekaran, A., Dubey, R., & Fosso Wamba, S. (2017b). Big data and analytics in operations and supply chain management: Managerial aspects and practical challenges. *Production Planning & Control, 28*(11-12), 873–876.

Perona, M., Saccani, N., & Bressanelli, G. (2018). Digitale e sostenibilità: come le tecnologie 4.0 abilitano l'Economia Circolare. Disponibile su: https://www.industry4business.it/esperti-e-analisti/digitale-e-sostenibilita-come-le-tecnologie-4-0-abilitano-leconomia-circolare/

Pezzini, M. (2012). *An emerging middle class*. Retrieved from https://oecdobserver.org/news/fullstory.php/aid/3681/An_emerging_middle_class.html

Potting, J., Hekkert, M. P., Worrell, E., & Hanemaaijer, A. (2017). *Circular economy: Measuring innovation in the product chain* (No. 2544). PBL Publishers.

Ranta, V., Aarikka-Stenroos, L., & Mäkinen, S. J. (2018). Creating value in the circular economy: A structured multiple-case analysis of business models. *Journal of Cleaner Production, 201*, 988–1000.

Reuter, M. A. (2016). Digitalizing the circular economy. *Metallurgical and Materials transactions B, 47*(6), 3194–3220.

Romero, D., & Molina, A. (2012). Green virtual enterprise breeding environments: A sustainable industrial development model for a circular economy. In *Working Conference on Virtual Enterprises* (pp. 427–436). Berlin: Springer.

Romero, D., & Noran, O. (2017). Towards green sensing virtual enterprises: Interconnected sensing enterprises, intelligent assets and smart products in the cyber-physical circular economy. *IFAC-PapersOnLine, 50*(1), 11719–11724.

Rosa, P., Sassanelli, C., Urbinati, A., Chiaroni, D., & Terzi, S. (2020). Assessing relations between circular economy and industry 4.0: A systematic literature review. *International Journal of Production Research, 58*(6), 1662–1687.

Schäfers, P., & Walther, A. (2017). Modelling circular material flow and the consequences for SCM and PPC. *Global Journal of Business Research, 11*(2), 91–100.

Shao, J., & Ünal, E. (2019). What do consumers value more in green purchasing? Assessing the sustainability practices from demand side of business. *Journal of Cleaner Production, 209*, 1473–1483.

Siggelkow, N. (2007). Persuasion with case studies. *Academy of Management Journal, 50*(1), 20–24.

Song, B., Yeo, Z., Kohls, P., & Herrmann, C. (2017). Industrial symbiosis: Exploring big-data approach for waste stream discovery. *Procedia CIRP, 61*, 353–358.

Soroka, A., Liu, Y., Han, L., & Haleem, M. S. (2017). Big data driven customer insights for SMEs in redistributed manufacturing. *Procedia CIRP, 63*, 692–697.

Stahel, W. R. (2016). The circular economy. *Nature, 531*(7595), 435–438.

Ünal, E., Urbinati, A., & Chiaroni, D. (2019). Managerial practices for designing circular economy business models: The case of an Italian SME in the office supply industry. *Journal of Manufacturing Technology Management, 30*(3), 561–589.

Unruh, G. (2018). Circular economy, 3D printing, and the biosphere rules. *California Management Review, 60*(3), 95–111.

Urbinati, A., Bogers, M., Chiesa, V., & Frattini, F. (2019). Creating and capturing value from Big Data: A multiple-case study analysis of provider companies. *Technovation, 84*, 21–36.

Urbinati, A., Chiaroni, D., & Chiesa, V. (2017). Towards a new taxonomy of circular economy business models. *Journal of Cleaner Production, 168*, 487–498.

Van Schaik, A., & Reuter, M. A. (2016). Recycling indices visualizing the performance of the circular economy. *World of Metallurgy, 69*(4).

Voss, C., Tsikriktsis, N., & Frohlich, M. (2002). Case research in operations management. *International Journal of Operations & Production Management, 22*(2), 195–219.

Wang, X. V., & Wang, L. (2019). Digital twin-based WEEE recycling, recovery and remanufacturing in the background of Industry 4.0. *International Journal of Production Research, 57*(12), 3892–3902.

Weber, R. P. (1990). *Basic content analysis* (No. 49). Sage.

WEF (World Economic Forum). (2016). *Shaping the future of construction: A breakthrough in mindset and technology*. Retrieved from https://www3.weforum.org/docs/WEF_Shaping_the_Future_of_Construction_report_020516.pdf

Yin, R. K. (2003). *Case study research* (Vol. 5). Thousand Oaks, CA.

Davide Chiaroni is Full Professor of Strategy & Marketing at Politecnico di Milano, where he obtained in 2007 his Ph.D. in Management, Economics and Industrial Engineering. His research interest is in the management of innovation, with a particular focus on energy, sustainability and smart ecosystems (grid, buildings, communities, cities). He is also among the most cited authors in the field of Circular Economy, where he studies the implications of the adoption of circular business models. The results of his research are documented by an intense scientific production. Davide Chiaroni is author of two books with international editors, one with an Italian publisher and more than 150 contributions on international and national journals, edited books, and conference proceedings.

Matteo Orlandi is an Associate at Arup Italy. He is a Building Engineer as a background and graduated from the Polytechnic of Milan. He currently leads the Technology Team, operating in the field of design and innovation. His role covers various activities, including technical advice and consultancy, design management, and business development. The team is specialized in advanced design and engineering, materials consultancy with a specific focus on Circular Economy practices and the development of digital processes and tools. Matteo was nominated Digital Champion, thus responsible for the Digital Transformation of Italy Group.

Andrea Urbinati, is Assistant Professor of Strategy and Business Design at the School of Industrial Engineering of LIUC Universitá Cattaneo (Italy). He is also Member of the Core Faculty and Director of the Center on Technological and Digital Innovation of LIUC Business School, the School of Management of LIUC Università Cattaneo. His research interests are in the fields of circular economy, business model design, and digital technologies. Andrea has more than seventy publications, as papers on international journals, book chapters, national and international conferences. Andrea is Associate Editor of the International Journal of Innovation and Technology Management, Member of the Editorial Board of Sustainability, Review Editor on the Editorial Board of Frontiers in Sustainability (specialty section on Circular Economy), and Ordinary Member of the International Society for Circular Economy (IS4CE).

The Impact of the Novel Coronavirus Outbreak on the Development of Digital Economy in Commodity Countries

Galimkair Mutanov and Aziza Zhuparova

1   Introduction

The coronavirus pandemic, which has already affected more than 200 countries, had far-reaching consequences for the global economy: the closure of small enterprises, the transfer of employees to their home office, and the closure of schools and universities. The outbreak has led many companies to pay more attention to the provision of online services. Companies that provide online business management tools are currently benefiting the most, indicating that crises of this kind are opening up opportunities for online businesses. This is due to the fact that enterprises, faced with a crisis, seek to reduce their costs, seek to efficiently distribute their resources, and look for any possible sources of income in order to compensate for losses. Current economic conditions require the digitization of industries and the digitization of everyday life.

The continuous spread of digital technology over a long period determines the paths of economic and social development that constantly lead to fundamental changes in people's lives. The formation and development of the digital economy is one of the key priorities of economic leaders and countries, including the United States, Britain, Germany, Japan, etc. This has allowed such countries to quickly switch to the digital format of doing business in the face of the current crisis. Nevertheless, countries with economies in transition, where innovation processes and the development of the digital economy are still in their infancy, have set a serious challenge for government policy and pointed out the need to support programs for the widespread adoption of digital technologies.

After the crisis, commodity countries are waiting for another economy if they can create the conditions for digital transformation and industry 4.0, but such crises are usually longer and more difficult, since it takes time to find new solutions.

G. Mutanov · A. Zhuparova (✉)
al-Farabi Kazakh National University, Almaty, Kazakhstan

© The Author(s), under exclusive license to Springer Nature Switzerland AG 2021   59
D. R. A. Schallmo, J. Tidd (eds.), *Digitalization*, Management for Professionals,
https://doi.org/10.1007/978-3-030-69380-0_4

Unfortunately, at one time, countries with a developing innovative system did not pay special attention to the development of digital technologies, which led to a collapse during the coronavirus pandemic. Although digital economy is currently growing in developing countries, Kazakhstan and most of other post-soviet countries lag behind the leading countries. The main reason for the slow growth of domestic innovative companies is the lack of investment. Crowdfunding platforms can be singled out as an important tool for attracting investments. The introduction of innovative digital technologies has a positive impact on the labor market. In addition, digital technologies contribute to the social and financial involvement of the population and increase the accessibility, quality, and convenience of receiving services in such important areas as medicine, education, municipal and public services, and culture. The use of digital technology can increase the availability and efficiency of public services, and helps improve the business and investment climate. The following should be singled out as the main directions of the development of the digital economy: competent IT regulation, developed infrastructure, national centers of competence, and digital platforms.

2   Literature Review

Digitalization provides fundamental transformations in all spheres of human life and activity. Technology is becoming not only the engine for the development of new industries but also gaining important social roles, making a significant contribution to solving social problems, such as aging populations, social stratification, environmental problems, and climate change (Acemoglu and Robinson 2013). With the help of advanced science and technology, a "smart" society arises, based on new values of orientation to human needs, flexibility, creativity. Under the influence of digitalization, the labor market, healthcare, education, and spatial development are cardinally changing.

The introduction of new technologies and radical changes in the life sciences (bioinformatics, genomics, cell technology, synthetic biology) make it possible to modernize and personalize modern medicine by constantly monitoring the health status of each person, increasing the speed of medical care, and selecting individual therapy options, all this makes it possible to treat previously non-incurable (incurable) diseases. The development of bioinformatics allows the analysis of new DNA, RNA, or protein sequences only through in silico methods, which significantly reduces the time and material costs of conducting experiments. Bionics (biomimetics) is being developed rapidly, studying the possibilities of applying the principles of organization and functioning of living matter in the creation of technical systems and devices (Robosapiens 2017), for example, exoskeletons—mobile, wearable, robotic, electrified, or mechanized structures designed to complement the user's physical abilities (Bender 2019). Neurotechnologies not only help to create systems similar to the human brain in algorithms but also to study the mechanisms of behavior and the potential for brain development. In the future, this will contribute to the development of a person's cognitive abilities, increase his working capacity, and overcome the negative consequences of stressful situations (Tremblay et al. 2017).

Digitalization is causing technological complication and the disappearance of a number of traditional professions due to the automation of the corresponding labor operations and at the same time the emergence of new professions and the growing demand for non-algorithmic work and creativity, the so-called human in man (Beil et al. 2005). A significant part of labor relations and entire segments of employment is moving into the virtual environment, the flexibility of forms of which is significantly increased (the share of nonstandard, partial and unstable, one-time employment, etc.).

Digitalization requires the formation of new competencies in the labor market, which entails the restructuring of the entire education system. Transnational forms of education are developing (cross-border education), and a highly competitive environment is being formed in the rapidly growing global educational market, where both traditional (USA, UK) and new providers of educational services from East and Southeast Asia, Eastern Europe, and the Middle East coexist. The number of students entering universities in another country after graduation is growing by 10% per year and by 2020 will reach 8 million. Many countries, including Russia, have already adopted and are implementing education export support programs. In the near future, the labor market will experience an increasing influence of the exit of young workers, representatives of Generation Z, using digital technologies almost from birth (digital natives) and having unlimited access to information and developed digital competencies. Their share by 2025 will reach 25% of the total global employment (BCG 2017). The key motivating factor for them is the possibility of personal development (including those not related to work), and not just career growth and the level of remuneration, as in previous generations.

Accordingly, companies will have to change the tactics of hiring and retaining personnel, taking into account the values of the new generation (Shiu and Lam 2008).

Online technologies and the forms of education based on them are increasingly becoming part of the educational process at universities. The development of mass online education, the emergence of high-quality mass opens online courses (MOOCs), the abundance of information in open sources lead to the loss of a monopoly on knowledge transfer by universities. At the same time, open-access training courses of leading world universities have a significant impact on educational technologies (Myovella et al. 2019). The audience of such courses can reach millions of people, and training can be done in a user-friendly schedule and anywhere in the world. However, the digitalization of education also introduces a number of difficulties, requiring the solution of the issues of adapting the educational system to the digital environment, working out the ethical aspects of the use of digital technologies in the long term (Njoh 2017). The transition to personalized learning makes it necessary to implement a system of adaptive education and assessment that allows you to take into account the needs, level, and interests of the student. The teacher becomes more of a mentor and navigator in the educational process and not a "reproducer" of information.

The rapidly growing volume of data significantly exceeds the ability of a person to assimilate it, which determines the demand for artificial intelligence technology and electronic assistants. An increase in the speed of information exchange and its application requires an increase in the information literacy of the population, which raises the issue of digital inequality and the risks of a "digital split" on the agenda (Pradhan et al. 2014). At the same time, the reduction in the cost of technology leads to the emergence of intelligent devices that ensure active social inclusion of people with disabilities, single elderly people, etc., and the use of technology in public places allows solving social problems through cooperation. At the same time, the "smarter" access devices become, the higher the owner's vulnerability level. The spread of the Internet of things will make a person virtually transparent to any interested parties and structures, which, in turn, creates a demand for the development of information security technologies and cybercrime technologies.

3 Methodology

In this study, a comparative analysis of the institutional changes which should be implemented by countries of such as Kazakhstan in the face of the coronavirus outbreak in order to prevent its spread was carried out. The reason behind choosing the aforementioned countries was the fact that the economies of these nations are highly dependent on energy sales.

4 Findings

Oil is the most important export item both in the world as a whole and in Kazakhstan, where it accounts for more than 80% of all commodity exports of Kazakhstan. Thus, if Kazakhstan continues to specialize in the extraction of oil and other natural resources, it is unlikely to achieve a significant increase in the average per capita income in the medium term. In addition, it is unclear how long Kazakhstan's existing reserves of natural resources will last. According to available estimates, existing oil fields in Kazakhstan will be sufficient for oil production at the current rate for 20 years. This is relatively short term: Kazakhstan's reserves, for example, are believed to last for more than 60 years, Saudi Arabia for more than 70 years, and the United Arab Emirates for more than 90 years.

The concentration of commodity-dependent economies in the oil industry determines their high dependence on the situation in the world oil market. It means that a significant part of the state budget revenues of these states is generated through the sale of raw materials on foreign markets and, accordingly, any decrease in oil prices leads to a decrease not only in exports and government revenues, but also contributes to a slowdown in economic growth. This demonstrates that the fall in oil prices in the face of coronavirus outbreak once again emphasizes the need to shift away from the raw material orientation and the need to diversify the economy, including the development of the digital economy and the development of alternative forms of conducting business.

Today, the world is on the verge of new global changes. The innovations that came into our lives with the advent of the Fourth Industrial Revolution (Industry 4.0)—the wider use of information and telecommunication technologies, the use of the Internet by about 60% of the world population (this figure increased against the backdrop of the COVID-19 coronavirus pandemic), robotics and artificial intelligence technologies, the Internet of Things (IoT—Internet of Things), big data (Big Data) and digitalization resulting from all of the above open up new opportunities for us. These opportunities are now revealing themselves more than ever.

In connection with the infection of the coronavirus that began in China earlier this year and the declaration of the virus (COVID-19) as a pandemic by the World Health Organization on March 11, millions of people in homes and offices began to use digital platforms more actively. The coronavirus pandemic that has swept the whole world resembles the phenomenon of the Black Swan (the term used by the American economist and writer Nassim Talebi in his book Black Swan Under the Sign of Unpredictability—meaning a global phenomenon that is difficult to predict and has significant influence). This time, the emergence of a new type of coronavirus epidemic caused the debate in the world on digitalization of the economy and various fields of activity and accelerated the transition to the digital economy.

Coronavirus gives impetus to the use of new generation technologies, bringing digital technology to the fore.

At the moment, the Black Swan phenomenon, in addition to opening the door to changes in the economy at the global level, can also change our behavior—to change both people and organizations. Against the backdrop of the pandemic, the heads of government refuse international tête-à-tête meetings, preferring conferences in Skype, Zoom, and other similar programs to them; business, education, and other various fields are moving to the online platform. As a result of working at remote workstations and video conferences, the wider use of connection services, and the work of millions of people outside the office from home, costs are significantly reduced. Experts believe that in the fight against a pandemic, fast delivery without people and contact fully demonstrates its advantages. Service robots, self-service stores without sellers, etc.—form a new direction and help reduce the risk of infection. The spread of infection in the world isolated many cities in America, Europe, and Asia and seriously affected the development of digital technologies in the economy. Fearing a virus infection, people and companies now prefer offline trading to its online counterpart, which increases the share of e-commerce.

The current situation leads to a great demand for online applications, digital technologies, and this, in turn, makes it necessary to exist and build a sustainable infrastructure in the countries of the world. So, thanks to the transfer of millions of people to their home working hours, the demand for connection services is growing rapidly, the volume of content transmitted over the Internet is increasing, which makes the development of infrastructure necessary.

Currently, authorized bodies, private companies, and scientists are trying to find new ways to combat the virus. In China, police using drones monitored people who did not wear masks in areas at risk of infection, and Internet giants (Google, Facebook, Amazon, etc.) launched a campaign to combat false information related to the virus. The Canadian company "BlueDot" collects information from around the world about cases of new infections and, using artificial intelligence, is trying to predict the presence of infections in new territories in China and other countries of the world. The American start-up "AIME" (Artificial Intelligence in Medical Epidemiology—Medical Epidemiological Artificial Intelligence) has been using the capabilities of artificial intelligence since 2015 to analyze epidemics and predict them.

China's real-time fight against coronavirus has shown the world the power of modern technology and superApps (special mobile applications that combine several services). At the end of December 2019, cases of infection that erupted in China began to decrease by February due to the mobilization of the country and the use of all possible means to combat the virus. The use of artificial intelligence applications from large Chinese companies such as Baidu, Alibaba, Alipay, and others has led to significant effects. More than 50% of the requests received in the medical system were transferred to the online format, as carriers of the virus could transmit it during a visit to the doctor. For this, a connection to a high-speed 5G network was created and the widespread use of a telemedicine system began. At the same time, medical applications were provided for use, providing patients with communication with doctors, pharmacies, as well as applications that provide useful tips on combating the virus. What is happening demonstrates that mitigation of the damage caused by epidemics is made possible thanks to information technology, including, thanks to the Internet—digitalization has changed the approach of mankind to the diagnosis and monitoring of many diseases.

For spatial processes of development of digital economy are of great importance among economic institutions. When these institutions work well, firms and people are encouraged to innovate as a source of revenue from their activities. Good institutions also attract investment from foreign firms with new technological competencies that are not necessarily related to the existing production structure in the country or region. New digital technologies involve costs, but firms are encouraged to bear these costs because they can expect to make a profit in the case of success.

Therefore, it is very important to develop institutions for the development of the digital economy in commodity countries.

The first and most important is the availability and reliability of the telecommunications infrastructure. The availability of broadband Internet should become a state-guaranteed social minimum. All state institutions should be connected to it, and most houses in settlements should be able to connect. In addition, mobile Internet also becomes a necessary social minimum where it is impossible to connect broadband Internet. Now, for example, in Kazakhstan and in Russia, mobile operators for their towers receive land on a common basis or rent it from private owners. Therefore, communication coverage may not only develop but may even worsen due to the fact that the number of towers in a particular place has decreased. It is necessary to allocate a special category of land for them and in any master plans, detailed planning plans to allocate land for them already, since they are very small.

The second should be a digital state. Right now, in Kazakhstan they give out material assistance through an application sent to the E-government platform, and immediately there were problems with access to the site, because, apparently, it was not designed for such a number of requests. Accordingly, the state should approach the filling of its sites and services with maximum responsibility. President Tokayev has already talked about introducing the institute of digital officers in state bodies, but in my opinion, there is still a need for constant checks on the occupancy and relevance of state websites. Everything that the state does, except classified information, should be available on the Internet.

Thirdly, trade should move to the Internet. Now in Kazakhstan, the share of online commerce is about 4%. This is very small. We must reach the level of 20–25%. Online trading will help to significantly reduce the volume of smuggling, counterfeiting and tax-free trading. At the same time, it is necessary to ensure free online trading throughout the territory of the Eurasian Economic Union without various restrictions, certificates, and so on.

For example, for example, we can buy goods in Russian stores, but on the contrary, it can sometimes be difficult due to restrictions of state bodies of other countries. It should be understood that it is impossible to limit duty-free trade with third countries. The threshold of 200 euros of duty-free purchases should remain on; otherwise, the Russian Internet giants will monopolize the entire market.

Fourthly, the work of mail and various delivery services is an extremely important factor. Payments are sent through the mail, pension and social payments are received through the mail, goods are ordered and received from the catalogs, well, in addition, there is still the opportunity to receive financial services. For the country-side, mail is an island of life. Therefore, by the way, the US Post constantly works at a loss to itself, but it ensures the coherence of the entire US economic space. Well, now, sitting in quarantine, we see that delivery is becoming a vital element of the urban economy. Without couriers, life would have become generally unbearable. And, perhaps, the courier will become one of the most important forms of employ-ment for young people and, in general, for low-skilled labor. Therefore, it is very important that couriers have some kind of social guarantees, and delivery services have certain preferences for official vehicles, warehouses, and personnel.

The fifth important component of the digital economy is warehouses. The presence of large warehouses with automated loading and unloading systems is an essential element of urban security. Indeed, it is only thanks to them that the city can live in quarantine. Therefore, it is extremely harmful to think that warehouses with railway dead ends have no place inside the city. As you can see, under the conditions of quarantine, such warehouses are an ideal solution for the whole city—the goods are imported with minimal labor force participation, there is no need to organize a large flow of trucks from the region to the city.

The sixth part of the digital economy is a system of automated and remote work. Nowadays, employers are increasingly realistically evaluating both the amount of labor and the maintenance of offices. As we always remember, the human factor is always the most vulnerable. Automated accounting systems, document management, order tracking, collaboration on documents, and so on—that is the future. And, of course, systems that allow you to work remotely from anywhere in the world. In general, there will be a big reevaluation of the role of staff and the office in the life of each company.

A seventh of the new digital economy is distance education. Now it is possible only as a second higher, but most likely, it will be necessary to make it possible and the first in certain specialties or subjects. Of course, this requires much more responsible students, but it is necessary to raise the level. In fact, the university should mainly provide and emphasize the practical work of students, as close as possible to the real requirements of employers. You need to invest not so much in buildings as in laboratories, libraries, and software.

In this study, an analysis of the institutional changes implemented by Kazakhstan in the face of the coronavirus outbreak in order to prevent its spread was carried out. The reason behind choosing the aforementioned countries was the fact that the economies of these nations are highly dependent on energy sales.

Acknowledgments This work was supported by the Postdoctoral Fellowship provided by al-Farabi Kazakh National University.

References

Acemoglu, D., & Robinson, J. (2013). *Why nations fail*. New York: Crown Publishers.

BCG. (2017). Россия 2025: от кадров к талантам. Retrieved from http://d-russia.ru/wpcontent/uploads/2017/11/Skills_Outline_web_tcm26-175469.pdf

Beil, R., Ford, G., & Jackson, J. (2005). On the relationship between telecommunications investment and economic growth in the United States. *International Economic Journal, 19*(1), 3–9. https://doi.org/10.1080/1351161042000320399.

Bender, S. (2019). Robo sapiens japanicus: Robots, gender, family, and the Japanese nation. *Social Science Japan Journal, 22(2)*, 329–332. https://doi.org/10.1093/ssjj/jyz00.

Myovella, G., Karacuka, M., & Haucap, J. (2019). Digitalization and economic growth: A comparative analysis of Sub-Saharan Africa and OECD economies. *Telecommunications Policy, 101856*. https://doi.org/10.1016/j.telpol.2019.101856.

Njoh, A. (2017). The relationship between modern information and communications technologies (ICTs) and development in Africa. *Utilities Policy, 50*, 83–90. https://doi.org/10.1016/j.jup.2017.10.005.

Pradhan, R., Arvin, M., Bahmani, S., & Norman, N. (2014). Telecommunications infrastructure and economic growth: Comparative policy analysis for the G-20 developed and developing countries. *Journal of Comparative Policy Analysis: Research and Practice, 16*(5), 401–423. https://doi.org/10.1080/13876988.2014.960227.

Robertson, J. (2017). *Robo sapiens japanicus Robots, gender, family, and the Japanese nation.* University of California Press. https://doi.org/10.1525/9780520959064

Shiu, A., & Lam, P. (2008). Causal relationship between telecommunications and economic growth in China and its regions. *Regional Studies, 42*(5), 705–718. https://doi.org/10.1080/00343400701543314.

Tremblay, S., Iturria-Medina, Y., Mateos-Pérez, J. M., Evans, A. C., & De Beaumont, L. (2017). Defining a multimodal signature of remote sports concussions. *Eur J Neurosci, 46*, 1956–1967.

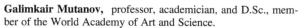

Galimkair Mutanov, professor, academician, and D.Sc., member of the World Academy of Art and Science.

His excellent management skills and commitment facilitated KazNU to gain a solid foothold in international higher education. The use of innovative result-oriented management contributed to the transformation of KazNU into a world-class research university.

He started managing universities in his early years. In 2002, he became the first Vice-minister of Education and Science of Kazakhstan. Author of more than 500 scientific publications. Selected works reviewed by the Nobel Prize winner, John Nash. Awards: ISESCO Prize in Mathematics and many others.

Aziza Zhuparova postdoctoral fellow at the Higher School of Economics and Business. She has publications devoted to the economic diversification of Kazakhstan, development of innovative economy. Aziza defended her Ph.D. entitled "Effectiveness of Innovative development of Kazakhstan" in 2014. She participated in Summer School at the University of New Delhi (India) on conducting scientific research and publishing scientific papers in top-rated journals. Completed international internships in Malaysia and Germany.

Part II

Digital Maturity

Digital Maturity Models: A Systematic Literature Review

Rafael-Leonardo Ochoa-Urrego and José-Ismael Peña-Reyes

1 Introduction

Due to the technological development, the digitalization is a crucial element in modern life. As a consequence, the transformation led by this development has caused outstanding changes in organizations (Schwer et al. 2018). Such has been the effect of the digitalization process into the business world, that these transformations are comparable to the ones that emerged in the first Industrial Revolution (Westerman et al. 2014); it has opened a huge extent of improvement in all business areas (Ministerio de Tecnologías de la Información y las Comunicaciones 2018).

One of the most promising technological and business opportunities for organizations nowadays is the digital transformation, which has been called Industry 4.0 or Fourth Industrial Revolution. This phenomenon is used to name a hypothetical fourth mega stage of the technological and economic evolution of the humanity. This revolution is based on the inclusion of better processing capacities of an increasing amount of available information. An essential element of this transformation is the Artificial Intelligence AI, which is deeply related to the massive information processing—Big Data—the usage of advanced computer algorithms and the massive interconnection among devices and people. Under this new technological development paradigm, the use of expressions such as Big Data, Internet of things (IoT), Blockchain, 3D Impression, Cyber-physical Systems, Cyber manufacturer, etc. is common (Colli et al. 2018; Lichtblau et al. 2015; Catlin et al. 2015).

Therefore, one of the first inconveniences for organizations when facing the digital transformation process is to know their current digital development status (Blatz et al. 2018); at this point, the digital maturity models undertake a crucial role. These models foster the assessment of the technological incorporation in the organizations (Schwer et al. 2018). Nonetheless, the descriptive function is not the

R.-L. Ochoa-Urrego (✉) · J.-I. Peña-Reyes
Universidad Nacional de Colombia, Bogota, Colombia
e-mail: rlochoau@unal.edu.co; jipenar@unal.edu.co

© The Author(s), under exclusive license to Springer Nature Switzerland AG 2021
D. R. A. Schallmo, J. Tidd (eds.), *Digitalization*, Management for Professionals,
https://doi.org/10.1007/978-3-030-69380-0_5

only one in the maturity models. Additionally, these models are useful to define an action plan directed to achieve higher maturity models; they also work as referents to establish a comparison with other organizations within the same economic sector or compare the digital development level of different sectors (De Carolis et al. 2017).

The historical referent in the assessment of digital technologies incorporation is the Capability Maturity Model (CMM). This model assesses the digital integration level in software engineering and software development organizations. Additionally, other models responding to bigger needs have been developed and they are focused on the Information Technologies IT Government. Under this viewpoint, the most popular model is the one promoted by the COBIT standard (Nolasco-Vázquez and Ojeda Ramírez 2016).

Nevertheless, and due to the high interest generated by the digital transformation in organizations and the academy, the CMM and the COBIT models are not the only ones existing in this case. Certainly, a great quantity of new models has been proposed, and it makes it complex for an organization to decide a unique strategy to develop their digital capabilities. Consequently, this document seeks to make a systematic review of the literature with the idea to consolidate the available models and make a comparison of them in the light of the enterprise architecture.

To achieve this purpose, this chapter starts with a discussion around the definition of digital maturity and its relationship with the concept of digital strategy. Later, the methodology implemented in the construction of these results is explained. In the third section of the chapter, the findings of this systematic review are presented. Finally, some conclusions and future projects are summarized.

2   Methodology

In order to accomplish the systematic review of literature already mentioned, the methodological proposal of Tranfield et al. (2003) was considered. This methodological proposal divides the systematic review into three stages: planning the review, conducting the review, and finally reporting and dissemination. Table 1 summarizes the stages and phases proposed by Tranfield, Denyer, and Smart.

The main objective of this systematic review is to make an inventory of the existing maturity models and understanding how these models permeate the different enterprise architecture layers. Therefore, the Scopus, EBSCO, ProQuest, and Web of Science databases were consulted with the search strategy "Digital Maturity." First of all, 1944 articles were found, and they were filtered in five different stages. The exclusion criteria designed for each one of the stages are shown in Table 2. The aim was to include documents designing or applying formal maturity models.

As a result of applying the five filters, 16 documents to be compared were selected. The number of resulting documents after the application of the five filters is shown in Table 3.

In addition to these 16 documents, there were included six models that are frequently referenced in the analyzed literature. Likewise, it was included a model

Table 1 Stages of the systematic review

Stage	Phase
I. Planning the review	0. Identification for the need for a review 1. Preparation of a proposal for a review 2. Development of a review protocol
II. Conducting a review	3. Identification of research 4. Selection of studies 5. Study quality assessment 6. Data extraction and monitoring progress 7. Data synthesis
III. Reporting and dissemination	8. The report and recommendations 9. Getting evidence into practice

Source: David Tranfield, Denyer David, and Smart Palminder. "Towards a Methodology for Developing Evidence-Informed Management Knowledge by Means of Systematic Review." *British Journal of Management,* 14 (2003): 214

Table 2 Exclusion criteria

Filter	Criteria
1	Include just peer-reviewed sources
2	Eliminate duplicates among databases
3	Review of the title and abstract
4	Available to be downloaded
5	Models for service provider companies

Source: Author's creation

Table 3 Search and selection of literature

Database	Search parameter	Filter 1	Filter 2	Filter 3	Filter 4	Filter 5
Scopus	57	51	34	19	15	10
Web of Science	28	24	17	11	10	4
ProQuest	1773	60	53	7	7	2
EBSCO	86	18	13	4	4	0
Total	1944	153	117	41	36	16

Source: Author's creation

presented by the Ministry of Information, Technologies and Communications in Colombia.

3 Maturity and Digital Strategy

Contrary to popular belief, the digital transformation process is not exclusively related to the acquisition of digital technologies and the abilities to use them (Flott et al. 2016). The starting point in the configuration of a digital company is the creation of a digital strategy; this strategy must be precise and coherent with the general organizational strategy (Lorenzo Ochoa 2016). This means that organizations must align their organizational structure, their human talent development, the financing mechanisms, and their performance indicators with the digital strategy selected (Catlin et al. 2015).

In general terms, a digital strategy embraces the digitalization intentions of the companies. This concept includes the application of digital technologies for the productive processes, the products or services provided, or even the transformation or creation of business models based on these digital technologies (Schallmo et al. 2018). Therefore, the success of the digital strategy does not only rely on the type of technology adopted; on the contrary, this success depends on the ability of organizations to invest in relevant digital abilities to be aligned with both the digital strategy and the general strategy of the organization (Catlin et al. 2015).

The question to be answered by organizations when starting their digital transformation process is where and how to start doing it; in order to achieve this purpose, it is necessary to know the current digital maturity level of the organization. This assessment allows to be aware of the available capabilities and the possible action scenarios (Blatz et al. 2018). The digital maturity concept is born in the public organizations field and the improvement of its service (Flott et al. 2016).

This concept is related to a comparison between the current condition of an organization or a process and a perfect or fully ready state (Schumacher et al. 2016). The maturity models can be used to evaluate and compare improvement processes with the purpose to generate a report of the achieved advances in the development of a capability in a specific organizational area (De Bruin et al. 2005).

It is important to state that unless it has been usually used as a synonym, a maturity model is not a readiness model because the second one assesses the system preparation to undertake a technological intervention, while the maturity model shows the current state of this system toward a particular framework (Schumacher et al. 2016). In other words, as it was previously said, the maturity models must be understood as useful tools to understand the status-quo of the organizational abilities with the purpose to construct measures toward their improvement (Becker et al. 2009).

Likewise, a maturity model supports organizations to assure their digitalization process. In this pathway, the organizations besides acquiring the technologies required to understand how to interoperate with other systems and the way in which this interoperation can impact the value delivered to their final customers (Flott et al. 2016). Equally, digital maturity is acquired not only when the productive processes are digitalized, but also when the thoughts and the organizational culture is transformed into a digital perspective and they lead the organizational performance (Álvarez Marcos et al. 2019). In other words, the inclusion of technologies, such as the Big Data, the contents digitalization, or the Search Engine Optimization (SEO), is crucial in the transformation process. Nevertheless, the generation of a strong and adaptative digital culture can be useful to relieve the impact of lacking these technologies (Catlin et al. 2015). As a consequence, the digital transformation is not a process that concerns only the technology areas, but it also involves activities within multiple decision units (Colli et al. 2018).

As it can be understood, the maturity models see the digital transformation as an evolving pathway, which goes through sequential digital stages that are characterized by an increasing digital integration (Colli et al. 2018). According to Kane, the organization learns to respond accurately to the competitive emerging digital environment (Álvarez Marcos et al. 2019). In this sense, the different maturity models are grounded around a specific framework, which besides providing the concept and assessing the maturity of an organization or a process compared with an objective status (Schumacher et al. 2016), work as action plans to execute the transformation of activities and organizational processes (De Carolis et al. 2017).

4   Results

The 23 selected documents were analyzed in two different levels. In the first level, the following elements were identified: type of document (journal paper, conference proceeding, report or book chapter), the sector where the model is directed, the number of maturity levels included, the number of dimensions and items included in the evaluation and the type of application used to define the maturity level (applied, self-applied, or public). The results of this analysis are summarized in Table 4.

In the second level of analysis, the dimensions proposed by each one of the models were compared with the architecture ArchiMate 3.0.1; the purpose of this comparison is to identify the architecture layers that are included in the different proposals. ArchiMate 3.0.1. is a language intended to describe, analyze, and communicate different aspects of the enterprise architecture and their change over time, as well as aspects related to the business model of the organization, and the IT systems inside them (The Open Group 2017). This architecture presents six layers: strategy layer, business layer, application layer, technology layer, physical layer, and implementation and migration layer. The strategy layer includes the resources, capacities, and action plan to manage the digital transformation process. The business layer includes the active and passive elements, as well as the activities comprised in the digitalized business models. In third place, the application layer groups the people involved (active elements), the activities and physical elements (passive elements) that are necessary to manage the digital relationship with customers and other participants of the value chain. Next, the technology layer includes the management of the technological platform that supports the business model. Referring to the physical elements layer, it includes all the technologies supporting the direct processes of transformation and value aggregation. Finally, the implementation and migration layer embrace the necessary elements to fulfill the transition processes between the traditional model and the digital model (The Open Group 2017).

The analysis results of each one of the documents in the light of the ArchiMate 3.0.1. is shown in Table 5.

Table 4 General analysis of the selected documents

ID	Authors	Type	Sector	Levels	Dimensions	Items	Application
A1	Westerman et al. (2014)	Book	General	4	2	20	Self-applied
A2	KPMG (2014)	Report	General	N/A	5	18	Applied
A3	Lichtblau et al. (2015)	Report	Manufacture	6	6	19	Self-applied
A4	Catlin et al. (2015)	Journal paper	General	N/A	3	11	Self-applied
A5	Valdez-De-Leon (2016)	Journal paper	Services	6	7	N/A	Self-applied
A6	Nolasco-Vázquez and Ojeda Ramírez (2016)	Journal paper	Education	N/A	3	58	Public information
A7	Schumacher et al. (2016)	Journal paper	Manufacture	5	9	62	Self-applied
A8	De Carolis et al. (2017)	Conference proceedings	Industry	5	4	N/A	N/A
A9	Solar et al. (2017)	Conference proceedings	Government	4	4	42	Self-applied
A10	Jugo et al. (2017)	Conference proceedings	Education	5	5	37	Mixed
A11	D'Antonio et al. (2017)	Conference proceedings	Industry		1	6	Self-applied
A12	Berghaus et al. (2017)	Report	General	5	9	N/A	N/A
A13	Durek et al. (2018)	Conference proceedings	Education	5	7	33	Self-applied
A14	Colli et al. (2018)	Conference proceedings	General	6	5		Applied
A15	Seitz and Burosch (2018)	Conference proceedings	General	5	4	4	Applied
A16	Isaev et al. (2018)	Journal paper	Services	4	7	29	Self-applied
A17	Gatziu Grivas et al. (1992)	Book chapter	General	4	9	N/A	N/A
A18	Blatz et al. (2018)	Conference proceedings	SME	3	6	N/A	Self-applied

A19	Pulkkinen et al. (2018)	Conference proceedings	General	5	6	69	Self-applied
A20	Balaban et al. (2018)	Journal paper	Education	5	5	37	Mixed
A21	Ministerio de Tecnologías de la Información y las Comunicaciones (2018)	Report	General	4	4	9	Self-applied
A22	Guarino et al. (2019)	Journal paper	Arts	2	1	19	Self-applied
A23	Álvarez Marcos et al. (2019)	Journal paper	Press	5	6	60	Self-applied

Source: Author's creation

Table 5 Summary of the second-level analysis for the selected papers

Authors	Strategy	Business	Application	Technology	Physical	Implementation and migration
Westerman et al. (2014)	X	X	X	X		
KPMG (2014)	X	X	X		X	
Lichtblau et al. (2015)	X	X	X	X	X	
Catlin et al. (2015)	X	X	X	X	X	
Valdez-De-Leon (2016)	X	X	X	X	X	
Nolasco-Vázquez and Ojeda Ramírez (2016)	X	X		X		
Schumacher et al. (2016)	X	X	X	X	X	
De Carolis et al. (2017)		X			X	
Solar et al. (2017)	X		X	X		X
Jugo et al. (2017)	X	X	X	X		
D'Antonio et al. (2017)				X		
Berghaus et al. (2017)	X	X	X	X	X	
Durek et al. (2018)	X	X	X	X	X	
Colli et al. (2018)	X	X	X	X		
Seitz and Burosch (2018)	X	X	X		X	
Isaev et al. (2018)	X	X	X	X	X	
Gatziu Grivas et al. (1992)	X	X	X	X		
Blatz et al. (2018)	X	X	X	X		
Pulkkinen et al. (2018)	X	X	X			
Balaban et al. (2018)	X	X	X	X		
Ministerio de Tecnologías de la Información y las Comunicaciones (2018)	X	X			X	
Guarino et al. (2019)				X		
Álvarez Marcos et al. (2019)	X	X	X	X	X	

Source: Author's creation

5 Discussion and Results

In this section, the main findings from this systematic review will be presented. The detail of the dimensions' association with each one of the ArchiMate 3.0.1 architecture layers is summarized in Appendix.

When analyzing all the models together, it is clearly observed the multidimensional orientation of the *frameworks* used for their design. As a matter of fact, just two models (Guarino et al. 2019; D'Antonio et al. 2017) are exclusively focused on the assessment of technological aspects.

Furthermore, the biggest interest is oriented toward the strategy and business layers; (De Carolis et al. 2017; D'Antonio et al. 2017; Guarino et al. 2019) in the case of the business model layer. In each one of these two layers, the 32 dimensions related were found.

Also, the 18 models suggest one or more assessment dimensions in the technology and application layers. The models proposed by De Carolis et al. (2017) and the Ministerio de Tecnologías de la Información y las Comunicaciones (2018) do not present dimensions related to any of these two layers and the models of Seitz and Burosch (2018) and Pulkkinen et al. (2018) do not consider exclusive assessments over the use of technological elements. This situation can be understood by the fact that some models consider that the exclusive use of technologies cannot guarantee any transformation process. Referring to the number of dimensions associated with these two layers, 23 dimensions in the application layer and 22 dimensions in the technology layer were found.

Likewise, it was found that 12 of the models consider assessment indicators for the physical elements that support the adding-value activities; these indicators are immersed in 14 dimensions.

Finally, as the most remarkable element, it was found that the model proposed by Solar et al. (2017) considers the assessment of actions for the implementation of new technologies and business models. This aspect could become of outstanding importance to guarantee the success of a strategy implementation; at this point, it would be interesting to undertake actions oriented to develop maturity models that consider from the strategic planning of the business (strategy layer), until the results of the business model (business and application layers), while including specific actions associated to the change management (implementation and migration layer).

6 Conclusions

By means of the systematic review developed, it was possible to demonstrate the importance of the digital transformation process for the organizations and the academy. It can be stated with the 1944 reviewed documents in the selected databases.

A remarkable advancement was the identified agreement in the literature that recognizes the digital transformation process as a multidimensional phenomenon that surpasses the exclusive inclusion of technologies in the organizational processes and activities. Consequently, there is an emphasis on the necessity to propose a clear and precise strategy capable to guide the organizational efforts intending to integrate the organization and its digital focus. Additionally, it is mandatory to adapt the business model of the organization to guarantee its accurate response to the particularities of the digital competitive environment.

Furthermore, it is clear that the main tool to start and guide both the digital strategy and the transformation process is a maturity model; it is useful to support the organization in recognizing its technological capacities and future status, which is expected to be achieved. These aspects help to design the specific actions that will guide the organization through its digital transformation process.

Appendix: Analysis of the Dimensions of the Maturity Models

Table / ID	Strategy — Resources	Strategy — Capabilities	Strategy — Course of action	Business — Internal active structures	Business — Event	Business — Internal passive structure	Application — Internal active structures	Application — Event	Application — Internal passive structure	Technology — Internal active structures	Technology — Event	Technology — Internal passive structure
A1	Leadership capabilities			Digital capabilities			Digital capabilities					
A2	Innovation capability			Business model	Competitive dynamics		Focus on client					
A3	Strategy and organization; Employees			Data-oriented services			Intelligent products			Smart factory		
A4	Strategy			Agile culture; Talent connections			Data-empowered decision-making		Connectivity			Two-speed IT
A5	Strategy; Capabilities			Organization		Ecosystem	Customer		Technology			
A6	Political compromise; Public–private association; Teacher development			Use of ICT in teaching; Technological infusion								Infrastructure
A7	People		Strategy	Culture			Clients		Products	Technology		
A8	Governance			Organization								
A9	General abilities						Citizen-oriented services; Open government			Enablers of digital government		
A10	Planning, management, and leadership; Development of digital competences			ICT in learning and teaching			ICT culture			ICT infrastructure		
A11												CAD; PDM; ERP; PLM; MES; SCM
A12	Strategy; Transformation management			Organization; Collaboration; Culture and expertise			Client experience		Product innovation	IT		

(continued)

Table ID	Strategy			Business			Application			Technology		
	Resources	Capabilities	Course of action	Internal active structures	Event	Internal passive structure	Internal active structures	Event	Internal passive structure	Internal active structures	Event	Internal passive structure
A13	Leadership, planning, and management			Learning and teaching; Scientific research work		Technology transfer and service to society	ICT Culture			ICT resources and infrastructure		
A14	Governance			Competence			Value creation			Technology		Connectivity
A15	Digital mindset			Digital business models					Digital marketing and sales strategy			
A16	Strategy			Organization; Innovation		Partnership	Relationships with users			Technology		
A17	Strategy; Governance			IT alienation/business; Organization			IT service management			Architecture; IT control		Cloud computing/security
A18	Strategy and leadership			Company culture and organization			Product			Data maturity	Process and operation	IT Infrastructure
A19	Strategy			Business model; Performance indicators/processes				Information flow	Interfaces			
A20	Leadership, planning, and management	Digital capabilities development		ICT in learning and teaching			ICT culture			ICT infrastructure		
A21	Management; Administration			Marketing and Sales								
A22										Infrastructure		
A23	Strategy; Digital transformation management			Technological convergence			Contents convergence			Digital intensity		

ID	Physical			
	Internal active structures	Event	Internal passive structure	Implementation and migration
A1				
A2	Business processes			
A3	Intelligent operations			
A4	Process automation			
		Real-time monitoring		
A5				
A6				
A7	Operations			Monitoring and control
A8	Process	General abilities	Technology	
A9				General abilities
A10				
A11				
A12	Process digitalization			
A13	Quality assurance			
A14				
A15	Digital business operations			
A16	Operations			
A17				
A18				
A19				
A20				
A21	Operations			
A22				
A23	Professional convergence			

References

Álvarez Marcos, J., Capelo Hernández, J., & Álvarez Ortiz, J. I. (2019). La madurez digital de la prensa española. Estudio de caso. *Revista Latina de Comunicación Social, 74*, 499–520. https://doi.org/10.4185/RLCS-2019-1342.

Balaban, I., Redjep, N. B., & Čalopa, M. K. (2018). The analysis of digital maturity of schools in Croatia. *International Journal of Emerging Technologies in Learning, 13*(6), 4–15. https://doi.org/10.3991/ijet.v13i06.7844.

Becker, J., Knackstedt, R., & Pöppelbuß, J. (2009). Developing maturity models for IT management. *Business and Information Systems Engineering, 3*, 213–222. https://doi.org/10.1007/s12599-009-0044-5.

Berghaus, S., Black, A., & Kaltenrieder, B. (2017). *Digital maturity & transformation report 2017.* https://doi.org/10.1007/s13398-014-0173-7.2.

Blatz, F., Bulander, R., & Dietel, M. (2018). Maturity model of digitization for SMEs. Maturity model to measure the status of digitization in SMEs. In *2018 IEEE International Conference on*

Engineering, Technology and Innovation, ICE/ITMC 2018 – Proceedings (pp. 1–9). https://doi. org/10.1109/ICE.2018.8436251.

Catlin, T., Scanlan, J., & Willmott, P. (2015). Raising your digital quotient. *McKinsey Quarterly, June,* 1–13. [Online]. Retrieved from http://search.ebscohost.com/login.aspx?direct=true& db=buh&AN=110711834&site=ehost-live.

Colli, M., Madsen, O., Berger, U., Møller, C., Vejrum Wæhrens, B., & Bockholt, M. (2018). Contextualizing the outcome of a maturity assessment for Industry 4.0. *IFAC-PapersOnLine, 51* (11), 1347–1352. https://doi.org/10.1016/j.ifacol.2018.08.343.

D'Antonio, G., Macheda, L., Bedolla, J. S., & Chiabert, P. (2017). PLM-MES integration to support industry 4.0. In *IFIP Advances in Information and Communication Technology* (pp. 129–137). https://doi.org/10.1007/978-3-319-72905-3_12.

De Bruin, T., Freeze, R., Kaulkarni, U., & Rosemann, M. (2005). Understanding the main phases of developing a maturity assessment model. In *Australasian Conference on Information Systems (ACIS)* (p. 109). https://doi.org/10.1108/14637151211225225.

De Carolis, A., Macchi, M., Negri, E., & Terzi, S. (2017). A maturity model for assessing the digital readiness of manufacturing companies. In *Advances in production management systems. The path to intelligent, collaborative and sustainable manufacturing* (pp. 298–305). https://doi.org/ 10.1007/978-3-319-66926-7.

Durek, V., Kadoic, N., & Begicevic Redep, N. (2018). Assessing the digital maturity level of higher education institutions. In *2018 41st International Convention on Information and Communication Technology, Electronics and Microelectronics, MIPRO 2018 – Proceedings* (pp. 671–676). https://doi.org/10.23919/MIPRO.2018.8400126.

Flott, K., Callahan, R., Darzi, A., Mayer, E., & Urol, F. (2016). A patient-centered framework for evaluating digital maturity of health services: A systematic review. *Journal of Medical Internet Research, 18*(4), 1–10. https://doi.org/10.2196/jmir.5047KEYWOR.

S. Gatziu Grivas, M. Peter, C. Giovanoli, and K. Hubli, "FHNW maturity models for cloud and enterprise IT," in *Business Information Systems and Technology 4.0. New trends in the ages of digital change*, 1st ed., vol. 43, 4, D. Rolf, Ed. Basel: Springer, 1992, p. 365.

Guarino, M., Di Palma, M. A., Menini, T., & Gallo, M. (2019). Digital transformation of cultural institutions: A statistical analysis of Italian and Campania GLAMs. *Quality and Quantity*. https://doi.org/10.1007/s11135-019-00889-3.

Isaev, E. A., Korovkina, N. L., & Tabakova, M. S. (2018). Evaluation of the readiness of a company's IT department for digital business transformation. *Information Systems Technology Business, 2*(44), 55–64. https://doi.org/10.17323/1998-0663.2018.2.55.64.

Jugo, G., Balaban, I., Pezelj, M., & Begicevic Redjep, N. (2017). Development of a model to assess the digitally mature schools in Croatia. In *IFIP Advances in Information and Communication Technology* (pp. 169–178). https://doi.org/10.1007/978-3-319-74310-3_19.

KPMG. (2014). *Survival of the Smartest 2.0.*

Lichtblau, K., et al. (2015). *Industrie 4.0 readiness*. Report. [Online]. Retrieved from https://www. industrie40-readiness.de/?lang=en.

Lorenzo Ochoa, O. (2016). Modelos De Madurez Digital: ¿En Qué Consisten Y Qué Podemos Aprender De Ellos? *Boletín de Estudios Económicos, 71*(219), 573–590. [Online]. Retrieved from https://search.proquest.com/openview/937dd70ffd989152b0dde42abed3c418/1?pq-origsite=gscholar&cbl=1536340.

Ministerio de Tecnologías de la Información y las Comunicaciones. (2018). *Modelo de madurez para la transformación digital.*

Nolasco-Vázquez, P., & Ojeda Ramírez, M. M. (2016). La evaluación de la integración de las TIC en la educación superior: fundamento para una metodología. *Revista de Educación a Distancia, 48*(9), 1–24. https://doi.org/10.6018/red/48/9.

Pulkkinen, A. J., Vainio, V. V., Leino, S.-P., & Anttila, J.-P. (2018). Modelling of digital extended enterprise. In *Proceedings of the 20th International Dependency and Structure Modeling Conference, DSM 2018* (pp. 139–148).

Schallmo, D., Williams, C. A., & Lohse, J. (2018). Clarifying digital strategy-detailed literature review of existing approaches. In *The XXIX ISPIM Innovation Conference – Innovation, The Name of the Game* (pp. 1–22).

Schumacher, A., Erol, S., & Sihn, W. (2016). A maturity model for assessing industry 4.0 readiness and maturity of manufacturing enterprises. *Procedia CIRP, 52*, 161–166. https://doi.org/10.1016/j.procir.2016.07.040.

Schwer, K., Hitz, C., Wyss, R., Wirz, D., & Minonne, C. (2018). Digital maturity variables and their impact on the enterprise architecture layers. *Problems and Perspectives in Management, 16*(4), 141–154. https://doi.org/10.21511/ppm.16(4).2018.13.

Seitz, J., & Burosch, A. (2018). Digital value creation. In *2018 IEEE International Conference on Engineering, Technology and Innovation, ICE/ITMC 2018 – Proceedings* (pp. 1–5). https://doi.org/10.1109/ICE.2018.8436380.

Solar, M., Murua, S., Godoy, P., & Yañez, P. (2017). Correlation between ICT investment and technological maturity in public agencies. In *International Conference on Electronic Government* (pp. 411–420). https://doi.org/10.1007/978-3-319-64677-0_34.

The Open Group. (2017). ArchiMate 3.0.1 Specification. *ArchiMate 3.0.1*. Retrieved from http://pubs.opengroup.org/architecture/archimate3-doc/chap01.html#_Toc489945945.

Tranfield, D., Denyer, D., & Smart, P. (2003). Towards a methodology for developing evidence-informed management knowledge by means of systematic review. *British Journal of Management, 14*, 207–222.

Valdez-De-Leon, O. (2016). A digital maturity model for telecommunications service providers. *Technology Innovation Management Review, 6*(8), 19–32. [Online]. Retrieved from http://www.timreview.ca/sites/default/files/article_PDF/Valdez-de-Leon_TIMReview_August2016.pdf.

Westerman, G., Bonnet, D., & McAfee, A. (2014). *Leading digital. Turning technology into business transformation*. Boston, MA: Harvard Business Review Press.

Rafael-Leonardo Ochoa-Urrego is a researcher at Universidad Nacional de Colombia. He has a doctorate in Engineering—Industry and Organizations with master's degrees in Administration of the Universidad Nacional de Colombia, and E-business: Telecommunications and New Business Models of the Cantabria University, Spain. He is a system Engineer of the Universidad Nacional de Colombia. Nowadays, he is a postdoctoral researcher.

José-Ismael Peña-Reyes is a professor at Universidad Nacional de Colombia. He is a system engineer from the Universidad Nacional de Colombia with master's degrees in Philosophy of Sciences, Education, Information Systems Management and Management Technology. He has a doctorate in Management Sciences from Université de Grenoble-Alpes. Nowadays, he is the National Director of Third Mission, Innovation and Intellectual Property of the Universidad Nacional de Colombia.

An Approach for a Digital Maturity Model for SMEs Based on Their Requirements

Daniel R. A. Schallmo, Klaus Lang, Daniel Hasler, Katharina Ehmig-Klassen, and Christopher A. Williams

1 Introduction

"Digitalization" and "digital transformation" are currently some of the most used buzzwords in consulting, economics, and management sciences. The media constantly seems to report that Germany is at risk of losing touch with the latest trends, but, according to the digital economy and society (DESI) index of the European Commission, Germany is placed slightly above average with countries such as Finland, Sweden, the Netherlands, and Denmark leading the field (European Commission 2019). Some might speak of "Digital Darwinism" (Kreutzer and Land 2015), suggesting that technology and society are changing faster than businesses can adjust.

The bigger the company, the higher their perception of digital maturity (Lichtblau et al. 2018; Brandt 2018). Taking a deeper look, it is particularly the German SMEs that will have to adapt their current business models to new consumption patterns and disruptive technologies or risk losing their competitive advantages in a globalized marketplace. Only one in four companies uses digital marketing or sales concepts, reorganized workflows to prepare for the digital age, or digitalized their products and services (Zimmermann 2019).

A possible and efficient solution to correctly determine the status quo of a company's state of digitalization can be the use of a digital maturity model (DMM). Maturity models are rather practical tools that have been present in different areas of actions, e.g., project management (Cook-Davies 2002: 16–20), for quite some time but have become extremely popular in recent years in the context of

D. R. A. Schallmo · K. Lang · D. Hasler · K. Ehmig-Klassen (✉)
Neu-Ulm University of Applied Sciences, Neu-Ulm, Germany
e-mail: katharina.ehmig-klassen@hnu.de

C. A. Williams
Johannes Kepler University, Linz, Austria

digital transformation (Hess 2019). In our understanding, a DMM serves to clarify the current state of digitalization of a company based on different questions and variables, sometimes compared to other companies in the same sector or cross-sectoral and recommends further actions to improve the company's state of digitalization.

Although the Internet is currently being flooded with practical tools provided by different stakeholders, there is little theoretical consensus on what a DMM is. The problem here lies within the lack of clarity of tools and literature as well as objectivity when it comes to the application, execution, and analysis of a DMM in practice. Therefore, we seek to provide insight into what requirements SMEs have and how they can be integrated into future DMMs.

2   Theoretical Background

A common opinion or standard procedure is not apparent regarding either maturity models or the degree of DT.

Digital Transformation

Various definitions of DT have been presented (e.g., BMWi 2015; Bowersox et al. 2005; Bouée and Schaible 2015; PwC 2013). In our understanding, DT can be seen as follows:

> ...the networking of actors such as businesses and customers across all value-added chain segments, and the application of new technologies. As such, DT requires skills that involve the extraction and exchange of data as well as the analysis and conversion of that data into actionable information. This information should be used to calculate and evaluate options, in order to enable decisions and/or initiate activities. In order to increase the performance and reach of a company, DT involves companies, business models, processes, relationships, products, etc. (Schallmo et al. 2017)

Maturity Models

Becker et al. (2009b: 2–3) state that many maturity models often deal with similar topics, deriving from the field of business informatics or considering the use of information technologies in companies or other organizations. For example, there have been around 30 different maturity models in the domain of "project management" (Cook-Davies 2002: 16–20) and even 150 maturity models for "IT service capability, strategic alignment, innovation management, program management, enterprise architecture, or knowledge management maturity" (Bruin et al. 2005: 3).

The authors criticize that only in rare cases is it even disclosed how the development of a new maturity model was motivated, in which steps it was developed, who was involved in these steps, and whether and how it was evaluated that the new model fulfilled its function (Becker et al. 2009b: 2–3).

Degree of Maturity

Basically, the degree of maturity of a research object deals with the fulfillment of certain objectives, characteristics, or indicators (Becker et al. 2009a: 213). The characteristic values or dimensions necessary to achieve a degree of maturity are generally predefined (CMMI Product Development Team 2011: 464); the point in time can be arbitrary (Pfeifer-Silberbach 2005) but is usually the actual state of a company and its products, services, business model, and processes considering the point in time of the measurement.

Digital Maturity Models

Considerable research has been done on maturity models focusing on digital capabilities in the areas of IT management (Becker et al. 2009b) and business processes (Tarhan et al. 2016; Williams et al. 2019). Maturity models for digitization in companies must summarize certain characteristics in particular dimensions at a specific time (Becker et al. 2009a; Pfeifer-Silberbach 2005; CMMI Product Development Team 2011: 464). They serve to determine the current state and the degree of digital maturity in the context of DT (e.g., regarding competence, performance, and level of experience) and allow recommendations for future actions deriving from the current degree of maturity.

Small and Medium Enterprises and Their Requirements

According to the Institut für Mittelstandsforschung (2020), SMEs are companies that employ fewer than 500 persons and have an annual turnover not exceeding 50 million euros.

SMEs are also typically seen as long-term, stable, and independent (Bundesverband der Deutschen Industrie e. V. 2015). Therefore, they have their own needs and requirements, especially when it comes to new and radically changing issues like DT. They do not rely much on theoretical approaches and prefer quick and easy pragmatic solutions. Their requirements must consist of practical facts and recommendations for action.

Furthermore, Arendt (2008: 93–108) found that knowledge and skills were the biggest barriers for SMEs with regard to digital initiatives. Zimmermann (2019: 11) adds data security and governance as well as Internet infrastructure.

3   Research Questions and Research Design

Research Questions

Based on the previous sections, we propose the following research questions:

- What are their main requirements for the creation of a DMM to support SMEs?
- What DMMs exist?
- What does a suitable maturity model for SMEs look like?

Research Design

Our research design consists of three parts. First, we collected practical qualitative data by interviewing SMEs for their requirements regarding DMMs. Second, we conducted a systematic literature review (SLR) to gain insight into existing approaches for DMM. In the last step, we compared theoretical and practical results to see how DMMs for SMEs can be improved in the future.

For the qualitative data, we used action research as this method helps to "address complex real-life problems and the immediate concern of practitioners" (Avison et al. 1999: 95), and we can test and refine a DMM approach for SMEs with the help of SMEs' feedback.

In the context of the InnoSÜD research project "Digitaler Reifegrad@Mittelstand" at the University of Applied Sciences Neu-Ulm, in various workshops and interviews with regional SMEs, we are currently in the process of obtaining data and requirements for developing and testing an SME-oriented DMM. The goal of the InnoSÜD university network is to use innovative transfer formats to facilitate a sustainable and effective exchange between science, business, and society. The focus is on topics that are important for the region, such as transformation management. In this case, the transfer refers to SMEs. With the support of the Institute for Digital Transformation of the University of Applied Sciences Neu-Ulm, they should determine their digital maturity to be able to derive a digitization strategy and implement it in their own company.

We interviewed five regional SMEs on the topics of digital maturity and DT in their companies to determine the necessary requirements for an SME-oriented DMM.

The central questions asked were:

- What is the status quo of your company regarding the DT?
- Where do you see the biggest problem field in your company regarding the DT?
- Where do you see the greatest need for action regarding digitalization in your company?
- What are your expectations for determining digital maturity?

Furthermore, we conducted an SLR to gain insight into existing approaches for DMMs as "[s]ystematic reviews are undertaken to clarify the state of existing research and the implications that should be drawn from this" (Feak and Swales 2009: 3). This formal and methodical approach aims to reduce bias in choosing literature selectively and to increase the reliability of the chosen literature (Tranfield et al. 2003).

For the SLR, we used the keywords "Digitalisierung," "digitalization," "Digitaler Reifegrad," "digital maturity," "Reifegradmodell," "maturity model," "digital assessment," "digital readiness," and "digital fit" to retrieve sources from the Internet as well as Web of Science, SpringerLink, Ebsco, Emerald, ScienceDirect, and Wiley databases.

To refine the review, we applied the following exclusion criteria. First, we only kept sources for analysis that were available in German or originated in Germany, Austria, or Switzerland. We conducted our workshops and interviews in Southern Germany (Bavaria and Baden-Wurttemberg), and our objective was to rely on available additional data with a minimum of cultural-related bias as DT and maturity might be perceived differently in other areas of the world.

Second, we focused on maturity models with the core topic of DT. As mentioned above, maturity models are present in various areas of action, but our focus is on digitalization and DT.

Third, sources had to be generally or at least cross-sectionally applicable. To achieve transparency and possible comparison among the different SMEs interviewed, it was not possible to rely only on industry-specific DMMs.

Sources were further examined using the following criteria:

- Group: Who designed the model?
- Sector: What are the main target sectors of the maturity model?
- Methodology: How was the survey conducted, and how were data collected?
- Model structure: How is the model structured? How many questions, dimensions, rating levels (degrees of maturity) does it consist of?

The results are summarized in Table 3 in the appendix of this chapter. As a last step, we present the following four DMMs and compare them to SME requirements from the interviews:

- Digitaler Reifegrad of Schweizer KMU, (Wyss 2017)
- Industrie 4.0 Readiness Modell, (Digital in NRW n.d.)
- Industry 4.0/Digital Operations Self-Assessment, (Geissbauer et al. 2016)
- Potentialanalyse Arbeit 4.0, (Offensive Mittelstand – Gut für Deutschland 2018)

These were chosen because (1) the questions were simple, understandable, and minimally complex so that they could be used in a workshop context; (2) each of them comes from a different group; and (3) they all include recommendations for further actions and therefore seem to have a good overall fit for an application to SMEs.

4   Findings

We analyzed four DMMs and examined how they meet the requirements of SMEs deriving from interviews and workshops of the InnoSÜD research project "Digitaler Reifegrad@Mittelstand." None of the existing models met all of the requirements. Consequently, suggestions for improving future model constructs can be derived.

Requirements for SMEs Based on "Digitaler Reifegrad@Mittelstand"

The results of the workshops are summarized in Table 1. We clustered the SMEs' responses into various dimensions, such as (digital) strategy; the interaction with partners and suppliers via a partner interface; the company's processes, employees, and used technologies; the interaction with customers via a customer interface; and the company's products and services.

The most important areas for improvement are internal processes, products, and services and the overall digital strategy. Processes are often "highly analog" and "still use a lot of paper," which "impedes the processing of important data" internally and toward customers, partners, and suppliers. In this context, IT systems are very old or the IT infrastructure is not harmonized.

Regarding products and services, the potential of new technologies, such as artificial intelligence or mobile apps, to upgrade existing products and expand the service portfolio has already been detected, but these initiatives progress slowly due to a lack of capacity and knowledge of the company's employees.

This leads to the third core topic: digital strategy. The companies know that "something has to be done" but often "do not know where to start." Determining the digital maturity is seen as a good way to discover "potentials and recommendations for further actions" as well as to create a "digitalization roadmap including priorities."

Table 1 Required dimensions for digital maturity models provided by SMEs

Requirements/dimensions	SME 1	SME 2	SME 3	SME 4	SME 5
Strategy		●		●	●
Partner interface			○	●	●
Processes	●		●	●	●
Employees	○	○		○	●
Technologies		○	○	●	●
Customer interface		○	○	●	●
Products and services		○	●	●	●

●—Strong need for further actions (top priority)
○—Need for further actions
Blank—No immediate need for further actions

Existing Approaches for Digital Maturity Models

Table 3 in the appendix of this chapter summarizes the results of the SLR. In general, there is a large number of maturity models, which are based on different dimensions and are therefore neither generally comparable nor applicable. Studies differ in terms of the industries and sectors, company sizes, and the number of participating companies.

A wide variety of methodologies have been applied from (online) questionnaires and online self-checks (e.g., Hochschule Neu-Ulm [(HNU)], minnosphere GmbH 2017; Techconsult n.d.; Mittelstand 4.0 Kompetenzzentrum Kaiserslautern n.d.) over conceptual modeling (Westerman et al. 2012) and literature reviews (Back et al. 2016, 2017) toward more qualitative methods, such as interviews (Geissbauer et al. 2016), focus groups, workshops (e.g., Acatech n.d.; H&D 2016), and assessments (fme AG n.d.).

We see the following main groups as creators of DMMs:

- Consulting firms use DMMs as a practical supporting tool for providing information and consultancy services to companies needing to improve their digital strategy. Their objective is profit-orientated, like the companies they are consulting, operating in one or various industry sectors.
- Associations are representations of a sum of companies with the intention to inform and strengthen the industry sector in which the respective companies are operating. Digital maturity should help create benchmarks and comparisons for the members.
- Universities and research institutes, in this context, have the goal to inform, educate, and support the public, e.g., companies, citizens, etc., on actual topics like digitalization, DT, and digital maturity.
- Big companies, e.g., Deutsche Telekom (Techconsult n.d.), sometimes create their own DMM to improve their status quo with regard to DT and to collect market data.

We also encountered various combinations of the groups, e.g., an association contracting a research institute for conducting a survey on digital maturity (e.g., IMPULS-Stiftung 2015), a university partnering with a company for transforming research results into a product or service (e.g., Universität St. Gallen and Crosswalk AG 2016, 2017), or a company using their knowledge for their own consulting branch (e.g., Rockwell Automation 2014).

Moreover, the model structures differ largely in the number of dimensions, questions, and rating levels. While some DMMs only deal with three (Rockwell Automation 2014), others consist of up to nine different dimensions (e.g., Frauenhofer Austria Research GmbH 2017) while the majority presents five central fields of action. The number of questions range from 15 (Digital in NRW. (n.d.).) to 166 (Offensive Mittelstand – Gut für Deutschland 2018). The number of different degrees of maturity is usually in between three and six rating levels. Only one DMM (Industrie- und Handelskammer [(IHK)] München & Oberbayern n.d.) offers 11 different maturity degrees.

Furthermore, not all information on dimensions, questions, and rating levels have been publicly available, which complicates detailed comparison of existing approaches.

Comparing SME Requirements to Existing Approaches

As Table 2 shows, none of the four analyzed DMMs fully considers every dimension of digitalization mentioned by the interviewed SMEs during the InnoSÜD research project "Digitaler Reifegrad@Mittelstand." The four existing models, however, all consider to some extent the aspects of the company (processes, employees, and technologies) as well as the overall digital strategy. The latter as well as the internal processes have been detected as the most important areas of improvement by the interviewees as well. The partner interface and sometimes the customer interface are neglected in some of the analyzed existing approaches.

Nevertheless, an approach for a DMM for SMEs should consist of all of the requirements mentioned in Tables 1 and 2. For the upcoming data collection process, the questionnaire has to include questions to determine the digital maturity of all aspects of digitalization.

5   Contributions

This study aims to determine the requirements that are currently lacking in DMMs for companies through analysis and a deductive method. The results give readers a deeper look into the requirements of SMEs in relation to DMMs. These results and

Table 2 Existing digital maturity models vs. SME requirements

Requirements/ dimensions	Industrie 4.0- readiness- Modell	Digitaler Reifegrad von Schweizer KMU	Industry 4.0/Dig. operations self- assessment	Potentialanalyse 4.0
Strategy	○	●	●	○
Partner interface		○		○
Processes	○	●	●	●
Employees	○	●	●	●
Technologies	○	●	●	●
Customer interface		●	●	○
Products and services	○	●		●

●—Included in the model
○—Partly included in the model
Blank—Not included in the model

the indication that requirements are lacking in current DMMs can be used in the development of future DMMs.

6   Practical Implications

First of all, practitioners will get an overview of and deeper insights into existing DMMs. In addition, they will find the analysis of the requirements of SMEs for DMMs and first approaches to build a model that meets the requirements of SMEs.

7   Limitations

This chapter aimed to report our current research-in-progress regarding the necessary requirements for standardized DMMs to meet stakeholder interests. We see the following limitations to this paper. Due to our focus on the German-speaking area, the results may not be generalizable on a global level.

Furthermore, it is debatable whether companies are willing to publish their data on digital maturity for a common goal. Although it would be helpful to create more transparency in the context of benchmarking, they could interpret this as an exposure of their own shortcomings, endangering their market position.

8   Recommendations for Further Research

Practitioners should be even more included in further research as the model could intensively be tested and more company data would be available for comparison. It would be interesting to create an overall accessible and anonymized database to be able to strengthen which dimensions are truly necessary for a DMM. This database would allow researchers to get insights from different industries, regions, or countries; practitioners would get a reliable benchmarking tool providing recommendations for further actions inside their companies.

Annex

Table 3 Digital maturity models

Maturity model	Group	Sector	Methodology	Structure
Industry 4.0 Maturity Model Frauenhofer Austria Research GmbH (2017)	University/ Research institute	Industry, production, manufacturing	Questionnaire, software supported calculation, visualization and report in a roadmap	9 dimensions 62 questions 5 rating levels
The Connected Enterprise Maturity Model Rockwell Automation (2014)	Consulting, Company	Industry, production, manufacturing	Five steps: assessment, secure and updated network and controls, defined and organized working data capital, analytics, collaborations	3 dimensions ? questions 5 rating levels
Industry 4.0/Digital Operations Self-Assessment Geissbauer et al. (2016)	Consulting	Industry, production, manufacturing	Interviews and surveys	7 dimensions ? questions 4 rating levels
The Digital Advantage MIT Center for Digital Business and Capgemini Consulting (Westerman et al. 2012)	Consulting	Industry, production, manufacturing	Conceptual model but refers to data (no references) with MNCs	? dimensions ? questions 4 rating levels
Digital Maturity & Transformation Study Universität St. Gallen, and Crosswalk AG (Back et al. 2016, 2017)	University/ Research institute, Company	Cross-sectoral	Literature review, expert interviews, focus groups	9 dimensions 64 questions 5 rating levels
IDT-Quickcheck— Digitales Reifegrad-Analysetool Hochschule Neu-Ulm (HNU), minnosphere GmbH (2017)	University/ Research institute, Company	Cross-sectoral	Online self-assessment, based on answering 10 core questions on the current status and the planned status in 3 years	5 dimensions 50 questions 5 rating levels
Digitalisierungsindex Deutsche Telekom (Techconsult n.d.)	Company	Cross-sectoral (selection at the beginning)	Online self-check to determine your own degree of digitalization	5 dimensions 71 questions 5 rating levels
Industrie 4.0-Readiness-Modell IdW Köln for VDMA IMPULS-Stiftung, with FIR e.V. Aachen IMPULS-Stiftung (2015)	University/ Research institute, Association	Cross-sectoral with focus on technological aspects	Online self-check to determine the individual industry 4.0 maturity level	6 dimensions 27 questions 6 rating levels

(continued)

Table 3 (continued)

Maturity model	Group	Sector	Methodology	Structure
Readiness Check Mittelstand 4.0 Kompetenzzentrum Kaiserslautern (n.d.)	Consulting	Cross-sectoral	Online self-check	5 dimensions 25 questions 5 rating levels
Leitfaden Industrie 4.0 Industrie- und Handelskammer (IHK) München and Oberbayern (n.d.)	Association	Cross-sectoral with focus on technological aspects	Online self-check for digital maturity level with a total of 19 main questions	4 dimensions 19 questions 11 rating levels
Quick Check Industrie 4.0 Reifegrad Digital in NRW (n.d.)	University/ Research institute	Cross-sectoral with focus on technological aspects	Online questionnaire with five possible answers to each question for self-evaluation	9 dimensions 15 questions 5 rating levels
Industrie 4.0-Readiness-Index H&D (2016)	Consulting	Cross-sectoral with focus on technological aspects	Cooperative maturity analysis in cooperation with the respective company	5 dimensions ? questions ? rating levels
Industrie 4.0-Maturity-Index Acatech (n.d.)	University/ Research institute	Cross-sectoral	Identification of status quo of industry 4.0 in companies via workshops	4 dimensions ? questions 6 rating levels
Digitaler Reifegrad von Schweizer KMU Hochschule Luzern (Wyss 2017)	University/ Research institute	Cross-sectoral with focus on SMEs	Study/survey	7 dimensions 54 questions 5 rating levels
Digital Maturity and Value Assessment Mc Kinsey (n.d.)	Consulting	Public sector	Survey— representative sample of authorities/ departments	4 dimensions 76 questions 3 rating levels
Digital Maturity Model tmforum (n.d.)	Association	Cross-sectoral	Online presentation with different implementation ideas	5 dimensions 110 questions ? rating levels
fme Reifegradmodell für die dig. Transformation fme AG (n.d.)	Consulting	Cross-sectoral	Assessment	5 dimensions 25 questions 5 rating levels

(continued)

Table 3 (continued)

Maturity model	Group	Sector	Methodology	Structure
Potentialanalyse 4.0 Offensive Mittelstand – Gut für Deutschland (2018)	Association	Cross-sectoral with focus on SMEs	Self-check with implementation support	6 dimensions 166 questions 3 rating levels

? means the number of questions/dimensions is unknown here and in the lower columns

References

Acatech. (n.d.). *Industrie 4.0 maturity index* [online]. Retrieved January 2020, from https://www.acatech.de/projekt/industrie-4-0-maturity-index/

Arendt, L. (2008). Barriers to ICT adoption in SMEs: How to bridge the digital divide? *Journal of Systems and Information Technology, 10*(2), 93–108.

Avison, D., Lau, F., Myers, M., & Nielsen, A. (1999). Action Research: To make academic research relevant, researchers should try out their theories with practitioners in real situations and real organizations. *Communications of the ACM, 42*(1), 94–99.

Back, A., Berghaus, S., & Kaltenrieder, B. (2016). *Digital maturity & transformation report 2016*. Universität St. Gallen (Institut für Wirtschaftsinformatik) and Crosswalk AG.

Back, A., Berghaus, S., & Kaltenrieder, B. (2017). *Digital maturity & transformation report 2017*. Universität St. Gallen (Institut für Wirtschaftsinformatik) and Crosswalk AG.

Becker, J., Knackstedt, R., & Pöppelbuß, J. (2009a). Developing maturity models for IT management. *Business & Information Systems Engineering, 1*(3), 213–222.

Becker, J., Knackstedt, R., & Pöppelbuß, J. (2009b). *Dokumentationsqualität von Reifegradmodellentwicklungen*. Working Paper 2009 (123) [online]. Retrieved January 2020, from https://www.econstor.eu/bitstream/10419/59549/1/718173538.pdf

BMWi. (2015). *Industrie 4.0 und digitale wirtschaft—impulse für wachstum, beschäftigung und innovation*. Berlin: Bundesministerium für Wirtschaft und Energie.

Boueé, C., & Schaible, S. (2015). *Die digitale transformation der industrie*. Studie: Roland Berger und BDI.

Bowersox, D. J., Closs, D. J., & Drayer, R. W. (2005). The digital transformation: Technology and beyond. *Supply Chain Management Review, 9*(1), 22–29.

Brandt, M. (2018). *Je größer desto digitaler* [online]. Statista GmbH. Retrieved January 2020, from https://de-statista-com.ezproxy.hs-neu-ulm.de/infografik/14216/einschaetzung-von-unternehmen-in-deutschland-zum-eigenen-stand-bei-der-digitalisierung/

Bruin, T., Freeze, R., Kulkarni, U., & Rosemann, M. (2005). Understanding the main phases of developing a maturity assessment model. *16th Australasian Conference on Information Systems, Sydney* [online]. Retrieved December 2019, from http://aisel.aisnet.org/acis2005/109/

Bundesverband der Deutschen Industrie (BDI) e. V. (2015). *Faktencheck* [online]. *Mittelstand und Familienunternehmen*. Retrieved January 2020, from https://bdi.eu/media/presse/publikationen/mittelstand-und-familienunternehmen/Faktencheck_Mittelstand_Familienunternehmen_230915.pdf

CMMI Product Development Team. (2011). *CMMI® für Entwicklung. Version 1.3* (p. 464). Software Engineering Institute, Carnegie Mellon University.

Cook-Davies, T. (2002). Project management maturity models. Does it make sense to adopt one? *Project Manager Today*, pp. 16–20.

Digital in NRW. (n.d.). *Online-Fragebogen zur Bewertung des Industrie 4.0-Reifegrades* [online]. Retrieved January 2020, from https://www.digital-in-nrw.de/de/termine-themen/workshop/online-fragebogen-zur-bewertung-des-industrie-4-0-reifegrades

European Commission. (2019). The digital economy and society index (DESI). *EC website*. Retrieved January 2020, from https://ec.europa.eu/digital-single-market/en/desi

Feak, C. B., & Swales, J. M. (2009). *Telling a research story: Writing a literature review*. University of Michigan Press.

fme AG. (n.d.). *Digitaler reifegrad* [online]. Retrieved January 2020, from https://www.fme.de/lan/digitaler-reifegrad/

Frauenhofer Austria Research GmbH. (2017). *Jahresbericht 2017: industrie 4.0 reifegradmodell* (pp. 20–21) [online]. Retrieved January 2020, from https://www.fraunhofer.at/de/publikationen/jahresbericht2017_e-paper.html

Geissbauer, R., Vedso, J., & Schrauf, S. (2016). *Industry 4.0: Building the digital enterprise* [online]. Retrieved January 2020, from https://www.pwc.com/gx/en/industries/industries-4.0/landing-page/industry-4.0-building-your-digital-enterprise-april-2016.pdf

H&D. (2016). *Industrie 4.0. forschungsprojekt smartTCS gestartet: service-plattform vernetzt produktionshalle mit technischem kundendienst* [online]. Retrieved January 2020, from https://www.hud.de/2016/02/15/industrie-4-0/

Hess, T. (2019). *Digitale transformation strategisch steuern. Vom Zufallstreffer zum systematischen Vorgehen*. Berlin: Springer.

Hochschule Neu-Ulm (HNU), minnosphere GmbH. (2017). *Digitales reifegrad analysetool* [online]. Retrieved January 2020, from http://reifegradanalyse.hs-neu-ulm.de/

IMPULS-Stiftung. (2015). *Industrie 4.0-readiness-modell* [online]. Retrieved January 2020, from https://www.industrie40-readiness.de/

Industrie und Handelskammer (IHK) München & Oberbayern. (n.d.). Digitalisierung im Mittelstand [online]. *Leitfaden Industrie 4.0*. Retrieved January 2020, from https://ihk-industrie40.de/

Institut für Mittelstandsforschung. (2020). *Institut für mittelstandsforschung - IfM Bonn*. Zugriff am 31. März 2020 [online]. Retrieved January 2020, from https://www.ifm-bonn.org/definitionen/

Kreutzer, R. T., & Land, K.-H. (2015). *Digital Darwinism – branding and business models in jeopardy*. Berlin: Springer.

Lichtblau, K., Schleiermacher, T., Goecke, H., & Schützdeller, P. (2018). Digitalisierung der KMU in Deutschland [online]. *IW Consult*. Retrieved January 2020, from https://www.iwconsult.de/fileadmin/user_upload/projekte/2018/Digital_Atlas/Digitalisierung_von_KMU.pdf

McKinsey & Company, Inc. (n.d.). Digital Digital Maturity and Value Assessment f'r den öffentlichen Sektor. Retrieved January 2020, from https://docplayer.org/8484104-Mckinsey-digital-digital-maturity-and-value-assessment-fuer-den-oeffentlichen-sektor.html

Mittelstand 4.0 Kompetenzzentrum Kaiserslautern. (n.d.). *Readiness-check* [online]. Retrieved January 2020, from https://kompetenzzentrum-kaiserslautern.digital/readiness-check/

Offensive Mittelstand – Gut für Deutschland. (2018). *Potentialanalyse Arbeit 4.0* [online]. Retrieved December 2019, from https://www.offensive-mittelstand.de/om-praxisvereinbarungen/potenzialanalyse-arbeit-40

Pfeifer-Silberbach, U. (2005). *Ein beitrag zum monitoring des reifegrades in der entwicklung eines produktes*. Aachen: Shaker.

PwC. (2013). *Digitale transformation – der größte Wandel seit der Industriellen Revolution*. Frankfurt: PricewaterhouseCoopers.

Rockwell Automation. (2014). *The connected enterprise maturity model* [online]. Retrieved January 2020, from https://literature.rockwellautomation.com/idc/groups/literature/documents/wp/cie-wp002_-en-p.pdf

Schallmo, D., Williams, C. A., & Boardman, L. (2017). Digital transformation of business models—best practice, enablers, and roadmap. *International Journal of Innovation Management, 21*(08).

Tarhan, A., Turetken, O., & Reijers, H. A. (2016). Business process maturity models: A systematic literature review. *Information and Software Technology, 75*, 122–134.

Techconsult. (n.d.). *Digitalisierungsindex* [online]. Retrieved December 2019, from https://www.digitalisierungsindex.de/

Tmforum. (n.d.). *Digital maturity model overview* [online]. Retrieved December 2019, from https://www.tmforum.org/digital-maturity-model-metrics/model-overview/

Tranfield, D., Denyer, D., & Smart, P. (2003). Towards a methodology for developing evidence-informed management knowledge by means of systematic review. *British Journal of Management, 14*(3), 207–222.

Westerman, G., Tannou, M., Bonnet, D., Ferraris, P., & McAfee, A. (2012). *The digital advantage: How digital leaders outperform their peers in every industry* (pp. 2–23). MA: MITSloan Management and Capgemini Consulting.

Williams, C., Schallmo, D., Lang, K., & Boardman, L. (2019). *Digital maturity models for small and medium-sized enterprises: A systematic literature review.* Florence: The ISPIM Innovation Conference.

Wyss, M. (2017). *Digitaler Reifegrad von Schweizer KMU.* Hochschule Luzern - Informatik.

Zimmermann, V. (2019). KfW-Digitalisierungsbericht Mittelstand 2018 [online]. *Digitalisierung erfasst breite Teile des Mittelstands – Digitalisierungsausgaben bleiben niedrig.* Retrieved January 2020, from https://www.kfw.de/PDF/Download-Center/Konzernthemen/Research/PDF-Dokumente-Digitalisierungsbericht-Mittelstand/KfW-Digitalisierungsbericht-2018.pdf

Daniel R. A. Schallmo is an economist, management consultant, lecturer, and author. He is a professor for digital transformation and entrepreneurship at the Neu-Ulm University of Applied Science, director of the Institute for Entrepreneurship, and member of the Institute for Digital Transformation. His research focuses on digitalization (digital maturity, digital strategy, digital transformation of business models, and digital implementation) and the development and application of methods to the innovation of business models, mainly in business-to-business markets. He is the author of numerous publications (10+ books, 20+ articles) and speaker (100+ speeches; 7000+ participants). He is a member of various research societies and a reviewer.

Klaus Lang is a management consultant and professor for corporate management and IT management at the Neu-Ulm University of Applied Sciences. As a business scientist, he did his doctorate in the field of business process modeling. He began his career as a consultant at Sietec Consulting in Munich, further positions were Siemens Business Services, where he headed a consulting unit.

He built the Institute for Digital Transformation (IDT) at the Neu-Ulm University of Applied Sciences, which he has headed since then. As the Dean of Studies, he is responsible for quality management in the Faculty of Information Management.

His work and research focus on the field of digital transformation: development of digital strategies, development of maturity models, the transformation of business models and agile methods.

Daniel Hasler is a research assistant for digital transformation at the Neu-Ulm University of Applied Sciences and a member of the Institute for Digital Transformation.
He is a Ph.D. candidate, whose research is focused on digitalization (digital maturity, digital transformation in SMEs, digital business models and digital platforms/ecosystems in particular), design thinking, and agile methods as well as start-ups and entrepreneurship.
Before returning to academia, Daniel acquired several years of practical experience in marketing, business development and sales working for German and multinational software SMEs. He studied International Marketing Management in Germany with semesters abroad in France and Peru.

Katharina Ehmig-Klassen is a research assistant for digital transformation, design thinking, business models, and entrepreneurship at the Neu-Ulm University of Applied Science and a member of the Institute for Digital Transformation. Her research focuses on digitalization (digital maturity, digital transformation in SMEs), design thinking, and agile methods as well as start-ups and entrepreneurship. Katharina Ehmig-Klassen has several years of practical experience in marketing and is a consultant for marketing, communication, and corporate development.

Christopher A. Williams is a strategic management researcher, consultant, and author. He is currently completing his Ph.D. in the field of Innovation Management at Johannes Kepler University Linz. He holds a BA in Communication, an MBA in General Management, and an MA in Learning, Technology, and Education from the University of Nottingham. His research focuses on strategic management topics, learning and instruction, human resources management, and corporate communication. He brings this practical experience and hard-won insights to bear when consulting companies in the development and implementation of new digital maturity models, corporate communication strategies, and blended learning educational programs.

Developing Strategies for Digital Transformation in SMEs with Maturity Models

Christoph Pierenkemper and Jürgen Gausemeier

1 Introduction

Although "digital transformation" has been one of the core issues in companies for many years, various studies show that especially small and medium-sized enterprises (SMEs) still face difficulties in implementing digitalization. There are a variety of reasons: unclear objectives, unmanageable risks, nonobvious potential benefits, no specific budget, etc. (Horváth et al. 2018). In addition, companies are faced with the challenge of identifying precisely those from the variety of implementation options that promise success for their own position (Bley et al. 2016). Furthermore, in numerous business units are reservations regarding the cost–benefit ratio (Demary et al. 2016). This leads to SMEs testing digital applications only in the form of pilot applications, prototypes, and stand-alone solutions. There is no overarching vision or a strategic plan for the comprehensive implementation of digital transformation (e.g., Hoberg et al. 2015). This situation is worrying for numerous reasons:

- Ninety percent of all companies worldwide are SMEs (World Bank 2019). They are responsible for an essential part of the value chain and have to ensure their international competitiveness.
- Among the most successful companies in the context of digitalization are large corporations such as Microsoft, Apple, Google, Amazon, and Facebook. Their market power is continuously increasing. SMEs must counteract this decisively in order to survive.
- In contrast to global players, SMEs often still pursue classic and rigid innovation approaches. Digitalization, however, requires a rethink: value creation structures and the way innovations are created will change significantly. Given the fact that

C. Pierenkemper (✉) · J. Gausemeier
Heinz Nixdorf Institute, University of Paderborn, Paderborn, Germany
e-mail: christoph.pierenkemper@contech.de

© The Author(s), under exclusive license to Springer Nature Switzerland AG 2021
D. R. A. Schallmo, J. Tidd (eds.), *Digitalization*, Management for Professionals,
https://doi.org/10.1007/978-3-030-69380-0_7

digitalization is seen as one of the main drivers of innovation, urgent action is needed.

However, there is currently a lack of a methodology for SMEs in particular to quickly and easily develop their individual strategy for digital transformation. This chapter presents a methodology that allows SMEs to quickly and easily develop a comprehensive strategy for digital transformation in consideration of the own needs.

2   Cyber-Physical Systems as a Key Driver for Digital Transformation

Information and communication technology has been continuously driving technological development in mechanical engineering and related industries for years. Intelligent technical systems are being created that communicate and cooperate with each other via the Internet. These so-called cyber-physical systems (CPS) are increasingly finding their way into industrial production. These systems are based on the close cooperation between disciplines such as mechanics, electronics, and software. The use of these systems in industrial production is often declared as Smart Factory. This refers to the ability to network intelligent machines, operating resources, storage and transport machines, etc. on an ad hoc basis to form efficient value-added networks (Gausemeier and Plass 2014). This opens up a wide range of opportunities for manufacturing companies to increase performance, for example, through more flexible production processes, more customer-specific products, or new forms of human–machine interaction (Kagermann et al. 2013). In view of this diversity, however, SMEs in particular are confronted with almost unmanageable alternatives for action. Furthermore, for many companies, the goals and potential benefits of digitalization are not apparent. Therefore, it is necessary to approach the topic step by step. Maturity models for digital transformation with clearly defined development stages based on each other offer a suitable approach to solve this problem. They have two major advantages: Firstly, the performance levels make the benefits of the digital transformation more tangible. Secondly, they simplify to estimate the monetary costs of implementing digitalization in a company (VDMA Forum Industrie 4.0 2016). They are particularly suitable for the systematic and evolutionary planning of a digital transformation in SMEs. The starting point of the transformation process is the determination of the actual position by evaluating the current performance with the help of performance levels. Based on this, a demand-oriented target position can be formulated, which primarily results from the business strategy of the company. The path from the actual to the target position can be concretized with the help of a digital transformation strategy.

3   Maturity Models as a Tool for Digital Transformation

With the help of maturity models, companies can systematically record their performance status in the context of digital transformation. Determining the status quo leads to the question "In which direction do we want to develop in the future?" Against the background that, for various reasons, companies are not always able to introduce what is basically possible, the answer to this question is not trivial. If a company is supposedly aware of its target position, external influences often make it more difficult to achieve the goal, which often results in an adjustment of the target position. It is important to take these circumstances into account at the planning stage. Figure 1 provides a schematic illustration of the ramp-up of performance enhancement processes with maturity models.

The left side represents the organization at the present time (current position). The performance level can be determined with the help of a maturity model. Once the performance levels have been determined in the maturity level model, the current performance profile can be created. The next step is to determine which position the organization wants to achieve in the future (target position). In order to answer this question, the corporate strategy or corporate goals must be taken into account. It depends to a large extent on what future maturity level the organization should reasonably have. In order to answer the question of the future, a strategic foresight must be carried out first. Established methods such as trend analysis or the scenario

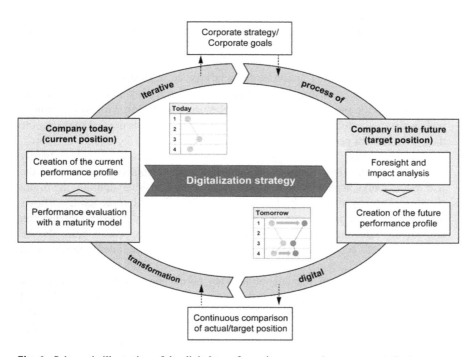

Fig. 1 Schematic illustration of the digital transformation process (own representation)

technique exist for this purpose. They can be easily adapted to the digitalization context. Then it is necessary to evaluate the effects of these future developments on the organization. The findings flow into the creation of the company-specific performance profile. From the target/actual comparison of the performance levels contained in the profile, the need for performance improvement is immediately apparent. The implementation of the performance increase must be mapped in the form of a strategy for digital transformation. It describes the path (transformation process) from the company today (current position) to the organization in the future (target position). This schematically represented procedure must be iteratively run through. In a continuous implementation and premise controlling, it must be checked whether the organization is on the right path. The purpose of premise controlling is to check whether the assumptions made in the strategy are still correct. Implementation controlling checks whether the measures introduced are carried out as planned and are effective. If deviations are detected in implementation and premise controlling, the strategy must be adjusted immediately.

4 State of the Art

There are several approaches dealing with the development of digitalization strategies. An extensive literature research has shown that these mainly consist of three generic phases: Analysis of the initial situation, determination of the target definition, and planning of implementation measures. The discussion of these approaches with experts from research and industry has led to the following findings:

- The analysis of the initial situation is usually carried out with the help of classical analysis methods (SWOT analysis, gap analysis, etc.). However, the application of these methods often leads to different evaluation results and is also strongly dependent on the previous knowledge of the user about digital transformation as well as his methodological experience. Additional support is needed to determine their own current position.
- The determination of the target position is usually intuitive and is hardly supported by foresight methods. In addition, respondents often expressed the fear that essential aspects were inadvertently overlooked when defining the future position. There is also a lack of a detailed methodological approach that shows how the current position can be developed toward the defined target picture, considering relevant environmental developments. This approach must also be able to take into account the limited resources of SMEs when defining the target position.
- The implementation of digitalization often takes place with action plans or roadmaps. Their consistency in terms of content depends largely on the skills of the creator. Interdependencies, obstacles, or synergies between the measures and strategic programs are not systematically derived. However, SMEs in particular need methodological support to ensure the effectiveness and consistency of their strategy.

5   Methodology for the Development of Digitalization Strategies

The methodology for the development of digitalization strategies presented below is the result of a research project based on the Design Research Methodology (DRM) according to Blessing and Chakrabarti (2009). It was funded by the German Federal Ministry of Economics and Energy (BMWi) and the European Regional Development Fund (EFRE). The procedure is explained in detail below. It consists of four phases (Fig. 2).

For a better understanding, the method is explained using an example from industry at a medium-sized automotive supplier. The goal of this project was the strategic planning of the digitalization of production in the course of the fourth industrial revolution—in Germany often referred to as "Industry 4.0." Due to the confidentiality of the information, the contents have been anonymized.

Performance Assessment

The performance assessment in the context of digitalization is the starting point of the methodology. It serves to determine the current performance of a company from a socio-technical point of view using a selected maturity model. Against the background that digitalization not only has an impact on the technical components of a company, the socio-technical approach has become established in many cases. The aim is to determine the current performance profile, which reflects the current position of the company. It reveals strengths and weaknesses as well as starting points for performance enhancement.

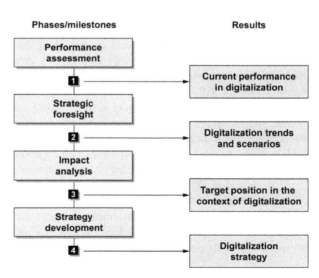

Fig. 2 Methodology for the development of digitalization strategies

Table 1 Examples of criteria and corresponding performance levels

Criteria	Performance Level 1	Performance Level 2	Performance Level 3	Performance Level 4
Horizontal integration	No interconnection of IT systems along the value chain.	Partial networking of the IT systems in individual stages of the value chain within the company, e.g. production or dispatch.	Extensive interconnection of IT systems within the company and across company boundaries, e.g. with logistics service providers.	Complete integration of all IT systems along the value chain, from the supplier to the producer to the customers.
Vertical integration	No interconnection of the company layers.	Communication between closely linked levels, e.g. interconnection of ERP and MES systems	Communication between several company layers, e.g. connecting ERP and MES systems and the field level.	Complete integration from the field level to the corporate management level across all levels
Systems engineering	The engineering is carried out in a discipline-specific manner. Classic development methods are used.	The engineering is based on interdisciplinary approaches such as the V-model (VDI 2206).	The idea of systems engineering is widely established. A holistic and interdisciplinary development of the system takes place.	There is an extended understanding of „classical" systems engineering, which also takes into account the early phases of product development (advanced systems engineering).
...	...	...	...	...

The first step is to identify a suitable maturity model. The suitability of a maturity model depends on various factors (e.g., included evaluation criteria, effort to carry out the evaluation in terms of time, personnel). The decisive factor is that the maturity model has various criteria (also called entities or indicators) with several performance levels. Table 1 shows examples of such criteria and corresponding performance levels.

In some maturity models, these criteria are combined into fields or areas. Depending on the maturity level models, this subdivision is named differently. Ideally, the criteria and performance levels should be accompanied by concise descriptions that specify them in more detail. A performance level is considered to have been reached when the criteria contained in the description are completely fulfilled (Christiansen 2009). Maturity models with detailed descriptions are particularly suitable for developing strategies. There are a large number of digitalization maturity models with different focuses. Therefore, companies must first determine the requirements for a maturity model before making a decision. A classification can provide support in the selection of a maturity model. Such a classification is a partial result of our research. It is visualized in Fig. 3. For this purpose, 15 selected maturity models in the field of digitalization have been combined into four maturity model classes. The classification was carried out using cluster analysis (cf. Backhaus et al. 2016; Bacher et al. 2010). The visualization is done by means of multidimensional scaling (cf. Dichtl et al. 1979; Green and Tull 1982). In order to arrive at such a classification, it is necessary to determine the most differentiated and independent characteristics and characteristic values for maturity models. This can be supported by using methods such as relevance and networking analyses. Examples for

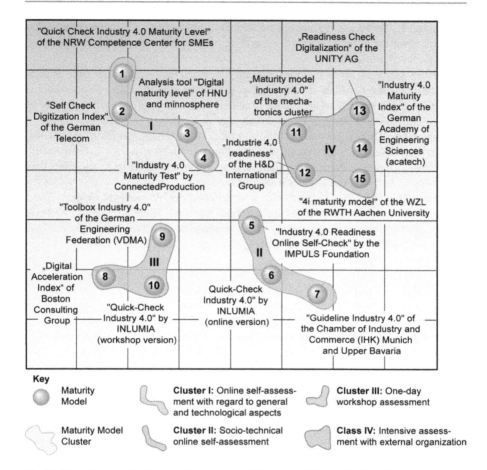

Fig. 3 Visualization of Industry 4.0 maturity models in a multidimensional scaling

characteristics and characteristic values are the object of investigation (functional area, plant, entire company) or the form of execution (online self-check, internal employee workshop, project with external experts). Each maturity model must be characterized on the basis of these values in order to describe them as accurately as possible.

The distances between the classes shown in the map provide information about their similar (small distance) or dissimilar (wider distance) characteristics. With the help of this classification, companies are in a position to select the appropriate class and a suitable maturity model. Criteria for the selection can be, for example, the time or financial expenditure for the application of a maturity level model. Each class is provided with a description:

- **Cluster I:** These are maturity models that enable online self-assessment. The focus is on the investigation of general and especially technological aspects of industrial digitalization.
- **Cluster II:** This class includes maturity models that also allow online self-assessment. In contrast to the first class, however, they investigate socio-technological aspects of industrial digitalization—they thus additionally focus on employees and changes in work and organization.
- **Cluster III:** This class contains maturity models that enable performance assessment in one-day workshops. They are more comprehensive than online self-assessments and often lead to sharper assessment results due to the intensive discussion between the experts involved.
- **Cluster IV:** This class contains the most comprehensive maturity models. They require intensive cooperation with external partners. Their application extends over multiple days. The accuracy of the evaluation results is the highest of all classes, but the implementation is also associated with a large effort.

In the further course of developing the digitalization strategy, the workshop version of the maturity model from the INLUMIA research project from class III will be used ("Quick-Check Industrie 4.0"). INLUMIA is a German acronym for "instrumentation for performance improvement of companies by Industry 4.0." According to socio-technical considerations, the maturity model divides its elements of action into the three dimensions of technology, business, and human in line with Ulich's HTO concept (cf. Ulich 2013). However, the "organization" provided in this concept is extended in the INLUMIA maturity model by criteria of benefit and business orientation (e.g., business models) and is therefore called "business" (Fig. 4). In total, the maturity model contains 59 criteria. By determining the current performance level for each criterion, the current performance level in digitalization (current position) is recorded. Each dimension contains four areas for action. In the Technology dimension, these are, for example, the technical organization, engineering, production, and the product. Each area of action contains criteria, each with four performance levels. Examples of criteria in the technical organization are horizontal or vertical integration. The detailed descriptions of the performance levels allow an exact assessment of the current performance for each criterion. The current digitalization performance capability of a company can thus be determined in workshops with experts from various disciplines within the company. Furthermore, under "desired target position" a first estimation can be made as to which target position would be desirable in the future. A detailed determination of the target position (phase 2 of the methodology) cannot replace this estimation. However, it serves to prepare the next step.

Following the evaluation, it is recommended that the criteria in the maturity model be prioritized with the help of a relevance assessment. On the one hand, this serves to reduce complexity. In addition, this step is suitable for obtaining a manageable number of criteria from the total of 59 criteria, which are then examined in detail for potential improvements with the help of so-called depth analyses. The relevance assessment can be carried out in various ways. A pragmatic approach in

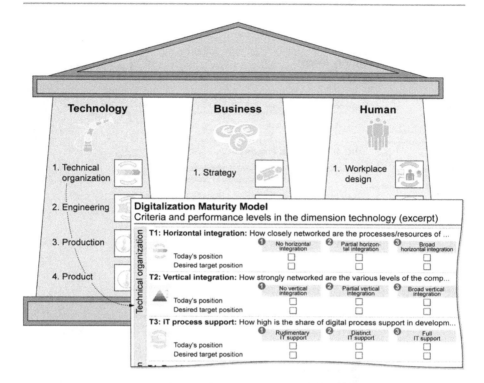

Fig. 4 Structure of the INLUMIA maturity model (cf. Knospe et al. 2018)

the pilot project workshops carried out has proven to be "point bonding." Each workshop participant receives a defined number of bonding points (usually 3–5 pieces), which he can assign to any criteria with individual weighting. The workshop posters thus quickly show the criteria for which the experts believe there is the greatest need for action.

Of course, other forms of evaluation are also conceivable at this point. Optionally, the most relevant criteria can be grouped into fields of action with similar criteria (Fig. 5). They can be addressed together in strategy development. In addition, they are suitable for determining depth analysis methods that simultaneously examine as many criteria as possible with regard to the potential improvements. In this example, several criteria were combined to form the field of action "production processes." For a better understanding, the fields of action are provided with a short description and guiding questions, which will be answered in the following analyses.

For the detailed analysis of the identified fields of action, a methodology kit was developed in the underlying research project. It contains already established as well as specially developed methods for the identification of improvement potentials in the context of digitalization. Improvement potentials represent potential weak points and serve as a starting point for an increase in performance in the company. The methodology kit contains tools that are suitable for investigating the criteria in the

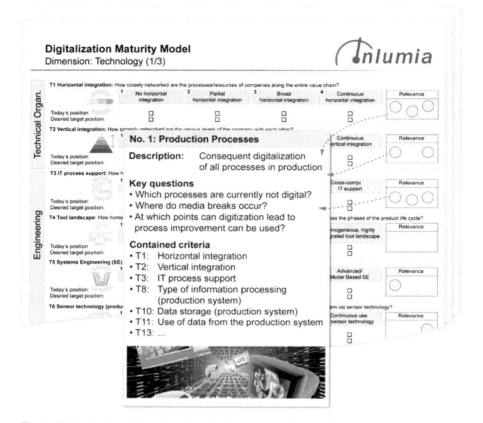

Fig. 5 Field of action derived from the criteria of the maturity model

maturity model. For the identified fields of action and the criteria contained in, this makes it possible to determine directly suitable methods for identifying the potential for improvement (Fig. 6). Examples of the methods included are OMEGA (Object-oriented method for business process modeling and analysis) or a method for mapping the value creation system of a company.

It is recommended that these methods be applied in workshops within the company. Experts from various disciplines and levels of management should participate in order to obtain a comprehensive assessment of the performance capability from various perspectives. We have found that the joint application of the methods and the overarching discourse reveal numerous potentials for improvement. It can hardly be avoided that some of these potentials are similar. It is important to summarize them in the best possible way. Since not all potentials are equally important or can be tapped simultaneously, prioritization is necessary. For example, an evaluation of all improvement potentials with regard to the two dimensions of benefit and development effort is suitable for this purpose. The result can be

Methods for deep analyses (examples)

Method for business process modelling and analysis

Kartons beschaffen

Method for mapping the value creation system of a company

Field of action

No. 1: Production Processes

Description: Consequent digitalization of all processes in production

Key questions
- Which processes are currently not digital?
- Where do media breaks occur?
- At which points can digitization lead to process improvement can be used?

Contained criteria
- T1: Horizontal integration
- T2: Vertical integration
- T3: IT process support
- T8: Type of information processing (production system)
- T10: Data storage (production system)
- T11: Use of data from the production system
- T13: …

Fig. 6 Examples of methods to analyze the fields of action

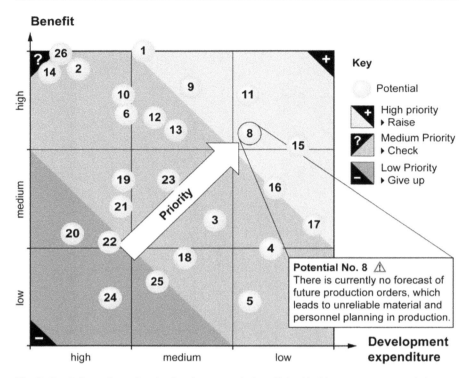

Fig. 7 Portfolio to determine the development priority of identified improvement potentials

transferred into a portfolio from which the prioritization of the potentials can be read (Fig. 7).

The exploitation of improvement potentials at the bottom left of the portfolio provides minor benefits with a high development effort. They should be neglected at first. The priority of the potentials in the middle of the portfolio should be checked. It must be decided on a case-by-case basis whether the potentials should be processed immediately or should be put on hold for the time being. Potentials in the upper right-hand corner of the portfolio should be tapped immediately. They offer considerable advantages at low development costs. These so-called low hanging fruits help to significantly increase performance in the context of digitalization within a short time. In the present case, for example, the company has decided that potential no. 8 should be one of the first to be processed. The interim findings at this point are the current performance profile of the company and the potentials for improvement. In order to obtain an estimation of which position the company should take in the future, strategic foresight is essential. The next phase will therefore create a comprehensive understanding of future developments in the context of digitalization.

Strategic Foresight

The systematic foresight of markets, technologies, and business environments serves to identify a promising future position for the company in the field of digitalization. A precise vision of the future is required in order to align the subsequent strategy accordingly. Two established methods are used for strategic foresight: trend analysis and the scenario technique (cf. Gausemeier and Plass 2014). They are suitable for determining two target positions with different time horizons that build on each other step by step.

In order to estimate the medium-term digitalization developments (time horizon approx. 5 years), a trend analysis is first carried out. A trend is a possible future development that can already be observed to a certain extent today and which will have an influence on future business due to its probability of occurrence and impact strength. The trend analysis is divided into four steps:

- **Identification of digitalization trends:** Relevant digitalization trends are first identified with the help of suitable sources such as studies, specialist publications, or expert interviews. Web crawlers or bibliometric analyses have also proven to be useful tools. Given a socio-technical view of digitization, these should also take organizational and social developments into account in addition to the technical perspective.
- **Documentation of trends:** Subsequently, the trends are documented in an appropriate manner. This can be done with the help of trend profiles. These contain a detailed description of the trend as well as the associated opportunities and risks. In addition, they can be provided with further relevant information (e.g., trend drivers).
- **Trend evaluation:** In the next step the trends are evaluated. The occurrence probability and impact have proven to be suitable evaluation criteria to prioritize the trends. The probability of occurrence expresses how strongly it can be assumed that a trend will actually occur. The strength of impact indicates how strongly a company will be affected by a trend (Liebl 1996; Klopp and Hartmann 1999).
- **Creation of a trend radar:** With the help of the evaluation, a trend radar can be set up (Fig. 8). The trend radar visualizes the results of the evaluation and provides information about which trends are of particular importance for tomorrow's business.

Each yellow bullet in the trend radar represents a digitalization trend. The closer a trend is to the center of the radar, the higher is its probability of occurrence. The diameter of a circle provides information about the strength of the impact. The assignment to the areas Technology, Business, and Humans indicates the dimension to which a trend is assigned. All trends with a high probability of occurrence and a large impact must be given special consideration in the further course of events.

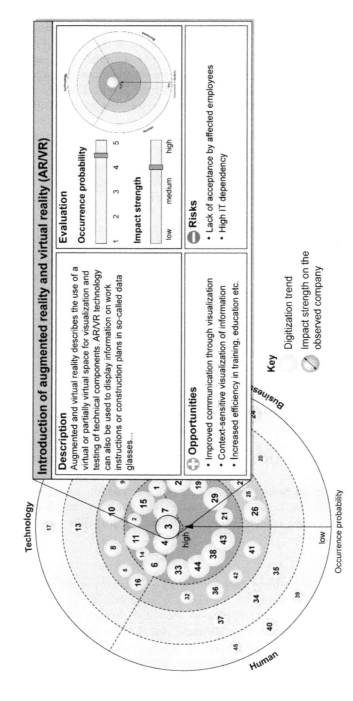

The figure contains the following text:

Introduction of augmented reality and virtual reality (AR/VR)

Description

Augmented and virtual reality describes the use of a virtual or partially virtual space for visualization and testing of technical components. AR/VR technology can also be used to display information on work instructions or construction plans in so-called data glasses....

Opportunities
- Improved communication through visualization
- Context-sensitive visualization of information
- Increased efficiency in training, education etc.

Evaluation

Occurrence probability

1 2 3 4 5

Impact strength

low   medium   high

Risks
- Lack of acceptance by affected employees
- High IT dependency

Key

Digitization trend

Impact strength on the observed company

Technology

Business

Human

Occurrence probability

high   low

Fig. 8 Trend radar with digitalization trends

Key factor No. 2: Breakthrough of ICTs

Description
The penetration of information and communication technology is influenced by technical developments in this area. These developments often trigger further innovations in other branches of industry and therefore act as enablers. The willingness or ability of people to integrate new information and communication technologies into their everyday lives plays a major role in their diffusion. Thus, the increasing penetration of information and communication technology can be perceived "as a blessing" or "as a curse".

Projections

2A) Connected world
The rapid penetration of the world of work and leisure with information and communication technology has continued to increase in recent years. Everyone has access to information and services at all times and everywhere. The use of semantic technologies enables an efficient management of the abundance of available information [...].

2B) Information elites
The amount of data produced daily has reached new dimensions. Many see undreamt-of possibilities in this. As predicted by many, the enormous amount of data proves to be the gold of the 21st century. But the free availability of data is deceptive. Only a few succeed in exploiting the technological possibilities and generating information and knowledge from data: creating information elites [...]

2C) IT frustration
The ICT hype of the leisure world has not found its way into production. The necessary high demands on the reliability of IT systems are not being met. The expected increases in efficiency have not materialised. In private life, scepticism about ICT is growing strongly because the consequences of "relaxed" use are now gradually becoming apparent [...].

Fig. 9 Example of a key factor with associated projections

The trend analysis is followed by an assessment of the long-term development of digitalization (time horizon approximately 10 years). The scenario technique is applied. With the help of the scenario technique, future developments are systematically anticipated within the framework of the forecast. Future scenarios are generally understandable descriptions of possible future situations. They describe various conceivable development possibilities of a particular area of consideration with a selectable planning horizon and are also suitable for estimating longer-term developments.

The methodological approach (simplified) is to first identify relevant key factors. These are factors that particularly characterize the object of investigation (in this case digitalization). Subsequently, several conceivable development possibilities (so-called projections) are described for each key factor (Fig. 9). As a rule, 10–20 key factors with 3–5 projections each are obtained. To obtain a consistent picture of the future, the compatibility of all projections with each other is checked by a consistency analysis. Projection bundles are formed on the basis of this analysis. A projection bundle is a chain of projections, with exactly one projection for each key factor. A scenario is therefore a combination of future projections that fit together well. The chains of projections are finally verbally elaborated. They ultimately form the future scenarios. As a rule, these are 3–5 of them. These scenarios are then evaluated and prioritized. The result can be transferred into a portfolio. It is possible to select the so-called reference scenario that is used for further planning (Gausemeier and Plass 2014).

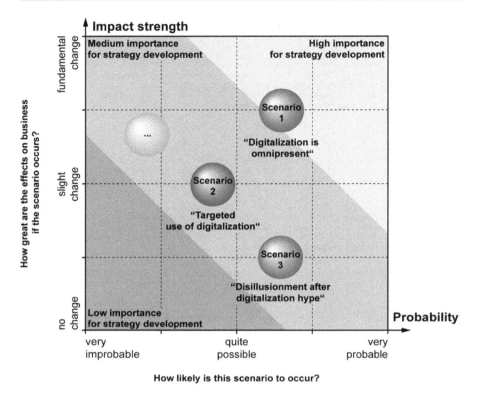

Fig. 10 Portfolio for selecting the reference scenario

The aim is to select a reference scenario that describes a future picture of the digitalization as accurately as possible. In order to select this reference scenario, the future scenarios created must first be evaluated. Once again, the probability of occurrence and the impact strength have proven to be the evaluation criteria. The evaluation of the scenarios can be represented in a portfolio (Fig. 10). In this example, Scenario 1 was selected because of its high occurrence probability. In addition to the digitalization trends already identified, it serves as an additional input variable for the impact analysis.

Impact Analysis

An impact analysis is carried out following the forecast. The influence of the previously projected environmental developments on the medium- and long-term target position is examined here. It is determined whether the trends or a reference scenario hinder or favor an increase in performance. It is clarified whether higher levels of performance can be achieved taking environmental developments into

Impact matrix Assessment of the extent to which a digitization trend will facilitate the achievement of a higher performance level.	Digitalization trends	Increase of big data applications	Use of cloud computing	Increased use of digital platforms	Increasing spread of smart services	New forms of work organization	Skill shortage	Sum	Medium-term target position
Prioritized criteria	No.	T1	T2	B1	B2	H1	H2	Σ	Level
Horizontal integration	T1	0	1	0	0	0	0	0	0	0	0	0	0	6	8	Level 3
		1	1	1	1	1	1	0	0	1	1	0	0	36	25	
IT process support	T3	0	0	0	0	0	0	0	0	0	0	0	0	4	16	Level 2
		1	1	1	1	0	The increased use of digital platforms promotes platform-based ad-hoc co-operation in a temporary value-added network.						13	3	
...																
Value creation cooperations	B4	0	0	0	0	0							7	7	Level 3
		1	1	0	1	1	1	0	0	1	1	-1	-1	41	32	
		0	1	0	0	0	0	0	0	0	0	0	2	6	Level 2
		0	0	0	0	0	0	0	0	0	0	5	1	
		0	0	0	0	0	0	0	0	-1	-1	2	12	Level 2
		1	0	1	0	0	0	0	-1		10	7	
		0	The lack of skilled workers hinders the central documentation of personal knowledge in the company.		0	9	9	Level 2
		0			0	2	7	

Key

The achievement of **level 1** for criterion i (row) is promoted (1), not influenced (0) or hindered (-1) by trend j (column).

The achievement of **level 2** for criterion i (row) is promoted (1), not influenced (0) or hindered (-1) by trend j (column).

L1	L2
L3	L4

The achievement of **level 3** for criterion i (row) is promoted (1), not influenced (0) or hindered (-1) by trend j (column).

The achievement of **level 4** for criterion i (row) is promoted (1), not influenced (0) or hindered (-1) by trend j (column).

Fig. 11 Determining the impact of digitalization trends on performance improvement

account. An impact matrix is used to assess the medium-term and long-term target positions (Fig. 11).

The structure of the impact matrix is explained below:

- In the first column, the prioritized criteria are listed. These were already determined at the beginning.
- The first row lists the identified digitalization trends. It is recommended to consider a selection of the most relevant trends here. Particularly important trends can be read from the trend radar.
- Four fields each are available for a pairwise comparison of a criterion with a trend or a future projection (see highlighting). The four fields are used to assess the influence of future developments on the achievement of a performance level in the maturity model. The evaluation scale for each field ranges from −1 ("The achievement of performance level X of criterion i (line) is hindered by trend j (column)") to 0 ("The achievement of performance level X of criterion i (line) is not influenced by trend j (column).") to 1. ("The achievement of performance level X of criterion i (line) is promoted by trend j (column).")
- The column "Sum" provides information on the ideal performance level that can be achieved taking trends into account.
- The medium-term target position can be read in a simple way in the last column and be used to create the medium-term line profile.

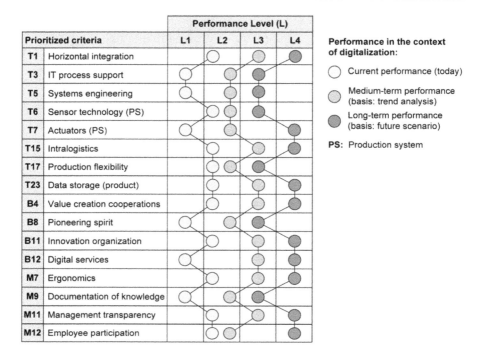

Fig. 12 Current and future performance profiles following Westermann (2017)

The same procedure can be used to estimate the long-term target positions. The influence matrix presented above is also used for this. However, instead of digitalization trends, the projections contained in the reference scenario are listed in the first row. This allows the assessment of the impact of future projections on performance improvement.

From the impact analysis, a medium- and long-term performance profile can be now derived (Fig. 12). This shows the need for action for the prioritized criteria in the next 5 or 10 years. The individual needs for action can now be transferred into a superordinate strategy.

Note: As already shown in the MDS above, an online version of the used maturity model exists. In this online version, the current and future performance can also be determined. The evaluation results of the participating companies are stored in a database. In addition, different company characteristics are queried for each participant in order to classify the data sets of similar companies. At the end of the performance evaluation, each participating company receives its own certificate and a comparison with evaluations and future plans of similar companies (anonymized). From this, valuable conclusions can be drawn for the own strategy development and target profiles can be sharpened further.

Strategy Development

The current and future performance profile can now be used to set up the strategy (cf. Bensiek 2013). It makes sense to plan the achievement of the targeted performance levels in more detail. A suitable tool for this is a roadmap (Fig. 13). This presents a challenge. Even if the determined performance profiles give the impression that some performance levels can be achieved simultaneously, there are interdependencies between the performance levels of the different criteria that hinder this. An example: In the long term, according to the upper profiles, performance level 3 of criterion 6 and performance level 4 of criterion T15 should be achieved simultaneously. However, since extensive use of sensor technology in the production system is a requirement for autonomous intralogistics, this must be taken into account in the strategy. The development of level 3 of criterion T6 is, therefore, to be preferred. Taking these dependencies into account, the complete digital transformation can ultimately be represented in the strategy.

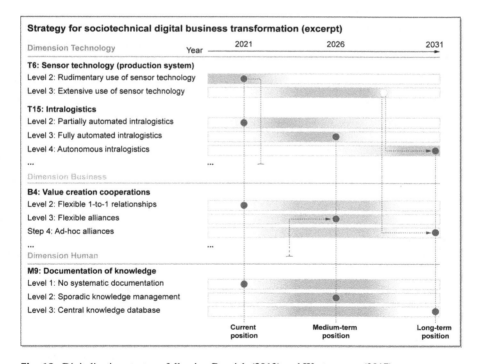

Fig. 13 Digitalization strategy following Bensiek (2013) and Westermann (2017)

6   Conclusion and Outlook

This chapter provides a procedure that allows the simple development of a digitalization strategy using a maturity model. In contrast to already existing approaches to the development of digitalization strategies, environmental influences and their effects are extensively considered. Target positions can be defined at two different points in time, which supports the gradual digital transformation of a company. Especially SMEs get a suitable tool to identify the relevant aspects of digitalization and plan their implementation in a strategy. With regard to future research work the following aspects can be stated:

- The methodological approach currently does not yet take sufficiently into account the interdependencies between the criteria of the maturity model, which are to be developed further. Identified interdependencies must be taken into account during implementation in order to make the best possible use of synergies. This consideration of interdependencies is currently still done manually and often only in the implementation planning. It is mainly based on the experience of the user. A methodical support can provide considerable added value here.
- To continuously monitor the implementation of the strategy, continuous implementation and premise controlling is essential. The review of the premises can be carried out by continuously checking the developments in the environment and their tendencies. However, implementation controlling can be supported even better. Indicators that monitor the development progress in the implementation of the performance improvement may be suitable here. The methodological procedure should be expanded to include this aspect.
- In order to achieve the targeted performance levels in the digitalization strategy, it is advisable to define concrete measures for implementing each performance level. The progress of individual measures is easier to track and supports the monitoring of digital transformation.

References

Bacher, J., Pöge, A., & Wenzig, K. (2010). *Clusteranalyse. Anwendungsorientierte Einführung in Klassifikationsverfahren* (3rd extended, completely revised and redesigned ed.). Munich: Oldenbourg. Accessed December 12, 2019, from http://www.oldenbourg-link.com/isbn/9783486710236.

Backhaus, K., Erichson, B., Plinke, W., & Weiber, R. (2016). *Multivariate Analysemethoden. Eine anwendungsorientierte Einführung* (14th, revised and updated ed.). Berlin: Springer Gabler.

Bensiek, T. (2013). *Systematik zur reifegradbasierten Leistungsbewertung und -steigerung von Geschäftsprozessen im Mittelstand* (Vol. 357). Dissertation, Faculty of Mechanical Engineering, University of Paderborn. HNI-Verlagsschriftenreihe.

Blessing, L. T. M., & Chakrabarti, A. (2009). *DRM, a Design Research Methodology*. London: Springer. Accessed December 12, 2019, from http://site.ebrary.com/lib/alltitles/docDetail.action?docID=10310350.

Bley, K., Leyh, C., & Schäffer, T. (2016). Digitization of German Enterprises in the Production Sector. Do they know how "digitized" they are? In *Surfing the IT innovation wave. 22nd*

Americas Conference on Information Systems (AMCIS 2016): San Diego, CA, 11–14 August 2016. Americas Conference on Information Systems; Association for Information Systems; AMCIS (pp. 736–746). Red Hook, NY: Curran Associates Inc.

Christiansen, S.-K. (2009). *Methode zur Klassifikation und Entwicklung reifegradbasierter Leistungsbewertungs- und Leistungssteigerungsmodelle* (Vol. 264). Dissertation, Faculty of Mechanical Engineering, University of Paderborn. HNI-Verlagsschriftenreihe.

Demary, V., Engels, B., Röhl, K.-H., & Rusche, C. (2016). *Digitalisierung und Mittelstand. Eine Metastudie.* Cologne, Institut der deutschen Wirtschaft Medien GmbH, IW-Analysen, No 109.

Dichtl, E., Schobert, R., & Beeskow, W. (1979). *Mehrdimensionale Skalierung. Methodische Grundlagen und betriebswirtschaftliche Anwendungen.* Munich: Vahlen.

Gausemeier, J., & Plass, C. (2014). *Zukunftsorientierte Unternehmensgestaltung. Strategien, Geschäftsprozesse und IT-Systeme für die Produktion von morgen* (2nd ed.). Munich: Hanser.

Green, P. E., & Tull, D. S. (1982). *Methoden und Techniken der Marketingforschung.* Stuttgart: Poeschel.

Hoberg, P., Krcmar, H., Oswald, G., & Welz, B. (2015). *Skills for digital transformation.* Research Report 2015. Hg. v. Technical University of Munich, Chair for Information Systems. Accessed December 12, 2019, from https://www.i17.in.tum.de/fileadmin/w00btn/www/IDT_Skill_Report_2015.pdf.

Horváth, P., Reichmann, T., Baumöl, U., Hoffjan, A., Möller, K., & Pedell, B. (Eds.). (2018). *Transformation im Controlling. Umbrüche durch VUCA-Umfeld und Digitalisierung* (1st ed. (Controlling, Special Edition 2018)). Munich: Vahlen Franz.

Kagermann, H., Wahlster, W., & Helbig, J. (2013). *Recommendations for implementing the strategic initiative INDUSTRIE 4.0.* Final report of the Industrie 4.0 Working Group. acatech – Deutsche Akademie der Technikwissenschaften e.V., Berlin.

Klopp, M., & Hartmann, M. (Eds.). (1999). *Das Fledermaus-Prinzip. Strategische Früherkennung für Unternehmen.* Stuttgart: Logis.

Knospe, O., Drewel, M., Mittag, T., Pierenkemper, C., & Hobscheidt, D. (2018). Leistungssteigerung durch Industrie 4.0 für kleine und mittlere Unternehmen. *ZWF, 113*(1–2), 83–87. https://doi.org/10.3139/104.111867.

Liebl, F. (1996). *Strategische Frühaufklärung. Trends, issues, stakeholders.* Munich: Oldenbourg.

Ulich, E. (2013). Arbeitssysteme als Soziotechnische Systeme – eine Erinnerung. *Psychology of Everyday Activity, 6*(1), 4–12.

VDMA Forum Industrie 4.0. (2016). *Guideline Industrie 4.0. Guiding principles for the implementation of Industrie 4.0 in small and medium sized businesses.* Frankfurt am Main.: VDMA Verlag.

Westermann, T. (2017). *Systematik zur Reifegradmodell-basierten Planung von Cyber-Physical Systems des Maschinen- und Anlagenbaus* (Vol. 375). Dissertation, Faculty of Mechanical Engineering, University of Paderborn. HNI-Verlagsschriftenreihe.

World Bank. (2019). *Small and Medium Enterprises (SMEs) Finance: Improving SMEs' access to finance and finding innovative solutions to unlock sources of capital.* Accessed December 12, 2019, from https://www.worldbank.org/en/topic/smefinance.

Christoph Pierenkemper was a research assistant at the Heinz Nixdorf Institute of the Paderborn University in the department "Advanced Systems Engineering." His research focus was on strategic planning and innovation management. He was responsible for a research project on performance improvement of companies through Industry 4.0 and a research project on the development of a digital platform for AI applications in the product development process. Furthermore, he was active in teaching and worked on various industrial projects on the digital transformation of manufacturing companies in the mechanical and plant engineering sector. He studied industrial engineering and management with a focus on mechanical engineering and innovation management at the Paderborn University. Today, he works as an assistant to the management of an electronics company.

Jürgen Gausemeier is a senior professor at the Heinz Nixdorf Institute of the University of Paderborn and chairman of the board of the Leading-Edge Cluster "Intelligente Technische Systeme Ostwestfalen-Lippe (OWL)," which was initiated by the Federal Ministry of Education and Research. He was a speaker of the Collaborative Research Centre 614 "Self-Optimizing Concepts and Structures in Mechanical Engineering" and a member of the German Council of Science and Humanities from 2009 until 2015. Jürgen Gausemeier is an initiator and chairman of the Supervisory Board of the consulting company UNITY AG. Since 2003 he is a member of "acatech—German Academy of Science and Engineering" and since 2012 vice president.

Part III

Digital Strategy

Same Same, But Different: An Exploration of Alternative Business Model Disruptions Across German Industries

Alexander Lennart Schmidt

1   Introduction

From observations across industries and by reviewing current scholarly debates, we can conclude that business models can lead to disruptive change in hitherto established industries (Christensen et al. 2018). For instance, Spotify's business model disrupted the music industry and displaced pay-per-song business models. Moreover, Airbnb's model disrupted the hospitality industry by offering a matching platform, connecting hosts and guests to circumvent established hotel chains. Given the current increase in pace and impact of these disruptive dynamics, management scholars have begun to label the current times an era of continual disruption (Kumaraswamy et al. 2018).

Disruptive innovation describes a specific process, in which a new market entrant (usually equipped with relatively little resources) is able to challenge established industry incumbents by introducing new offerings. These offerings gain a foothold in the niche before they increasingly attract mainstream customers through constant improvements. Whereas these dynamics were initially assigned to technological innovations, current debates underline the strategic positioning of the disruptive innovation in the market (Christensen et al. 2018). Hence, the business model has become the relevant unit to further the understanding of disruptive dynamics (Hopp et al. 2018; Kumaraswamy et al. 2018).

Against this background and based on empirical observations, it appears that there exist communalities of disruptive business models. The platform model, which allowed Spotify to disrupt the music industry, can also be identified in the case of Airbnb. Contrarily, low-cost models as applied by Ryanair or Fintech companies

A. L. Schmidt (✉)
FH Münster | Münster University of Applied Sciences, Science-to-Business Marketing Research Centre, Münster, Germany

Zuyd University of Applied Sciences, Maastricht, The Netherlands
e-mail: alexanderlennart.schmidt@fh-muenster.de

disrupt their mainstream counterparts by using very different mechanisms related to just good-enough products and services.

To better understand these similarities and differences between disruptive business models, we interviewed more than 80 company representatives across German industries, systematically collected a vast amount of secondary data, and attended a large number of practitioner conferences. Based on the acquired domain knowledge, this paper builds on the following question: "How are disruptive business models similar (or different) across German industries?" Consequently, eight exemplary cases of disruptive business models are explored within the scope of this paper. Based on a qualitative content analysis, similarities and differences of business model disruptions are presented. Ultimately, this paper presents conclusions and avenues for further research.

2 Theoretical Background

Business Models as the Vehicle for Disruptive Innovation

Disruptive innovation describes a process in which an entrant with fewer resources challenges established incumbents in the mainstream market by introducing initially underperforming offerings (Christensen et al. 2018). The emerging customer segments, which are targeted by the entrant, are rooted in the low-end and largely overlooked by the incumbents (Christensen et al. 2018; Schmidt and Druehl 2008). However, by gaining a market foothold, entrants can continuously improve their new offerings along the alternative performance trajectory, ultimately growing and moving up the market. Thereby, entrants establish their offering within the mainstream market and erode incumbents' market shares (Adner 2002).

When the phenomenon of disruptive innovation was conceptualized in the mid-1990s, the focus was on technological invention. However, since 2006, scholarly and practitioner debates agree that the reason market incumbents are disrupted lies in the corresponding strategic positioning of the innovation (Christensen 2006; Markides 2006). Consequently, disruptive innovation is more of a competitive process than an innovation process and, hence, it is best approached by studying business models. In other words, business models can be understood as the vehicle that drives disruptive dynamics across industries (Cozzolino et al. 2018; Snihur et al. 2018).

Despite the emphasis on the business model, recent theoretical contributions highlight that there is no "one size fits all" approach to initiate disruptive dynamics in an industry. In particular, there is only limited knowledge regarding the strategic approaches of how companies design their disruptive business models (Christensen et al. 2018; Hopp et al. 2018). Consequently, there is a need to further explore how far business models underlying disruptive dynamics show similarities or differences in characteristics.

Similarities of Business Models

Over the past years, the concept of the business model gained considerable interest among scholarly and practitioner debates. Indeed, the concept is considered suitable to conceptualize value creation beyond physical products and services (Amit and Zott 2001; Foss and Saebi 2017; Schneider and Spieth 2013; Zott et al. 2011). Thereby, the business model allows to study competitive processes that emerge and evolve regardless of underlying radical technological inventions. Scholars have built on the business model concept to discuss how companies do business, which processes are performed, and how these processes are interlinked (Foss and Saebi 2017; Schneider and Spieth 2013).

Despite diverging understanding in the early years (Wirtz et al. 2016), the understandings of the business model concept are increasingly converging. Current literature increasingly agrees on these three dimensions, which are being ascribed to a business model: value propositions, value creation, and value delivery (Foss and Saebi 2017; Teece 2010). First, a business model depicts which value propositions are delivered to the market. Second, value creation defines the activities from input factors to customers that result in new market offerings (Chesbrough 2006). Finally, the value capture refers to how revenue sources and pricing capture the created value (Teece 2018).

Based on this multidimensional understanding, scholars argued for similarities of business models. In fact, Teece (2010) argues that business models are, to a certain, degree "*'shared' by multiple competitors*" (p. 179). Baden-Fuller and Morgan (2010) state that business models can be used as recipes. Against this background, business model researchers continuously engage in discussing similarities and differences across successful business models (Bocken et al. 2014; Fielt 2014; Gassmann et al. 2014; Ritter and Lettl 2018). For instance, Ritter and Lettl (2018, p. 2) describe the discussed similar business models as "generic logics of how firms do business" (p. 2). Famous illustrative examples of such similar business models are the "razor and blade" model of Gillette (and printer-cartridge models of, e.g., Hewlett Packard), or the "low-cost carrier model" of Southwest Airlines (and the similar model of Ryanair) (Fielt 2014).

Building on these discussions, researchers recently engaged in likewise studies in the context of disruptive innovation. First, Amshoff et al. (2015) focus on a particular disruptive technology (i.e., condition monitoring) and discuss similarities across related business models. Second, Garbuio and Lin (2019) investigate similarities across disruptive business models in the healthcare industry. Third, Trabucchi et al. (2019) study similarities of business models of big-bang disruptors—a specific form of disruption characterized by a zero marginal cost structure (Downes and Nunes 2014).

Whereas these studies contribute to a better understanding of similarities and differences of disruptive business models, they either focus on a particular industry (or technology) or a based on the specificities of Big-Bang disruptions. Hence, to further advance research on disruptive innovation, a cross-industry exploration of business model similarities appears timely and relevant. Such an exploration would provide practical guidelines for decision-makers on how to design business models to pursue disruptive opportunities (Hopp et al. 2018; Teece 2010).

3   Methodology

Case Selection and Data Collection

To explore the research question, an in-depth analysis of multiple cases has been carried out. Purposeful theoretical sampling of the informative cases has been performed by referring to previous studies that highlight disruptive developments within certain industries. Further, the sampling of cases was based on the continuous in-depth discussions with decision-makers across industries.

Within the identified "disruption-prone" industries, eight cases of business model disruption have been selected. In-depth interviews with key informants (i.e., CEO, COO, business developer) have been conducted from August 2017 until December 2019. Within these interviews, the focus was on the design of the business models along the three dimensions of value proposition, value creation, and value capture and the relative sustaining business model (i.e., how business models are positioned in relation to the existing ways of doing business in the mainstream). Furthermore, based on previous research on disruptive innovation (e.g., Ansari et al. 2016; Cozzolino et al. 2018), archival material has been systematically accessed via LexisNexis. Thereby, a more complete picture of the studied disruptive business models and their underlying generative mechanisms could be obtained. The subsequent table presents an overview of the eight cases (Table 1).

Data Analysis

To better understand the collected thick data of the eight cases, abductive coding (Saldaña 2016) has been applied. For coding, the content analysis feature in MAXQDA18 has been used. The qualitative content analysis was focused on how the data describe the disruptive business models.

In the first coding cycle, segments were coded based on the three business model dimensions: (1) value proposition: how are products/services, customer segments, and customer relationships described; (2) value creation: how are key activities, required resources, partners, and underlying technologies described; (3) value capture: how are revenue and cost structures described. Hence, the material was coded to identify the mechanisms behind the studied business model disruption. Subsequently, the coded business models were pairwise compared for grouping and identification of similarities and differences. Grouping was performed, when the identified similarities were representative of underlying mechanisms propelling the particular business model disruption.

Table 1 Case overview

Industry reasoning	Company	Interviewee(s)	Interview date(s)	Length of interview transcript (word count)	Length of archival data (word count)	Disruptive business model	Anchor quote(s) for disruptive business model	Relative sustaining business model	Business model disruption approach
Consulting; Christensen and Raynor (2013)	Consulting_Alpha	Co-founder	21.08.2017	7355	6792	Data analytics as a service	"We build a web platform for the customer from open source components, so we work completely as-a-service based, we offer Data Analytics as-a-Service, in a self-service."	Data consultancy (i.e., selling consultant days), Selling on-premise software licenses	Flexibilizing
Insurance; Braun and Schreiber (2017), Christensen et al. (2018)	Insurance_Alpha	COO	20.06.2019, 20.08.2018	16,571	22,851	Digital private health insurance	"If I want to do health management, I need exactly the opposite. I need a lot of contact with the customer, how else can I talk to them about their health?"; "We have relied very heavily on standard products"	Private health insurances with little customer interaction and analog value creation processes	Reducing

(continued)

Table 1 (continued)

Industry reasoning	Company	Interviewee(s)	Interview date(s)	Length of interview transcript (word count)	Length of archival data (word count)	Disruptive business model	Anchor quote(s) for disruptive business model	Relative sustaining business model	Business model disruption approach
Insurance; Braun and Schreiber (2017), Christensen et al. (2018)	Insurance_Beta	Head of Business Development, CEO	18.10.2017, 06.12.2019	8453	4946	Digital development platform for insurance products	"Basically [we have] a B to B to C business model. [...] That means we also work with business partners, therefore B to B. But we provide the complete value chain, i.e. the entire value chain, right through to the customer"; "We provide insurance solutions, so that partners can make their end customers happy, of course we immediately have quite an end-to-end relationship as far as the solution is concerned and that is why we speak of a platform."	Classic insurance, i.e., an insurance broker or an insurance agent	Connecting

Fashion Retail; Christensen et al. (2018), Markides (2006)	Retail_Alpha	Co-founder	10.11.2017	11,395	6305	Live video shopping assistant	"The core idea has been that you communicate with each other via live video. But and that was just the hurdle, how do I make it so that it replicates the shopping experience and conversation in the store?"	Face-to-face shopping in offline stores	Reducing
Fashion Retail; Christensen et al. (2018), Markides (2006)	Retail_Beta	Co-founder	15.08.2017	8642	3921	Digital matchmaking platform for outfit suggestions	"An app that uses self-learning algorithms to present women with individual outfit suggestions based on weather and occasion."	Traditional high street fashion boutique with individual assistance	Connecting
Manufacturing; Nagy et al. (2016), Hahn et al. (2014)	Manufacturing_Alpha	Co-founder	06.11.2017	4219	2278	3D printing-as-a-service	"The print service was created to give people the opportunity to purchase 3D print parts without having their own 3D print production."	3D printing with on-premise printers	Flexibilizing

(continued)

Table 1 (continued)

Industry reasoning	Company	Interviewee(s)	Interview date(s)	Length of interview transcript (word count)	Length of archival data (word count)	Disruptive business model	Anchor quote(s) for disruptive business model	Relative sustaining business model	Business model disruption approach
Automotive; Ferras-Hernandéz et al. (2017), Christensen and Raynor (2003)	Automotive_Alpha	Senior Business Developer	09.10.2017	8239	64,935	Minute-based car sharing service	"Car sharing, I mean, we offer the ride at a per-minute rate. Of course, [this] means that we don't necessarily have exclusive cars, but that the topic of mobility should work, the technology, in terms of access to the vehicles and the whole ecosystem around them, billing, wear and tear, renting, etc."	Selling cars (i.e., customer owns the vehicle), long-term car rental	Flexibilizing
Hospitality; Akbar and Tracogna (2018)	Hospitality_Alpha	CEO	04.12.2017	8316	9709	Digital, no-frill hotel with self-service	"I only book my room online, there is no receptionist, I get my bill online, I actually only get everything through my app and can finally decide when I go to the hotel, when I go out."	Full service hotels	Reducing
			Total	73,190	121,737				

4   Findings

Overview of Analyzed Cases and Their Business Models

Based on the formulated research question, the following eight cases of business model disruption have been studied.

Consulting_Alpha is an entrant in the consulting industry and started operations in 2017. The business model is built around the claim to provide data mining processes in self-services. Consequently, personnel-intensive consulting services present the sustaining counterpart. Consulting_Alpha designs its value proposition in a way that allows the analysis of data in self-service. Consequently, the value creation is based on highly automatized processes and a focus on standardization of features. Moreover, the self-service logic makes a significant customer integration necessary. Customers take over large parts of the actual value creation themselves. The value capture mechanisms allow for relatively low financial entry barriers, as there is no need for investments in large consulting projects or on-premise software. Revenue is generated on a subscription-based income stream, which mirrors the notion of the self-service-based value proposition.

Insurance_Alpha is an entrant in the digital private health industry and launched its business in 2017. The entrant designed a business model, which enables continuous customer relationship building via digital channels. Thereby, Insurance_Alpha envisions to position its business model more as a healthcare manager than a traditional insurance company. The sustaining counterpart business model is the traditional private health insurance with little customer interaction and analog value creation processes. Insurance_Alpha designs its value proposition as a human-centered digital health management solution. Consequently, value creation processes are highly automatized and digitalized to save resources and provide a digital experience. Insurance_Alpha acquired external investments from beyond the insurance industry to comply with strict (financial) industry regulations, yet maintaining strategic flexibility.

Insurance_Beta entered the insurance industry in 2017 with a business model for B2B2C. Hence, the entrant offers a digital platform via which new insurance solutions can be developed and offered "white label" to other market players (beyond the insurance industry). Insurance_Beta's sustaining counterpart is the classic insurance companies, which sell their insurances via brokers or agents. The entrant's value proposition can be characterized as a digital platform for developing new insurance services. To allow for the co-creation of new insurance products and a flexible and open collaboration with industry partners, Insurance_Beta's value creation is designed openly (e.g., via open APIs). The value capture logic is designed to lower the financial risks for associated industry partners, with whom the new insurance products are designed. In particular, Insurance_Beta takes over significant long-term liabilities, which enables an easy entry into new collaborations.

Retail_Alpha's business model encompasses a live video shopping assistant solution and started business in 2015. Hence, Retail_Alpha's sustaining counterpart business model can be characterized as the traditional face-to-face shopping experience in fashion retailing. The entrant, however, designed a value proposition, which integrates offline and online shopping experience by using its live shopping video assistant. For value creation, the entrant relies heavily on existing technological solutions to limit the need for new developments. Furthermore, value is captured via a commission-based logic. Hence, whenever a shopping transaction is completed successfully via the digital assistant, the entrant earns a commission.

Retail_Beta is an entrant in the fashion retail industry, too. The entrant's business model was introduced in the market in 2016 and designed to ease everyday fashion decisions by using self-learning algorithms. The sustaining counterpart is traditional high street fashion boutiques, which provide face-to-face professional fashion assistance. Retail_Beta designed a value proposition, which eases the process of fashion outfit selection for users. Therefore, the entrant set up value creation processes that match users (who search for new fashion outfit suggestions) with suppliers from the fashion industry. Whenever a matching transaction is successfully completed, Retail_Beta captures value based on a commission (i.e., affiliate marketing).

Manufacturing_Alpha designed a business model based on 3D printing services on demand. Hence, other than its sustaining counterpart, customers no longer need on-premise 3D printing facilities. Accordingly, the value proposition of Manufacturing_Alpha can be described as a flexible access to 3D printing technology to manufacture customized products. The entrant set up a value creation process, which allows for high flexibility. Moreover, a partner network has been set up to cater to specific customer needs, while upholding a high level of flexibility. The value capture dimension of Manufacturing_Alpha's model is based on a pay-per-use logic.

Automotive_Alpha designed a business model for a flexible use of cars on a pay-per-minute logic. Hence, the corresponding sustaining innovation can be characterized as long-term car rentals or even the traditional car selling business. Accordingly, Automotive_Alpha's value proposition is designed to allow very short-term car rentals, thereby limiting the usage barriers. The value creation processes are designed in close collaboration with Automotive_Alpha's parent organization, which provides the vehicle fleet. Moreover, value creation processes integrate the customer via digital channels to enable customized service provision. The value capture dimension is based on a flexible pay-per-minute logic.

Hospitality_Alpha's business model encompasses a digital, no-frill hospitality solution. Whereas the sustaining counterpart of full-service hotel chains offer the full spectrum of personal assistance and add-ons, Hospitality_Alpha designed a value proposition that is reduced to the basic functionality of providing a place to stay. The value creation processes are designed accordingly. Hence, the used assets are reduced to a minimum and the customer is integrated into the value creation process through digital interfaces (i.e., smartphone app). The value capture dimension is built on relatively low-cost revenue streams.

The subsequent paragraphs present how the studied business models enabled dynamics of disruptive innovation by showing similarities and differences. By exploring the eight cases of disruptive business models, it can be concluded that business model disruption across industries is "same same, but different."

Connecting

The analyzed data suggest a first approach for performing business model disruption, which can be labeled as the "connecting" approach. Retail_Beta and Insurance_Beta can be categorized here. Their business models are designed in a way to match market sides and to connect with external partners to create the value proposition. To facilitate this connecting paradigm, business models are based on a digital platform technology and enable users to complete transactions (Retail_Beta) or to cocreate new solutions (Insurance_Beta).

Moreover, efficient processes have been identified as being essential within the value creation logic of these business models. The efficiency orientation paves the way for relatively low-cost transactions. Hence, for instance, "*algorithms virtually learn what fits together when, how, and under which conditions*" [Retail_Beta], thereby underlining the importance of the automated optimization of processes.

Regarding the value capture design of business model disruption based on "connecting" market sides, flexibility in cost and revenue streams appears to be key.

The use of underlying technologies allows the automation of transactions and ensures low operational costs. Hence, value is captured based on a subscription logic or based on a charged fee per transaction. The co-founder of Retail_Beta explains:

> So the app itself is free, we earn something from it when you buy it and, of course, if you don't return it, so if you buy 500 items and don't keep any of them, we don't earn anything, but only for what you really keep. [Retail_Beta]

Further, Retail_Beta's model is described as:

> [the user] is also immediately forwarded, [. . .] called affiliate links within the app; if you see a part that you would like to have, you can put it on your wish list or click directly into the shop and then land on the website or in the app of the respective partner and can buy it there directly. [Retail_Beta]

Consequently, customers no longer pay surcharges for having intermediaries in the process, the customers "only" pay a transaction fee for the successful connection with needed market sides.

In the case of the Insurance_Beta co-creation platform, this highly flexible value creation logic results in a situation,

> where we really run the full risk when it comes to innovative new products that they have to sell on the market. [Insurance_Beta]

Summarizing, business model disruption based on "connecting" market sides and partners allows to customize market transactions, thereby limiting under- or overserving of any market player. While these mechanisms spur disruptive dynamics, however, the value capture logic is highly flexible, which poses significant uncertainty for the entrant.

Reducing

Second, the data suggest an approach for business model disruption through "reducing." Retail_Alpha, Hospitality_Alpha, and Insurance_Alpha can be assigned to this approach. Core to business model disruption through "reducing" is the focus on efficiently standardizing the value creation logic, while lowering the complexity of the value proposition to an absolute minimum. By making the value propositions easy to understand, the respective entrants can offer scaled-down solutions to hitherto unaddressed customer segments.

Entrants realize the fundamental form of low-end disruptive innovations by introducing good enough value propositions compared to existing market alternatives. Hence, even hitherto complex value propositions are scaled down to an absolute minimum, which allows targeting fringe customer segments. Retail_Alpha's co-founder revealed about their digital live video shopping assistant that:

> there is somehow a way that you can simply recreate the advice, the experience in the shop as closely as possible. [Retail_Alpha]

Consequently, relative to this expensive mainstream business model of face-to-face assistance in offline shopping, Retail_Alpha transferred its value proposition to the digital world in a just good enough manner, thereby reducing costs significantly.

Hence, targeting customers *"exclusively via the digital distribution channel"* [Insurance_Alpha] makes hitherto dominant intermediaries in value networks redundant, which in turn positively affects the cost-effectiveness of business model disruption through "reducing."

Moreover, the value creation logic is automatized and is based on rules and norms, ultimately resulting in faster completion of value creation activities. Indeed, in the case of Insurance_Alpha, *"everything runs digitally and via app—billing, patient records, customer contact. That saves on personnel. And provides the insurance company with almost complete knowledge about the state of health of its members"* [Insurance_Alpha].

Ultimately, the value capture mechanisms are flexibilized to focus on the reduction of fixed costs. Hence, non-core value creation processes for the business models are outsourced to externals. which is typical for no-frill value propositions. This is explained by Hospitality_Alpha's CEO:

> The software should be organized and [the hotel should] not [be] permanently staffed when I don't need it. In order to finally achieve an economic model in the operation of the hotel, that is, I can run a hotel without much effort or a hotel director. [Hospitality_Alpha]

Flexibilizing

A third approach for business model disruption can be labeled as "flexibilizing." Consulting_Alpha, Manufacturing_Alpha, and Automotive_Alpha can be categorized here.

In contrast to delivering a value proposition via the traditional sale of goods, the actual use of products and services is the core of this approach of business model disruption. Essential to this approach is the flexible use of resources for value creation. Whereas conventional business models are often based on the sale of goods, these business models design a value proposition that allows customers to make use of the companies' resources. For instance,

> the focus is no longer necessarily on the ownership of the vehicle, [. . .] in the sense of an automobile manufacturer, the customers will also break away [Automotive_Alpha]

Second, Consulting_Alpha's co-founder described:

> we build a web platform for the customer from open source components, that is, we work completely as-a-service-based, we offer data analytics as-a-service, in a self-service. [Consulting_Alpha_U196]

Third, Manufacturing_Alpha created its 3D printing service:

> to give people the opportunity to purchase 3D printed parts without having their own 3D printing production. [Manufacturing_Alpha_U177]

To this end, related business models create value through standardized processes so that the basic value propositions are uniform, while specific customer needs are addressed by flexibly building upon external value creation (i.e., via partners). This collaboration with externals is realized as follows:

> We do not have metal printers ourselves, for example. But we do have a network where we can buy installation space. This is something we have worked out, because it would not be worthwhile for us to put up a 1.5 million euro machine. [Manufacturing_Alpha]

Moreover, the customers of these business models require less specific knowledge, which allows them to benefit from the value proposition ad hoc. For Consulting_Alpha, the CEO revealed that:

> we provide the complete IT infrastructure for our customers, we provide the know-how, we provide the skilled workers. And the customer actually only needs [. . .] departmental knowledge in this case, because the statistical knowledge is not the decisive factor, but his professional expertise. [Consulting_Alpha_U199]

Consequently, the data suggest that relatively non-technology-savvy customers are likely to be attracted by this type of business model disruption.

Ultimately, business model disruption based on the "flexibilizing" approach, frequently include a free trial period, which eases customers' first access by lowering entry barriers. This is particularly relevant for first-time customers having relatively little (technological) experience. Indeed, the co-founder of Consulting_Alpha underlined:

> We would like to give the product away. That would be the ideal business model. We would go to the market for free. [Consulting_Alpha_U210]

Consequently, customers do not face potential high entry barriers (i.e., initial investments). Indeed, the "flexibilizing" paradigm is mirrored in the value capture dimension, when margins are calculated on a flexible, per-use basis.

5   Conclusions

We started this paper by asking how disruptive business models are similar (or different) across German industries. To explore this question, eight cases of disruptive business models have been analyzed by means of qualitative content analysis. For analysis, the three dimensions of value proposition, value creation, and value capture served as an agreed-upon framework for discussing similarities and differences across disruptive business models. This article joins debates that ask for an abstraction and consolidation of disruptive innovation dynamics to further the emergence of this intellectual field (Christensen et al. 2018; Hopp et al. 2018).

The data suggest three different approaches of business model disruption, thereby underlining that business models are "same, same" in that they induce disruptive dynamics, yet being different in how they let these dynamics unfold. In particular, the approaches of "connecting," "reducing," and "flexibilizing" could be classified. Consequently, this paper adds to calls for a clearer picture of how companies bring about business model disruption. Indeed, Christensen et al. (2018) state that business models underlying disruptive innovation have only been *"tentatively specified."*

Indeed, the analysis suggests that the three distilled approaches present alternatives for business model disruption, thereby extending the hitherto accepted criteria of disruptive innovation (Govindarajan and Kopalle 2006). Moreover, the presentation of a triad of approaches for business model disruption can be seen as timely and relevant, as disruption is accelerating in pace and frequency across industry and contexts (Kumaraswamy et al. 2018).

6   Implications and Limitations

From the study, implications for managers within incumbent organizations as well as for entrepreneurs can be derived. In fact, there is little guidance for managers on how to design disruptive business models (Schiavi and Behr 2018). Hence, the presented alternative approaches for business model disruption may assist practitioners in understanding disruptive innovation better, while reducing parts of its inherent complexity through abstraction.

In particular, the triad of approaches may be used as guidelines in a workshop setting, assisting brainstorming for new business model design or response strategies for potential disruptive developments.

This study is not without limitations. First, it relies on a selected set of eight cases and corresponding in-depth interviews, and archival data. This empirical setting is, thus, limited to historical data. Future research should take a real-time approach and study business model disruption in becoming (Burgelman 1994). Moreover, the selection of "only" eight cases limits the claim for completeness. Consequently, further research should engage in a broader and more systematized analysis of business model disruption to follow-up on a discussion on abstraction and generalization of the disruptive innovation phenomenon.

Acknowledgement This research paper is part of a larger research project on "Innovative Business Models for coping with Disruptive Change in small and medium Enterprises," which was funded by the German Ministry for Education and Research (Grant: 03FH031PX5).

References

Adner, R. (2002). When are technologies disruptive? A demand-based view of the emergence of competition. *Strategic Management Journal, 23*(8), 667–688. https://doi.org/10.1002/smj.246.

Akbar, Y. H., & Tracogna, A. (2018). The sharing economy and the future of the hotel industry: Transaction cost theory and platform economics. International Journal of Hospitality Management, 71, 91–101. https://doi.org/10.1016/j.ijhm.2017.12.004

Amit, R., & Zott, C. (2001). Value creation in E-business. *Strategic Management Journal, 22*(6–7), 493–520. https://doi.org/10.1002/smj.187.

Amshoff, B., Dülme, C., Echterfeld, J., & Gausemeier, J. (2015). Business model patterns for disruptive technologies. *International Journal of Innovation Management, 19*(03), 1540002. https://doi.org/10.1142/S1363919615400022.

Ansari, S. S., Garud, R., & Kumaraswamy, A. (2016). The disruptor's dilemma: TiVo and the U.S. television ecosystem. *Strategic Management Journal, 37*(9), 1829–1853. https://doi.org/10.1002/smj.2442.

Baden-Fuller, C., & Morgan, M. S. (2010). Business models as models. *Long Range Planning, 43*(2–3), 156–171. https://doi.org/10.1016/j.lrp.2010.02.005.

Bocken, N. M. P., Short, S. W., Rana, P., & Evans, S. (2014). A literature and practice review to develop sustainable business model archetypes. *Journal of Cleaner Production, 65*, 42–56. https://doi.org/10.1016/j.jclepro.2013.11.039.

Braun, A., & Schreiber, F. (2017). The current InsurTech landscape: Business models and disruptive potential. Institute of Insurance Economics I.VW-HSG, University of St. Gallen

Burgelman, R. A. (1994). Fading memories: A process theory of strategic business exit in dynamic environments. *Administrative Science Quarterly, 39*(1), 24. https://doi.org/10.2307/2393493.

Chesbrough, H. (2006). *Open business models: How to thrive in the new innovation landscape.* Harvard Business Review Press. Retrieved from http://public.eblib.com/choice/publicfullrecord.aspx?p=5181926.

Christensen, C. M., & Raynor, M. E. (2003). The innovator's solution: Creating and sustaining successful growth. Harvard Business School Press

Christensen, C. M. (2006). The ongoing process of building a theory of disruption. *Journal of Product Innovation Management, 23*(1), 39–55. https://doi.org/10.1111/j.1540-5885.2005.00180.x.

Christensen, C. M., & Raynor, M. E. (2013). The innovator's solution: Creating and sustaining successful growth. Harvard Business Review Press.

Christensen, C. M., McDonald, R., Altman, E. J., & Palmer, J. E. (2018). Disruptive innovation: An intellectual history and directions for future research. *Journal of Management Studies, 55*(7), 1043–1078. https://doi.org/10.1111/joms.12349.

Cozzolino, A., Verona, G., & Rothaermel, F. T. (2018). Unpacking the disruption process: New technology, business models, and incumbent adaptation. *Journal of Management Studies, 55*(7), 1166–1202. https://doi.org/10.1111/joms.12352.

Downes, L., & Nunes, P. (2014). *Big bang disruption: Strategy in the age of devastating innovation*. Retrieved from http://search.ebscohost.com/login.aspx?direct=true&scope=site&db=nlebk&db=nlabk&AN=1123617

Ferràs-Hernández, X., Tarrats-Pons, E., & Arimany-Serrat, N. (2017). Disruption in the automotive industry: A Cambrian moment. Business Horizons, 60(6), 855–863. https://doi.org/10.1016/j.bushor.2017.07.011

Fielt, E. (2014). Conceptualising business models: Definitions, frameworks and classifications. *Journal of Business Models, 1*(1), Inaugural issue. https://doi.org/10.5278/ojs.jbm.v1i1.706.

Foss, N. J., & Saebi, T. (2017). Fifteen years of research on business model innovation: How far have we come, and where should we go? *Journal of Management, 43*(1), 200–227. https://doi.org/10.1177/0149206316675927.

Garbuio, M., & Lin, N. (2019). Artificial Intelligence as a growth engine for health care startups: Emerging business models. *California Management Review, 61*(2), 59–83. https://doi.org/10.1177/0008125618811931.

Gassmann, O., Frankenberger, K., & Csik, M. (2014). *The business model navigator: 55 models that will revolutionise your business*. Pearson.

Govindarajan, V., & Kopalle, P. K. (2006). The usefulness of measuring disruptiveness of innovations ex post in making ex ante predictions*. *Journal of Product Innovation Management, 23*(1), 12–18. https://doi.org/10.1111/j.1540-5885.2005.00176.x.

Hahn, F., Jensen, S., & Tanev, S. (2014). Disruptive Innovation vs Disruptive Technology: The Disruptive Potential of the Value Propositions of 3D Printing Technology Startups. Technology Innovation Management Review, 10.

Hopp, C., Antons, D., Kaminski, J., & Oliver Salge, T. (2018). Disruptive innovation: Conceptual foundations, empirical evidence, and research opportunities in the digital age. *Journal of Product Innovation Management, 35*(3), 446–457. https://doi.org/10.1111/jpim.12448.

Kumaraswamy, A., Garud, R., & Ansari, S. (2018). Perspectives on disruptive innovations. *Journal of Management Studies, 55*(7), 1025–1042. https://doi.org/10.1111/joms.12399.

Markides, C. (2006). Disruptive innovation: In need of better theory*. *Journal of Product Innovation Management, 23*(1), 19–25. https://doi.org/10.1111/j.1540-5885.2005.00177.x.

Nagy, D., Schuessler, J., & Dubinsky, A. (2016). Defining and identifying disruptive innovations. Industrial Marketing Management, 57, 119–126. https://doi.org/10.1016/j.indmarman.2015.11.017

Ritter, T., & Lettl, C. (2018). The wider implications of business-model research. *Long Range Planning, 51*(1), 1–8. https://doi.org/10.1016/j.lrp.2017.07.005.

Saldaña, J. (2016). *The coding manual for qualitative researchers* (3rd ed.). SAGE.

Schiavi, G. S., & Behr, A. (2018). Emerging technologies and new business models: A review on disruptive business models. *Innovation & Management Review, 15*(4), 338–355. https://doi.org/10.1108/INMR-03-2018-0013.

Schmidt, G. M., & Druehl, C. T. (2008). When is a disruptive innovation disruptive? *Journal of Product Innovation Management, 25*(4), 347–369. https://doi.org/10.1111/j.1540-5885.2008.00306.x.

Schneider, S., & Spieth, P. (2013). Business model innovation: Towards an integrated future research agenda. *International Journal of Innovation Management, 17*(01), 1340001. https://doi.org/10.1142/S136391961340001X.

Snihur, Y., Thomas, L. D. W., & Burgelman, R. A. (2018). An ecosystem-level process model of business model disruption: Business model disruption: The disruptor's gambit. *Journal of Management Studies, 55*(7), 1278–1316. https://doi.org/10.1111/joms.12343.

Teece, D. J. (2010). Business models, business strategy and innovation. *Long Range Planning, 43* (2–3), 172–194. https://doi.org/10.1016/j.lrp.2009.07.003.

Teece, D. J. (2018). Business models and dynamic capabilities. *Long Range Planning, 51*(1), 40–49. https://doi.org/10.1016/j.lrp.2017.06.007.

Trabucchi, D., Talenti, L., & Buganza, T. (2019). How do Big Bang Disruptors look like? A business model perspective. *Technological Forecasting and Social Change, 141*, 330–340. https://doi.org/10.1016/j.techfore.2019.01.009.

Wirtz, B. W., Pistoia, A., Ullrich, S., & Göttel, V. (2016). Business models: Origin, development and future research perspectives. *Long Range Planning, 49*(1), 36–54. https://doi.org/10.1016/j.lrp.2015.04.001.

Zott, C., Amit, R., & Massa, L. (2011). The business model: Recent developments and future research. *Journal of Management, 37*(4), 1019–1042. https://doi.org/10.1177/0149206311406265.

Alexander Lennart Schmidt is a lecturer for Innovation and Entrepreneurship at Zuyd University of Applied Sciences in Maastricht (The Netherlands). He is alumni of the Science-to-Business Marketing Research Centre (S2BMRC) at the Münster School of Business at Münster University of Applied Sciences. Alexander Lennart did his Ph.D. in a cooperative Ph.D. program at the Vrije Universiteit (VU) Amsterdam and Münster University of Applied Sciences. He is researching the topic of innovation management while focusing on disruptive innovation and business model innovation.

Productivity Paradox in Digital Innovation for SMEs

Insights from a Participatory Inquiry

Matthias Hartmann, Ralf Waubke, and Leonhard Gebhardt

1   Introduction

Digital innovations promise to invent new business models and to improve the efficiency of business processes. However, experience has shown that this promise is not always kept. In other words, digital technologies have not been able to increase productivity sufficiently. Productivity, in turn, is a simple concept that describes the output per unit of input (Brynjolfsson and Lorin, 1998). In this light, the Productivity Paradox (PP) has been discussed for more than 30 years (e.g., Skinner 1986; Solow 1987; Elstner et al. 2018; Krishnan et al. 2018). In simple terms, the PP, therefore, describes a mismatch between the high productivity potential of digital innovations on the one hand and a low actual productivity increase after implementation of the digital innovations on the other hand.

In over 30 years of discussion, the PP was discussed both at the economic level (see Brynjolfsson and Hitt 1998; Adalet McGowan et al. 2015) and at the business level (e.g., Skinner 1986). This approach is reasonable if one is looking for a holistic understanding of the PP: an economy is constituted by the totality of the enterprises within it (enterprises as subsystems of the national economy system). The examination of the PP and the productivity underlying it seems to be useful because it is responsible for the long-term increase in the standard of living and prosperity of nations (Brynjolfsson and Hitt 1998) or as stated by Adalet McGowan et al. (2015, p. 3) "Productivity is the ultimate engine of growth in the global economy." It is therefore hardly surprising that the topic was discussed in detail at nearly all levels of analyses. In particular, innovation barriers in managing digital innovations have been discussed deeply (see for an overview of innovation barriers Hueske and Guenther 2015). However, these barriers are still hindering success in digital transformation.

M. Hartmann · R. Waubke · L. Gebhardt (✉)
HTW Berlin - University of Applied Science, Berlin, Germany
e-mail: leonhard.gebhardt@htw-berlin.de

© The Author(s), under exclusive license to Springer Nature Switzerland AG 2021   145
D. R. A. Schallmo, J. Tidd (eds.), *Digitalization*, Management for Professionals,
https://doi.org/10.1007/978-3-030-69380-0_9

A common explanation from a business perspective is that Top Management (TM) still approaches such innovations unsystematically. Examples of unsystematic approaches include, staff being insufficiently trained or the organization not being restructured in a viable way. In this context, we consider small and medium-sized enterprises (SMEs) to be more flexible than larger companies when it comes to the implementation of organizational changes. On the other hand, SMEs tend to have fewer resources. In short, the management of digital innovation in SMEs faces different challenges than in large companies (Dans 2001). In this context, it is surprisingly under-researched how SMEs, confronted with inadequate managerial skills and limited resources, drive digitalization (Li et al. 2018).

Therefore, we investigate the following research question: How does TM of SMEs deal with the implementation of digital innovations in order to overcome the PP? Consequently, this paper aims to identify and explore how SMEs TM address the implementation of digital innovations out of a productivity paradox perspective.

2   Theoretical Grounding

Thirty years ago, Skinner (1986), Solow (1987), and Brynjolfsson (1993) already pointed out that innovations in Information, Communication and Technology (ICT) must be approached fundamentally and holistically. Skinner, in particular, stated that SME management has to think and act as system innovators to avoid the PP. Any narrow focus on cost reduction, volume output, and punctual optimization does not lead to increased productivity and improved competitiveness.

After considerable increases in productivity in the 1990s and the early 2000s, the PP, also known as the Solow Theorem (ST), was seemingly overcome. However, recent studies contradict this finding. For example, Krishnan et al. (2018) asked whether the ST has made a comeback and stated: "that Digitization isn't stimulating productivity growth—yet."

The initial ST may be interpreted as showing that the first wave of innovation, triggered by new ICT possibilities, was gradually understood and thus only meaningfully embedded in companies after a period of transition. However, the full potential of these earlier ICT technologies is currently almost exhausted. Lately, the appearance of the ST may be interpreted as appearing due to a new wave of digital innovations, which according to Case (2017) (3rd wave) will be triggered by the Internet of Everything, and not yet fully understood and therefore not optimally embedded in enterprises.

Moreover, it is not clear whether the initial ST has been solved for SMEs. For example, it is sufficient for the largest—and often also the most resourceful—firms in an economy to achieve high productivity gains in order to achieve significant macroeconomic productivity growth. Indeed, the growth of the world's most productive businesses has continued to be stable in the twenty-first century. Nevertheless, the gap between these world-leading companies and the rest has widened over time (Adalet McGowan et al. 2015). However, this does not imply a general statement on SMEs.

This phenomenon pertains to SMEs in particular, and puts their competitiveness at stake (Madrid-Guijarro et al. 2009; Ussman et al. 2001). We define SMEs as non-subsidiary, independent firms with less than 250 employees. These firms often lack the abilities to bridge innovation barriers (Chesbrough 2010). Most recent, OECD (2019, p. 8) asserts that technology adoption remains an issue for most SMEs. Companies as them "face more difficulties in undertaking the complementary investments in skills and organizational changes that are needed to adopt and benefit from technology" (OECD 2019, p. 8).

In this sense Elstner et al. (2018) identify four reasons for the PP: (1) Financial constraints limit investment in innovation, (2) Stabilization and thus decline in IT productivity following the high productivity of Year 2 Kilo (Y2K), (3) Some firms have, other firms do not have high productivity growth, (4) Measurement errors exist.

Whereas reason (2) and (4) tend to raise macroeconomic issues, reason (1) and (3) raise many questions for the innovation management of SMEs. This relationship is in line with the EOGI model (Hueske and Guenther 2015). In our view, the causes of the PP can be attributed to innovation barriers such as the organization (O) itself, as well as group (G) and individual (I)-related barriers. Based on the Upper Echelons Theory (Hambrick 2007), we consider top managers (I) or top management teams (G) to be particularly critical for SMEs in order to overcome innovation barriers in general and the PP in particular.

3   Research Design

To be able to answer the research question fully and to gain profound insights, we considered it appropriate to become "insiders" of the organizations under investigation. Accordingly, we considered participatory action research well suited for our purpose (e.g., Kemmis et al. 2013). In short "participatory action research is practical and collaborative because it is inquiry completed 'with' others rather than 'on' or 'to' others. In this spirit, advocacy/participatory authors engage the participants as active collaborators in their inquiries" (Creswell 2007, p. 22). We claim that active participation in the innovation process helps to make the role of TM more visible. Consequently, we have actively participated in digitization projects of SMEs.

Sampling

We conducted an intensive field study of 39 SMEs over 3½ years (July 2016 to December 2019) in the city of Berlin. We used data from interviews, workshops, and observations and relied on purposive sampling (Yin 2009).

To identify SMEs that wanted to initiate an innovation process in the research time frame, we decided to cooperate with institutions that have access to many SMEs in Berlin. The European Regional Development Fund (ERDF) supported the conducted research. We also cooperated with a regional bank and a chamber of crafts to approach their clients/members actively. As we were looking for SMEs that are willing to promote the digitization process actively, this was a suitable opportunity to make a pre-selection. Thus, only companies that were interested in the progress of digitization contacted us. Our described approach resulted in a pre-sample of 75 SMEs.

Our first goal was then to identify a joint digitization project in which we could actively participate. To do so, we determined the business model (Osterwalder and Pigneur 2010), the digital maturity level (Hartmann 2018), and the digital agenda in a first discussion with the TM of interested SMEs. The research team accompanied the project with the highest priority given by the SME TM. By doing so, we aimed to ensure from the very start of the project that the TM would remain committed to the project over time.

The second phase, the planned implementation of digital innovation involved 39 SMEs. The drop-out of 36 resulted from a variety of the following reasons. Some companies prioritized projects that did not have a high enough demand for implementation. These did not appear to be suitable for barrier research. Other companies had unrealistic project ideas exceeding the project scope, and lastly, some companies hesitated in their commitment to the digital innovation implementation.

In the third phase, the project was implemented jointly with the 39 SMEs (Hartmann 2018, 2019). The creation was company-specific and varied in duration and content. Even though joint projects were completed in 27 of 39 SMEs, we were able to make essential observations in the 12 unsuccessful projects. Our final sample was, therefore, the 39 SMEs with whom we started a joint project.

Data Collection and Analyzing

For the data collection, we used semi-structured interviews, workshops, observations, and documentation. Besides, we observed the project progress throughout the cooperation. We documented activities (e.g., phone calls) and our evaluations in protocols. To be fully absorbed in the insider role and to minimize communication barriers, we considered it consistent with our research approach not to record conversations or interviews.

We analyzed our data using our database to identify similarities and differences. Because we were deeply immersed in the cases and gained an insider's perspective, we ensured that at least one team member did not have direct contact with a company, so that a more objective perspective could be added to the interpretation.

4   Findings

After an initial analysis, our data indicate that the success of digital innovation at the organizational level depends primarily on the existing knowledge and open-mindedness of TM. We observe considerable differences between SME TMs.

Although all TMs committed themselves to a digital innovation project at the beginning of the process, only a few of them kept the process going.

Many TMs give up digital innovation projects very early. If, for example, initial resistance arises from within the organization, resources are immediately withdrawn. As a result, projects are repeatedly postponed and suffer repeated ramp-up times, or are buried entirely. In many cases, no experts are assigned to projects. This is why interns, working students, or high performing employees without IT knowledge lead digital innovation projects. Also, external consultants are hardly ever called in, and fast, cheap, and therefore, mostly unsystematic solutions are pushed forward. The consequences are usually not understood. Our study shows that this process is self-reinforcing. The fast solutions do not bring the expected gains, which leads TM to conclude that digital innovations are not as productivity-enhancing as they are made out to be. For this reason, future projects tend to be allocated even fewer resources, which again results in low output. The TM thus gets more and more entangled in the PP. As a result, some TMs cannot recognize the opportunities offered by digitization and thus do not take advantage of them. We consider it as the PP of many SMEs, making it more challenging to adopt digital innovations. Paradoxically, this also means that the potential of digital innovations cannot be exploited.

On the other hand, the observed successful TMs continuously expand their knowledge and perspective. Participation in business networks, work with institutions such as universities and the involvement of external consultants are more common practice than an exception. As a consequence, digital innovation projects in successful SMEs tend to be approached systematically and holistically. The resulting productivity gains strengthen TM's confidence in innovation efforts, which in turn leads to more resources being allocated to future projects.

In short, a successful TM manages to overcome the following four identified groups of barriers to innovation: (1) Limited management competencies in innovation management, (2) A lacking IT basis, (3) Limited knowledge about digitization, (4) Biased focus on cost management.

5 Contribution

Based on our findings, we suggest the PP about digital innovation is linked to the upper echelon theory (UET). UET postulates that TM's personal interpretations are the trigger for their entrepreneurial actions, which in turn affect the organization. Therefore, we consider organizational results in strategic outcomes as well as in performance as reflections of the values and cognitions of TM (Hambrick 2007).

In that light, our results suggest that the TM of underperforming SMEs are unable to see their limitations in digital innovations. Hence, we hypothesize that the productivity boundary of digitization in Luhmann's sense (2018), is a horizon that TM cannot spot. The very limit itself is not perceived at all as TM will not see what TM cannot see. The TM is not looking for the possibilities on the other side of the boundary either. Even more, the TM does not know that there is a boundary and thus anything beyond it. Luhmann would call this situation paradoxical: The link between innovation management and the UET contributes a better understanding of innovation barriers in digital transformation for SMEs.

Besides, the assumption that the PP has never been solved for many SMEs is strengthening. Even though the largest and most successful companies have mastered the first wave (Case 2017) of digital innovation, many TMs still do not know how to embed basic digital technologies into the organization profitably. Thus, we do not fully agree with Krishnan et al. (2018), who argued that the PP was solved and only reappeared with the advent of new digital technologies. Instead, we agree the PP may have been solved when looking at macroeconomic data and thus across all firms. However, for many firms in general and SMEs, in particular, the PP never vanished in the first place.

6   Practical Implications

The findings of this study are relevant for researchers as well as for practitioners. The perspective on management behavior can add value to companies that are currently undergoing innovation processes in digitization. The TM of SMEs can be given a more precise starting point and roadmap for digitization.

Most notably, TM of SMEs must think systemically and anticipate barriers to innovation. Therefore, it is necessary to broaden one's horizons continually. TM should, therefore, critically question whether it is already trapped in the PP. For this purpose, participation in formats such as business networks to facilitate low-threshold knowledge transfer is recommended. Furthermore, cooperative research projects between theory and practice appear to be beneficial. For smaller SMEs especially, it is beneficial to reduce the reluctance of contact with external institutions and consultants.

References

Adalet McGowan, M., Andrews, D., Criscuolo, C., & Nicoletti, G. (2015). The future of productivity. *OECD study*.

Brynjolfsson, E. (1993). The productivity paradox of information technology. *Communications of the ACM, 12*.

Brynjolfsson, E., & Hitt, L. (1998). Beyond the productivity paradox. *Communications of the ACM, 41*(8), 49–55.

Case, S. (2017). *The third wave: An entrepreneur's vision of the future* (1st ed.). New York: Simon & Schuster Paperback.

Chesbrough, H. (2010). Business model innovation: Opportunities and barriers. *Long Range Planning, 43*, 354–363.

Creswell, J. W. (2007). *Qualitative inquiry and research design: Choosing among five approaches* (2nd ed.). Thousand Oaks, CA: Sage.

Dans E (2001) IT investment in small and medium enterprises: Paradoxically productive? *The Electronic Journal of Information Systems, 4*(1), 1–15.

Elstner, S., Feld, L. P., & Schmidt, C. M. (2018). *The German productivity paradox—Facts and explanations* (CESifo Working Paper Series 7231).

Hambrick, D. C. (2007). Upper Echelons theory: An update. *Academy of Management Review, 32* (2), 334–343.

Hartmann, M. (2018). *Impulse für digitale Lösungen: Empfehlungen für Kleine und Mittlere Unternehmen* (1st ed.). Berlin: BWV Berliner Wissenschafts.

Hartmann, M. (2019). *Digitale Transformation von KMU: Von der Strategie bis zum Werkzeug* (1st ed.). Berlin: Berliner Wissenschafts.

Hueske, A.-K., & Guenther, E. (2015). What hampers innovation? External stakeholders, the organization, groups and individuals: a systematic review of empirical barrier research. *Management Review Quarterly, 65*(2), 113–148.

Kemmis, S., McTaggart, R., & Nixon, R. (2013). *The action research planner: Doing critical participatory action research*. Berlin: Springer Science & Business Media.

Krishnan, M., Mischke, J., & Remes, J. (2018). *Is the Solow paradox back?* McKinsey Quarterly.

Li, L., Su, F., Zhang, W., & Mao, J.-Y. (2018). Digital transformation by SME entrepreneurs: A capability perspective. *Information Systems Journal, 28*(6), 1129–1157.

Luhmann, N. (2018). *Die Wissenschaft der Gesellschaft* (8th ed.). Suhrkamp: Frankfurt am Main.

Madrid-Guijarro, A., Garcia, D., & van Auken, H. (2009). Barriers to Innovation among Spanish Manufacturing SMEs. *Journal of Small Business Management, 47*(4), 465–488.

OECD (2019). *OECD SME and entrepreneurship outlook 2019*. https://www.oecd-ilibrary.org/sites/34907e9c-en/index.html?itemId=/content/publication/34907e9c-en. Accessed April 2020.

Osterwalder, A., & Pigneur, Y. (2010). *Business model generation: a handbook for visionaries, game changers, and challengers*. Hoboken, NJ: Wiley.

Skinner, W. (1986). The productivity paradoxon. *Management Review, 75*(9), 41–45.

Solow, R. (1987). We'd better watch out. *New York Times Book Review, (12)*, 36.

Ussman, A., Almeida, A., Ferreira, J., Mendes, L., & Franco, M. (2001). SMES and innovation. *The International Journal of Entrepreneurship and Innovation, 2*(2), 111–118.

Yin, R. K. (2009). *Case study research: Design and methods, Applied social research methods series* (4th ed.). Los Angeles: Sage.

Matthias Hartmann was a professor at the HTW Berlin (Hochschule für Technik und Wirtschaft, Berlin), an University of Applied Sciences. At HTW Berlin, he lectured in the fields of Operations Management and Business Simulation and conducted seminars on Digital Business. From 2016 to 2020, he was the head of the research group, "Digital Value" which carries out multiple projects on digital transformation with SMEs. Before his professorship, he has worked as a management consultant at A.T. Kearney, specialised in Strategy Management and Strategic Information Technology. He obtained his PhD in the field of Technology Management from the University Erlangen-Nuremberg.

Ralf Waubke is a PhD candidate at the University of Potsdam and works at the HTW Berlin. Within his work, he supports SMEs to better understand the impact and potential of digitalization on their value chains and to make holistic decisions for a sustainable digital transformation.

Leonhard Gebhardt Besides digital transformation, Leonhard Gebhardt is particularly interested in sustainable entrepreneurship and entrepreneurial ecosystems. His dissertation about these fields is supervised by Prof. Dr Katharina Hölzle, HPI, University of Potsdam. He is a research associate in the Digital Value project at HTW Berlin, which supports SMEs in digitalizing their value creation. In addition, he is a lecturer for Digital Business and General Management, also at HTW Berlin. Leonhard studied nonprofit management and public governance, economics, and art history in Berlin, Jena, and Madrid. He gained professional experience in international NGOs in Berlin and Mexico City.

Five Topics for Which Industry Needs Innovation Managers

A Job Advertisement Analysis

Chris C. Gernreich, Christian Ahlfeld, and Sebastian Knop

1   Introduction

Since digital change is still a relatively new topic, the need for the integral management of this change and the associated innovations is growing within companies (Maier and Brem 2017). The extent of this change is often unclear to management-level employees, and at times they possess minimal knowledge of its potentials and risks (Hofmann and Rüsch 2017). As a result, an increasing number of medium-sized companies have established the role of innovation manager in their companies. This employee generally deals with topics of digital change and introducing new ideas into the company (Dziatzko and Steinwandt 2011; Noss 2002). However, increasingly complex environments challenge innovation managers in new ways that are not yet fully understood (Nambisan et al. 2017). This study contributes to the exploration of the formal and informal roles of innovation managers (Dziatzko and Steinwandt 2011; Maier 2014; Maier and Brem 2017) by answering the following question:

What competences do companies expect from innovation managers?

In the following section, a literature review provides information about the state of research to date on the competences of innovation managers. First, the typical tasks and required competences for innovation managers are explained. Next, job advertisements are examined with quantitative text analysis, using topic modeling, and the five resulting topics are discussed and compared to previous findings. Finally, practical implications are summarized and direction is provided for future research.

C. C. Gernreich (✉) · C. Ahlfeld · S. Knop
Ruhr-Universität Bochum, Bochum, Germany
e-mail: chris.gernreich@rub.de; christian.ahlfeld@rub.de; sebastian.knop@rub.de

153

2   Literature Background

Innovation Managers' Common Tasks

There are several tasks essential to the management of innovations within companies. Among them are the creation of generally favorable structures and the establishment of a corporate climate that fosters progress (Vahs and Brem 2015). These tasks are handled by institutionalized innovation management, and in medium-sized companies, the responsibility is typically assumed by a specialized individual (Schon 1963; Sim et al. 2007)—the innovation manager. Acting as a kind of interface between the companies and their environment, innovation managers ensure that business opportunities are identified and utilized. They outline potentials and alternatives; coordinate existing knowledge within their company; and access knowledge sources in the company's environment (Freiling et al. 2008; Wöhlert 2000). They are also responsible for preparing decisions and gaining the support of management for initiating innovative projects (Gershman and Thurner 2016; Vahs and Schmitt 2010). In this way, the many responsibilities of innovation managers foster innovation at various levels of their organizations.

One superordinate area of responsibility is defining a basic innovation strategy. When formulating this strategy, innovation managers identify relevant trends, taking into consideration their company's product and service portfolio (Dziatzko and Steinwandt 2011; Vahs 2007). Building on this, they define the change in corporate culture and organization that would be required to achieve the objectives formulated in the innovation strategy. Indeed, it is corporate culture that creates a foundation for communication (Dziatzko and Steinwandt 2011; Trott 2012; Vahs 2007) and collaboration (Chesbrough 2006), which in turn enable the emergence and development of new ideas and innovations within a company. Innovation managers adapt or develop the processes necessary to turn an idea into an innovation. Once all the prerequisites have been met, they analyze these ideas and innovations by considering their potentials and risks; implementing them within the company; and continually evaluating them to ensure success (Cacaci 2006; Oakland and Tanner 2007; Stolzenberg and Heberle 2013; Vahs 2007).

Required Competences

Companies that lack institutionalized innovation management must see their innovation managers as highly skilled generalists who fulfill the tasks of both an innovation manager and a relationship manager (Dziatzko and Steinwandt 2011). To cope with this wide range of tasks, innovation managers need the appropriate competences, which can be developed over time when knowledge is applied successfully (Ortmann 2014). These skills, in turn, are used to solve problems that arise across a diverse range of situations.

Research on the tasks of innovation managers has already produced a variety of insights. One example of a competence described in previous research is the ability to set overarching goals, orient oneself towards them, and act on one's own initiative (Dziatzko and Steinwandt 2011; Gerybadze 2004). Scientific and technological competences have been found to be necessary, as they assist in the understanding of relevant objectives and the associated uncertainties for a company (Tidd 2001). Legal knowledge is less relevant to an innovation manager's work. Although companies do consider it a relevant competence for innovation managers (Dziatzko and Steinwandt 2011), they generally purchase legal consultancy as a service instead of requiring it of innovation managers. Nevertheless, legal knowledge, as it relates to how new technologies are accepted by customers or partners (e.g., data security and contractual agreements between parties), has been shown to influence a company's ability to innovate (Kagermann et al. 2013). An innovation manager may therefore find it necessary to acquire legal knowledge. To implement innovations in a company, innovation managers also need decision-making and execution competences (Vahs and Schmitt 2010). The fact that innovation managers are required to have these competences is an expression of their authority to issue directives and their decision-making scope, which is granted by the management of the company. It is also of great importance for innovation managers to build a sound understanding of existing problems and future challenges by identifying and applying adequate methods (Dziatzko and Steinwandt 2011), searching for information relevant to solving the problems or challenges, and evaluating this information (Kepner and Tregoe 1997; Simon 1982). Therefore, innovation managers must possess comprehensive linguistic skills that they are able to successfully apply in order to more fully understand the complexity of the options available to them. Furthermore, they must be able to assess the scope and impact of their decisions. They also need solid technical knowledge to execute their decisions, and a fundamental scientific-technical competence serves as a central prerequisite for this (Leiponen 2005). Lastly, innovation managers must be able to convincingly argue their points, motivate people to act, and successfully obtain the support of their company (Armstrong 2017; Dziatzko and Steinwandt 2011). This is of paramount importance when dealing with team collaboration and communication (Dziatzko and Steinwandt 2011). Native language competence, and foreign-language competence, if necessary, are fundamental for communication and collaboration with company partners (Ritter and Gemünden 2003).

3 Methodology

Data Collection

Germany is one of the most innovative countries in the world, and its industry is in the midst of a digital transformation. As a result, the German job market provides suitable search results for this research. Search queries were launched in the largest job portals in Germany, i.e., Monster (https://www.monster.com/), XING (https://www.xing.com/), LinkedIn (https://www.linkedin.com/), StepStone (https://www.stepstone.com/), Jobware (https://www.jobware.com/), and Indeed (https://de.

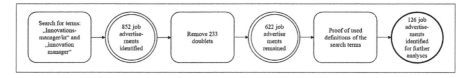

Fig. 1 Procedure for identifying relevant job advertisements

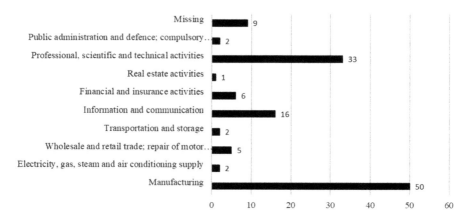

Fig. 2 Sample description according to economic activities

indeed.com/). Search queries for the English term "innovation manager" and its German translation returned 852 hits in the first stage (see Fig. 1). A search was done in English to account for the international activities of many German companies and the increased use of English terms in their job advertisements (van Meurs et al. 2015). Also, a full-text search ensured that job advertisements with different job titles but similar content were also selected for further analysis. Consequently, job advertisements containing only one of the two search terms were also listed among the hits.

Companies often post job advertisement in multiple job portals, which inevitably led to duplicates within the sample. All 852 job advertisements were therefore subject to a qualitative examination, and each was included in the sample only once, resulting in 622 unique job advertisements. Of these, a large number of job advertisements were removed from the sample because they did not use the term "innovation manager" as defined in this study or because the terms "innovation" and "manager" were used in separate contexts; for example, a car dealership was looking for an "innovative sales manager." After adjusting the sample to account for these postings, the sample contained 126 job advertisements and consisted mainly of manufacturing companies; professional, scientific, and technical activities; and companies from the information and communication sector, which represented 82.5% of the sample (see Fig. 2).

Data Analysis

A variable for the profiles defined in the job advertisements was modeled to create the data set for statistical analysis. Since there are larger and better-tested databases available in English for analyzing terms, job advertisements written in German were translated into English. Job advertisements in English were not modified in any way. In addition to the usual stop words, expressions were removed that are common across all types of job advertisements and therefore do not serve to differentiate them well (e.g., "innovation" and "manager"). For further analysis, all of the text was transformed to lowercase, to prevent identical words with different capitalization from being identified as different words. Subsequently, according to the Porter algorithm (1980), the remaining words were stemmed to their root in order to identify the same word written in its singular and plural forms as identical. Finally, all words with fewer than three letters were removed to obtain interpretable terms.

After processing the data, 506 unique terms remained for the competences that companies list in their job advertisements. Using the R software environment and the extensions topicmodels (Grün and Hornik 2011) and tm (Meyer et al. 2008), the remaining terms were transferred into a document-term matrix. This matrix is the starting point for the calculation of linguistically related groups based on the Latent Dirichlet Allocation, one of the most commonly used text analysis methods (Lee et al. 2010). The matrix shows the frequency with which the terms appear in the job advertisements, with the columns representing the terms and the rows representing the numbered job advertisements.

Subsequently, the job advertisements were analyzed using topic modeling, with the aim of uncovering underlying semantic structures (Blei et al. 2003; Blei and Lafferty 2007). Topic modeling reveals the extent to which a document contains certain terms. It determines the probabilistic distribution of terms, or the so-called "loading," and groups these terms (Blei 2012; Griffiths and Steyvers 2004). This method identifies correlations between terms and groups them into numbered topics for further interpretation (Blei 2012). We used the heuristic approach of Zhao et al. (Zhao et al. 2015) to determine the number of topics to analyze. In texts where the number of topics is not known a priori, the number of topics used can affect how the results are interpreted. Introducing too many topics could lead to complex results, wherein each topic is defined by the high loading of only one term, with the other terms loading comparatively lower. On the other hand, if the number of topics is too low, the topics will be defined by terms with low values for correlation, which also complicates the interpretation of the results. Perplexity is a measurement of how well a statistical model describes a dataset (Zhao et al. 2015). Zhao et al. (2015) formulated an approach that calculates the change in perplexity as the number of topics modeled changes. Since their approach determined that utilizing five topics results in the optimal perplexity (Zhao et al. 2015), the number of topics for the Latent Dirichlet Allocation was set at five, corresponding to five overarching competences.

4   Results

Figure 3 shows the five groups of terms (Topics 1–5) that form the basis for deriving the higher level competences. In Topic 1, the term "English" is of particular importance, but "German" also has a high loading, as does "excel." The terms "design" and "present" load comparatively low in Topic 1. Both the term "analyt" and "science" are strongly correlating in Topic 2, with "creative" not far behind. The terms "digit" and "compare" load similarly. In Topic 3, the stemmed terms "technology" and "communic" are by far the most strongly loading terms, whereas the terms "process" and "structure" load lower, and the term "initi" loads the lowest. For Topic 4, the terms "communic," "team," and "intern" are the strongest, followed by "travel" and "develop." In Topic 5, the term "econom" plays a particularly important role, while the word stems "environ," "consult," "develop," and "market" all load comparatively lower but with similar strength.

5   Discussion

According to the European Commission's definition (2018), the ability to collect and process information is typically associated with linguistic competences. Topic 1 is distinguished by its strong loading of the term "English," which can be understood as an indication of the indispensability of foreign-language competences. English, in particular, dominates many aspects of the professional world (Küchler 2017; Northrup 2013): Employees who are proficient in English have access to international knowledge repositories and networks (Löfgren 2014; Patsch and Zerfass 2017). These employees are able to analyze existing company knowledge and identify their company's inadequacies and deficiencies in the broader context of international knowledge networks. Consequently, they can facilitate the change in perspective needed to develop knowledge, methods, and technologies within their own companies (Küchler 2017). In this way, our findings contribute additional understanding to previous research, finding that innovation managers assume the role of gatekeeper of their company's knowledge management. They work at the intersection of their organization and sources of knowledge, just as employees in the sales force do (Peltokorpi and Vaara 2014; Welch and Welch 2008). Mastering native language competences ("German") is then important for internally

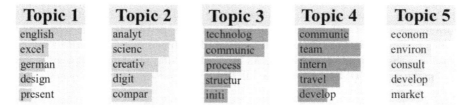

Fig. 3 Identified topics of competences

communicating knowledge gathered from external sources. The related terms "present" and "design" might also serve as indicators of the necessity for innovation managers to be able to handle, process, prepare, design, and present new information or knowledge. However, if IT departments do not provide dedicated software for these tasks, many companies manage their data using standard tools, as indicated by the term "excel" (Galipoglu and Pöppelbuß 2017). In summary, Topic 1 could be interpreted as the need for presentation and expression competences. However, Topic 1 highlights the importance of competences that were not identified as relevant in previous research. It is possible that companies view these competences as valuable and expect them of their innovation managers while innovation managers not explicitly mentioned them in previous studies that researched their competences.

Our interpretation of Topic 2 is made difficult by the diversity of the terms within it: mathematical and basic scientific-technical competences, as well as digital competences, can be identified. The importance of analytical competences ("analyt") has already been demonstrated to be crucial for the success of innovation managers (Dziatzko and Steinwandt 2011; Leiponen 2005). In addition, "science" could mean the ability to scientifically approach and understand a problem and apply a structured decision-making process. Terms such as "compare" or "creative" might stand for requirements concerning comparing alternatives for the development of ideas, which corresponds to the ability to work creatively. After a problem has been analyzed and understood, creativity is indispensable for the further development of ideas (Huber et al. 2014; Maier 2014; Ohly et al. 2006). The term "digit" may represent a need for digital competence, which is also expressed in Topics 2 and 1, although the term "digit" on its own requires further interpretation. The term "digit" may underline that innovation managers should be able to use digital tools to accomplish all of the previously mentioned tasks (analyzing, comparing, being creative). Being generally able to scientifically or analytically compare alternatives might not be enough for innovation managers. They need to be able to transfer these competencies to the digital world, since IT-supported processing of information and knowledge within an organization requires the corresponding digital competences (European Commission 2018; Pearlson et al. 2016). All in all, we can interpret Topic 2 as the requirement for a competence similar to the decision and execution skills that Vahs and Schmitt (2010), and Dziatzko and Steinwandt (2011) have identified; in this research, however, these skills are enhanced by aspects of digital work.

Topic 3 represents a digital knowledge management competence that could serve as an answer to the challenges arising in response to the technological developments of recent years. The term with the strongest loading in Topic 3 is "technology," leading to the conclusion that companies require candidates to be able to handle technical issues with products or services, or that they at least should be familiar with the use of technology. The loading of the term "communic" is also strong. Combined with "technology" it indicates the requirement for a sound understanding of communication via different technologies, since communication technology as an accelerator of innovations (Fischer et al. 2017) can support the optimization of an organization's structure and processes. Technology can be used to simplify and implement decentralized organizational structures to increase the efficiency of communication and decisions (Bloom et al. 2014). Since the terms "process" and "structure" are also present in Topic 3 alongside "technology" and "communic," companies might be requiring a competence that involves organizing knowledge repositories and the distribution of knowledge. In this context, the stem "initi" indicates that innovation managers should be capable of taking initiative and changing an organization's processes and structure, as well introducing new technologies, thus creating the basis for successful knowledge management (Dalkir 2005; Luo and Bu 2016). This would confirm previous findings regarding the required initiative and goal-oriented actions of innovation managers (Dziatzko and Steinwandt 2011; Gerybadze 2004; Tidd 2001). To conclude, Topic 3 and the terms it includes might correlate to various areas of competence: language competences; mathematical and basic scientific-technical competences (for an understanding of technologies); digital competence; as well as personal initiative and entrepreneurial competence. Topic 3 thus represents the most comprehensive set of terms.

Topic 4 primarily addresses the social and linguistic competences of innovation managers. Unlike the technological orientation of Topic 3 illustrated by the term "communic," the terms in Topic 4 instead focus on communication in an interpersonal social context. Strong loadings of the terms "team" and "intern" indicate that internal communication is of paramount importance to the companies that posted the job advertisements. This supports the findings of Dziatzko and Steinwandt (2011), and Armstrong (2017), who stated that team communication is essential to an innovation manager's daily work. In general, working directly with other individuals sparks and develops creative ideas (Salter et al. 2015). However, this does not explain why the results did not explicitly represent issues such as establishing an innovation culture or a supportive climate. The positive effect that innovation culture has on innovative outcomes has been researched a time ago (Axtell et al. 2000; Baer and Frese 2003; Choi 2004; Collins and Smith 2006; Ekvall 1997). However, as in Topic 3, the ability to establish, manage, and utilize social ties is shown to be crucial for communication and knowledge management (Kwon and Adler 2014) and the quality of creative outcomes in general (Björk 2012; Björk and Magnusson 2009; Burt and Soda 2017; Perry-Smith and Shalley 2003). An innovation manager's ability to make use of their social ties presupposes social and civic competences (Dziatzko and Steinwandt 2011), for which the appropriate linguistic competences are necessary (European Commission 2018). However, the term "intern" can also be interpreted in conjunction with another term from Topic 4: the presence of the term "travel" can be understood as companies requiring their innovation managers to be more willing to travel internationally. Although a higher willingness to travel is not a component of any of the specific competences, it can be attributed to the personal initiative and entrepreneurial competence because it often signals increased independence and motivation. The last term of Topic 4, "develop," can be interpreted to imply that innovation managers must develop their team or general social network in order to make use of these social ties.

The specific combination of terms in Topic 5 has not previously been identified by studies researching innovation managers' tasks and competences. The correlation of terms in Topic 5 indicates that innovation managers must be aware of relevant developments in the economic environment of the company they are applying to work for ("econom," "environ") or the market in general ("market"). This general overview is crucial so that innovation managers can consider relevant trends when developing their own strategies (Dziatzko and Steinwandt 2011; Gershman and Thurner 2016; Vahs 2007). Accordingly, companies seem to expect innovation managers to be able to take on an advisory role ("consult") and develop recommendations for handling the opportunities and risks of these trends in their economic environment. Although innovation managers influence management decisions, they often have no decision-making or executive power of their own (Kaschny et al. 2015). Thus, Topic 5 could be seen as encapsulating the dominant understanding of innovation management in companies: the companies that posted the job advertisements analyzed in this study see innovation managers as consultants. In small- and medium-sized companies, flat hierarchical structures and proximity to company management typically compensate for the innovation manager's lack of decision-making power (Kaschny et al. 2015). The term "develop" indicates that companies expect their innovation managers to develop ideas until they are ready to be placed on the market as an answer to the identified trends. However, it remains unclear whether or not they also realize the ideas that they develop or only prepare them for further decision-making by upper management (Augsten et al. 2017).

Finally, when combining some of the identified topics, it turns out that the importance of absorbing and processing knowledge is evident in several of the identified topics. By monitoring the company's environment (Topic 5), analyzing the information available to them (Topic 2), and developing the company's structures and processes (Topic 3), innovation managers are expected to possess all the competences that correspond to dynamic capabilities. According to Teece (2007), dynamic capabilities are necessary for a company to adapt to new environmental conditions. He differentiates the dynamic capabilities into sensing, seizing, and transforming. In line with the terms in Topic 5, Teece uses the word "sensing" to refer to the identification of trends in the form of opportunities and risks in the company's environment. The identified opportunities then need to be systematically exploited according to Topic 2, for example, through further analyses, which he calls "seizing." The subsequent "transforming" in response to the insights from the seizing, which are needed to take advantage of new opportunities, refers to the reorganization of the organization's structures and processes. The requirement for an innovation manager to have the corresponding competences for reworking structures and processes is indicated by Topic 3. This way, it seems that the companies expect their innovation managers to represent dynamic capabilities in person.

6   Conclusion

This chapter examines job advertisements for innovation managers using topic modeling. Our findings show that companies do not demand single or standalone competences from future innovation management. Instead, they expect comprehensive competences. Although digital competences are important when identifying the dangers of digital change with regard to opportunities and risks, this importance does not emerge explicitly from the job advertisements studied. Several of the topics observed in this study confirmed previous findings to some degree. Some of the topic's terms might help to further analyze and understand the expectations of the companies and the definition of the formal role of innovation managers.

There are limitations to the conclusions drawn from this research. Although the sample consists mainly of manufacturing companies or those that are affiliated with industry, it is possible that the existence of different economic sectors within the sample could have distorted the results. On the other hand, examining single economic sectors exclusively would have led to much smaller samples and thus lower statistical validities. Further investigation could provide information on the extent to which the identified topics or competences are dependent on company size or the course of time. New trends might have an effect on the composition of terms of a topic. A high degree of heterogeneity among the competences that an innovation manager possesses has so far only been observed in smaller companies (Maier and Brem 2017) where a lack of financial or human resources results in one person providing the full range of competences needed to meet the requirements set by the company (Schon 1963; Sim et al. 2007). In larger companies, tasks are often divided among several innovation managers, and as a result each innovation manager may only need a subset of the competences required (Maier and Brem 2017). Additionally, it may be instructive to examine whether an innovation manager should lead a company through digital change as board support within the organizational boundaries or as an independent consultant. Further research could also show, which sectors of industry are concerned with the identified topics and whether they are looking for similar competences.

Finally, it is worth noting that recent economic developments have the potential to change companies' innovation management strategies. Some companies may drastically reduce their innovation activities because they lack the resources to introduce radical innovations into the market. Others may strengthen their innovation activities because the COVID-19 crisis and a low utilization of production capacity allow them to gradually and thoroughly innovate their processes and products. The boost in digitalization that began before the crisis has the potential to incite innovation managers to go further in their efforts to communicate, search for trends, and transform their companies according to what they find. However, recent developments could shift the priorities of the topics that have been identified in this chapter, and these new priorities should be researched in the context of the current economic climate.

Acknowledgments We would like to thank Nina DePalma for her tireless work in proofreading this chapter.

References

Armstrong, M. (2017). *How to be an even better manager: a complete A-Z of proven techniques and essential skills* (10th ed.). London: Kogan Page.

Augsten, T., Brodbeck, H., & Birkenmeier, B. (2017). *Strategie und innovation.* Wiesbaden: Springer Fachmedien. https://doi.org/10.1007/978-3-658-15684-8.

Axtell, C. M., Holman, D. J., Unsworth, K. L., Wall, T. D., Waterson, P. E., & Harrington, E. (2000). Shopfloor innovation: Facilitating the suggestion and implementation of ideas. *Journal of Occupational and Organizational Psychology, 73,* 265–285. https://doi.org/10.1348/096317900167029.

Baer, M., & Frese, M. (2003). Innovation is not enough: climates for initiative and psychological safety, process innovations, and firm performance. *Journal of Organizational Behavior, 24,* 45–68. https://doi.org/10.1002/job.179.

Björk, J. (2012). Knowledge domain spanners in ideation: knowledge domain spanners in ideation. *Creativity and Innovation Management, 21,* 17–27. https://doi.org/10.1111/j.1467-8691.2012.00627.x.

Björk, J., & Magnusson, M. (2009). Where do good innovation ideas come from? Exploring the influence of network connectivity on innovation idea quality. *Journal of Product Innovation Management, 26,* 662–670. https://doi.org/10.1111/j.1540-5885.2009.00691.x.

Blei, D. M. (2012). Probabilistic topic models. *Communications of the ACM, 55,* 77–84. https://doi.org/10.1145/2133806.2133826.

Blei, D. M., & Lafferty, J. D. (2007). A correlated topic model of science. *The Annals of Applied Statistics, 1,* 17–35.

Blei, D. M., Ng, A. Y., & Jordan, M. I. (2003). Latent Dirichlet allocation. *Journal of Machine Learning Research, 3,* 993–1022.

Bloom, N., Garicano, L., Sadun, R., & Van Reenen, J. (2014). The distinct effects of information technology and communication technology on firm organization. *Management Science, 60,* 2859–2885. https://doi.org/10.1287/mnsc.2014.2013.

Burt, R. S., & Soda, G. (2017). Social origins of great strategies. *Strategy Science, 2,* 226–233. https://doi.org/10.1287/stsc.2017.0043.

Cacaci, A. (2006). *Change management.* Wiesbaden: DUV. https://doi.org/10.1007/978-3-8350-9081-1.

Chesbrough, H. W. (2006). *Open innovation: the new imperative for creating and profiting from technology.* First Trade Paper ed. Boston: Harvard Business Review Press.

Choi, J. P. (2004). Tying and innovation: A dynamic analysis of tying arrangements. *The Econometrics Journal, 114,* 83–101. https://doi.org/10.1046/j.0013-0133.2003.00178.x.

Collins, C. J., & Smith, K. G. (2006). Knowledge exchange and combination: The role of human resource practices in the performance of high-technology firms. *Academy of Management Journal, 49,* 544–560. https://doi.org/10.5465/AMJ.2006.21794671.

Dalkir, K. (2005). *Knowledge management in theory and practice.* Amsterdam: Elsevier/Butterworth Heinemann.

Dziatzko, N., & Steinwandt, A. (2011). To be or not to be an innovation manager. *Z Für Innov Forsch Prax, 6,* 32–42.

Ekvall, G. (1997). Organizational conditions and levels of creativity. *Creativity and Innovation Management, 6,* 195–205. https://doi.org/10.1111/1467-8691.00070.

European Commission. (2018). Proposal for a council recommendation on key competences for LifeLong Learning. Brussels.

Fischer, S., Lubarski, A., Galipoglu, E., & Müller, F. (2017). Service innovation: Sensing with information systems. In *Information systems in the service innovation process. Presented at the Americas conference on information systems.*

Freiling, J., Gersch, M., & Goeke, C. (2008). On the path towards a competence-based theory of the firm. *Organization Studies, 29,* 1143–1164. https://doi.org/10.1177/0170840608094774.

Galipoglu, E., & Pöppelbuß, J., (2017). Service innovation practices in manufacturing companies and the role of information systems. *Presented at the international research symposium on service excellence in management, Porto.*

Gershman, M., & Thurner, T. (2016). New development: State-owned enterprises as powerhouses for innovation—the Russian case. *Public Money & Management, 36,* 297–302. https://doi.org/10.1080/09540962.2016.1162996.

Gerybadze, A. (2004). *Technologie- und Innovationsmanagement: Strategie, Organisation und Implementierung, Vahlens Handbücher der Wirtschafts- und Sozialwissenschaften.* München: Vahlen.

Griffiths, T. L., & Steyvers, M. (2004). Finding scientific topics. *Proceedings of the National Academy of Sciences, 101,* 5228–5235. https://doi.org/10.1073/pnas.0307752101.

Grün, B., & Hornik, K. (2011). Topicmodels: An R package for fitting topic models. *Journal of Statistical Software, 1*(13).

Hofmann, E., & Rüsch, M. (2017). Industry 4.0 and the current status as well as future prospects on logistics. *Computers in Industry, 89,* 23–34. https://doi.org/10.1016/j.compind.2017.04.002.

Huber, D., Kaufmann, H., & Steinmann, M. (2014). *Bridging the innovation gap.* Heidelberg: Springer. https://doi.org/10.1007/978-3-662-43925-8.

Kagermann, H., Wahlster, W., & Helbig, J. (2013). Recommendations for implementing the strategic initiative INDUSTRIE 4.0.

Kaschny, M., Nolden, M., & Schreuder, S. (2015). *Innovationsmanagement im Mittelstand: Strategien, Implementierung, Praxisbeispiele.* Wiesbaden: Springer.

Kepner, C. H., & Tregoe, B. B. (1997). *The new rational manager: An updated edition for a new world.* Cork: BookBaby.

Küchler, U. (2017). Wissenstransfer. In L. Kühnhardt & T. Mayer (Eds.), *Bonner Enzyklopädie der Globalität* (pp. 561–570). Wiesbaden: Springer Fachmedien. https://doi.org/10.1007/978-3-658-13819-6_46.

Kwon, S.-W., & Adler, P. S. (2014). Social capital: Maturation of a field of research. *Academy of Management Review, 39,* 412–422. https://doi.org/10.5465/amr.2014.0210.

Lee, S., Baker, J., Song, J., & Wetherbe, J. C. (2010). An empirical comparison of four text mining methods. In *2010 43rd HICSS. Presented at the 2010 43rd HICSS* (pp. 1–10). https://doi.org/10.1109/HICSS.2010.48

Leiponen, A. (2005). Skills and innovation. *International Journal of Industrial Organization, 23,* 303–323. https://doi.org/10.1016/j.ijindorg.2005.03.005.

Löfgren, A. (2014). International network management for the purpose of host market expansion: The mediating effect of co-innovation in the networks of SMEs. *Journal of International Entrepreneurship, 12,* 162–182. https://doi.org/10.1007/s10843-014-0129-1.

Luo, Y., & Bu, J. (2016). How valuable is information and communication technology? A study of emerging economy enterprises. *Journal of World Business, 51,* 200–211. https://doi.org/10.1016/j.jwb.2015.06.001.

Maier, M. A. (2014). What innovation managers really do—An empirical study about tasks, skills and traits of innovation managers in Germany (pp. 1116–1120). IEEE. https://doi.org/10.1109/IEEM.2014.7058812

Maier, M. A., & Brem, A. (2017). What innovation managers really do: a multiple-case investigation into the informal role profiles of innovation managers. *Review of Managerial Science.* https://doi.org/10.1007/s11846-017-0238-z.

Meyer, D., Hornik, K., & Feinerer, I. (2008). Text mining infrastructure in R. *Journal of Statistical Software, 25,* 1–54.

Nambisan, S., Lyytinen, K., Majchrzak, A., & Song, M. (2017). Digital innovation management: reinventing innovation management research in a digital world. *MIS Quarterly, 41,* 223–238. https://doi.org/10.25300/MISQ/2017/41:1.03.

Northrup, D. (2013). *How English became the global language.* Basingstoke: Palgrave Macmillan.

Noss, C. (2002). Innovationsmanagement—quo vadis? Kommentar zu Jürgen Hauschildts "Zwischenbilanz zum Stand der betriebswirtschaftlichen Innovationsforschung". In G. Schreyögg & P. Conrad (Eds.), *Theorien Des Managements* (pp. 35–48). Wiesbaden: Springer Gabler.

Oakland, J. S., & Tanner, S. (2007). Successful Change Management. *Total Quality Management and Business Excellence, 18*, 1–19. https://doi.org/10.1080/14783360601042890.

Ohly, S., Sonnentag, S., & Pluntke, F. (2006). Routinization, work characteristics and their relationships with creative and proactive behaviors. *Journal of Organizational Behavior, 27*, 257–279. https://doi.org/10.1002/job.376.

Ortmann, G. (2014). Können und Haben, Geben und Nehmen. Kompetenzen als Ressourcen: Organisation und strategisches Management. In A. Windeler & J. Sydow (Eds.), *Kompetenz* (pp. 19–107). Wiesbaden: VS Verlag für Sozialwissenschaften. https://doi.org/10.1007/978-3-531-19939-9_2.

Patsch, S., & Zerfass, A. (2017). Co-innovation and communication: The case of SAP's global co-innovation lab network. In N. Pfeffermann & J. Gould (Eds.), *Strategy and communication for innovation* (pp. 385–402). Cham: Springer. https://doi.org/10.1007/978-3-319-49542-2_23.

Pearlson, K. E., Saunders, C. S., & Galletta, D. F. (2016). *Managing and using information systems: a strategic approach* (6th ed.). Hoboken, NJ: Wiley.

Peltokorpi, V., & Vaara, E. (2014). Knowledge transfer in multinational corporations: Productive and counterproductive effects of language-sensitive recruitment. *Journal of International Business Studies, 45*, 600–622. https://doi.org/10.1057/jibs.2014.1.

Perry-Smith, J. E., & Shalley, C. E. (2003). The social side of creativity: A static and dynamic social network perspective. *Academy of Management Review, 28*, 89. https://doi.org/10.2307/30040691.

Porter, M. F. (1980). An algorithm for suffix stripping. *Program, 14*, 130–137.

Ritter, T., & Gemünden, H. G. (2003). Network competence: Its impact on innovation success and its antecedents. *Journal of Business Research, 56*, 745–755. https://doi.org/10.1016/S0148-2963(01)00259-4.

Salter, A., Ter Wal, A. L. J., Criscuolo, P., & Alexy, O. (2015). Open for ideation: Individual-level openness and idea generation in R&D: Open for ideation. *Journal of Product Innovation Management, 32*, 488–504. https://doi.org/10.1111/jpim.12214.

Schon, D. A. (1963). Champions for radical new inventions. *Harvard Business Review, 41*, 77–86.

Sim, E. W., Griffin, A., Price, R. L., & Vojak, B. A. (2007). Exploring differences between inventors, champions, implementers and innovators in creating and developing new products in large, mature firms. *Creativity and Innovation Management, 16*, 422–436. https://doi.org/10.1111/j.1467-8691.2007.00457.x.

Simon, H. A. (1982). *Models of bounded rationality*. Cambridge, MA: MIT Press.

Stolzenberg, K., & Heberle, K. (2013). *Change management*. Heidelberg: Springer. https://doi.org/10.1007/978-3-642-30106-3.

Teece, D. J. (2007). Explicating dynamic capabilities: the nature and microfoundations of enterprise performance. *Strategic Management Journal, 28*, 1319–1350. https://doi.org/10.1002/smj.640.

Tidd, J. (2001). Innovation management in context: environment, organization and performance. *International Journal of Management Reviews, 3*, 169–183. https://doi.org/10.1111/1468-2370.00062.

Trott, P. (2012). *Innovation management and new product development* (5th ed.). Harlow, England: Financial Times/Prentice Hall.

Vahs, D. (2007). *Organisation: Einführung in die Organisationstheorie und -praxis*, 6., überarb. und erw. Aufl. ed. Stuttgart: Schäffer-Poeschel.

Vahs, D., & Brem, A. (2015). *Innovationsmanagement: von der Idee zur erfolgreichen Vermarktung*, 5., überarbeitete Auflage. ed. Stuttgart: Schäffer-Poeschel.

Vahs, D., & Schmitt, J. (2010). Determinanten des Innovationserfolgs—Ergebnisse einer empirischen Studie. *Z Für Organ*, 40–46.

van Meurs, F., Planken, B., Korzilius, H., & Gerritsen, M. (2015). Reasons for using english or the local language in the genre of job advertisements: insights from interviews with Dutch job ad designers. *IEEE Transactions on Professional Communication, 58*, 86–105. https://doi.org/10.1109/TPC.2015.2423351.

Welch, D. E., & Welch, L. S. (2008). The importance of language in international knowledge transfer. *Management International Review, 48*, 339–360. https://doi.org/10.1007/s11575-008-0019-7.

Wöhlert, K. (2000). Innovationsmanager in KMU, In T. Lenk, S. Zelewski, Universität Leipzig, Universität Essen (Eds.), *ECOVIN: Enhancing competitiveness in small and medium enterprises via innovation—Handbuch zum Innovationsmanagement in kleinen und mittleren Unternehmen*. Univ. [u.a.], Leipzig.

Zhao, W., Chen, J. J., Perkins, R., Liu, Z., Ge, W., Ding, Y., & Zou, W. (2015). A heuristic approach to determine an appropriate number of topics in topic modeling. *BMC Bioinformatics, 16*(Suppl 13) https://doi.org/10.1186/1471-2105-16-S13-S8.

Chris C. Gernreich is a project manager at the German Federal Agency for Disruptive Innovation. He worked as a research assistant at the Chair of Industrial Sales and Service Engineering at the Faculty of Mechanical Engineering at the Ruhr-Universität Bochum. Additionally, he supports the International Society for Professional Innovation Management as a scientific coordinator. He holds a master's degree in technology-oriented management from the Technical University of Braunschweig. His main research interests are knowledge management, creativity and innovation management. In his dissertation, he is currently investigating how B2B customers can be involved in innovation activities.

Christian Ahlfeld works as a research assistant at the Chair of Industrial Sales Engineering at the Faculty of Mechanical Engineering at the Ruhr-Universität Bochum. He studied Sales Engineering and Product Management at the Ruhr-Universität Bochum from 2005 to 2011 before he received his doctorate in 2017. His research concentrates on selected topics in both product and sales management with the aim of gaining a deeper understanding of innovation and sales processes to improve the innovativeness and performance of small- and medium-sized companies in particular.

Sebastian Knop is a research assistant and doctoral student at the Chair of Industrial Sales and Service Engineering at the Faculty of Mechanical Engineering at the Ruhr-Universität Bochum. He holds a master's degree in Business Economics from the University of Bremen, Germany. His research interests include B2B marketing, data science, and innovation management. He is currently investigating the effects of branding within B2B companies. He has also written several papers that have been published at international conferences and in international journals.

Connecting the Corporate Brain: How Digital Platforms Accelerate Digital Transformation and Continuous Cultural Renewal

Tobias Kruft and Michael Gamber

1 Introduction: No Digital Transformation Without Cultural Renewal

For at least 20 years, digital transformation has presented and still presents a challenge to many industries. However, companies still struggle to continuously adapt to new digital demands and many industries are by now far behind. Netflix and Spotify have outpaced the music and film industry with digital business models, in the financial sector digital start-ups successfully challenge established companies, and in the pharmaceutical industry companies like Apple and IBM are about to take over the information market of the pharmaceutical companies' customers. If General Electric had not managed to counter SAP and other software and advanced analytics companies with a multibillion-dollar initiative in 2011, these companies would have turned General Electric into a commodity equipment provider. Furthermore, since many companies fear much worse consequences for themselves, they make an effort not to become casualties of the digital transformation as well (Iansiti and Lakhani 2014; Champagne et al. 2015; Schallmo and Williams 2018; Hess et al. 2019). The current pandemic also intensifies the need for transformation, which is why companies are obliged to take drastic measures: For example, in the airline industry, Lufthansa now cuts 20% of its management staff to become more responsive to cultural change through flatter hierarchies (Lufthansa 2020).

How can it be that digital transformation has been an issue for such a long time and established companies still struggle with it? The answer is growing cultural inertia. By now, large companies struggle with their rigid hierarchies and inflexible processes, but they further worsen their culture by almost desperately chasing every new trend instead of dominating it. If markets were to change radically only occasionally, even slower companies would have a chance to catch up, given the

T. Kruft (✉) · M. Gamber
Technische Universität Darmstadt, Darmstadt, Germany
e-mail: kruft@tim.tu-darmstadt.de; gamber@tim.tu-darmstadt.de

will to do so. However, industries are rarely subject to only one disruption. As soon as a disruption is in full swing, the next disruption is already underway: While several companies still focus on automation and most are in the process of digitization, significant changes are underway through machine learning and artificial intelligence, which only those companies that have already mastered automation and digitization can tackle (Rowles and Brown 2017). This eternal chasing after ever new and faster trend exhausts employees in large companies, as they feel they will never arrive at the promised goal before it changes again and therefore employees give up in frustration. Companies then adapt slower, lose more revenues, will have less budget for change, and will, thus, be even slower to adapt. Thus, inert corporate culture makes this process a vicious circle against which leadership must fight constantly and increasingly harder. The employees do not want to change (anymore), but leadership rightfully perceives change as necessary to survive and always tries out new methods, from different multistep change processes up to flipping where management time and again introduces small behavioral adjustments, so-called flips (Pflaeging and Hermann 2018).

How can companies avoid this vicious circle? They can avoid it through a renewing culture instead of an inert culture: when the company's culture is driven forward by employees and managers alike; when not the strategic destination of cultural change in itself is the focus but the daily, inspiring interchange among colleagues about finding the right journey; when people do not talk about change management but about new perspectives as part of their everyday life. Such a corporate culture adapts continuously and almost self-sustainingly to new trends and no longer requires dominant, management-driven change management. In order to differentiate the management-dominated terminology of *cultural change* from this new perspective, we call it *continuous cultural renewal*. Our approach, thus, ties in with a company's agile mindset—in which management provides room for individual talents' perspectives and mainly sets the direction while the teams determine the speed—consistently taking this approach even further at the company's cultural level (Cockburn and Highsmith 2001).

This process of cultural renewal is based on inspiring exchanges between management and employees at eye level. These exchanges can be very lengthy in multinational companies and are therefore difficult to realize with traditional exchanges since rapid adaptation capabilities are increasingly required. In the course of digitization, however, one particular solution becomes very relevant in terms of cultural renewal: company-internal digital platforms. Digital platforms have an enormous potential to connect all employees—independent of their geographical location—to a well-linked corporate brain. This connection fosters a rapid exchange of knowledge and values. This rapid exchange significantly accelerates the almost self-sustaining process of cultural renewal to a pace at which the resulting *digital* renewal process represents an efficient and competitive alternative or an effective complement to current cumbersome change processes. While digital cultural renewal basically facilitates adaptation to every new emerging trend, the digital nature of digital platforms accelerates the digital transformation even further.

After an introduction to the fundamentals of the cultural renewal mechanisms, we guide through the three steps that are necessary to establish a continuous cultural renewal process in a company: While in step 1, we first derive the basics for the introduction of digital platforms, in step 2 we explain in detail how companies can introduce and manage digital platforms effectively. Step 3 concludes the roll-out process by discussing important measures to keep the cultural renewal process running as efficiently as possible. The three steps are illustrated in Fig. 2 and will be derived in detail in the fundamentals section. Once the three steps have been successfully implemented in the company, the company only has to invest a comparatively small amount of time and effort to ensure that the process remains self-sustaining and continuously incorporates new trends into the company's cultural DNA.

This three-step process to achieve continuous cultural renewal is one of the important results of a three-year research project in which we performed a systematic, in-depth analysis of more than 40 listed companies to explore the interplay between corporate incubation (Kruft and Kock 2019a; Gamber et al. 2020a), digital platforms (Kruft and Kock 2019b; Kruft et al. 2019; Zhu et al. 2019; Gamber et al. 2020b), and cultural renewal (Kruft et al. 2018; Kruft and Kock 2019c; Gamber et al. 2020b). This chapter, therefore, summarizes this research project's overarching findings regarding the interplay between digital transformation and cultural renewal. The chapter, furthermore, enriches the findings with many different real-world examples (gray boxes) that we have collected during this time.

2 Fundamentals: The Process of Continuous Cultural Renewal

Rapid adaptability and a strong conviction that companies can and must continuously transform are central enablers to face disruptive trends as a company. However, it is not only adaptability and the willingness to change those challenge companies. Even if a company has decided to open up to digital transformation, it must surely know what this means in terms of precise targets. Becoming a digital organization not only means having digital products, services, and customer interactions but also means providing technologies to core activities and using these technologies to transform the organization's processes and business models to create a whole new manner of thinking for the entire organization (Hess et al. 2019). Consequently, the company must achieve tectonic changes in employees' tasks and individual behavior as well as changes in the manner they interact with others inside and outside the organization (Hemerling et al. 2018). Such changes arise predominantly as an essential component of the corporate culture, which, through its sum of values, norms, and basic assumptions shared by the employees' vast majority (Schein 1996), determines each company's and its employees' behavior. In fact, corporate culture and transformation processes cannot be examined in isolation; culture influences every single element of what a company does—or does not do—and even a strong corporate strategy alone cannot counteract this effect (Besson and Rowe 2012; Rowles and Brown 2017).

The strong influence of culture becomes clear when we consider how it affects the daily work practices of all employees. While many aspects of a corporate culture are not visible, they implicitly influence how employees think, decide, and act since the corporate culture determines what is perceived as appropriate and important within the company. Much more visible and tangible is the working climate, which results from the decisions and actions shaped by the corporate culture. It can best be described as the perceptions of the work environment, which result from the employees' collective behavior and mindset as the visible manifestation of the corporate culture (Abbey and Dickson 1983; Schein 1985; Ekvall 1996). The working climate thus consists of everything that employees absorb daily from their surroundings and what they themselves say and practice in relation to their colleagues. Now the influence of culture is suddenly evident. For example, if a department in a company with an inert corporate culture is exposed to technological disruption, their response to the technology will depend on how they can justify their response to other departments and superiors. If the company's cultural values hinder being open to new technologies, the department will refuse to embrace this technological trend. Likewise, most of the other departments will act accordingly because this inert corporate culture is omnipresent throughout the whole company as part of its corporate culture. Another example: If employees had long since ceased to engage in anything more than their daily work and stopped questioning existing processes or trying out new working methods, they would not adapt to changes since it would be against what they are accustomed to. In both examples, the consequence is a culturally rooted lack of acceptance and adoption of the technological trend, in our case digital transformation, which cannot just be overcome by a change initiative or a new strategy (Besson and Rowe 2012; Rowles and Brown 2017).

To understand how to prevent this cultural mismatch such that corporate culture *promotes* digital transformation instead, it is important to understand how cultural renewal takes place on a conceptual level. Archer (1995) describes a suitable approach in her much-cited morphogenetic cycle as part of her social realist theory. Figure 1 shows a simplified and adapted version of this process. The concept essentially states that cultural and structural circumstances always determine people's actions, which, in turn, maintain or modify the circumstances. While culture comprises the range of ideas, beliefs, values, and propositional knowledge, structures comprise the range of social positions, hierarchies, and roles (Porpora 2013). Simplified and related to our specific use case, this means that the employees' values and attitudes toward the digital transformation mirror the cultural side, while a digital transformation strategy and the strategy-executing leadership represent the structural side. The two perspectives, which are vastly different given a conservative corporate culture, collide in an environment where both leadership and employees are present: the departments' working environment. Here, countless interactions take place, which are dominated by social and socio-cultural factors, such as reputation, power, habits, religion, or ethnic identity. These interactions determine whether the structural or cultural perspective consolidates over time. In each case, however, the

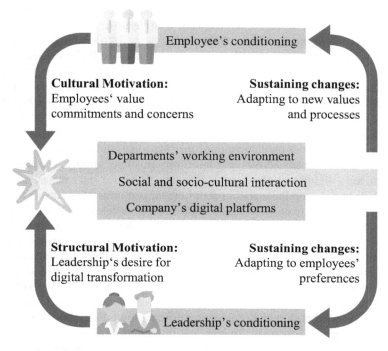

Fig. 1 Digital transformation as process of continuous cultural renewal; inspired by Archer (1995)

two sides align with each other and the perspectives become somewhat blended. The result of this interaction process then leads employees and managers to question their perspective, even if only slightly, and to adjust their perspective to a certain extent. This cycle thereby happens constantly: Every hour, minute, and second, people in departments exchange perspectives and over weeks, months, and years they adapt their values almost imperceptibly. These small adjustments add up over time and create an adapted set of values and, thus, an adapted corporate culture.

The problem with the previously described adaptation process is that it happens very slowly: It takes years to measure a cultural change in a corporate environment (Kruft and Kock 2019c). As we explained at the beginning, companies do not have this amount of time because the next megatrend is already underway, and the adaptation must happen as quickly as possible. Therefore, it is essential to speed up the adaptation process.

A highly effective means to speed up the cultural renewal processes is to increase the interactions' intensity between all people involved, which can generally be achieved via three levers: The more frequently people exchange perspectives, the more different their perspectives are, and the greater the impact of this interaction is, the faster a cultural renewal process will take place. The difficulty with traditional exchanges within departments is that especially the last two factors are not really a given: Within a department, the perspectives usually do not differ significantly and the discourse between colleagues from one department rarely influences other departments. Here, cross-functional teams or interdepartmental dialog can increase the diversity of exchange (Kahn 2001; Sethi et al. 2001) but the potential for genuinely effective exchange still remains largely untapped. Companies can only achieve a genuinely effective exchange when they use all three levers to their full potential, that is, if *every* employee and manager in the company can share perspectives with each other and *every* single employee and manager can be inspired by these specific perspectives—across site and country borders on a global scale. A technical solution that comes closest to or allows for this effective exchange is digital platforms. It should not go unmentioned that the successful introduction of digital platforms alone already drives digital transformation, simply because digital platforms are a digital tool. However, for the time being, we leave this advantageous effect aside to focus on the main impact of digital platforms.

Before we can explain why digital platforms can accelerate cultural change so profoundly, we must first clarify what we consider digital platforms to be. From a business perspective, a digital platform provides a place that creates value by facilitating exchanges of information, goods, or services between platform users. More technically speaking, a digital platform is a software-supported system that offers core functions extendable through modules and interfaces to support organizational processes (De Reuver et al. 2018). There are well-known examples of platforms in different domains, all serving different purposes: platforms for social media exchange like Facebook, Twitter, and Instagram; platforms for shared media consumption like YouTube and Spotify; platforms for knowledge exchange like Wikipedia, Quora, and StackOverflow; and service-oriented platforms like Uber and Airbnb. For this chapter, however, we focus exclusively on company-internal platforms that support a specific corporate purpose, that is, at least the promotion of knowledge and value exchange between employees and managers and, thus, cultural change.

Platforms with the greatest potential to fulfill this purpose are online ideation platforms, which offer employees the opportunity to submit and discuss ideas, as well as exchange and learning platforms, which enable employees to engage in learning activities and share success and failure stories throughout the whole company (Chapman and Hyland 2004; Beretta 2019; Zhu et al. 2019). These platforms should not be confused with other digital communication systems, such as videoconferencing, e-mail, and chat tools, which often already exist in companies. Although the latter tools are also used to exchange information within the company, this knowledge is not openly visible to all people in the company—most of the time for a good reason: E-mails are only sent to the relevant recipients owing to confidentiality reasons and during video conferences usually only a small group of people participate also to not distract others with trivial things. In contrast, digital platforms, such as online ideation platforms used for idea contests, deliberately serve to exchange information between as many people as possible. The following example illustrates what we mean by digital platforms.

What Can a Digital Platform Accomplish? A Hands-On Perspective

We talked to a multinational company that wanted to use a digital platform for gathering ideas among its employees to unlock new potential for the company. Collecting ideas within this multinational company has always been a complex task since smart employees are scattered all over the world but are not linked together in a large network. Instead of just running local think tanks, the company wanted to bring together all the worldwide people in the company and connect them to one big corporate brain such that every employee could have access to a fruitful exchange, communication, and cross-fertilization of new ideas. Besides just reaching out to the innovative people, the company also wanted to use this platform to explicitly promote less innovative minds within the company so as to slowly but surely activate them to participate in the ideation activities as well.

Once the digital platform infrastructure was in place, the central innovation unit developed targeted formats, such as online workshops (to teach new methods and perspectives) and technology and industry-specific idea contests (to connect people with similar expertise or motivation and generate novel ideas). During these competitions, not only the employees who submitted ideas exchanged experiences, but also employees who visited the platform purely out of interest in the creative environment gave feedback on the submitted ideas and participated in knowledge sharing.

The comments' number of views also revealed that for certain ideas, significantly more employees than those who actually participated followed the exchange of perspectives and experience. Once published on the platform, the ideas and comments, thus, served as multipliers for an exchange that could never have taken place offline—especially since the exchange took place across time zones and national borders and the submitted ideas and comments were read for a long time after they had been submitted.

Even though this platform was originally intended as a platform for finding new potentials for the company, such as new products, services, and business models, it also proved to be a powerful instrument for bringing people throughout the company closer together and promoting a targeted cultural exchange.

The potential to simultaneously reach all employees and managers regardless of time and place illustrates the full potential of digital platforms. Digital platforms offer easier access to a larger network of people in the company to exchange perspectives (Katz and Shapiro 1985; Rode 2016) that are, in turn, potentially visible to every platform user, resulting in a greater reach. The modularity of platforms enables the linking of databases, knowledge repositories, and other complementary technological tools (Rai and Tang 2010), which facilitates the exchange of views and even introduces new perspectives that are ideally aligned with the company's digital strategy. Digital platforms often reveal problems at an early stage to a large group of employees (Björk and Magnusson 2009) and create more competition in the search for solutions. Through this competition, participants exchange ideas to obtain feedback and improve their ideas and, thus, subconsciously share values that accelerate cultural change. Similarly, digital platforms increase the probability of receiving feedback compared to ideas that are only discussed within the boundaries of certain departments (Nylén and Holmström 2015; Zhu et al. 2019), as transaction costs and the effort of network participants decrease. In summary, digital platforms enable individual employees and managers to be connected to a vast, company-wide network, the corporate brain. The better this network is connected and used, the faster the adaptation processes take place and, thus, also cultural renewal in line with the digital transformation.

However, companies cannot exploit this concentrated potential if digital platforms are introduced but not used, because digital platforms, like all other changes in companies, depend on the employees' willpower to accept these changes. Implementing platforms can, therefore, only succeed if the employees—and thus the working climate—are sufficiently open to new perspectives, at least to the extent that employees do not entirely impede new perspectives (Kruft et al. 2018). In many companies, this is already the case because certain departments always have a few innovative minds that will take the opportunity to share their ideas with others. However, a systematic effort must be made to convince as many employees within the departments as possible to participate in the platforms from the very beginning. As such, a cultural renewal begins with a renewal of the working environment— more precisely a renewal of the working climate—because the working climate of departments can be changed much more quickly and selectively than the corporate culture. Thereby, an innovative working climate (or in short: innovation climate) enables easier implementation and acceptance of digital platforms. Subsequently, if the corporate brain is digitally connected, it is possible to achieve an accelerated but nonetheless sustainable cultural change. Through cultural change toward a more innovative corporate culture, barriers gradually fall away. Consequently, digital platforms and other changes that form part of the digital transformation increasingly resonate and the adaptation process accelerates further. Therefore, as soon as a certain tipping point has been passed, digital transformation can potentially become a sure-fire success.

In the following sections, we will guide through the process of accelerating digital transformation and cultural change via digital platforms (see Fig. 2). In Step 1, we describe how companies can achieve an innovation climate to pave the way for employees to be open to the introduction of digital platforms and, ultimately, digital transformation. Step 2 describes what companies need to consider when introducing digital platforms and what advantages this could have. Lastly, Step 3 focuses on how companies can preserve the efforts made such that the effort is not in vain.

Since digital platforms themselves represent a part of the digital transformation, companies may consider the process of introducing digital platforms representative of other digital infrastructure or the digital transformation implementation itself: It is also necessary to prepare the minds of employees and management for digital transformation, digital transformation must ultimately be introduced and special

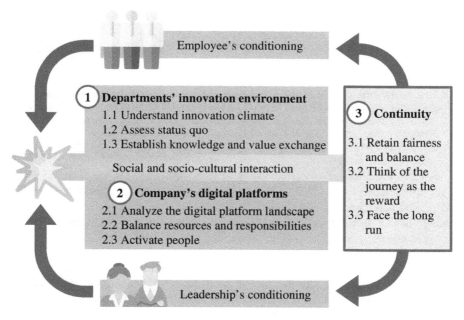

Fig. 2 Steps for the digital transformation as a process of continuous cultural renewal

attention must be paid to ensuring that the measures introduced are lived and therefore sustained. Nevertheless, this process specifically focuses on the introduction of digital platforms aimed at increasing the exchange between employees and thus accelerating the adaptation to the digital transformation. One can, therefore, consider transferring this process to other digital measures although it may not always be practical.

3   Step 1: Innovation Climate—Preparing the Corporate Brain

There are generally two fundamentally different approaches to ensure that a maximum number of people in the company—employees and managers—use digital platforms and exchange information on these: by actively opening up employees and managers *prior to* the implementation of digital platforms or through learning by doing *as a result of* the implementation. While a combined approach is usually the most effective, taking only the latter approach is the least effective. As with any change in the habits of an individual, all the people in a company must have at least somewhat open attitude toward this change to accept it (Hernández-Mogollon et al. 2010). The vast majority will in all likelihood not actually accept and use digital platforms properly if people, who in the worst case have not had to make any changes in their workplace habits for years, do not consciously open up to new situations. A simple learning-by-doing approach (or to put it more drastically: find out how to deal with it) as implemented by certain companies, therefore, involves a great deal of implementation failure risk. Besson and Rowe (2012, p. 105) formulate quite strikingly why this is the case:

> To understand the issues of organizational transformation, one must keep in mind the central paradox of organizing. Organizing means routinizing. Yet this action of routinization creates inertia by entrenching the organization and causing patterns to become rigid. In this perspective, transforming implies overcoming organizational inertia to realign the organization with its environment.

For this realignment, the company must first "unfreeze" the status quo (Lewin 1951; Besson and Rowe 2012), which only works if people understand the need for adaptation and therefore join forces. It is, thus, crucial to prepare everyone for the change before or at least during the implementation of digital platforms and other new technologies. In the following, we explain how this can work.

To prepare employees and managers for this change, companies should pursue the following three steps, which are further explained in the following sections: First, the company should acquire a clear understanding of what it means to create openness within the company (section "Understand the Innovation Climate"). The managers who are supposed to drive the implementation should not only develop this understanding but should also ensure that all people in the company understand what will be expected of them. Second, companies should assess their status quo (section "Assess the Status Quo"). This is important not only to be able to later evaluate whether the measures were successful but also to know what measures are actually necessary and where the working climate might already be sufficiently open. Third, once the first two steps are achieved, an open working climate must be established; we will refer to it later as innovation climate when it is defined (section "Understand the Innovation Climate"). To achieve an open working climate, it is necessary to introduce new impulses into the company that generates this openness. Before the company can introduce these impulses, it must determine what exactly these impulses, which mostly consist of knowledge and values, should be and where they are supposed to come from. Once these three steps are achieved, the company is ready for the successful launch of digital platforms.

Understand the Innovation Climate

We can define working climate as people's perceptions of the work environment, which result from the employees' collective behavior and mindset as the visible manifestation of the corporate culture (Abbey and Dickson 1983; Schein 1985; Ekvall 1996). Viewed across all departments of a company, the working climate provides a behavioral and mindset-based representation of the corporate culture (Denison 1996). At the departmental level, however, the working climate certainly differs within a company. Since the differences in mindset and behavior also alter the

Fig. 3 Dimensions of the innovation climate; according to Kruft et al. (2018)

culture in the long run, the corporate culture is always, even if very gradually, in a dynamic motion (see Fig. 1). At all times, the working climate mirrors this slow-moving quasi-stationary equilibrium (Lewin 1951), which, in principle, allows trends in corporate culture to be detected before they manifest over years. It can therefore be very useful to follow the working climate's development throughout the company in order to assess how the corporate culture develops.

The working climate encompasses a wide range of different perspectives on the employees' environment (Patterson et al. 2005). To understand how corporate culture influences companies' innovativeness and adaptability, we only need to focus on a single part of the working climate: the innovation climate. How exactly this part of the working climate is constituted, varies throughout innovation research literature. Kruft et al. (2018) reviewed this literature and found seven relevant dimensions that best reflect this literature—and therefore innovation climate. These dimensions are displayed in Fig. 3.

Except for psychological safety, which is a dimension by itself, all other dimensions form pairs, which are closely related to but still distinct from each other. The first pair covers the part of the innovation climate that deals with new perspectives. Both openness & flexibility are important factors for determining innovation climate, as low emphasis on work rules and high flexibility facilitate innovation (Damanpour 1991). Furthermore, scholars have shown that a flexible climate influences all stages of the innovation process significantly (Abbey and Dickson 1983), and also Amabile (1988) confirms that inflexibility—thus being opinionated, constrained, and unwilling to do things differently—inhibits creativity. Reflexivity is a similar dimension. Complementary to the more passive and reactive dimension of openness & flexibility, reflexivity represents the innovation climate's ability to foster the reflecting capabilities of each individual to proactively challenge the status quo (O'Reilly 1989; West 2000; Schippers et al. 2015).

The next pair of dimensions is mainly determined by the employees' direct supervisors. Supervisory support indicates the extent to which employees experience support and understanding from their immediate supervisor, which leads to a supportive work environment that improves creativity and ideation (Siegel and Kaemmerer 1978; Amabile et al. 1996; Ekvall 1996). Since supervisors, due to their position, have a high influence on the employees, the supervisors "facilitate innovation because the successful adoption of innovations depends largely on the leadership, support, and coordination managers provide" (Damanpour 1991, p. 559). Strongly linked to supervisory support, is the opportunity of employees to participate in decision-making processes. The extent to which employees have considerable influence over decision-making strongly depends on their supervisor. A supervisor who encourages employees to make choices and develop a sense of responsibility for their actions influences all stages of the innovation process and the innovation culture itself significantly (Abbey and Dickson 1983; O'Reilly 1989; Claver et al. 1998). Nevertheless, participation differs from supervisory support since participation means the employees' active participation in decision-making instead of the supervisors' support in executing already made decisions.

The third pair concerns two dimensions involving interactions between people. Without a communication-friendly environment, there would be a lack of "access to and availability of diverse knowledge, cross-fertilization of ideas, improved quality of decision-making and consideration of novel alternative solutions that yield innovation" (Hogan and Coote 2014, p. 1612). Without a collaborative climate, there would be no information and specialist resources from other functional areas to achieve successful and innovative outcomes (Baker and Freeland 1972, De Clercq et al. 2009; Hogan and Coote 2014).

As discussed variously in the literature (March and Shapira 1987; Craig et al. 2014; Tian and Wang 2014; Garcia-Granero et al. 2015), an enormously important dimension for innovation climate is a climate that fosters taking the risk and being tolerant to praiseworthy failures (Edmondson 2011) along with making the employees feel safe to think differently (Baer and Frese 2003; Tellis et al. 2009). Nowadays an organization cannot wait for complete and clearly defined information to make strategic decisions. Other competing organizations do not wait either and the success of even one innovative product could obstruct the efforts of hesitant organizations. Thus, a climate of psychological safety so as to take risks has to be implemented in development to overcome the lack of time in dynamic and uncertain environments (Saleh and Wang 1993) and to boost innovative creativity (Amabile 1988).

In order to achieve an open working environment in which employees are excited about new perspectives, all seven dimensions must reach a certain level. It is not enough for departments to have a high level of openness and flexibility, because if, for instance, there is no supervisory support and no psychological safety, the acceptance of new perspectives will prove to be very difficult—nobody will dare to try something new if they are afraid of the consequences. Moreover, the innovation climate as the sum of all seven dimensions can vary from company to company—and sometimes even from department to department—because the willingness to adapt is not only determined by the innovation climate but also by how new the employees perceive change to be (Kruft et al. 2018). Although the innovation climate may not be particularly strong in a software development department, the acceptance of digital platforms is still likely. On the other hand, a company's departments may in principle have a high innovation climate, but the introduction of digital platforms nevertheless turns out to be a major challenge, as their introduction requires the implementation of further necessary digital infrastructure that was not available before.

Assess the Status Quo

There are many advantages to assessing the innovation climate's status quo. First of all, the innovation climate can be measured very tangibly so that the differences between departments and the seven dimensions become noticeable. This allows not only to measure the change in innovation climate by repeated measurements at later points in time but also to evaluate the success of implemented measures. Furthermore, assessing the innovation climate's status quo enables the measures to be used selectively and purposefully as it becomes clear where improvement potential exists.

There are various approaches to measuring innovation climate. An easily scalable and feasible approach is a questionnaire, which every employee and supervisor in the company should ideally fill out. Kruft et al. (2018) translated the seven innovation climate dimensions into a total of 24 survey questions to ensure that these dimensions can be measured as validly as possible. To provide a sense of what an innovation climate assessment can resemble and what should be considered, we describe in the following the case of a listed technology company that has already carried out this assessment twice to review the influence of its measures.

Almost 9% in 2 Years: A Success?

The aerospace and chemical-pharmaceutical industries are characterized by lengthy development cycles lasting many years to develop new products. Particularly because product safety dominates the development process, the companies do not rush the development and proceed slowly and step by step. This mentality inevitably affects the corporate culture in these industries. This makes it all the more difficult to achieve an opening for new perspectives, although it is all the more essential to keep up with changing markets and not be outpaced by competition, precisely because of this rigid culture.

This case's company had to deal with exactly this challenge. Many activities have been initiated to open up the culture and create a stronger innovation climate in the departments. These activities included information events, lectures, training sessions, and workshops. For example, the company had initiated innovation summits where interesting personalities such as

---

(continued)

successful entrepreneurs reported on their experiences; there were regular "fuckup nights" where stories of professional failure were exchanged and discussed to capture the learning, and there were many opportunities for each employee to engage in informal exchange with start-ups and thought leaders from the company. Furthermore, the company offered employees professional workshops and training sessions focusing on methods, such as design thinking, the business model canvas, or prototyping. All these activities were mainly carried out to receive new ideas for business model development, but they also aimed at opening up the employees and providing them with new perspectives. "Over time, this should be noticeable in the working environment." This was the expectation of the manager in charge: "We surveyed almost 8,000 people, and this happened twice during the last two years. Answering the questions may not have taken more than ten minutes per participant and yet they quickly add up to large amounts for all of them. Hopefully, this effort was worth it."

Indeed, even after all biases were removed, the innovation climate across all departments had significantly improved by 9% on a scale of one to five and every dimension has even improved at least a little bit (see Fig. 4).

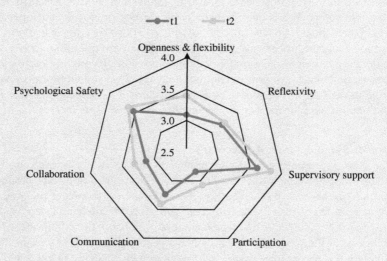

Fig. 4 The case company's innovation climate improvement after 2 years

"That was more than expected, to be honest," the manager said. In fact, it is a major achievement to affect so many employees in a relatively short time. What they discovered, was that a great number of employees did not participate in events at all. It appears as if the innovation mindset has spread throughout the company partially by itself through participants exchanging with their colleagues.

Establish Knowledge and Value Exchange

For this step, companies must now actually trigger an initial change toward a pronounced innovation climate. This will be easier if, by achieving the step outlined in section "Assess the Status Quo", the company knows in which dimensions the innovation climate is not yet so pronounced. Nevertheless, two things must be done to achieve the goal: finding suitable knowledge and value sources and promoting the dissemination of both within the company.

To understand why particularly knowledge and values are important for achieving a strong innovation climate, we need to delve a bit deeper into the topic of inertia. Companies consist of many processes that are frequently repeated, which results in routines that become stuck in people's heads. This happens automatically and is not necessarily bad because efficiency accompanies routine and efficiency is desirable in companies to save costs. Routines, however, also create inertia, complicating the implementation of changes (Besson and Rowe 2012). In companies, there are five types of inertia that impede an organizational transformation and an opening of the working climate (see Fig. 5).

Negative psychology inertia describes employees and/or managers being overwhelmed by negative emotions due to threat perception. This happens, for example, if they are afraid of losing their job due to the change or if they simply find changes cumbersome and time consuming. The natural consequence is that they refuse to face the threat and are not willing to adapt (Coch and French 1948). *Socio-cognitive inertia* describes resistance to changes resulting from the characteristics of individuals, departments, or entire industries that lead to the retention of norms and values. Thus, the airline industry differs significantly from the fast-moving consumer

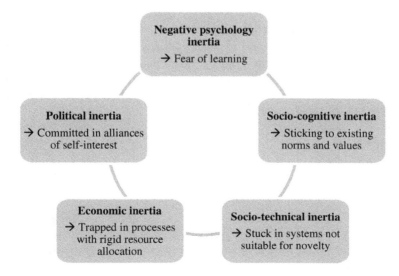

Fig. 5 Dimensions of organizational inertia; in accordance with Besson and Rowe (2012)

goods (FMCG) industry in its development cycles and therefore its adaptability. Likewise, the personality of individuals determines how much they are open to new perspectives (Dutton and Duncan 1987). *Socio-technical inertia* can be understood as the dependence on existing technical systems, which have taken considerable time and effort to build up and which now run smoothly. Adding new systems or changing the entire architecture can prove to be very time consuming and employees try to avoid this just as much as managers (Hannan and Freeman 1984). *Economic inertia* can best be understood as an impediment resulting from resources already being committed elsewhere and therefore no longer available. A common case is that resources are tied up in projects that serve to increase efficiency, which means that resources are no longer available for exploration and opening up to new perspectives (Gilbert 2005). *Political inertia*, lastly, means the motivation of people to defend their interests and stay in existing alliances to maximize their own advantage. The inertia arises because it takes time and effort to reshape such alliances; therefore, it is easier for people to remain in the old structures (Denis et al. 2001; Besson and Rowe 2012). The following practical example illustrates how inertia can cause attempts at improving the innovation climate to fail or even to be counterproductive.

It May Be Trash Ideas, but I Have Ten of Them!
This can happen when managers are not serious about realizing their goals or simply do not have time to pay attention to details. "At first we thought our idea contest was a huge success," recalls the innovation manager of a medium-sized industrial company. "We had over 240 ideas submitted in our idea campaign—we never had so many in the campaigns before!" However, it soon became apparent that almost 90% of the ideas were unusable: "No clue who comes up with submitting such stupid ideas. It was a huge effort to filter out the good ideas." The same applied to the comments: "Half of the comments were introduced to improve the idea; half of them were only 'I like your idea' and that was it. But, honestly, I did not pay too much attention to that." Retrospectively, the campaign team discovered the reason for the sudden rise of so many bad ideas: A number of supervisors had included in the target agreements with their employees that they should submit a certain number of ideas in idea contests.

This is the consequence of a typical mistake if the manager does not implement measures to promote more openness in the company correctly and this can then even achieve the opposite. Those who should actually take the time to explore new ideas and perspectives in order to open up, wrote down ten ideas within a very short time and submitted them in idea competitions. It did not take too much of their time. The burden had to be borne by those who were already committed to a strong innovation climate and new perspectives in the company: They had to invest plenty of time to sort out these ideas again; moreover, their effort and frustration level understandably increased noticeably. If managers were to commit more time, or as role models submit ideas themselves instead of merely including "creativity" in the target agreements, employees would probably submit much more ideas worth evaluating.

The employees referred to in the case box cannot be blamed alone for how the situation turned out. Probably they simply did not have enough time to submit convincing ideas because the supervisor did not grant them the time to do so (economic inertia, see Fig. 5). Perhaps the idea competition aimed at methods of increasing workplace productivity and the employees fought back by torpedoing the campaign (negative psychology inertia). Nevertheless, this department failed to establish an innovation climate because the supervisor was unaware of the value of good ideas or just not interested in a strong innovation climate due to his specific value concepts (socio-cognitive inertia). A strong innovation climate can only develop if it is created *together* with both employees and managers and not against their interests or capabilities—and that takes time; at least more time than formulating a goal and then waiting to see how the employees react to this goal.

Studying the five types of inertia, it should now become clear why implementing a new technology without reflecting on the background of the target environment is most likely doomed to failure. The barriers are often far too pronounced and are maintained by the people who benefit from them. It is therefore important that people understand why change is good and important such that they are willing to support this change on their own initiative. This can only work if the values the change brings with it correspond to the values that the employees themselves embrace (Klein and Sorra 1996). If the employees can be convinced of the new values, the first hurdle is overcome, although it is still not clear how the change can actually be achieved. This requires knowledge clarifying the necessary steps without which the change, even if the motivation for it exists, cannot be carried out. To put it in the words of Archer (1998, p. 104), culture changes through "the growth of knowledge, elaboration of beliefs, accumulation of literature and so forth." Plainly formulated, the values convey *why* people should change, while knowledge shows *how* adaptation can take place.

It becomes evident that knowledge and values are key to triggering organizational change and achieving a stronger innovation climate. However, where can companies obtain them from? The basic rule is that both must come from outside the company if they are not already present in certain parts of the company. As already shown in the box entitled "Almost 9% in 2 Years: A Success," there are many different formats to bring new values and knowledge into the company. These formats can range from information events, lectures, and training sessions to workshops lasting several days. The easiest means to achieve a knowledge and value exchange is to bring employees and managers together with people who already represent the new value system and possess the knowledge to implement the new technology (Kruft and Kock 2019c). These are often entrepreneurs or thought leaders who have followed new trends for years. Ideally, however, they also represent a few of the employees' and managers' values that they are supposed to change. It is also helpful if they can build on people's existing knowledge. Consequently, such entrepreneurs and thought leaders should at least come from a similar industry and may even have once represented the "old" values, which stand to be changed, that are still present in the company. This makes it much easier for employees and managers to identify with the entrepreneur or thought leader, and a value change and knowledge transfer take place much more easily (Gibbons and Stiles 2004; Mensmann and Frese 2019). It is crucial to stress once again that not only the employees but especially the managers have to undergo a value change. If managers' values do not change, there will most likely be no change in the innovation climate.

Injecting Knowledge and Values: Does It Hurt?

Values and many forms of knowledge can usually only be exchanged implicitly. In such cases, any format in which people are exposed to new perspectives without these perspectives being the main reason for the exchange is potentially appropriate. For example, we noticed several times in practice that there are workshops or ideation teams where internal and external perspectives are put together by forming joint teams comprising employees and external start-ups to actively collaborate, for instance, in ideation campaigns.

This not only enables combining the strengths of both groups, which could be a booster for the ideation process, but such combined teams or workshops can also have significant positive side effects: exchange of knowledge and values in terms of methods, tools, thinking patterns, and convictions. The convenient thing about knowledge and values is that people even exchange them subconsciously and take up the new perspectives without closing themselves off from the outset; therefore, it does not "hurt" at all. Especially when employees and entrepreneurs need to join forces to achieve a common goal, they learn to appreciate the other perspective and adopt parts of it. Furthermore, sometimes they do not even notice that they thereby alter their perspectives regarding values and new knowledge. Within a reasonable amount of time (maybe a few weeks), a change in perspective can be achieved, which can lead to innovation climate—if the majority of the departments' people is involved.

A challenge of such joint teams can be the governance of intellectual property created through the activity, for example, how to treat (confidential) information and know-how amongst the participants. As long as the boundary conditions are set in advance and both parties benefit from this exchange, the exchange of knowledge and values should be ensured.

In summary, the introduction of an innovation climate aims to spread the conviction within the company that digital platforms and the digital transformation as a whole make life easier, not harder. The key point is that the efforts for digital transformation should not lead to a duplication of existing work processes but rather improve the organizational system as a whole. By creating a pronounced innovation climate and aligning the user experience of the technologies to be introduced with the needs of the employees, companies create a scenario in which employees are willing to embrace the new technologies instead of being forced to do so.

4   Step 2: Digital Platforms—Shifting Interactions to the Digital World

Once the scene is set for the introduction of digital platforms, the company can begin to gradually shift the employees' exchange to the digital world. Particularly suitable for this purpose are platforms that at least promote a knowledge and value exchange between employees and managers. When choosing the type of platform, it is important to ensure that every employee and every manager in the company has the opportunity to exchange information with each other and that every single employee and manager can be inspired by this specific exchange. The platforms with the greatest potential for fulfilling this purpose are online idea contests, which give employees the opportunity to submit and discuss ideas, and learning platforms, which allow employees to participate in learning activities and share success and failure stories throughout the company (Chapman and Hyland 2004; Beretta 2019; Zhu et al. 2019).

At this point, we would like to emphasize again that these platforms should not be confused with other digital communication systems, such as videoconferencing, e-mail, and chat tools, which often already exist in companies. On the one hand, interactions via such tools only serve to exchange information with a specific number of people and not to disseminate information to all people within the company like digital platforms do; on the other hand, these interactions are not centrally coordinated, but platforms are. A dissemination of information that can be coordinated by a moderator is important to effectively accelerate cultural renewal and successfully achieve digital transformation. Digital platforms, like online idea contests and learning platforms, can offer exactly that. They can be designed to primarily promote company-wide exchange specifically on topics such as digital transformation. Thereby, digital platforms can also be used as an indicator for how well the digital transformation is set in motion, as participation rates and participant behavior can be tracked on digital platforms. If not already read, we recommend the gray box entitled "What can a digital platform accomplish? A hands-on perspective" in the fundamentals section of this chapter, as it illustrates vividly what a digital platform can contribute to cultural renewal.

In the next sections, we will elaborate step by step how companies can set up and operate a well-integrated and functioning platform in the company. Since the planning and development of a digital platform is an extensive undertaking and depends strongly on the organizational boundaries, the available budget, and the specific range of functionalities the platform should entail, we focus on the five most important aspects that should be considered when setting up and running any digital platform as we define it. The focus hereby lies on creating the most intensive exchange possible between all people in the company to accelerate cultural renewal and, thus, also the digital transformation. That the digital platforms can also be used for other purposes, such as the development of new products, services, and business models, is thereby neglected to better focus on the cultural renewal perspective.

In sections "Analyze the Digital Platform Landscape" and "Clear Responsibilities and Efficient Resource Allocation", we derive what needs to be considered to build up digital platforms. This includes primarily an analysis of the company's existing platform landscape ("Analyze the Digital Platform Landscape") as well as the allocation of responsibilities and a deliberate balancing of priorities in relation to the available resources and their use ("Clear Responsibilities and Efficient Resource Allocation"). Section "Activate People" then explains how platforms can be operated successfully once built up, especially how to activate people to use the platform.

Analyze the Digital Platform Landscape

A first major step before implementing digital platforms is to analyze the company's digital platform landscape. It happens frequently that a multitude of potentially relevant platforms are already being used in a rather local, small-scale setup throughout the company. Moreover, it is not uncommon for different departments to have separate licenses for the same software combined with non-uniform processes with which they meet their specific needs. Consequently, providing transparency into the company's digital platform landscape can have several advantages: First, platforms that have already been introduced locally offer the opportunity to test their suitability for the envisioned functionalities and also for scaling them up to a company-wide variant. Second, redundancies can be eliminated, and application gaps closed to create a uniform system that is not only easier to manage but that can also be more cost-effective. Third, platforms that have already been implemented offer a unique opportunity to build on the implementation success in the relevant departments and, thus, increase the acceptance of company-wide variants that are implemented later on. However, even more potential can be unlocked:

From Three in Three Make Four in One

In the discussion with practitioners, we were presented with a case in which the company-wide analysis of existing tools—as a mandatory step before the intended introduction of a new learning and exchange platform—brought interesting benefits. As already anticipated, the company could achieve considerable savings by merging single licenses, as this platform was already used independently in three different departments. However, the actually more valuable advantage was a completely different one: As also suspected, the acceptance for this platform was already very high in all three departments. However, what the people in charge had not expected, was the community that had already developed around the platform in the three departments. Not only did the company-wide version of the platform connect these three communities with each other on one platform, which meant that a large number of users were active on the platform right from the start, but the three communities even joined together and two of them also promoted the

(continued)

platform in other departments. Thereby, not only could costs be saved, synergies be developed, and existing acceptance be used, but the new platform also spread in the company, to a certain extent solely through the existing community.

Companies should not underestimate the advantage of an existing community that actively promotes the platform. A platform without active users hardly offers any added value and new, potential users who consequently usually do not remain active on the platform for long. However, if a large community is already active on the platform and consciously integrates new users, the probability is much higher than new users will remain active on the platform in the long term. This effect is also known as network effects and describes, in this case, how the benefit that a user derives from a platform increases when the number of other users increases.

Clear Responsibilities and Efficient Resource Allocation

In order to successfully run a platform, a company must answer two key questions that many companies face in this context: Who is responsible for which part of the process and how should one prioritize the available resources? Especially when companies introduce new supporting infrastructure, tools, or platforms as part of the digital transformation, the question regarding responsibilities for these new elements arise.

A question that often has to be answered during implementation is: Who is responsible for the platform implementation and who takes responsibility for the day-to-day operation? In a number of companies, the term "digital" appears to lead to an irreversible association with IT. This also means that the IT department is often considered as responsible for the company's entire digital transformation. This is wrong and usually will not work either. Digital transformation is neither an IT initiative nor a purely tech-centric activity. The digital transformation affects the entire company—the alignment of the business models to digital business models as well as the digitization of working methods. Digital transformation is, thus, about transforming the business and the people and, hence, it also goes along with a cultural renewal. Companies must identify and analyze the impact of this transformation on the business, the people, and the culture to be able to address the impacts proactively and involve the relevant functions that then also share responsibility.

Only in very few cases, there is an end-to-end responsibility. Owing to multiple internal stakeholders being involved, it is more likely that the responsibility for different steps is split between different functions in the firm. This lack of clarity is reinforced by the involved functions and departments having different processes and structures and often suffering from a lack of flexibility, which makes it difficult to work together smoothly. Furthermore, there is also often a lack of collaboration and communication between departments, which could have been avoided by an at least somewhat pronounced innovation climate (see Fig. 3).

Everything stated thus far can be applied on a general level to the digital transformation in a company as well as to single steps of the digital transformation such as the introduction of platforms to support the generation of ideas. Since this article is about tapping the corporate brain, we stick to the example of introducing an online ideation platform. All the distractions that homemade firm-internal complexity brings about form the actual task of driving the digital transformation by implementing and operating the ideation platform without friction. In order to reduce complexity and thus friction, and to allow to focus on digital transformation and boost the latter, an increasing number of companies create organizational structures that often manifest themselves in (central) digital/innovation labs. If these labs come along with clearly defined competencies and responsibilities, they set the scene for a focus on content and the people as source of creativity.

Stuck in the Middle? Platforms Between Exploration and Exploitation
One of the companies we spoke to face an unequivocal question: "Should we focus our resources on digital transformation and develop new business areas through innovation activities or should we focus on making the core business more efficient?"

This is a question that many companies have to ask or have already asked themselves. The answer the company had was pretty simple: It is both. The company's managers decided not to rely on only one or the other but to pursue both goals simultaneously. This approach demands, on the one hand, a clear differentiation of the various functions, while, on the other hand, a close coordination is indispensable in order to be able to leverage synergies and avoid inefficient overlaps. In the case of this company, a newly founded corporate innovation lab has been mandated. This innovation lab was tasked to connect both worlds and facilitate their interactions in order to maximize the overall impact on the company. Both worlds have very different, sometimes contradicting requirements that cannot simply be reconciled. Understanding these requirements and mediating these two areas of interest is a challenging, yet important step between the exploitation of the core business and the exploration of new businesses enabled by the digital transformation. What, therefore, did this innovation lab do to overcome the hurdles?

The company began to create an ideation ecosystem by introducing a company-wide idea platform that was accessible to every employee. To avoid friction between the IT department and the innovation lab, they decided that the IT department would provide and operate the platform and be responsible for software maintenance (e.g., updates) and technical user requests. All content-specific topics were, in turn, handled by the central innovation lab,

(continued)

with the aim of providing the ideators with a one-stop solution to ensure optimal support for their ideas.

Through this ecosystem, the IT department and the central innovation lab tried to bring the two perspectives together and consciously arrange for an exchange of both views. Thereby, both worlds should understand each other better and collaborate more easily. Several of the formats on the platform were even deliberately designed to pinpoint the conflict between the two sides and to find supporters from both sides. This was done to create as much attention as possible throughout the company and to stimulate a vigorous discourse. During such discourses, a lot of effort was invested in finding a mutual solution and, thus, prejudices from both sides—for example, that radical innovations always lead to the loss of jobs in the core business—were resolved and more understanding was created. In addition to the digital exchange, the IT department and the central innovation lab also invested a lot of effort in involving middle management in reflections and decision-making processes, as these often represent a major barrier when it comes to implementing innovations in the company later on.

Focusing on both exploration and exploitation at the same time without increasing the available resources can require prioritization of how available capacities ought to be used. There is no right or wrong—the firm's preconditions will determine which focus will be set. For the platform's success, it is important to create the necessary traffic by activating people to participate.

Activate People

If there are no people, there are no interactions. Moreover, without interactions, there is no platform use and, even more so, no cultural renewal. It is self-evident—and therefore almost superfluous—to emphasize that people represent the company's most important resource. Without the employees' consent, no new technology can be successfully implemented and without their conviction, the new technology will not be used properly. In terms of digital platforms, this means that employees will not exchange information via the platforms. However, cultural renewal only occurs in the first place when employees share their convictions.

There are two moments in the process where people can be consciously activated: before they decide to exchange ideas on platforms and while they are busy exchanging ideas. A strong innovation climate already addresses the first moment subconsciously (see step one: innovation climate). However, companies can also consciously encourage employees and leadership to exchange ideas on the platforms, for example, through ignition workshops as the following example illustrates.

Ignition: That Is How Fireworks Happen!

In 2017, one of our international case companies conducted a highly strategic and well-promoted digital research and development (R&D) idea contest to discover, promote, and drive radical and disruptive innovations. As with any digital exchange platform, participation in such international, company-wide competitions always leads to a strong exchange between people who have never spoken before to each other in the company. Ideas and convictions are exchanged and cultivated: the basis for cultural renewal.

The organizer team toured the company's various locations and conducted ignition workshops to encourage people to participate in the idea contest. The objective of these workshops was to enthuse both employees and managers about the competition and encourage them to exchange ideas on the platform. During the workshops, the organizer team also presented the idea competition's core search fields and then actively supported the ideators in the idea generation process to directly overcome the first hurdle of participation.

To foster collaboration between the participating employees and stimulate communication and interaction, the moderators actively engage in the discussion. By setting impulses and stimulating and guiding the discussions, the value of the idea generation's and participation's output increased.

In fact, the literature shows that such ignition workshops can increase both participation and the quality of ideas. Above all, however, ignition workshops increase the sharing of ideas on the platform, thus further promoting a knowledge and value exchange (Kruft and Kock 2019b). The increased number of interactions through such workshops primarily results from an increase in people's self-efficacy (faith in oneself and one's convictions). Through appreciation, active motivation, and the promotion of self-confidence, ignition workshops can increase self-efficacy and, thereby, overcome the resistance that has thus far prevented people from sharing their views on the platform (Larson 1989; Northcraft and Ashford 1990; Bandura 1997). These workshops' effects are further enhanced by the organizing team taking the extra effort to actually be active on the ground everywhere. This willingness to invest shows the commitment by the company and emphasizes the importance of the workshops' purpose—the exchange of information between people on the platform (Rhoades and Eisenberger 2002).

However, it does not always have to be extensive and expensive workshops. Especially when many people from all over the company are already active on the platform, there is something more substantial that motivates them to continue sharing convictions and knowledge: motives, which are "reasons people hold for initiating and performing voluntary behavior" (Reiss 2004, p. 179). To make this intangible term more manageable, it is advisable to split it up. Reiss (2004) distinguishes 16 different motives that drive people. Tasks, goals, or problems, which actively address these motives, will profit almost automatically from being

Table 1 Motives addressed by digital platforms; according to Reiss (2004) and Kruft (2020)

Motive	Explanation	Intrinsic feeling
Curiosity	Desire for knowledge and discovery	Wonder
Social Contact	Desire for peer companionship and exchange	Fun
Idealism	Desire for altruism, justice, and to improve society	Compassion
Appreciation	Desire for approval and support	Self-confidence
Status	Desire for social standing and attention	Self-importance
Power	Desire to influence (including leadership)	Efficacy
Challenge	Desire to even the score (including desire to compete, to win)	Vindication

tackled, aimed at, or solved. Digital platforms have an inherent potential to address at least seven of these motives (see Table 1), thereby disclosing a strong potential for the intrinsic motivation of individuals to participate in activities on these platforms (Vroom 1964; Kruft 2020).

The motive *curiosity* means the desire to learn purely for the sake of learning. Curious people are eager for knowledge and interested in finding out the truth or discovering new experiences. They become bored more quickly with routine tasks. The motive *social contact* is about striving for contact, interaction, and exchange with others. People with this motive usually have a high level of social competence, are friendly, sociable, and extroverted. *Idealism* means the need for social justice and fairness. People who have a strong pronounced motive for idealism want to contribute to the welfare of humanity and make the world a better place. People with a pronounced motive for *appreciation* strive for high self-esteem, which bases on the feedback of others. People with a strong pronounced motive for appreciation feel good when others support and confirm them. Striving for *status* means the desire for prestige in the social hierarchy. People with a high motive for status either want to do more or gain more than others and be respected for it. Status can be experienced and lived out materially or immaterially. Immaterial can be pride in skills, titles, or membership in a group or organization. The motive *power* means the desire for influence and challenges. People with this motive have the ambition to perform excellently. They want to lead others, take responsibility, and take control. A highly pronounced motive for power also means to stand up for one's convictions. The motive for *challenge* means wanting to win or defend oneself. People with a high pursuit of revenge like to compete with others. They are driven to top performance through competition. It is important for them to assert themselves and not to run away from offensive behavior (Reiss 2004).

How, therefore, can digital platforms inherently address these motives and easily motivate a multitude of different personalities to exchange ideas on digital platforms? *Addressing curiosity and social contacts:* Digital platforms offer various possibilities to facilitate and stimulate the search for new discoveries and to exchange ideas with others along the way. On the one hand, digital platforms offer access to large networks (Katz and Shapiro 1985), which have a wider reach than is possible at the workplace, and they offer many opportunities to make new social contacts (Rode 2016). On the other hand, digital platforms enable the integration of databases, trend scouts, intelligent search algorithms, and other tools that make new knowledge easier to access (Honig 2001; Chapman and Hyland 2004).

Addressing Idealism People with a distinct desire to help other people and contribute to a better world are encouraged on digital platforms. This encouragement takes place by giving them the opportunity to contribute to other ideas, help solve problems, and contribute with their own ideas. Moreover, digital platforms often make problems accessible to a large number of people at the outset, increasing the likelihood that the problems will be solved (Björk and Magnusson 2009). Such an environment fosters a commitment to help and collaborate with others and, conversely, to take more risks, which is a fertile basis for a fruitful exchange (Baer and Frese 2003).

Addressing Appreciation and Status On digital platforms, each activity is visible to everyone in the company. By using rewards, such as badges, ranks, or titles, employees can be rewarded for their dedication on the platform (Nicholson 2015). Rewards especially motivate people who strive for appreciation and status. Furthermore, the platforms' ease of use usually leads to fast and frequent feedback (Nylén and Holmström 2015; Zhu et al. 2019), as transaction costs and the effort for digital feedback are lower than those for offline feedback. According to Janssen (2000), open-minded exchange occurs when the relationship between effort expended and reward received is beneficial to the participants. If employees receive more and at the same time more visible rewards due to digital platforms, they perceive their own activities as more valuable, rewarding, and motivating—and therefore they more willing to continue to engage on the platform (Eisenberger and Selbst 1994; Eisenberger 2003; Fuller et al. 2006).

Addressing Power and Challenge In recent years, a growing field of research has focused on the gamification of digital content and, as an important part of this, on how to consciously challenge participants to stimulate their activities in digital media (Nicholson 2015). Time constraints, endless opportunities, difficult challenges, and benchmarking with other people on the platform can stimulate people who pursue motives of power and challenge. The ability of digital platforms to increase the activities' visibility, reach, and comparability in a network can increase the challenge among employees and, thus, their motivational power (Vroom 1964; Reiss 2004).

Even if platforms already inherently promote many of the motives mentioned, there is still a need for active moderation of interactions on digital platforms. Only then is it possible to ensure that the exchange of ideas is on the right track toward the targeted cultural renewal. The following practice case illustrates this in more detail.

The Moderator on the Back Seat

During our studies, we talked with several moderators of digital platforms, especially idea contests, who shared their experience with us. The moderators usually control the idea exchange process through targeted idea campaigns that are advertised on the company's intranet before their official launch. These campaigns are conducted to promote topic-specific exchange and to elicit new ideas for specific search fields. To allow the ideators to concentrate, large campaigns involving people from all business units of the company are organized such that they do not overlap. "For me, a campaign is not only about evaluating but also about enriching," said one of the moderators in this context.

Based on the firms we talked to, a timely and fast further development of the ideas is important in order to use the momentum generated in the idea generation phase and to maintain the motivation of the employees for further participation. "However, if you do not address the momentum immediately, discussions can develop a dynamic of their own that may no longer be conducive to achieve the set goals. [...] Occasionally, however, there are great discussions that we then mark as 'hot' so that many participants can see them and be inspired by them."

To keep motivation high on digital platforms, it is important to value all thoughts. "With a third of the ideas, maybe even a little less, we had most of the work, because we did not want to throw someone out by saying: 'Well, that' is inadequate, not enough elaboration.' [...] We actually tried to say: 'Idea first' [...] and really tried to reward those who take the plunge with new thoughts by giving them attention, understanding what they try to tell us, and then to help accordingly." Another moderator described this feeling quite aptly: "It is like steering a car without being behind the steering wheel. The participants themselves have to do it, otherwise they quickly lose their motivation."

5 Step 3: Continuity—Enabling a Sustainable Transformation

Once the company has arrived at this point, it is well on the way to becoming a real cultural athlete. Athletes who achieved a certain performance level want to keep it in the long term and even increase it further—this is also the case with digital transformation enabled by cultural renewal. To anchor the achievements, firms would usually rely on the third step of Lewin's (1951) change model: unfreeze, change, refreeze—and try to cement what has been achieved. However, this idea is only half the truth because a company should never stagnate but rather concentrate on being continuously in motion. In the context of digital transformation, the final status is not set since the world constantly evolves as is the case with the digital transformation already for more than 20 years (Schallmo and Williams 2018). Firms—depending on the level from which they start—usually have to invest a lot of effort into the digital transformation to catch up with their peers. As shown in the previous sections, it is often quite difficult to implement the necessary infrastructure, on the one hand, and to create the cultural prerequisites, on the other hand, to bring the digital transformation to a level that allows the generation of added value. Therefore, companies have to ensure that the level of digital transformation that has been achieved is not only maintained but even constantly increased. The ultimate goal would, therefore, be to anchor a digital process of cultural renewal in the company's DNA and embrace it on a daily basis (Kruft and Kock 2019c; Kruft 2020). Consequently, a company is prepared not only for further digital trends but also for other future megatrends, as the company's progress is continuously driven forward and the culture continuously renewed by employees and managers alike.

In order to maintain the process of cultural renewal in the company in the long term, three things are particularly important as we will explain in the following sections. In section "Retain Fairness and Balance", we address an important aspect that especially increases the self-sustaining character of the cultural renewal process and can, thus, save the company active maintenance costs if the systems are designed correctly: the retention of fairness and balance. In section "Think of the Journey as the Reward", we explain why it is important that people in the company, especially managers, understand the journey as the goal and why employees should not think too much about the cultural goal at all. Section "Face the Long Run" then focuses on the long run, which does not mean cultural renewal has to take a long time to happen but rather that it is important to keep an eye on future trends and be aware of the long-term consequences of continuous renewal.

Retain Fairness and Balance

Good prerequisites for the sustainability of digital platforms and their positive impact on employee behavior and culture are the motivation of the involved employees and their enjoyment of working on the platform. Generally speaking, simply providing the tool is not enough—specifications for its use must also be made. In addition to the platform as the necessary infrastructure, digital transformation requires rules and processes that define how to use the infrastructure. These rules and processes need to embody fairness and the belief that there is a balance between what the people invest and what they gain. Maintaining fairness and balance is the main reason why the process of cultural renewal is not completely self-sustaining because fairness and balance unfortunately do not arise automatically in digital systems where many people with different perspectives exchange thoughts. If fairness and balance are not actively monitored, this leads to deviant behavior and distrust, neither of which promotes healthy cultural renewal (Füller 2012; Kruft et al. 2019).

Deviance is a fundamental challenge: Digital platforms usually have clear rules and objectives that serve as a guideline for appropriate behavior. With regard to the platform's objectives, the company and the participants also build common expectations about the appropriateness of contributions. Disregarding these rules and expectations—for example, by sharing defamatory content—constitutes deviant behavior, which can lead to the community's mood turning bad or its motivation to collapse. Deviant behavior must therefore be actively addressed or removed by the moderators. However, deviant behavior is not always bad (Wolf and Zuckerman 2012). Not only humorous or provocative contributions but also deviance from social or technical norms can certainly initiate completely new perspectives, encourage reflection on issues, and spread these thoughts throughout the company. Gatzweiler et al. (2017, p. 781) describe a vivid example where, on a platform from Volkswagen, new ideas and prototypes for apps of Volkswagen's future infotainment system were explored:

> Among the 96 suggested prototypes was a 'worst possible front seat passenger.' The app consisted of a virtual avatar, which should help to improve drivers' skills and prevents them from getting bored; it included characters such as 'mom' or husband.

This deviant idea appeared to strike a certain chord, as it was taken up and developed further by others. Therefore, deviant behavior has to be distinguished very carefully such that it does not nip potential ideas in the bud that might be relevant for the business later on.

Another fundamental challenge is distrust. Distrust can simply mean that people are afraid to raise their voices on a company-wide digital platform because they fear personal consequences. Distrust can, however, also mean that people do not believe the company will be able to acknowledge the real potential of their ideas or that the company will not recognize them as originators of their ideas, for example, in terms of reputation or intellectual property ownership, if the company decides to develop them further (Gilliland 1993). Both aspects depend strongly on how fairly the participants feel treated on the platform. People who feel unfairly treated will initiate efforts to restore fairness—and if this is not possible, they will seek means to end the conflict. This can either end in no longer using the platform or, in addition, resigning from work. In contrast, if people feel valued and treated fairly by the company and the other platform participants, this can increase loyalty and identification with the company, which can lead to greater engagement on the platform and in the workplace (Franke et al. 2013). The importance of trust in an increasingly digital world and the resulting importance of a strong corporate culture are also reflected in PwC's Annual Global CEO Survey (Donkor et al. 2017):

> 69% of CEOs say that it's more difficult for business to gain and retain trust in a digitized world and 93% of CEOs say that it's therefore important to have a strong corporate purpose that's reflected in their organization's values, culture and behavior.

It becomes clear how serious the consequences can be if fairness and balance are not maintained. Therefore, this task must not be neglected but actively managed. In many firms, a central innovation unit carries out the platform management. Employees of these units not only define and monitor the processes and rules but also act as moderators and facilitators on the digital platform. Owing to the permanent monitoring of the platform, the innovation unit's employees can also develop an understanding of the digital transformation's progress and, in the event of opposing trends, set new impulses. Even without having to react to opposing trends, the moderators can provide impulses to initiate an exchange between employees and promote discussions. However, this task presents an enormous challenge, as the team, in most cases, lack the time, expertise, information, and/or motivation to address all the issues on the platform in a balanced and fair manner (Kruft et al. 2019). It is, therefore, especially important to be always transparent to the participants on the platform and to set incentives such that the participants can regulate their behavior as much as possible by themselves. In this manner, the effort of the moderator teams can be limited. The following practical example gives insight into how this could be implemented.

Define the Rules of the Game: For Both Sides

A company that prepared the launch of an ideation platform shared a few of their thoughts with us. Based on conversations with their employees as pre-launch preparation, it became obvious by this time that the use of a platform always requires users to not only trust the technology but also to trust in the fair treatment of the information and data entered. The manager of the company said: "Imagine what happens if the employees think of the idea platform as a kind of black box into which information is entered, but without knowing what consequences or relevance this has for you and what actually happens to the idea? That would certainly mean the end of the platform before it was really launched." Thus, the company invested effort in defining clearly formulated rules. These rules created the necessary transparency regarding the selection processes on the platform and the use of the data provided by the employees. Nevertheless, the company even went one step further by not only encouraging participation through transparency and clear rules of the game but also by implementing an incentive model to motivate employee participation. Special consideration was given to the question of how to strengthen the ideators' trust in this model. The solution to the problem of determining who submitted the idea first was a time stamp that uniquely assigns an idea to one or more employees when submitting an idea. This incentive model was also an answer to the employees' question regarding the balance of the effort the employees invest on the platform and the benefits they could achieve through their participation. The company is convinced that full transparency and the commitment of the company to seriously appreciate their ideas lead to a greater exchange on the platform. In fact, it was also the time stamp that motivated people to actively develop their ideas via the platform since it was always possible to prove in case of doubt what their contribution to the idea was.

Think of the Journey as the Reward

To regard the journey as the actual goal is just as important on the company level as on the people level. On a company level, thinking of the journey as the reward means having stamina. However, it also means to adjust to completely new perspectives from a value-creation perspective, which can drastically shift the core business. At Siemens, their digital factory initiative, which was announced in 2014, already accounted for 26% of total business revenue in 2019. Fujifilm transforms from a photography-centric firm to a healthcare and medical imaging company, which already accounts for 18% of their total revenue. Even companies that can already be described as digital continue to transform themselves. Adobe currently generates 27% of its total revenues with "digital experiences." In 2019, Netflix repositioned itself with original content that now accounts for 44% of its total revenues. Dell shifted from being a hardware company to being a cloud business, already generating 51% of its revenues with infrastructure and security (Anthony et al. 2019a).

It is neither the goal of these companies to generate 100% of their revenues from these new areas nor would it make sense: When the companies reach this point, there would be new trends to which they would have to adapt. It is, instead, more likely the goal of these companies to always be on a journey—the journey into the future in which the company performs even better.

Reflecting on this chapter's content, it is not surprising that companies like the abovementioned, which outperform their own transformation, grant their corporate culture a higher rank: They developed a culture that guides strategic decisions and brings clarity to daily tasks. One such example is Siemens (Anthony et al. 2019b, p. 6):

> Infusing a higher purpose into [Siemens' culture] called for pushing decision making out from the center to every business unit, so that managers and rank-and-file employees feel they have a stake in future success.

This cultural renewal spurred plans to divest the core oil and gas business and to shift capital to the Digital Industries and Smart Infrastructure businesses, which focus on energy efficiency, electric vehicle mobility, distributed power supply, and renewable energy storage (Anthony et al. 2019b). Such a significant change in the core business can, however, only work if the people develop with it; or even better, if the people in the company provide the impetus for these changes by themselves. Bernard Meyerson (2016, p. 30), Chief Innovation Officer at IBM, explains very well how important people are for the company:

> IBM has been innovating and reinventing itself for more than 100 years, and we've learned a great deal along the way about what it takes to innovate and to make innovation a part of our company's DNA. There are a number of key elements required to innovate, but the most important of them is people. People innovate. [. . .] I was a bench scientist, a physicist, for ten

years, and I loved it. I would love to go play with such things again today. However, my impact scales a lot better if I help a hundred or a thousand people do a great job than if I, as one physicist, do a great and glorious bit of personal research on my own. We all owe this support to the next generation.

This long-term perspective, which is entirely focused on employee development, shows the direction that managers should take to promote new long-term perspectives among employees. The journey and not the goal is the main focus: This is equally important at both the company level and the people level. This definitely does not mean that companies like Siemens and IBM did not have a goal in mind during their decade-long development journeys—otherwise they probably would not have been successful. Instead, it means that the idea should not be allowed to arise that management should dictate these goals to employees; in fact, the management should rather encourage employees such that they themselves come up with the new goals and carry them forward by means of a bottom-up approach (Kruft and Kock 2019c). This discrepancy also becomes apparent when we explore the differences in perception in corporate culture. Strategy& found in a global study that only about 40% of employees believe that corporate culture is lived as it is claimed, while over 70% of top management believes it is (Katzenbach 2018). This illustrates the relevance for a cultural renewal process very well: Living and continuously renewing culture does not mean that values are not only dictated top-down but rather that they are the result of how both management and employees live the values (see Fig. 1). This bilateral perspective on cultural development is the most effective means to ensure that the company does not leave its employees behind on their journey to address trends like digital transformation, and that the workforce always supports the company's goals, as these goals are the result of collaborative interactions about new perspectives as part of the employees' daily lives. Moreover, when the journey instead of the goal is celebrated, employees might no longer feel frustrated by chasing ever newer and faster trends that they believe they will never reach before the next goal is set.

Since people are very important for both cultural renewal and for corporate strategy development (Besson and Rowe 2012; Rowles and Brown 2017; Anthony et al. 2019b; Kruft and Kock 2019c), companies should also place a high value on empowering their employees as much as possible and providing them with the right tools and knowledge they need to take the right steps and draw the right conclusions. This can also be achieved via digital platforms, but only if the people in the company have already opened up to this technology well enough (see Fig. 3). The following example illustrates this approach.

Empowering People: Starting the Engine Instead of Pushing the Car

"I do not want to change employees—I want to equip them for our journey." This is a statement we heard from a manager when we asked her about the company's digital transformation. Since not all people are equally innovative, neither the employees nor the managers, a necessary step to embrace transformation is to empower the people to participate in innovation activities by educating them on platforms, processes, or even specific technological trends and topics as food for thought. Her company developed a dedicated platform to transfer the relevant knowledge to the people and also to allow them sharing their insights and thoughts on this new knowledge. The online training platform allows all employees—independent of their physical location, time zones, etc.—to access the relevant information at will. Another advantage of digital platforms for imparting knowledge becomes apparent in the current time during the pandemic when face-to-face training is difficult to implement and many companies have to switch to digital tools anyway.

Face the Long Run

The box entitled "Empowering people" focuses directly on the relevant topic for this section. Facing the long term does not mean to prepare for a lengthy cultural change; facing the long term means that the company should be aware of the long-term consequences of continuous renewal triggered by new trends from outside. As the corporate environment changes, so do the demands on the people in the company. Since the corporate culture is very people-driven, the new requirements are in constant interaction with the culture and influence each other: Not only do the new challenges influence the corporate culture, the corporate culture can also mitigate many new demands and compensate for their negative effects. An example of an employee clearly shows the consequences of new demands, in this instance a different skill set for coping with the digital transformation: "Previously a mechanic, nowadays a software engineer: Surely, this means a cultural change, as software engineers work differently and need a different working environment to that of mechanics" (Hartl 2019, p. 5). In this example, digital technologies were the driver for digital cultural change, which enabled new working practices but also required different skills. The different skills that were required led to changes in professional profiles and requirements.

This is not a unique case at all. In order to be armed for electromobility, Volkswagen currently prepares an entire site with 8000 employees to be ready for e-car production by 2021. Volkswagen thereby clearly demonstrates that it takes their employees with them into the new age (Volkswagen 2019). The example illustrates the following: While cultural renewal is initiated by employees and management alike, it is still the task of management to acknowledge the resulting consequences and address them in the overall interest of the company in order to be prepared for the future. However, "there is substantial evidence that some 70% of all change initiatives fail"—and evidence suggests that one "reason for this is a lack of alignment between the value system of the change intervention and of those members of an organization undergoing the change" (Burnes and Jackson 2011, p. 133). No matter how great the effort is that the company expends, the company can only remain an effective organization if goals and values stay consistent and are shared by the organization's leadership and employees through the change process (Detert et al. 2000; Burnes and Jackson 2011). Furthermore, the more exchange there is between people in the company, the sooner these values converge and the faster new impulses from outside are integrated.

What does this mean for companies in the long run? The more open the people in a company are to new perspectives in general, the easier it is for the company to take them on a journey—or do the people in the company perhaps take the company on a journey? If (1) the existing corporate culture promotes cultural renewal, (2) digital platforms accelerate the incorporation of upcoming trends just like the alignment of values within the company does, (3) skill sets are readily available to both managers and employees, and (4) the strategy of top management is an answer to the same upcoming trend, then it will probably be one and the same journey.

References

Abbey, A., & Dickson, J. W. (1983). R&D work climate and innovation in semiconductors. *Academy of Management Journal, 26*(2), 362–368.

Amabile, T. M. (1988). A model of creativity and innovation in organizations. *Research in Organizational Behavior, 10*, 123.

Amabile, T. M., Conti, R., Coon, H., Lazenby, J., & Herron, M. (1996). Assessing the work environment for creativity. *The Academy of Management Journal, 39*(5), 1154–1184.

Anthony, S. D., Trotter, A., Bell, R., & Schwartz, E. I. (2019a). The transformation 20—Strategic change rankings for 2019. In *Innosight—Strategy and innovation at Huron*.

Anthony, S. D., Trotter, A., & Schwartz, E. I. (2019b). The top 20 business transformations of the last decade. *Harvard Business Review*, 1–10.

Archer, M. S. (1995). *Realist social theory: The morphogenetic approach*. Cambridge: Cambridge University Press.

Archer, M. S. (1998). Addressing the cultural system. In: M. S. Archer, R. Bhaskar, A. Collier, T. Lawson, & A. Norrie (eds.) *Critical realism—Essential reading* (pp. 103–142).

Baer, M., & Frese, M. (2003). Innovation is not enough: Climates for initiation and psychological safety, process innovations, and firm performance. *Journal of Organizational Behavior, 24*(1), 45–68.

Baker, N. R., & Freeland, J. R. (1972). Structuring information flow to enhance innovation. *Management Decision, 19*(1), 105–116.

Bandura, A. (1997). *Self-efficacy: The exercise of control*. New York: Freeman.

Beretta, M. (2019). Idea Selection in Web-Enabled Ideation Systems. *Journal of Product Innovation Management, 36*(1), 5–23.

Besson, P., & Rowe, F. (2012). Strategizing information systems-enabled organizational transformation: A transdisciplinary review and new directions. *Journal of Strategic Information Systems, 21*(2), 103–124.

Björk, J., & Magnusson, M. (2009). Where do good innovation ideas come from? Exploring the influence of network connectivity on innovation idea quality. *Journal of Product Innovation Management, 26*(6), 662–670.

Burnes, B. & Jackson, P. (2011). Success and failure in organizational change: An exploration of the role of values. *Journal of Change Management*, 11 (2), 133–162.

Champagne, D., Leclerc, O., & Hung, A. (2015). *The road to digital success in pharma*. McKinsey Global Institute.

Chapman, R., & Hyland, P. (2004). Complexity and learning behaviors in product innovation. *Technovation, 24*(7), 553–561.

Claver, E., Llopis, J., Garcia, D., & Molina, H. (1998). Organizational culture for innovation and new technological behavior. *The Journal of High Technology Management Research, 9*(1), 55–68.

Coch, L., & French, J. R. P. (1948). Overcoming Resistance to Change. *Human Relations, 1*(4), 512–532.

Cockburn, A., & Highsmith, J. (2001). Agile software development, the people factor. *Computer, 34*(11), 131–133.

Craig, J. B., Pohjola, M., Kraus, S., & Jensen, S. H. (2014). Exploring relationships among innovation output in family and non-family firms. *Creativity and Innovation Management, 23* (2), 199–210.

Donkor, C., Slobodjanjuk, A., Cremer, K., & Weisshaar, J. (2017). The way we work – in 2025 and beyond. *HR Insights - PwC*, 1–33.

Damanpour, F. (1991). Organizational innovation: A meta-analysis of effects of determinants and moderators. *Academy of Management Journal, 34*(3), 555–590.

De Clercq, D., Menguc, B., & Auh, S. (2009). Unpacking the relationship between an innovation strategy and firm performance: The role of task conflict and political activity. *Journal of Business Research, 62*(11), 1046–1053.

Denis, J. L., Lamothe, L., & Langley, A. (2001). The dynamics of collective leadership and strategic change in pluralistic organizations. *Academy of Management Journal, 44*(4), 809–837.

Denison, D. R. (1996). What is the difference between organizational culture and climate? A native's point of view on a decade of paradigm wars. *Academy of Management Review, 21* (3), 619–654.

Detert, J. R., Schroeder, R. G., & Mauriel, J. J. (2000) A framework for linking culture and improvement initiatives in organizations. *Academy of Management Review, 25*(4), 850–863.

De Reuver, M., Sørensen, C., & Basole, R. C. (2018). The digital platform: A research agenda. *Journal of Information Technology, 33*(2), 124–135.

Dutton, J. E., & Duncan, R. B. (1987). The creation of momentum for change through the process of strategic issue diagnosis. *Strategic Management Journal, 8*(3), 279–295.

Edmondson, A. (2011). Strategies for learning from failure. *Harvard Business Review, 89*(4), 9.

Eisenberger, R. (2003). Motivation, reward and creativity. *Creativity Research Journal, 15*, 121–130.

Eisenberger, R., & Selbst, M. (1994). Does reward increase or decrease creativity? *Journal of Personality and Social Psychology, 66*(6), 1116–1127.

Ekvall, G. (1996). Organizational climate for creativity and innovation. *European Journal of Work and Organizational Psychology, 5*(1), 105–123.

Franke, N., Keinz, P., & Klausberger, K. (2013). "Does this sound like a fair deal?": Antecedents and consequences of fairness expectations in the individual's decision to participate in firm innovation. *Organization Science, 24*(5), 1495–1516.

Füller, J. (2012). *Die Gefahren des Crowdsourcing*. Harvard Business Manager.

Fuller, J. B., Marler, L. E., & Hester, K. (2006). Promoting felt responsibility for constructive change and proactive behavior: Exploring aspects of an elaborated model of work design. *Journal of Organizational Behavior, 27*(8), 1089–1120.

Gamber, M., Kruft, T., & Kock, A. (2020a). Balanced give and take—An empirical study on the survival of corporate incubators. *International Journal of Innovation Management*. https://doi.org/10.1142/S1363919620400058.

Gamber, M., Kruft, T., & Kock, A. (2020b). "Not-invented-here"—An empirical analysis of individual and climate-related antecedents. In: *Innovation and product development management conference (IPDMC)*.

Garcia-Granero, A., Llopis, O., Fernandez-Mesa, A., & Alegre, J. (2015). Unraveling the link between managerial risk-taking and innovation: The mediating role of a risk-taking climate. *Journal of Business Research, 68*(5), 1094–1104.

Gatzweiler, A., Blazevic, V., & Piller, F. T. (2017). Dark side or bright light: Destructive and constructive deviant content in consumer ideation contests. *Journal of Product Innovation Management, 34*(6), 772–789.

Gibbons, J. L., & Stiles, D. A. (2004). The thoughts of youth: Adolescents' ideal man and ideal woman in international perspective.

Gilbert, C. G. (2005). Unbundling the structure of inertia: Resource versus routine rigidity. *Academy of Management Journal, 48*(5), 741–763.

Gilliland, S. W. (1993). The perceived fairness of selection systems: An organizational justice perspective. *The Academy of Management Review, 18*(4), 694.

Hannan, M. T., & Freeman, J. (1984). Structural inertia and organizational change. *American Sociological Review, 49*(2), 16.

Hartl, E. (2019, August). A characterization of culture change in the context of digital transformation. In *Twenty-fifth Americas conference on information systems* (pp. 1–10).

Hemerling, J., Kilmann, J., Danoesastro, M., Stutts, L., & Ahern, C. (2018). It's not a digital transformation without a digital Culture. *Boston Consulting Group*, 1–11.

Hernández-Mogollon, R., Cepeda-Carrión, G., Cegarra-Navarro, J. G., & Leal-Millán, A. (2010). The role of cultural barriers in the relationship between open-mindedness and organizational innovation. *Journal of Organizational Change Management, 23*(4), 360–376.

Hess, T., Matt, C., Benlian, A., & Wiesböck, F. (2019). Options for formulating a digital transformation strategy. *MIS Quarterly, 15*(2), 123–125.

Hogan, S. J., & Coote, L. V. (2014). Organizational culture, innovation, and performance: A test of Schein's model. *Journal of Business Research, 67*(8), 1609–1621.

Honig, B. (2001). Learning strategies and resources for entrepreneurs and intrapreneurs. *Entrepreneurship: Theory & Practice, 26*(1), 21–35.

Iansiti, M., & Lakhani, K. R. (2014). Digital ubiquity: How connections, sensors, and data are revolutionizing business. *Harvard Business Review, 92*(11), 91–99.

Janssen, O. (2000). Job demands, perceptions of effort—reward fairness and innovative work behaviour. *Journal of Occupational and Organisational Psychology, 73*, 287–302.

Kahn, K. B. (2001). Market orientation, interdepartmental integration, and product development performance. *Journal of Product Innovation Management, 18*(5), 314–323.

Katz, M. L., & Shapiro, C. (1985). Network externalities, competition, and compatibility. *The American Economic Review, 75*(3), 424–440.

Katzenbach, J., (2018). *Global culture survey*. Strategy & Katzenbach Center.

Klein, K. J., & Sorra, J. S. (1996). The challenge of innovation implementation. *Academy of Management Review, 21*(4), 1055–1080.

Kruft, T. (2020). Digital platforms: Toward an efficient way to trigger employees' innovative behavior. In *Corporate incubation: How centralized, employee-focused innovation activities enhance the hosting companies' innovativeness* (pp. 81–110). TUprints.

Kruft, T., & Kock, A. (2019a). Towards a comprehensive categorization of corporate incubators: Evidence from cluster analysis. *International Journal of Innovation Management, 24* (8), 1–28.

Kruft, T., & Kock, A. (2019b). Exchange but stay focused: How social learning and workshop participation affect submission quality and quantity in corporate ideation contests. In: *The European Academy of Management Conference (EURAM)*.

Kruft, T., &Kock, A. (2019c). Behavioral change of innovation climate: How employee-focused, centralized innovation activities affect organizational innovation climate. In: *Innovation and product development management conference (IPDMC)*.

Kruft, T., Gamber, M., & Kock, A. (2018). Substitutes or complements? The role of corporate incubator support and innovation climate for innovative behavior in the hosting firm. *International Journal of Innovation Management, 22* (5), 1–29.

Kruft, T., Tilsner, C., Schindler, A., & Kock, A. (2019). Persuasion in corporate idea contests: the moderating role of content scarcity on decision making. *Journal of Product Innovation Management, 36*(5), 560–585.

Larson, J. R. (1989). The dynamic interplay between employees 'feedback-seeking strategies and supervisors' delivery of performance feedback. *Academy of Management Review, 14*(3), 408–422.

Lewin, K. (1951). Field theory in social science. In *Resolving social conflicts and field theory in social science*. American Psychological Association.

Lufthansa. (2020). Lufthansa decides on third package within restructuring program [online]. *Lufthansa Media Relations*. Available from: https://www.lufthansagroup.com/en/newsroom/releases/lufthansa-decides-on-third-package-within-restructuring-program.html.   Accessed 27 Oct 2020.

March, J. G., & Shapira, Z. (1987). Managerial perspectives on risk and risk taking. *Management Science, 33*(11), 1404–1418.

Mensmann, M., & Frese, M. (2019). Who stays proactive after entrepreneurship training? Need for cognition, personal initiative maintenance, and well-being. *Journal of Organizational Behavior, 40*(1), 20–37.

Meyerson, B. (2016). Embedding innovation in corporate DNA. *Research Technology Management, 59*(6), 30–35.

Nicholson, S. (2015). A recipe for meaningful gamification. In L. Wood & T. Reiners (Eds.), *Gamification in education and business* (pp. 1–20). New York: Springer.

Northcraft, G. B., & Ashford, S. J. (1990). The preservation of self in everyday life: The effects of performance expectations and feedback context on feedback inquiry. *Organizational Behavior and Human Decision Processes, 47*(1), 42–64.

Nylén, D., & Holmström, J. (2015). Digital innovation strategy: A framework for diagnosing and improving digital product and service innovation. *Business Horizons, 58*(1), 57–67.

O'Reilly, C. (1989). Corporations, culture, and commitment: motivation and social control in organizations. *California Management Review, 31*, 9–25.

Patterson, M. G., West, M. A., Shackleton, V. J., Dawson, J. F., Lawthom, R., Maitlis, S., Robinson, D. L., & Wallace, A. M. (2005). Validating the organizational climate measure: Links to managerial practices, productivity and innovation. *Journal of Organizational Behavior, 26*(4), 379–408.

Pflaeging, N., & Hermann, S. (2018). *Complexitools: How to (re)vitalize work and make organizations fit for a complex world*. Betacodex.

Porpora, D. V. (2013). Morphogenesis and social change. In M. S. Archer (Ed.), *Social morphogenesis* (pp. 25–37). Dordrecht: Springer.

Rai, A., & Tang, X. (2010). Leveraging IT capabilities and competitive process capabilities for the management of interorganizational relationship portfolios. *Information Systems Research, 21*(3), 516–542.

Reiss, S. (2004). Multifaceted nature of intrinsic motivation: The theory of 16 basic desires. *Review of General Psychology, 8*(3), 179–193.

Rhoades, L., & Eisenberger, R. (2002). Perceived organizational support: A review of the literature. *Journal of Applied Psychology, 87*(4), 698–714.

Rode, H. (2016). To share or not to share: The effects of extrinsic and intrinsic motivations on knowledge-sharing in enterprise social media platforms. *Journal of Information Technology, 31*(2), 152–165.

Rowles, D., & Brown, T. (2017). *Building digital culture: A practical guide to successful digital transformation*. London: Kogan Page.

Saleh, S. D., & Wang, C. K. (1993). The management of innovation: strategy, structure, and Organizational climate. *IEEE Transactions on Engineering Management, 40*(1), 14–21.

Schallmo, D. R. A., & Williams, C. A. (2018). *Digital transformation now! Guiding the successful digitalization of your business model*. Springer Briefs in Business.

Schein, E. H. (1985). *Organizational culture and leadership: A dynamic view*. San Francisco: Jossey-Bass.

Schein, E. H. (1996). Culture: The missing concept in organization studies. *Administrative Science Quarterly, 41*(2), 229.

Schippers, M. C., West, M. A., & Dawson, J. F. (2015). Team reflexivity and innovation. *Journal of Management, 41*(3), 769–788.

Sethi, R., Smith, D., & Park, W. (2001). Cross-functional product development teams, creativity, and the innovativeness of new consumer products. *Journal of Marketing Research, 38*(1), 73–85.

Siegel, S. M., & Kaemmerer, W. F. (1978). Measuring the perceived support for innovation in organizations. *Journal of Applied Psychology, 63*(5), 553–562.

Tellis, G. J., Prabhu, J. C., & Chandy, R. K. (2009). Radical innovation across nations: the preeminence of corporate culture. *Journal of Marketing, 73*(1), 3–23.

Tian, X., & Wang, T. Y. (2014). Tolerance for failure and corporate innovation. *Review of Financial Studies, 27*(1), 211–255.

Volkswagen. (2019). The largest training camp in the automotive industry [online]. *Volkswagen Newsroom.* https://www.volkswagen-newsroom.com/en/stories/the-largest-training-camp-in-the-automotive-industry-5533

Vroom, V. H. (1964). *Work and motivation.* New York: Wiley.

West, M. A. (2000). Reflexivity, revolution and innovation in work teams. In M. M. Beyerlein & D. A. Johnson (Eds.), *Product development teams* (pp. 1–29). Stamford, CT: JAI Press.

Wolf, B., & Zuckerman, P. (2012). Deviant heroes: Nonconformists as agents of justice and social change. *Deviant Behavior, 33*(8), 639–654.

Zhu, H., Kock, A., Wentker, M., & Leker, J. (2019). How does online interaction affect idea quality? The effect of feedback in firm-internal idea competitions. *Journal of Product Innovation Management, 36*(1), 24–40.

Dr. Tobias Kruft works as a business consultant in the domain of transformation architecture with focus on digital business models and innovation processes. Before, he was a post-doctoral researcher at the Technische Universität Darmstadt, Germany. His research focuses specifically on transformation processes reinforced by corporate incubators–including corporate entrepreneurship, ideation contests, innovation climate as well as strategic partnerships between organizations and start-ups.

Michael Gamber has been working in international consulting companies as well as in management functions in international companies in the last 15 years. Besides that he is an external doctoral student at Technische Universität Darmstadt, Germany. His practitioner and research focus are on corporate incubators and their interaction with the hosting company, innovation management and processes, innovation culture as well as the cooperation between companies and start-ups.

Development Process for Smart Service Strategies: Grasping the Potentials of Digitalization for Servitization

Christian Koldewey, Jürgen Gausemeier, Roman Dumitrescu, Hans Heinrich Evers, Maximilian Frank, and Jannik Reinhold

1   Introduction

In today's business environment, companies are more and more challenged to bring production in line with complex demands. This requires a substantial shift from the production of goods to the provision of knowledge-intensive systemic solutions (Morelli 2002). Servitization and digitalization—respectively Industry 4.0—are considered two of the most recent trends transforming industrial companies as well as whole industries. Managing these trends tends to be a great challenge for companies (Frank et al. 2019; Linz et al. 2017).

In terms of servitization, companies are changing their way of creating value by adding services to products (Baines et al. 2009). The concept of servitization was introduced by Vandermerwe and Rada, who stated that service should be an all pervasive part of the strategic mission and corporate planning (Vandermerwe and Rada 1988). Servitization is customer-driven, whether to improve the customer experience with product usage, to replace the purchase of a product with its use as a service, or to price the results of product usage (Vandermerwe and Rada 1988; Frank et al. 2019; Tukker 2004). The term servitization itself herby refers to the process shifting from a product-centric business to a service-centric approach (Kowalkowski et al. 2017). The resulting market offerings are called product-service-systems and are characterized as a marketable set of products and services capable of jointly fulfilling a user's need (Goedkoop et al. 1999). On the other hand, they can be also the result of service companies' "productization" of services (Baines et al. 2007).

Digitalization is an omnipresent phenomenon (Industry-Science Research Alliance 2013). It means representing, processing, storing, and communicating the widest range of matter, energy, and information as strings of ones and zeros

C. Koldewey (✉) · J. Gausemeier · R. Dumitrescu · H. H. Evers · M. Frank · J. Reinhold
Heinz Nixdorf Institute, University of Paderborn, Paderborn, Germany
e-mail: christian.koldewey@hni.upb.de

(Lyytinen et al. 2016). Hence, data becomes ubiquitous available, which creates vast opportunities for automation and interconnected systems (Böhmann et al. 2014). The exploitation of this convergence of the real and virtual world is to be expected one of the most powerful drivers for innovations in the years to come (Kagermann 2015). Resulting digital innovations are significantly new products or services that are either embodied in information and communication technology or enabled by them (Lyytinen et al. 2016).

Studies examining the potential of digitalization show that one of the most promising fields for digital technologies is industrial after-sales (Wee et al. 2016). In this field of tension, especially digital services that are interconnected with physical products ("smart services") gain in significance (Wünderlich et al. 2012). Hence, companies are well advised to complete their product and service portfolio with those smart services to remain competitive. However, until now, many pragmatic attempts to do so have failed because firms lack a resilient, competitive strategy for smart services (Biehl 2017). Thus, the research question arises *how can companies develop a suitable strategy to introduce smart services into the market and into the company itself?*

To answer that question, we propose a process model to develop smart service strategies. In this sense, we want to enable companies to tackle the mentioned challenges and improve their innovation capability.

The process model was developed using *the Design Research Methodology* (DRM) according to Blessing and Chakrabarti (2009). The DRM consists of four phases: (1) clarification of the research goal (CS), (2) First descriptive study (DS I), (3) Prescriptive study (PS), and (4) Second descriptive study (DS II). The clarification of the research goal includes the definition of the theoretical foundation, the state of the art, and the description of the goal (Sect. 1). The first descriptive study leads to a deeper understanding of the problem and the requirements for the methodological support derived from theory and practice (see Sect. 2). The methodology is developed during the prescriptive study and is based upon the experiences and requirements from DS I. The second descriptive study consists of the evaluation in practice (for PS & DS II see Sects. 3 and 4). By applying the methodology, the need for improvement is derived (Sect. 5). The research is part of a joint research project funded by the German ministry of education and research as well as the European Social Fund (ESF). Ten partners participate in the project: three research institutions, three technology suppliers as enablers, and four manufacturing companies as case studies.

2   Theoretical Background

In this chapter, the main topics of servitization, digitalization, and smart services are analyzed in order to create a common understanding and to derive requirements for the development of smart service strategies.

Servitization in Manufacturing Firms

The trend of servitization in business is increasingly visible across different industries and research disciplines (Martinez et al. 2017; Cusumano et al. 2015). Generally speaking the motives to do so are characterized as completive, demand-based, and economic (Oliva and Kallenberg 2003); and while differences may be dependent on the product complexity of the firms, they are ultimately unique and dependent on a number of factors (Raddats et al. 2016). In manufacturing firms, Cusumano and colleagues identify three categories of product-related services: (1) services, that smooth the product sale or usage without altering the product functionality significantly, (2) services, that adapt the product functionality, e.g., adding features, and (3) services, that substitute the purchase of the product (Cusumano et al. 2015). Those services are provided by service systems, which are "configurations of people, technologies, organizations and shared information, able to create and deliver value to providers, users, and other interested entities through services" (Maglio and Spohrer 2008). Consequently, because of these specificities of servitization, it is not that easy, nor natural, for a manufacturing firm to carry out a servitization strategy (Mathieu 2001). Various strategic avenues for extending the service business have been explored through service science, but at last, the performance of the service strategy heavily depends on its alignment with the determinants of service innovation (Lightfoot and Gebauer 2011). In recent years, technology (especially digital technology) is recognized as a central driver for novel service strategies (Huang and Rust 2017).

Digitalization of Market Offerings

Initially, the digitalization trend in the business to customer market became increasingly visible in the early 2000s with companies such as Amazon or eBay becoming popular. Nowadays, it is just as important in the manufacturing industry (Linz et al. 2017). This is expressed by wider popular terms like Internet of Things or Industry 4.0 (Kagermann et al. 2013). In relation to products there are numerous concepts (Novales et al. 2016); e.g., smart, connected products (Porter and Heppelmann 2015), intelligent technical systems (Gausemeier et al. 2014) or cyber-phyiscal systems (Broy 2010; Lee 2008). The resulting technical artifacts are increasingly equipped with globally usable digital functions in addition to their local physical functions (Anke and Krenge 2016; Fleisch et al. 2017). They combine the possibilities of embedded systems with global networks and create a direct link between the physical and digital world. Thus, they enable the monitoring and controlling of physical processes via communication over digital networks (Broy 2010; Lee 2008). Echterfeld and Gausemeier propose eight characteristics for digitized products based on a literature analysis: (1) adaptivity, (2) user-friendliness, (3) robustness, (4) foresightedness, (5) connectivity, (6) autonomy, (7) extensibility, and (8) multifunctionality (Echterfeld and Gausemeier 2018).

In terms of the digitalization of services, we follow Beverungen and colleagues, who define a digital service as the application of digital competencies through deeds, processes, and performances for the benefit of another entity or the entity itself (Beverungen et al. 2017). One of the most significant characteristics of digital services is that once they are developed and established, their upscaling cost should be ideally close to zero (Rifkin 2015). Basically, there are three use cases for digital services in manufacturing: improvement of the frontend operations, improvement of the backend operations, and introduction of new digitally enabled offerings (Coreynen et al. 2017). These characteristics make it obvious that CPS offers a significant potential for digital servitization (Mikusz 2014). Henceforth, the current level of digitalization of products, services, and processes calls for an integrated digital business strategy (Bharadwaj et al. 2013).

Smart Services as a Market Offering: An Update

The understanding of smart services has been evolving over time. Therefore, we updated this part of the paper to reflect the current understanding in the community. First, smart services were described by Allmendinger and Lombreglia, who understand them as data-based services. The data required to provide such a service comes from the sensors of an intelligent and networked product (Allmendinger and Lombreglia 2005). The term smart service originated from an evolution of various terms such as Teleservices, Remote Diagnostics, or Remote Services (Grubic 2014). The focus of the term formation was primarily on the term remote, which was intended to emphasize the spatial separation of the service provider and recipient (Klein 2017). Based on the initial definition by Allmendinger and Lombreglia, many other definitions emerged, that were refined and enriched by further characteristics. Figure 1 shows these characteristics which additionally are explained in the following. We differentiate between mandatory as well as conceivable characteristics. Most authors agree that a smart service is a digital, data-based service building up on some kind of product as a data provider. These mandatory characteristics are explained below:

- **Service Component:** The digital service component is the significant attribute of a smart service (Kampker et al. 2017). In addition, a physical service component is sometimes mentioned as a further (non-mandatory) component (Frank et al. 2018).
- **Data-Based:** Data is an essential requirement for smart services; it is the raw material (Oertel et al. 2015). From data the added value for the customer is derived (Steimel and Steinhaus 2017).
- **Type of Data Provider:** A physical product forms the basis for smart services. It is often mentioned differently in various sources: product or thing without any specifier (Frank et al. 2018), intelligent and/or networked product (Allmendinger and Lombreglia 2005; Tillotson and Lundin 2008; Wünderlich et al. 2015), Smart Products (Steimel and Steinhaus 2017) or CPS (Mittag et al. 2018) are common

Characteristics / Authors	Type of data provider				Service Component			Characteristics		Properties					
	Product / Thing	Networked product	Smart Product, intelligent product	Cyber-physical system (CPS)	Physical service is supplemented	Physical service is included	Digital service is a component	Independent market offering (service)	(Part of a) Product Service System	Data based	Smart Data	Customized	Platform based	Ecosystem	Different performance levels
SMART SERVICE WELT WORKING GROUP / ACATECH (2014)			X			X	X	(x)		X		X			
ACATECH (2018)		X					(x)	(x)	(x)	X	X	X			
ALLMENDINGER / LOMBREGLIA (2005)			X	X			(x)		(x)						
ANKE / KRENGE (2016)				X		X			X						
BARILE / POLSE (2010)	X					X	(x)						(x)		
BEVERUNGEN ET AL. (2017)			X		(x)	X	(x)		(x)					(x)	X
FRANK ET AL. (2018)	X				X	X	X	X		X					
JÜTTNER ET AL. (2017)			X			X	X		X	X	X	X	X		(x)
KAMPKER ET AL. (2017)			X		X	X			X	X			X		
KLEIN (2017), BIEHL (2017)		X					(x)	X		X					
MITTAG ET AL. (2018)	X	(x)				X	X		X	X					
OERTEL ET AL. (2015)			X				(x)	(x)		X	X				
PALUCH (2017)	X	(x)				X	(x)			X			(x)		X
RABE (2020)	X					X	X			X	X				
SCHÄFER ET AL. (2015)				X	(x)	(x)			X			(x)	X	X	(x)
STEIMEL / STEINHAUS (2017)			X				(x)	X		X					
STICH ET AL. (2019)	X					X	X		X	X		X			
TILLOTSON / LUDIN (2008)	X						(x)	X		(x)					
Percentage of mentions	39%	28%	39%	11% (100%)	6%	39%	100%	61%	44%	78%	17%	33%	22%	11%	22%

Legend: **X** Characteristic is **explicitly** named by the author (x) Characteristic is **implicitly** named by the author ☐ Characteristic is **not** named by the author

Fig. 1 Comparison of different Smart Service definitions updated according to Koldewey (2021)

terms. These terms can be used as synonyms in the broader sense as long as the product provides data. We recommend using the common term smart product.

The following characteristics are conceivable to the definition of smart services:

- **Smart Data:** Smart Data is data that has already been analyzed, interpreted, and enriched by other sources' raw data (Oertel et al. 2015; Kampker et al. 2017).
- **Customized:** A smart service can be tailored individually for each customer. The customer's requirements determine the composition of the service components (Jüttner et al. 2017; Stich et al. 2019).
- **Platform-Based:** Smart services are provided via a platform. The platform is the connection between the provider (company) and the recipient (customer) of the service (Jüttner et al. 2017; Paluch 2017; Schäfer et al. 2015).
- **Ecosystem:** Smart services are offered for smart products and are available on a platform. The platform itself is part of a larger ecosystem (Schäfer et al. 2015).
- **Different Performance Levels:** Smart services can fulfill different functions. Due to their complexity and impact on existing value networks, these can be divided into different performance levels. According to Porter and Heppelmann the following performance levels are possible: monitoring, control and monitoring, performance optimization, and automation (Paluch 2017; Porter and Heppelmann 2015).

Regarding the characteristic of the smart service, there is no unified perspective. Some authors define a smart service as part of a product-service-system (PSS) or as a descriptor for a PSS itself (e.g., Mittag et al. 2018). This implies, that the smart service cannot be traded as a separate entity. Other authors see smart services as **independent market offering**, which is not essential for the operation and the functionality of the product, but creates additional value for the customer (Klein 2017; Biehl 2017; Beverungen et al. 2017). This goes in line with the experiences we made in our case studies as well as an analysis of hundreds of smart services in practice (c.f. Koldewey et al. 2020a). As a conclusion, we found that Smart Services obviously depend on data from a physical product. Furthermore, the Smart Service's business model is mostly managed separately from the product's business model. That indicates Smart Services to be understood as independent market offerings, which requires a product as a prerequisite to unfold its value.

Planning of Smart Services and Associated Requirements

As shown, the need for companies to introduce smart services is obvious. But most companies struggle in practice; and there are good reasons for that: The planning and strategic alignment in the course of smart services is highly complex. In the following, we will introduce the most significant challenges from literature and the analysis of the market to derive requirements for our process model for developing a smart service strategy.

According to the definition, smart services build upon digitalized products. Hence, the planning of smart services has to be oriented by the companies given product portfolio (requirement R1). Consequently, smart services are provided by introducing CPS into digital service systems (Beverungen et al. 2017). These are complex socio-technical service systems that aim to create value and benefit for the customer. They can be approached interdisciplinary, integrating business functions, technology, and human resources (Drăgoicea et al. 2015; Carrol 2012; Beaumont et al. 2014) (R2). To successfully establish smart services systems in the market the company needs a competitive business strategy for smart services, that clearly states the strategic impact direction (R3 & R4) (Biehl 2017).

Since most companies have a wide product portfolio, they have to define where to start introducing smart services respectively which products are suitable for smart services (Kampker et al. 2017) (R5), and what kinds of smart services are in the customers' particular interest (R6) (acatech 2015). As the smart service builds up on the products data, the accessible data for the chosen products has to be evaluated to check the use cases (R6) (Allmendinger and Lombreglia 2005). As a business strategy, the smart service strategy has to include the targeted market offerings (smart services) (Gausemeier and Plass 2014), hence the process must include the identification and evaluation of smart service ideas bringing together market pull and technology push (Geum et al. 2016) (R7). By analyzing 175 Smart Services in different industries we discovered that most of them are part of a larger smart service portfolio, e.g., at DMG Mori. Thus, the strategy should include steps to plan the portfolio (R8). Since every smart service is a standalone market offering and therefore requires a specific business model (Frank et al. 2018) and the strategy has to provide the guidelines for the business models (Casadesus-Masanell and Ricart 2010), companies have to plan multiple business models for their smart service business (R9). Different business models in a single portfolio tend to generate synergies and cannibalization dependent on their design (Aversa et al. 2017), which should be exploited by the strategy (R10). Another challenge is the organizational transformation required (acatech 2015), which should also be addressed (R11). At last, every strategy has to be future oriented (Gausemeier and Plass 2014). Especially the scalability of the smart service business has to be taken into account in this regard (R12) (acatech 2016).

The consolidated requirements resulting from challenges are shown in Fig. 2. They can be structured into three categories. Overarching requirements, that result from the goal and the characteristics of smart services. The requirements for smart service planning address the questions regarding the market offering. The way the company wants to create value with the market offerings is considered by the requirements for business planning.

Requirements and Their Validation in Practice

To validate the requirements for the methodology we conducted four case studies with companies from the manufacturing industry. We performed a workshop each with specialists and managers and asked them to name the relevant elements of the smart service strategy. In addition, we carried out interviews in which we were able to evaluate the requirements in terms of relevance for the company. Figure 3 shows the results of the validation. It shows that the literature-based requirements are practically oriented and suitable for the development of a methodology for the

Overarching Requirements

R1	Portfolio-oriented development of smart service strategies	R3	Viewing smart services as the market offering of a socio-technical system
R2	Derivation of a strategic thrust for smart services	R4	Compliation of the smart service strategy

Requirements for Smart Service Planning | | **Requirements for Business Planning** |

R5	Structuring and analyzing of the product and service portfolio	R9	Design of the business model portfolio for smart services
R6	Analysis of accessible data and consideration of stakeholder needs	R10	Evaluation of synergy and cannibalisation effects in business
R7	Identification and evaluation of smart service ideas	R11	Design of an efficient smart service organization
R8	Development of a consistent product and service portfolio	R12	Future-oriented planning taking scalability into account

Fig. 2 Requirements for the development of a smart service strategy

Case Studys				Requirements											
No.	Business purpose	Employees	Status	1	2	3	4	5	6	7	8	9	10	11	12
1	Manufacturer of air compressors	<1000	Single smart service package												
2	Manufacturer of tooling machines	>5000	Multiple smart services												
3	Manufacturer of food processing tools	<250	First concepts												
4	Manufacturer of electric drive components	<100	Conceptualized solutions												

Legend: Requirement mentioned by company / Requirement not mentioned by company

Fig. 3 Requirements as mentioned in the case studies

development of a smart service strategy. Therefore, the requirements are used in the following to develop the process.

3 State of the Art

There are few approaches for the planning of smart services in general. Bayrle et al. focus on the development of data-based service business models (Bayrle et al. 2018), as do (Harland et al. 2017). Gerberich and Schweigart (2017) present a method for the development and implementation of smart services. These approaches represent a good starting point, but do not meet all the requirements for the development of a smart service strategy. There is a lack of consideration of the existing product ranges and strategic orientation. Biehl (2017) provides general design guidelines for smart services from a strategic point of view as well as a generic process, but he does not offer any concrete application steps for companies. Other smart service-specific approaches, e.g., (Geum et al. 2016), only address singular requirements, they should be considered developing the methodology. Traditional methods of service engineering, e.g., (Klein 2007; Shostack 1984), can make a contribution, but they are usually not specific enough to be applied to smart services. In summary, it can be said that smart services are a new and little-researched field, especially from the strategic management perspective. Evidence from a managerial perspective shows that current decision-making lacks theoretically grounded approaches (Biehl 2017). Henceforth there is a need for action regarding a development process for smart service strategies that enable companies to plan their smart service business holistically.

4   A Development Process for Smart Services Strategies

This chapter introduces the development process for smart services strategies. The process model consists of five phases and is shown in Fig. 4.

In the first phase, the competitive situation of the company and the given technological basis of the manufactured products are analyzed. Based on these insights the strategic thrust is derived. The second phase aims at the analysis of

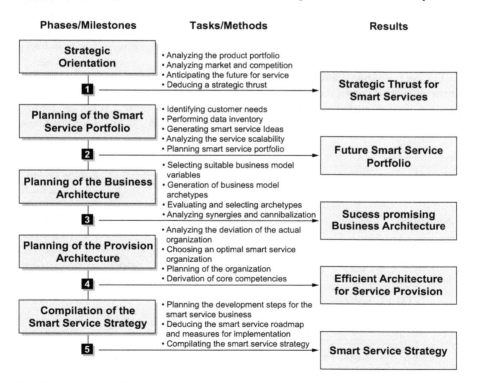

Fig. 4 Process model for the development of smart service strategies

today's and future customer needs. Following, smart service ideas are generated considering technological possibilities as well as the customer needs. The result is the targeted smart service portfolio. Then a suitable business architecture is planned in the third phase. That is done by defining few business model archetypes, which can be detailed to business model variants for specific smart services. Furthermore, in the fourth phase, the smart service organization and required core competences are determined. The last phase consists of the compilation of the strategy. Here, the evolution of the service business is outlined as well as the smart service roadmap. The result of the process is the smart service strategy, which summarizes the strategic targets and the measures to achieve them. The process model is explained by means of an industrial robotic manufacturer, which is an alienated excerpt from one of our projects.

Strategic Orientation

The aim of the first phase is the deduction of a strategic thrust for smart services. Since most manufacturing companies have a product portfolio of a multitude of product families to settle smart services on, first the given product portfolio is analyzed. For the customer, product families are represented by few properties (Schuh et al. 2012). Properties from the customer's point of view are, for example, "main technology," "field of application" etc. Taking the properties into account, we came up with three product families: "service robotics," "simple 3-axis industry robotics," and "6-axis high performance robotics."

For each product family then a characteristic performance indicator regarding smart services is determined. This is done by means of a pairwise comparison of the product families attributes. For example, for the "3-axis industrial robotics" family, the robot control was the significant characteristic (Fig. 5). It has three attributes,

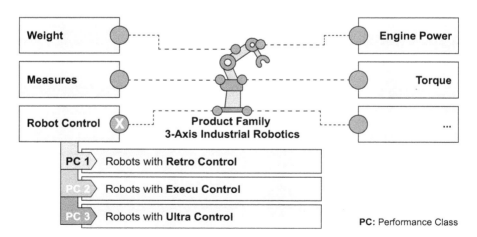

Fig. 5 Identification of performance classes for the product family 3-axis industrial robotics

Target Contribution Matrix Question: Does the CPS-Ability i (row) contribute to realize the smart service use case j (column)? Evaluation: 0 = no contribution 1 = low contribution 2 = moderate contribution 3 = high contribution		Smart Service Use Cases	Condition Monitoring	Remote Contro	Analytics	...	Predictive Maintenance	Broad effect (in %)	Depth effect	Target contribution	Target contribution (weighted, in %)
CPS-Component	CPS-Ability	Nr.	U1	U2	U3		U22				
Actuators	Process intervention	A1	0	0	0		0	25	1,5	0,38	1,53
Actuators	Postitioning accuarcy	A2	0	0								
Sensors	Measurement signals	A3	3	2								
Sensors	Source of information	A4	2	2								
Data	Data storage	A16	3	2								
Data	Data analysis	A17	1	1								
Data	Usage of external	A18	1	3								

Broad effect:
Describes the overall influence of a CPS-Ability on all smart service usecase.

Depth effect:
Describes the influence of a CPS-Ability on the smart service usecases in arithmetic mean.

Target contribution:
Total contribution of a CPS-Ability to realize a smart service usecase by multiplying the broad and depth effect.

Fig. 6 Target contribution matrix inspired by Westermann (2017)

which form the so-called *performance classes*: "Robots with Execu Control," which includes all products with the "Execu Control" control, "Robots with Retro Control," and "Robots with Ultra Control."

These performance classes are then evaluated in detail. This is based on a maturity model for cyber-physical systems. According to Westermann (2017), a cyber-physical system consists of six partial models: information processing, sensor technology, communication, data, actuators, and human–machine interface. For each partial model, there are several elements specifying it. But not all elements are equally relevant for the evaluation of cyber-physical systems regarding their suitability for smart services. We analyzed around 400 smart services in the market extending the work of M. Frank et al. (2019) to derive 22 reference smart services, which represent the typical use cases for smart service, e.g., *"condition monitoring."* Then we evaluated each element of the maturity model regarding their importance for each of the use cases. This results in the target contribution of each element of the maturity model. Figure 6 shows and elaborates the corresponding matrix.

Each performance class is then analyzed for their CPS-level in each element. The overall CPS-performance score is calculated by multiplying the target contribution with the evaluation score for each element and then summing them up resulting in the weighted average mean. This is shown in Fig. 7.

Performance Class 2: Robots with Execu Control							
CPS-Component	**CPS-Ability**	**TC* (in %)**	**Performance Level**				
			1	2	3	4	5
Actuators	Process intervention	1,53				▦	
	Positioning accuracy	1,02				▦	
Sensors	Measurement signals	11,2					▦
	Source of information	10,2				▦	
Information Processing	Control	0				▦	
	Identificaion & adaptation	1,02				▦	
	Optimization	2,03		▦			
Communication Systems	Vertical integration	7,65				▦	
	Horizontal integration	4,07			▦		
	Connectivity	10,7				▦	
	Network connection	11,2	▦				
	Security	7,12		▦			
Human Machine Interface	Functionality of HMI	5,59				▦	
	Location of HMI	2,54	▦				
	Multimodality	3,05	▦				
Data	Data storage	9,64			▦		
	Data analysis	5,58		▦			
	Usage of external data	5,94	▦				
CPS-Performance-Score: (weighted arithmetic mean)			**3,0**				

*TC: Target Contribution

Fig. 7 CPS-Performance-Diagram inspired by Westermann (2017) for performance class 2

In regard to the situation in the market and competition, we use a market offerings-market segments-matrix to analyze the market and an in-depth research- and clustering-approach to analyze the competition. We analyzed which smart services were implemented by each competitor, matched them to the reference services and derived a conclusion for the competitive situation.

At last, we used the scenario-technique according to Gausemeier and Plass (2014) to anticipate the future of the market environment for the considered company. Five scenarios for the time horizon 2030 emerged. Based on the evaluation in the project team we chose one scenario as our reference scenario: *"The robotics business depends heavily onto digital service solutions, the assets became commodities."*

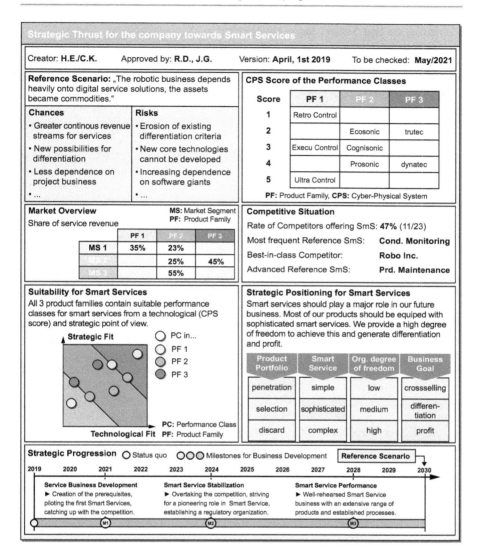

Fig. 8 Profile for the strategic thrust

Based on the analyses in the first phase, the strategic thrust is derived and documented in a strategic thrust profile (Fig. 8), which includes statements regarding the market and competitive situation, the anticipated future, related opportunities and risks, an evaluation of the product portfolio, the suitability of the performance classes for smart services rated by strategic and technological fit. Other statements address the envisioned strategic position based upon the analysis as well as a raw path for the strategic progression.

Planning of the Smart Service Portfolio

The aim of the second phase is the generation of a coherent smart service portfolio, that creates value for the customer and supports the strategic thrust. Hence, the first step is to analyze the customers' use of the targeted performance classes (e.g., *robots with ultra control*). To that we identify application scenarios of the product and use a customer journey to identify pains and gains for promising application scenarios (Fig. 9).

As smart services build up on the product data to create value by means of a digital service, the next step includes the inventory of the associated data of the product. To that we analyze three kinds of data sources (Fig. 10): (1) the product and its sensory data, (2) the data warehouses the product is connected to, e.g., MES systems, (3) the environment, which influences the product. The identified data is then evaluated regarding their importance and availability by the project team resulting in an ordered data inventory.

The insights from the customer journeys and the data inventory can be used to generate ideas for new smart services. In that way, the market pull and the technology push innovation approach are integrated (Geum et al. 2016). To that, we use the smart service ideation canvas, which is inspired by the value proposition canvas (Osterwalder et al. 2014). It consists of the customer profile including customer jobs, pains, and gains on the left hand, and the product data profile including the data sources (sensors, IT-Systems), data sinks (actuators, IT-Systems), and data inventory on the right hand. In the center is the smart service. The smart service is composed of the context in which it generates value, the insights it provides for the stakeholder, and the data processing. It is connected to the customer through the value proposition it provides and the interactions necessary. It is based on the data given from the product delivered via connectivity solutions. The aim is to find suitable ideas for the

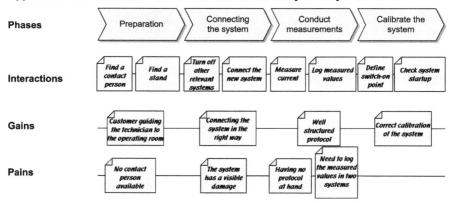

Fig. 9 Exemplary customer journey for an application scenario of the performance class robots with ultra control

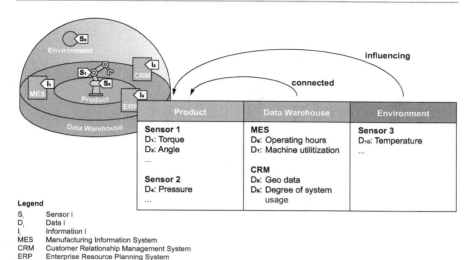

Fig. 10 Data inventory of the performance class robots with ultra control

given situation, that fit both customer profile and product data profile. Furthermore, future needs regarding the customer are to be identified as well as future requirements regarding the product data. The result is a comprehensive smart service idealist. Figure 11 shows the canvas with an alienated example from our project.

To complete the smart service portfolio two steps are necessary. First, the scalability of the smart services must be evaluated. This is done by performing a knockout (K.O.)-analysis and answering five guiding question for each of four scaling-options. The scaling options are (1) retrofit of old products, (2) usage for further new products, (3) smart service adaption for products of the competition, and (4) IP-commercialization (Koldewey et al. 2018a). The smart services are then associated with the relevant scaling options in a matrix consisting of four fields. Figure 12 shows this process for our example. It is performed for all smart services regardless of the performance class from which the idea resulted.

After the analysis of the scalability, the smart services are finally evaluated, to choose the right ones for the resulting smart service portfolio. We recommend using a simple evaluation regarding broad impact, economic attractiveness, and fit to the strategy to select the most promising smart services for further consideration.

Planning of the Business Architecture

The third phase aims towards the generation of business model archetypes, which describe few but significant basic elements of how a company wants to generate, impart, and secure value (Koldewey et al. 2018b). They can be understood as combinations of business model variables (e.g., *digital infrastructure*) and their characteristics (e.g., *third-party IoT-platform*). Business model archetypes are the

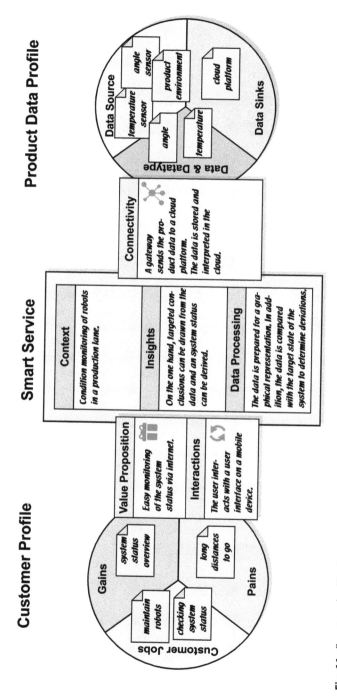

Fig. 11 Smart service ideation canvas

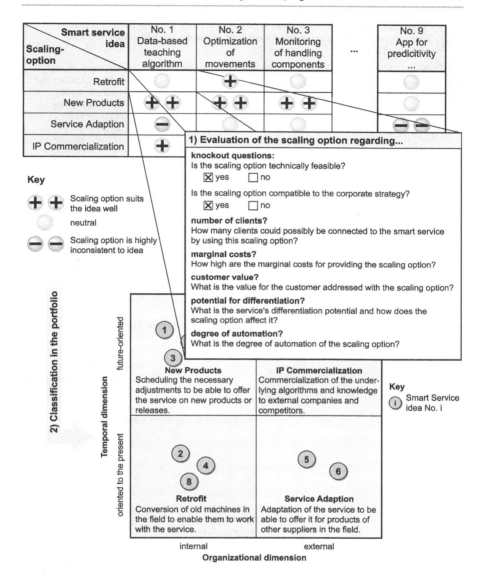

Fig. 12 Analysis of the smart service scalability

foundation for a detailed business model for each smart service (business model variants) building the business model portfolio. For that, we used different sources as inspiration. Figure 13 explains the whole process of generating archetypes. The process consists of six steps: (1) Identification and documentation of sources for business model characteristics, (2) Analysis to derive suitable business model characteristics, (3) Clustering and aggregation of characteristics to business model

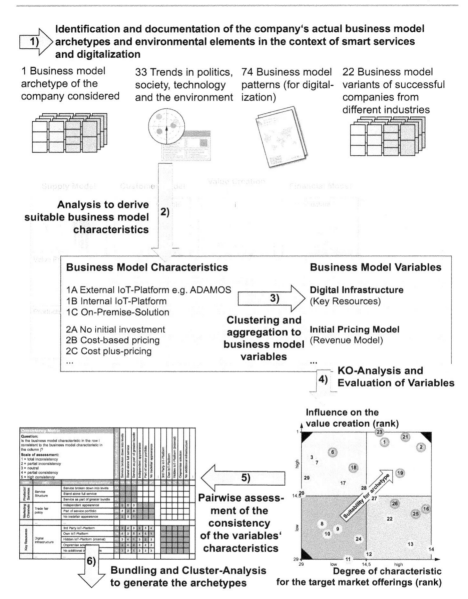

Fig. 13 Procedure for developing business model archetypes (Koldewey et al. 2018b)

variables, (4) K.O.-analysis to reduce the number of suitable variables and evaluation of the remaining variables in detail, (5) Pairwise assessment of the consistency of the chosen variables' associated characteristics, (6) Generation and clustering of highly consistent bundles of characteristics with the clusters representing business model archetypes.

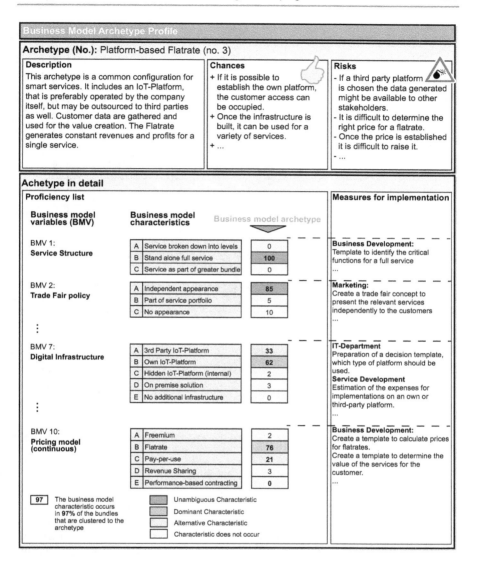

Fig. 14 Archetype profile (Koldewey et al. 2018b)

In our project six archetypes for the whole smart service portfolio regardless of the performance classes resulted from the analysis. They are then described by means of archetype profiles (Fig. 14). The profile consists of a brief description of the archetype, associated chances, and risks, as well as a list of the characteristics included and measures to implement the characteristics. The title of the archetype is obtained from the most relevant characteristics; in our project, we chose *pricing model (continuous)* and *digital infrastructure* in consultation with the company.

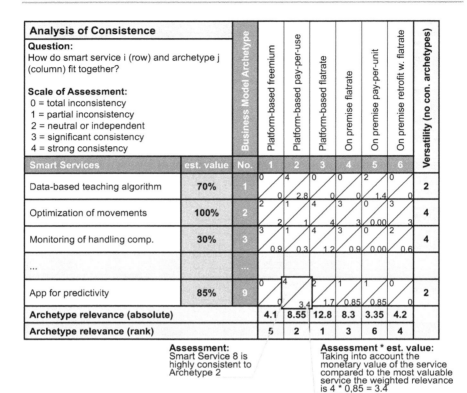

Fig. 15 Selection of suitable business model archetypes for the strategy (Koldewey et al. 2018b)

Next, the archetypes are evaluated regarding their suitability for the smart services, which is done by means of a consistency analysis (Fig. 15). The consistency matrix contains the smart services in the rows and the archetypes in the columns. For the smart services, the monetary value is estimated and given as a percentage of the most valuable service. In the cells the assessment of consistency takes place. The scale of assessments reaches from 0 *total inconsistency* to 4 *strong consistency*. The assessment is weighted with the services' value. The column sum indicates the business relevance of the archetypes and allows for a ranking order. In our project we chose one archetype that seemed highly promising: *3) Platform-based flat rate* (Koldewey et al. 2018b). Then we analyzed the interdependences with the core business models following (Koldewey et al. 2018b) and searched for cannibalization effects. Since the archetype leads to quite simple business models (and does not include the servitization of the whole product), no cannibalization effects were found. Synergies were also little.

Planning of the Provision Architecture

Given the smart service portfolio and the business architecture, the next design step of the strategy process is the planning of an efficient architecture to operate the smart service business. To that, we choose an organizational form and identify core competences to foster.

A suitable organizational structure is derived by analyzing the given structure of the company and evaluating whether it is suitable or not. For ,that, we use guiding questions for each core task of the smart service reference process (management, development, provision, and billing) to check how much deviance there is between the given structure of the company and the optimal configuration for a smart service business. The higher the deviance the further away the smart service business should be implemented from the core business. Figure 16 shows how to calculate the deviance factors for the four core processes and how to choose a suitable organizational structure from the total deviation score. For the chosen structure requirements are derived, e.g., how processes should be implemented. In our project, it seemed sensible to create a new business unit for smart services.

A significant aspect of a business strategy is the required core competences (Gausemeier and Plass 2014). To identify core competences, we analyze the smart service portfolio, the business model archetype(s), and the organizational

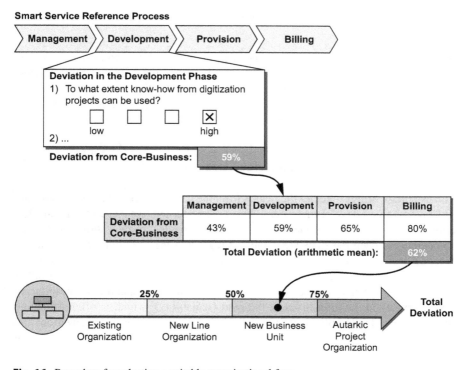

Fig. 16 Procedure for selecting a suitable organizational form

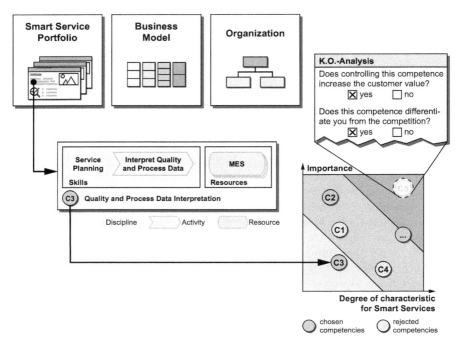

Fig. 17 Procedure for deriving core competences

requirements. This results in a competence inventory. Each competence is then evaluated regarding the importance for the business and the degree of characteristic. At last we use the three criteria customer value, differentiation from the competition, and expandability according to Hamel and Prahalad to perform a K.O. analysis for choosing the right core competences (Prahalad and Hamel 1990) (Fig. 17).

Compilation of the Smart Service Strategy

The last phase brings together the results from the earlier phases. First, the results are broken down into development steps. This is done for the five elements of consideration: smart services, scalability, business models, organization, and core competences. Then the steps are evaluated regarding the question *"does the step a function with the interim step b?"* The result of the evaluation is nine consistent overarching interim steps that span all five elements. Figure 18 shows the resulting implementation canvas. For example, the first step includes a condition monitoring pilot (service) for test machines in the field (scalability), which is offered for free (business model not implemented). A data analyst should be hired (organization) and the software development for neuronal networks should be learned (core competence).

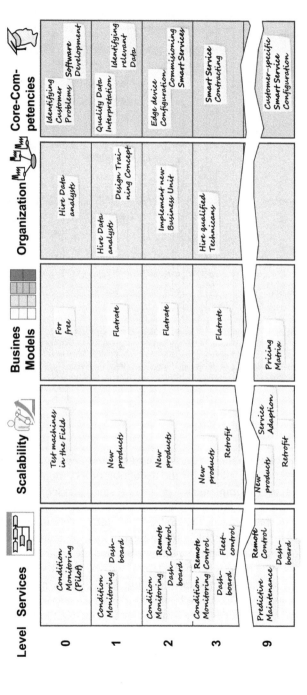

Fig. 18 Implementation canvas

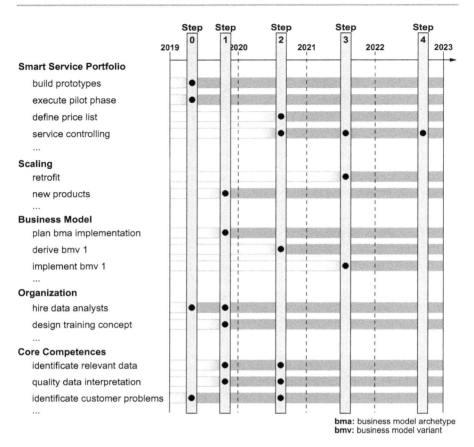

Fig. 19 Implementation roadmap

Based on the implementation canvas, measures and consequences are derived from the interim steps. This allows for the deduction of a comprehensive roadmap, that shows in detail, how to implement a promising smart service business (Fig. 19).

The last step is the aggregation of the results into the strategy profile (Fig. 20). This makes it easy to communicate the strategy and creates a common understanding of the measures to be implemented in the company and the reasons for them. The strategy profile comprises the implementation plan, and the smart services offerings matrix, that shows which performance classes will be targeted by which smart services. Furthermore, the information regarding the business model archetype is mentioned, as well as the measures and goals for the transformation of the organization. At last the core competences to be fostered are included in the profile. The result is the smart service strategy.

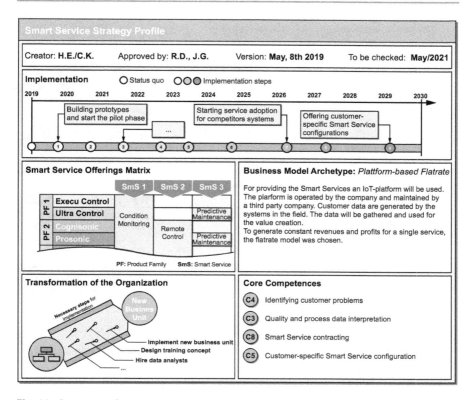

Fig. 20 Strategy profile

5   Discussion, Conclusion, and Retrospective

The convergence of digitalization and servitization revolutionizes today's product-service-systems and has a massive impact on companies' business decisions. Especially in the course of smart services, companies lack methods, tools, and processes as decision-making support from a managerial point of view. To the best of our knowledge, there is no suitable and detailed methodology to position a company considering smart services strategically. By our process model, we deliver an approach to close this research gap. The process model introduces a step-by-step approach to develop smart service strategies shaping the most critical design factors (e.g., business models). It integrates methods and tools from the state of the art, e.g., (Westermann 2017; Osterwalder et al. 2014; Köster 2014; Gausemeier and Plass 2014), and integrates them into a coherent process model adapting them for decision support in regards of smart services. Furthermore, we introduce new concepts (e.g., business model archetypes) into the process model.

The research is based on four comprehensive case studies. Hence, we provide insight into the process of strategy development in the course of smart services,

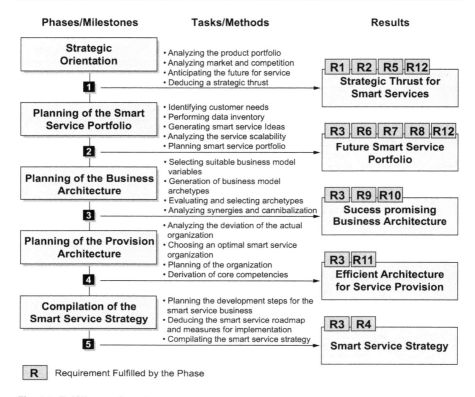

Fig. 21 Fulfillment of requirements

which is desperately needed given the failure of "hands-on" approaches. The process model enables practitioners to transfer our insights into their own companies and gain tangible benefits: The process model allows them to (1) access new potentials for their business through smart services, (2) choose a strategic direction for smart services, and (3) develop a specific strategy for their smart service business taking into account the most critical design factors. The method thus fulfills the requirements (Fig. 21).

With regards to the application in practice, we make the following recommendations based on our experience: (1) The establishment of a smart service business is a multidisciplinary approach, which should be represented by the team; (2) As smart services have a significant impact on the company, an early initiation of a change process is crucial; (3) There is often a great deal of uncertainty as to where the new business is to be anchored in the organization or how to implement the strategy. A distinctive premise controlling must be established in order to be able to make necessary price corrections at an early stage.

This paper was first published at the 2019 ISPIM Innovation Forum (Koldewey et al. 2019a). It was slightly updated to reflect the current understanding of smart services (c.f. Sect. 2). Since its first publication, two further iterations of the

DRM-process were run in late 2019/early 2020 applying the methodology and learning from further feedback. This lead to the development of design knowledge for the methodology in terms of smart service functionalities for idea generation (c.f. Koldewey et al. 2020a), generic strategies for strategic orientation (c.f. Koldewey et al. 2020b), and a Smart Service reference model (c.f. Frank et al. 2020). In addition, further methodological refinement and extension of the methodology were conducted focusing on idea generation and documentation (c.f. Koldewey et al. 2019b) as well as organizational questions regarding centralization of the smart service business and competencies (c.f. Koldewey et al. 2020c). An extended procedure for the development of smart service strategies will be published in 2021 (c.f. Koldewey 2021). Hence, the paper presented at the ISPIM has served as a solid backbone for further research.

Future research should focus on the operationalization of smart service strategies regarding processes, competencies, and IT-systems. Furthermore, significant challenges regarding the configuration of the smart service value network were obvious in our case studies.

Acknowledgment The original paper was presented at the ISPIM Innovation Conference in Florence (Koldewey et al. 2019a). The research at hand is part of the IMPRESS project (funding code: 02L17B070) and is funded by the Federal Ministry of Education and Research and the European Social Fund as part of the Future of Work program. The authors would like to thank the project partners Fraunhofer Institute for Mechatronics Design, Technical University Chemnitz, Weidmüller Interface, Diebold Nixdorf, the FIWARE Foundation, BOGE KOMPRESSOREN Otto Boge, DMG Mori, FREUND Maschinenfabrik, and MSF Vathauer for their cooperation and input.

References

acatech. (Ed.) (2015). *Smart service welt: recommendations for the strategic initiative web-based services for businesses*. Berlin.

acatech. (Ed.) (2016). *Smart Service Welt: Digitale Serviceplattformen—Praxiserfahrungen aus der Industrie, Best Practices*. Munich.

acatech. (Ed.) (2018). *Smart Service Welt 2018: Wo stehen wir? Wohin gehen wir?* Munich.

acatech, Smart Service Welt Working Group (Eds.). (2014). *Smart service welt—Recommendations for the strategic initiative web-based services for businesses*. Berlin.

Allmendinger, G., & Lombreglia, R. (2005). Four strategies for the age of smart services. *Harvard Business Review, 83*(10), 131–145.

Anke, J., & Krenge, J. (2016). Prototyp eines Tools zur Abschätzung der Wirtschaftlichkeit von Smart Services für vernetzte Produkte. In: *Multikonferenz Wirtschaftsinformatik (MKWI), Ilmenau, 9–11 Mar 2016* (pp. 1275–1286).

Aversa, P., Haefliger, P., & Reza, D. G. (2017). Building a winning business model portfolio. *MIT Sloan Management Review, 58*(4), 49–54.

Baines, T. S., et al. (2007). State-of-the-art in product-service systems. Proceedings of the Institution of Mechanical Engineers. *Part B: Journal of Engineering Manufacture, 221*(10), 1543–1552.

Baines, T. S., Lightfoot, H. B., Benedettini, O., & Kay, J. M. (2009). The servitization of manufacturing. *Journal of Manufacturing Technology Management, 20*(5), 547–567.

Barile, S., & Polese, F. (2010). Smart service systems and viable service systems—Applying systems theory to service science. *Service Science, 2*(1/2), 21–40.

Bayrle, C., Ohmer, C., & Seiter, M. (2018). Service-business-innovation-lab. In M. Bruhn & K. Hadwich (Eds.), *Service business development* (pp. 497–518). Wiesbaden: Springer.

Beaumont, L. C., Bolton, L. E., McKay, A., & Hughes, H. P. N. (2014). Rethinking service design: A socio-technical approach to the development of business models. In D. Schaefer (Ed.), *Product development in the socio-sphere*. Cham: Springer.

Beverungen, D., Matzner, M., & Janiesch, C. (2017). Information systems for smart services. *Information Systems and e-Business Management, 15*(4), 781–787.

Bharadwaj, A., El Sawy, O. A., Pavlou, P. A., & Venkatraman, N. (2013). Digital Business Strategy: Toward a next generation of insights. *MIS Quarterly, 37*(2), 471–482.

Biehl, S. (2017). *Design guidelines for smart services: A strategic-logic perspective on seeking competitive advantage with digitized servitization strategies*. Dissertation, University of St. Gallen.

Blessing, L. T. M., & Chakrabarti, A. (2009). *DRM, a design research methodology*. London: Springer.

Böhmann, T., Leimeister, J. M., & Möslein, K. (2014). Service Systems Engineering. *Business & Information Systems Engineering, 6*(2), 73–79.

Broy, M. (2010). *Cyber-Physical Systems: Innovation Durch Software-Intensive Eingebettete Systeme*. Berlin: Springer.

Carrol, N. (2012). *Service science: An empirical study on the socio-technical dynamics of public sector service network innovation*. Dissertation, University of Limerick.

Casadesus-Masanell, R., & Ricart, J. E. (2010). From strategy to business models and onto tactics. *Long Range Planning, 43*(2–3), 195–215.

Coreynen, W., Matthyssens, P., & van Bockhaven, W. (2017). Boosting servitization through digitization: Pathways and dynamic resource configurations for manufacturers. *Industrial Marketing Management, 60*, 42–53.

Cusumano, M. A., Kahl, S. J., & Suarez, F. F. (2015). Services, industry evolution, and the competitive strategies of product firms. *Strategic Management Journal, 36*(4), 559–575.

Drăgoicea, M., Falcão e Cunha, J., & Pătraşcu, M. (2015). Self-organising socio-technical description in service systems for supporting smart user decisions in public transport. *Expert Systems with Applications, 42*(17-18), 6329–6341.

Echterfeld, J., & Gausemeier, J. (2018). Digitising product portfolios. *International Journal of Innovation Management, 22*(5).

Fleisch, E., Weinberger, M., & Wortmann, F. (2017). Business models and the internet of things (extended abstract). In: *Interoperability and open-source solutions for the internet of things, Split, Croatia, 18 Sept 2017* (pp. 6–10).

Frank, M., Koldewey, C., Rabe, M., Dumitrescu, R., Gausemeier, J., & Kühn, A. (2018). Smart Services: Konzept einer neuen Marktleistung. *Zeitschrift für wirtschaftlichen Fabrikbetrieb (ZWF), 113*(5).

Frank, A. G., Mendes, G. H. S., Ayala, N. F., & Ghezzi, A. (2019). Servitization and Industry 4.0 convergence in the digital transformation of product firms: A business model innovation perspective. *Technological Forecasting and Social Change, 141*, 341–351.

Frank, M., Gausemeier, J., Hennig-Cardinal von Widdern, N., Koldewey, C., Menzefricke, J. S., & Reinhold, J. (2020). A reference process for the Smart Service business: development and practical implications. In: *Proceedings of the 2020 ISPIM Connects (Bangkok): Partnering for an innovative community, Bangkok, Thailand, 1-4 Mar 2020*.

Gausemeier, J., & Plass, C. (2014). *Zukunftsorientierte Unternehmensgestaltung: Strategien, Geschäftsprozesse und IT-Systeme für die Produktion von morgen*. Munich: Hanser.

Gausemeier, J., Rammig, F. J., & Schäfer, W. (Eds.). (2014). *Design methodology for intelligent technical systems: Develop intelligent technical systems of the future*. Berlin: Springer.

Gerberich, C. W., & Schweigart, T. (2017). Smart Services und die Dematerialisierung der Geschäfte. In A. Borgmaier, A. Grohmann, & S. F. Gross (Eds.), *Smart Services und Internet der Dinge: Geschäftsmodelle, Umsetzung und Best Practices* (pp. 109–122). Munich: Carl Hanser.

Geum, Y., Jeon, H., & Lee, H. (2016). Developing new smart services using integrated morphological analysis. Integration of the market-pull and technology-push approach. *Service Business, 10*(3), 531–555.

Goedkoop, M. J., van Halen, C. J. G., te Riele, H. R. M., Rommens, P. J. M. (1999). Product Service systems: Ecological and Economic Basics. The Report No. 1999/36 Submitted to Ministerje van Volkshuisvesting, Ruimtelijke Ordening en Milieubeheer, Hague.

Grubic, T. (2014). Servitization and remote monitoring technology. *Journal of Manufacturing Technology Management, 25*(1), 100–124.

Harland, T., Husmann, M., Jussen, P., Kampker, A., & Stich, V. (2017). Sechs Prinzipien für datenbasierte Dienstleistungen in der Industrie. In A. Borgmaier, A. Grohmann, & S. F. Gross (Eds.), *Smart Services und Internet der Dinge: Geschäftsmodelle, Umsetzung und Best Practices* (pp. 55–90). Munich: Carl Hanser.

Huang, M.-H., & Rust, R. T. (2017). Technology-driven service strategy. *Journal of the Academy of Marketing Science, 45*(6), 906–924.

Industry-Science Research Alliance (Ed.) (2013). Prosperity through research: What tasks lie ahead for Germany? IRB Mediendienstleistungen Fraunhofer-Informationszentrum Raum und Bau IRB, Stuttgart.

Jüttner, U., Windler, K., Schäfer, A., & Zimmermann, A. (2017). Design von Smart Services—Eine explorative Studie im Business-to-Business-Sektor. In M. Bruhn & K. Hadwich (Eds.), *Dienstleistungen 4.0: Geschäftsmodelle—Wertschöpfung—Transformation* (pp. 335–361). Wiesbaden: Springer.

Kagermann, H. (2015). Change through digitization—Value creation in the age of industry 4.0. In H. Albach, H. Meffert, A. Pinkwart, & R. Reichwald (Eds.), *Management of permanent change*. Wiesbaden: Springer.

Kagermann, H., Wahlster, W., & Helbig, J. (Eds.) (2013). Recommendations for implementing the strategic initiative INDUSTRIE 4.0: *Final report of the Industrie 4.0 Working Group*. Berlin: acatech.

Kampker, A., Frank, J., & Jussen, P. (2017). Digitale Vernetzung im Service. *WiSt—Wirtschaftswissenschaftliches Studium, 46*(5), 4–11.

Klein, R. (2007). *Modellgestütztes Service Systems Engineering: Theorie und Technik einer systemischen Entwicklung von Dienstleistungen*. Wiesbaden: Deutscher Universitäts.

Klein, M. M. (2017). *Design rules for smart services. Overcoming barriers with rational heuristics*. Dissertation, University of St. Gallen

Koldewey, C. (2021). Systematik zur Entwicklung Smart Service-Strategien im produzierenden Gewerbe. Submitted Dissertation, University of Paderborn.

Koldewey, C., Frank, M., & Gausemeier, J. (2018a, June 17–20). Planning of scalable smart services. In: *Proceedings of the 2018 ISPIM innovation conference (Stockholm): Innovation, the name of the game, Stockholm, Sweden*.

Koldewey, C., Echterfeld, J., Gausemeier, J., & Reilender, M. (2018b, December 3–5). Business model portfolio planning for smart services. In: *Proceedings of ISPIM connects Fukuoka: solving challenges through innovation, Fukuoka, Japan*.

Koldewey, C., Evers, H. H., Dumitrescu, R., Frank, M., Gausemeier, J., & Reinhold, J. (2019a, June 16–19). Development process for smart service strategies. In: *Proceedings of The XXX ISPIM innovation conference, Florence, Italy*.

Koldewey, C., Gausemeier, J., Fischer, S., & Kage, M. (2019b). Entwicklung von Smart Service Strategien. In: J. Gausemeier, W. Bauer, & R. Dumitrescu (Eds.), *Vorausschau und Technologieplanung. HNI-Verlagsschriftenreihe 390, Paderborn* (pp. 151–190).

Koldewey, C., Meyer, M., Stockbrügger, P., Dumitrescu, R., & Gausemeier, J. (2020a). Framework and functionality patterns for smart service innovation. *Procedia CIRP, 91*, 851–857.

Koldewey, C., Frank, M., Gausemeier, J., Bäsecke, A., Chohan, N., & Reinhold, J. (2020b). Systematische Entwicklung von Normstrategien für Smart Services. *ZWF Zeitschrift für wirtschaftlichen Fabrikbetrieb, 115*(7–8), 524–528.

Koldewey, C., Gausemeier, J., Chohan, N., Frank, M., Reinhold, J., & Dumitrescu, R. (2020c, November 25–27). Aligning strategy and structure for smart service businesses in manufacturing. In: *2020 IEEE international conference on technology management, operations and decisions (ICTMOD), Marrakech, Morocco* (in press).

Köster, O. (2014). *Systematik zur Entwicklung von Geschäftsmodellen in der Produktentstehung.* Dissertation, University of Paderborn, HNI-Verlagsschriftenreihe 326, Paderborn.

Kowalkowski, C., Gebauer, H., Kamp, B., & Parry, G. (2017). Servitization and deservitization: Overview, concepts, and definitions. *Industrial Marketing Management, 60*, 4–10.

Lee, E. A. (2008, June 5–7). Cyber physical systems. Design challenges. In: *Proceeding of the 11th IEEE symposium on object oriented real-time distributed computing (ISORC), Orlando, FL* (pp. 363–369).

Lightfoot, H. W., & Gebauer, H. (2011). Exploring the alignment between service strategy and service innovation. *Journal of Service Management, 22*(5), 664–683.

Linz, C., Müller-Stewens, G., & Zimmermann, A. (2017). *Radical Business Model Transformation: Gaining the Competitive Edge in a Disruptive World.* London: Kogan Page.

Lyytinen, K., Yoo, Y., & Boland, R. J., Jr. (2016). Digital product innovation within four classes of innovation networks. *Information Systems Journal, 26*(1), 47–75.

Maglio, P. P., & Spohrer, J. (2008). Fundamentals of service science. *Journal of the Academy of Marketing Science, 36*(1), 18–20.

Martinez, V., Neely, A., Velu, C., Leinster-Evans, S., & Bisessar, D. (2017). Exploring the journey to services. *International Journal of Production Economics, 192*, 66–80.

Mathieu, V. (2001). Service strategies within the manufacturing sector: benefits, costs and partnership. *International Journal of Service Industry Management, 12*(5), 451–475.

Mikusz, M. (2014). Towards an Understanding of Cyber-physical Systems as Industrial Software-Product-Service Systems. *Procedia CIRP, 16*, 385–389.

Mittag, T., Rabe, M., Gradert, T., Kühn, A., & Dumitrescu, R. (2018, May 29–31). Building blocks for planning and implementation of smart services based on existing products. In: *10th CIRP conference on industrial product-service systems (IPS2 2018), Linköping.*

Morelli, N. (2002). Designing product/service systems: A methodological exploration. *Design Issues, 18*(3), 3–17.

Novales, A., Mocker, M., & Simonovich, D. (2016, August 11–14). IT-enriched "digitized" products: Building blocks and challenges. In: *Surfing the IT innovation wave: 22nd Americas conference on information systems (AMCIS 2016), San Diego, California.*

Oertel, C., Ruehle, T., & Falk, S. (2015). Getting smarter: How smart services are disrupting the manufacturing industry. https://www.accenture.com/t20160811T030546__w__/de-de/_acnmedia/PDF-28/Accenture-Strategy-Getting-Smarter.pdf. Accessed May 2019.

Oliva, R., & Kallenberg, R. (2003). Managing the transition from products to services. *International Journal of Service Industry Management, 14*(2), 160–172.

Osterwalder, A., Pigneur, Y., Bernarda, G., Smith, A., & Papadakos, T. (2014). *Value Proposition Design: How to Create Products and Services Customers Want.* Hoboken, NJ: Wiley.

Paluch, S. (2017). Smart Services—Analyse von strategischen und operativen Auswirkungen. In M. Bruhn, & K. Hadwich (Eds.), *Dienstleistungen 4.0: Geschäftsmodelle—Wertschöpfung—Transformation.* Wiesbaden: Springer.

Porter, M. E., & Heppelmann, J. E. (2015). How smart, connected products are transforming companies. *Harvard Business Review, 93*(October), 97–114.

Prahalad, C. K., & Hamel, G. (1990). The core competence of the corporation. *Harvard Business Review, 69*(3).

Rabe, M. (2020). *Systematik zur Konzipierung von Smart Services für mechatronische Systeme.* Dissertation, University of Paderborn.

Raddats, C., Baines, T. W., Burton, J., Story, V. M., & Zolkiewski, J. (2016). Motivations for servitization: the impact of product complexity. *International Journal of Operations & Production Management, 36*(5), 572–591.

Rifkin, J. (2015). *The Zero Marginal Cost Society: The internet of things, the collaborative commons, and the eclipse of capitalism.* New York: Palgrave Macmillan.

Schäfer, T., Jud, C., & Mikusz, M. (2015). Plattform-Ökosysteme im Bereich der intelligent vernetzten Mobilität: Eine Geschäftsmodellanalyse. *HMD Praxis der Wirtschaftsinformatik, 52*(3), 386–400.

Schuh, G., Arnoschtt, J., & Schiffer, M. (2012). Innovationscontrolling. In G. Schuh (Ed.), *Innovationsmanagement: Handbuch Produktion und Management 3.* Berlin: Springer.

Shostack, G. L. (1984). Designing services that deliver. *Harvard Business Review, 65*(1).

Steimel, B., & Steinhaus, I. (2017). Neue Geschäftspotenziale mit Smart Services: Praxisleitfaden Internet der Dinge. https://www.smarter-service.com/download-assets/Praxisleitfaden_IoT_2017.pdf. Accessed May 2019.

Stich, V., Jussen, P., Moser, B., & Harland, T. (2019). Smart Service Design—Planung und Steuerung der Entwicklung von Smart Services. In S. von Engelhardt & S. Petzolt (Eds.), *Das Geschäftsmodell-Toolbook für digitale Ökosysteme* (pp. 148–165). Frankfurt/Main: Campus.

Tillotson, J., & Lundin, S. (2008). The art of smart services—Volume 2: Smart Cleantech The Clean Component of the Smart Services Equation. https://www.qualcomm.com/media/documents/files/the-art-of-smart-services-smart-clean-tech.pdf. Accessed May 2019.

Tukker, A. (2004). Eight types of product–service system: eight ways to sustainability? Experiences from SusProNet. *Business Strategy and the Environment, 13*(4), 246–260.

Vandermerwe, S., & Rada, J. (1988). Servitization of business: Adding value by adding services. *European Management Journal, 6*(4), 314–324.

Wee, D., Breunig, M., & von der Tann, V. (2016). Industry 4.0 after the initial hype: Where manufacturers are finding value and how they can best capture it. München.

Westermann, T. (2017). *Systematik zur Reifegradmodell-basierten Planung von Cyber-Physical Systems des Maschinen- und Anlagenbaus.* Dissertation, University of Paderborn, HNI-Verlagsschriftenreihe 375, Paderborn

Wünderlich, N., von Wangenheim, F., & Bitner, M. J. (2012). High tech and high touch. *Journal of Service Research, 16*(1), 3–20.

Wünderlich, N., Heinonen, K., Ostrom, A. L., Patricio, L., Sousa, R., Voss, C., & Lemmink, J. G. A. M. (2015). "Futurizing" smart service: implications for service researchers and managers. *Journal of Services Marketing, 29*(6/7), 442–447.

Christian Koldewey, born in 1989, studied mechanical engineering at the University of Paderborn and the University of Applied Sciences Bielefeld with a focus on production engineering. Since 2015 he has been a research assistant at the Heinz Nixdorf Institute of the University of Paderborn at the chair of Professor Gausemeier as well as at the chair Advanced Systems Engineering of Professor Dumitrescu. Since 2020 he leads the research area strategic planning at the latter. His particular research topics are digital service innovation and strategy, and business model generation.

Prof. Dr.-Ing. Jürgen Gausemeier is a senior professor at the Heinz Nixdorf Institute of the University of Paderborn and chairman of the board of the Leading-Edge Cluster "Intelligente Technische Systeme Ostwestfalen-Lippe (it's OWL)." He was a speaker of the Collaborative Research Center 614 "Self-Optimizing Concepts and Structures in Mechanical Engineering" and member of the German Council of Science and Humanities from 2009 until 2015. Jürgen Gausemeier is initiator and chairman of the Supervisory Board of the consulting company UNITY AG. Since 2003 he is member of "acatech—German Academy of Science and Engineering" and since 2012 vice president.

Prof. Dr.-Ing. Roman Dumitrescu is the director at the Fraunhofer Institute for Mechatronics System Design IEM and head of the working group Advanced Systems Engineering at the Heinz Nixdorf Institute of the University of Paderborn. His research focus is on the product creation of intelligent technical systems. In personal union, Prof. Dumitrescu is managing director of the Leading-Edge Cluster "Intelligente Technische Systeme Ostwestfalen-Lippe (it's OWL)." He is, among other things, a member of the expert group of the German Federal Government's Innovation Dialog, the research advisory board of the 3-D MID e.V. research association, the steering committee of the NRW state government's Initiative Wirtschaft & Arbeit 4.0, and the administrative board of the RKW competence center.

Hans Heinrich Evers , M. Sc., studied industrial engineering with specialization in mechanical engineering at the University of Paderborn. His focus was on innovation and production management. From 2017 to 2019 he was a student assistant at the Heinz Nixdorf Institute, University of Paderborn, and worked at the chairs of Professor Gausemeier and Professor Dumitrescu. Since 2020, he is working as a technology consultant at Zielpuls GmbH and supports customers in the successful implementation of systems engineering and the design of Advanced Driver Assistance Systems in the automotive industry.

Maximilian Frank , born in 1987, studied industrial engineering at the University of Kassel and the Technical University of Berlin. From 2016 to 2020 he was a research assistant at the Heinz Nixdorf Institute of the University of Paderborn. He worked in the Strategic Planning and Innovation Management team at the chair of Professor Gausemeier as well as at the chair Advanced Systems Engineering of Professor Dumitrescu. His research topics are digital service innovation, business model generation, and competence management. In these areas, he managed and worked on numerous research and industrial projects.

Jannik Reinhold, born in 1991, studied industrial engineering with focus on electrical engineering at the University of Paderborn. Since 2018 he is research associate at Heinz Nixdorf Institute of the University of Paderborn. He works in the research group Advanced Systems Engineering at the chair of Professor Dumitrescu and leads the team for strategic planning. His research topics are foresight, strategy development, and especially the planning of value networks considering pattern-based approaches. Addressed topics are mainly digitization and smart services. In these fields, he is working on numerous research and industry projects.

Problem Structuring to Enable Innovation in Business/IT Projects

Tatiana Porté, Gil Regev, and Alain Wegmann

1   Introduction

Companies use digitization to reap the benefits of innovation, but technological change is impossible without organizational change (Wade and Marchant 2014). We think that achieving the business and IT alignment is a key factor for successful digital transformation. How can we ensure this harmony between IT and people who affected by the changes to enable innovation?

We consider innovative IT projects as ill-structured problems—they include multiple actors, multiple perspectives, conflicting interests, and key uncertainties (Rosenhead and Mingers 2001). In business/IT analysis of complex IT problems problem structuring methods are used to model the structure of a situation that some people want to change (Rosenhead 2013). This chapter addresses how to structure problems in order to reduce the complexity and achieve business/IT alignment in IT projects.

We propose a problem structuring method in which we analyze the viewpoints of all the actors involved in a project—of the company of interest, of the company's customers, of customers of the customers, and of the regulators if necessary. We think that the understanding of viewpoints is a key to accommodation between them. We analyze the gaps between the current and desired state of affairs, using service and appreciation models. Instead of concentrating on process modeling as in BPMN we concentrate on service offering and service adoption; instead of concentrating on short-term goals, we concentrate on ensuring the long-term survival of the company. The described method differs from traditional techniques, e.g., root cause analysis (Solé et al. 2017), which concentrates on problems, and not on who sees the problem and why it is a problem.

T. Porté (✉) · G. Regev · A. Wegmann
Ecole Polytechnique Fédérale de Lausanne, Lausanne, Switzerland
e-mail: tatiana.porte@epfl.ch

© The Author(s), under exclusive license to Springer Nature Switzerland AG 2021   239
D. R. A. Schallmo, J. Tidd (eds.), *Digitalization*, Management for Professionals,
https://doi.org/10.1007/978-3-030-69380-0_13

This method, called SEAM, is used in IT consulting and innovation coaching and taught in EPFL marketing and business/IT courses in Computer Science Master's program. It was also taught in a digital transformation module in the EMBA program at EPFL. For teaching, we use problem-based learning in which students role-play consultants to understand the context and the structure of the company, analyze issues perceived by stakeholders, enumerate possible solutions, choose the solution that represents a trade-off between the goals of stakeholders and the survival of the company, and ultimately design the implementation.

SEAM is being developed since 1997 in the Systemic Modeling Laboratory of EPFL (Regev et al. 2013). The SEAM method is based on systems thinking principles while SEAM modeling is based on software engineering principles, particularly RM-ODP (Wegmann et al. 2007). With it, it is possible to use heuristics on similar problems from very different domains (e.g., marketing strategy, organizational strategy, IT strategy).

2   Case Study

We illustrate the method on a project of a Society of Family Doctors (SFD) faced with a problem of change management and digital transformation. The SFD case is used as an example of a concrete illustration of our method.

The project has started with a need to develop a database for the SFD to manage the internship information used in the coaching of post-graduate medical students who are doing post-graduate training to become family doctors (FD). We use contextual inquiry (Beyer and Holtzblatt 1995) as a way to gather information. A written transcript given in Annex 1 describes the results of the contextual inquiry.

Based on the transcripts and collected information we create service models "as-is" to analyze the problem and later design a service model for the solution "to-be." A service is the behavior of a system, observed from the system's environment (Wegmann et al. 2007), that brings value to another system in the same environment (for example, a customer of a company). All models are results of what people interpret from the reality, the business actors as well as the business analyst. The main principle of SEAM is interpretivism, all people in the project need to align their viewpoints in order to achieve the project goals—to develop a shared interpretation of what they consider of interest in the universe around them. Ensuring the alignment of developed models (viewpoints) help us find where the reality observed by different actors is not consistent.

Regulator Viewpoint: Understanding the Context of the Organization

As we stress the importance of viewpoints, we present different models that represent the actors' viewpoints on the situation. First, we will model the regulators'

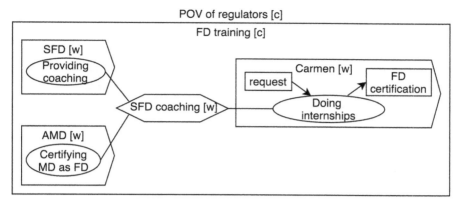

Fig. 1 The viewpoint of the "FD training" regulator

viewpoints. Regulators' norms are shared or taken into account by other actors so understanding their point of view allows us to understand the context of the problem.

When analyzing a group of actors with different viewpoints, we need to model their motivation. In a typical case, there exists a regulator, an actor whose values are shared by other actors to ensure the regulation (Regev and Wegmann 2011). Regulators and company management have the same motivation—to maintain the stability of a system by taking regulative actions when the norms are violated.

Note that not all projects have an explicit regulator present but searching for it can reveal tacit information shared by all actors involved in a project.

To analyze the behavior of the actors involved in the project, we do a SEAM service model where we show what actions on macro-level (services) actors perform. In SEAM we use a model element "working object" for a system which is a conceptualization of reality by an observer (Regev et al. 2013). To be able to observe the inside of a working object, we model it as a "composite"—a white box, denoted as [c] on the model. The "whole" view of a working object is a black box, denoted as [w], which means that we cannot observe the behavior of the actors inside it.

The regulator can be explicit (e.g., a legislative body) or implicit (e.g., a lobby). In the SFD case, there are two explicit regulators:

1. The Association of Medical Doctors (AMD)—as shown in Fig. 1—specifies what is required to be certified as a family doctor. A graduate medical student should do post-graduate training which includes a minimum of 6 years of internships in hospitals. The AMD specifies the minimum set of disciplines that should be practiced there. A federal certificate then allows one to open a practice as an independent practitioner. AMD's motivation is to guarantee FD's competencies.
2. Regional Department of Health—as shown on Fig. 2—maintains an adequate number of FDs in a region, it authorizes new family doctors to open practice in the region and provides funding to the SFD for medical students who became family doctors after coaching.

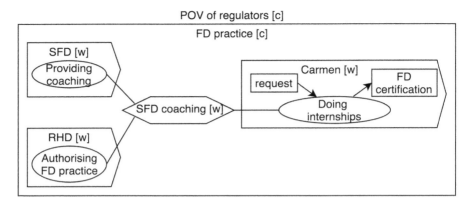

Fig. 2 The viewpoint of the "FD practice" regulator

We consider the viewpoint of regulators as two ecosystems "FD training" and "Regional practice" which help us group the actors based on what they do together. The "FD training" includes all actors relevant to the training of family doctors (universities, hospitals, student housing, medical students, etc.). The "Regional practice" contains all actors relevant in providing and benefiting from health services (doctors, nurses, hospitals, patients, etc).

The number of ecosystems is a design choice and does not have to be exhaustive and can be amended in the process of analysis, It is our perception that each ecosystem develops its own set of norms with or without an explicit regulator. For each ecosystem, we can observe a set of domain terms used by the actors.

Customer Viewpoint: Understanding What Is Provided to the Environment

Then we analyze the view of the customer of the organization which allows us to understand what services are provided to the environment—everything besides the considered system. In Fig. 3 we model all actors as perceived by the customer (Carmen).

In the service model from the customer point of view "as-is" (Fig. 3), we model all actors that interact (regardless of the organization in which they belong). We model companies as composite working objects and value networks, and people as working object as "whole." We show what services they perform and what information they exchange in the process. In the case, the direct customer of the SFD is personified in Carmen, a graduated medical student whose goal is to get certified as FD and open practice in her home region. It is preferred to base the model on a real person that can be observed in a contextual inquiry. We claim that the direct observation of a customer brings more insight than working with an abstract persona. Even if we consider a functional role filled by many people, we model a concrete person.

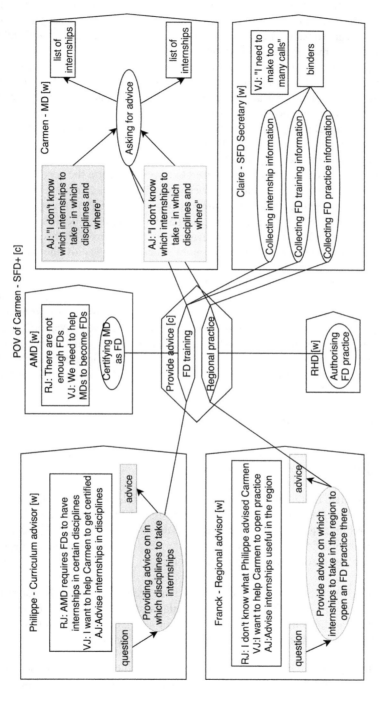

Fig. 3 Service model "as-is" from the point of view of a postgrad medical student

We do not concentrate on the organizational boundaries of the companies during business analysis. At the same time, for a company of interest (typically the project sponsor), we can consider the organizational view of the legal entity with related constraints in the management viewpoint.

The appreciation modeling in SEAM is based on Vickers's appreciative systems (Regev et al. 2011). For practical usage, we suggest scoping modeling of reality (RJ), value (VJ), norms, and action judgments (AJ) of all actors to only relevant ones—the customer and the customer of the customer. We show relevant judgments on the service model in Fig. 3. For relevant actors, we consider the gaps between the reality the actors perceive and their values and norms. The resulting value judgments describe the problems faced by different actors.

We model information which actors need to have to perform the service. We can note which interpretations are shared between actors and which are not. We use the model element "working object" to represent what other people conceptualizes as "system." We believe that we can develop a shared interpretation between the actors of a project only by showing a model. When considering actors with different points of views, it is extremely important to note what properties of the model are interpreted by the actors differently.

On the service model "as-is" we can observe how the SFD advisors are providing regional and curriculum advice to Carmen, how the SFD secretary collects information about internships and student status. From inquiry, it is already known that internship binder is not useful for students (service model shown in Annex 2, Fig. 6), but modeling "as-is" helps uncover other discrepancies in the shared conceptualization of actors. An analyst, as an external observer, can have a different interpretation of the universe of discourse than other actors which should be captured for analysis. Analyst notes can be of two kinds:

- Scoping notes (what is shown and what is not shown for the purpose of the model)
- Analysis notes (if there is a discrepancy between the analyst observations and reality judgments of actors as observed by the analyst)

We concentrate on the problem of the customer and its customer. In the case, the analyst notes that Carmen is asking what internships she needs to take to fulfill the disciplines requirement for certification and, at the same time, what internships can help her open practice in the same region later. But advisors receiving the same question give her inconsistent advice because of:

1. Not-shared interpretation—both of them provide advice in form of list internships to take but, under influence of the regulator's norms, one of them treats internships as disciplines and the other advisor as regional opportunities.
2. Not sharing data on student curriculum and previously given advice.

These findings show that problem cannot be solved just by the development of a cloud database as requested by the project sponsor, the business processes inside the company need to change as well, along with the norms of people involved in the project to ensure that they act accordingly to the technological change.

Management View: Understanding How the Environment Helps the Company to Survive

Then we consider the viewpoint of the organization's management which is either complimentary to the viewpoint of the customer or the customer of the customer and describes what the organization provides to its environment. The view of the management describes how the environment helps the company to survive, we call this view metabolic.

When we consider the viewpoint of the customer, we are modeling a functional service that the company is providing. But according to homeostasis principles (Regev et al. 2012), the company needs to ensure its long-term survival. We postulate that finding the actor who provides the means for the continuing survival of the company. In this case it is especially evident since the functional service of SFD—coaching of students—is free. The customer of the SFD is the Regional Health Department (Fig. 4) which provides funding and thus ensures the SFD's survival.

The funding is dependant only on the conversion rate in the "FD," therefore solutions involving ceasing regional advice are counter-productive. At the same time, reducing advice in the first ecosystem leads to a reduced number of certified FDs that can open practice, therefore removing curriculum advice to avoid confusion is also impossible.

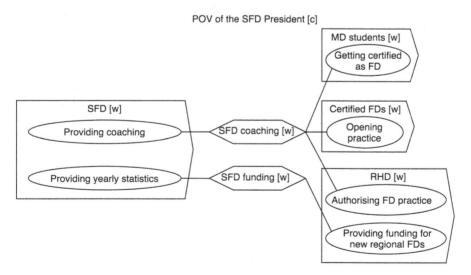

Fig. 4 Service model from the point of view of the customer of the customer

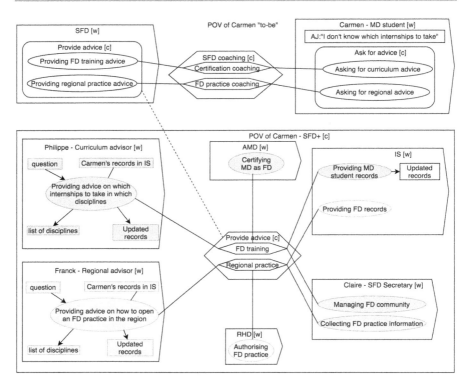

Fig. 5 Service model "to-be" from the point of view of a postgrad medical student

Aligning Viewpoints: Serving the Environment to Get the Means for Survival

Finally, we construct the updated service model from the point of view of the customer to design a solution to the problem. Here we design a service that provides value to the environment while ensuring that the environment values the service.

We believe that the selection of a solution is indistinguishable from the way we define the problem in the process of problem structuring. In this case, we have defined the problem as the ambiguity of terms and shared information between actors, therefore the designed solution restructures service offering to remove the ambiguity and improve information management.

In this case, we have identified the ambiguity of terms and information exchanged between actors. The designed functional service "to-be" (Fig. 5) provides the following changes:

– Tracking of internships is replaced with tracking of coaching. It is counter-intuitive to the original project brief but was validated with stakeholders.
– Regional advisors now provide networking contacts in the region instead of quickly expiring internships.

- The secretary manages the community of family doctors instead of updating binders with internships and student information.
- The information system provides secure access to the shared curriculum and student information to ensure shared interpretation.

Once the solution is selected, we do the behavior model "to-be" where we describe the service offering and service implementation. After the solution is selected and the behavior of actors "to-be" is defined, we do an information model "to-be" as a viewpoint of IT of the company of interest.

When we do perform service design, it is important to pay attention to what actors are inside and outside of the system boundary. The system boundary defines which parts of the system we can change and control and guarantee the service. We postulate that the system boundary denotes the area where the actors inside of it can "guarantee" the service which is implemented for the problem solution, sometimes explicitly with an SLA. The selected boundary should not only address the function of the company of interest but also ensure the survival of it through metabolic service. To check the validity of this relationship, we can do a reverse model with the company of interest as the customer of those who is providing the means for its survival, as shown previously in Fig. 4.

3   Discussion

Problem structuring for business/IT projects using the SEAM method means constructing a set of service models as a way of conceptualizing the observed reality in a systemic way. The word "system" is not a model element, it is a way to conceptualize reality and it is extremely observer-dependent and it is always based on tacit knowledge (Lakoff and Johnson 1980). Those models can be combined in different ways for their purpose—as viewpoints of actors, as many service layers of customer and customer of the customer, as ecosystems, etc. There is a trade-off between the number of people modeled and the number of things that can be seen in parallel.

How do we know that the project is complete? All models have relevance and rigor for a purpose and within a selected scope. For example, the sketch models done in the earlier stages of contextual inquiry for the purpose of structuring all the actors do not require the same level of rigor as the models done for software implementation requirements. In the academic environment, we postulate that the students have finished the project when the developed set of models has an appropriate level of relevance and rigor. In an industry environment, e.g., in consulting or business analysis, the analyst needs to make sure that all stakeholders agree on the shared interpretation captured in the models.

Model Validation

For validation of the service models with stakeholders to ensure shared conceptualization of the outcome of the service and its implementation, we propose the following relevance levels:

- Relevant with shared interpretation
- Relevant without shared interpretation
- Irrelevant

A transcript produced after an interview or a contextual inquiry typically lacks shared interpretation. Validating a service model with stakeholders ensures the correctness of the model. It can also lead to the reconciliation of not-shared interpretation if the analyst brings discrepancies in interpretations of different actors to their attention. The shared service model is a model all stakeholders agree about (Regev et al. 2013). Scoping criterion—we model all entities necessary for the purpose of the model but as few as possible. We need to avoid modeling actors where we are sure of the execution of the service.

Model Verification

We check the ontological correctness for model verification to make sure that the model can be used for IT implementation. We propose the following rigor criteria:

- Actors need to share necessary information within a working object to perform their service.
- The relationship between "composite" and "whole" view of a working object is well-formed (the model has input and output local properties; service-process relationships are defined).

IT Applicability

For business analysis purposes the model in "as-is" does not have to be formally verifiable (Therefore the "flat" view is allowed) but formally verifiable "to-be" model using declarative semantics can be used to generate specifications for executable software code (Rychkova et al. 2008).

The resulting service model can also be used as input parameters for software as a service (SaaS). To make the link more precise, the service model notation can be extended with code capturing the relationships between actors and properties in text.

4   Conclusion

In this chapter, we have presented an IT consulting case illustrating how to structure information to solve a problem. We present a set of models and heuristics on how to construct them in order to reconcile and share conceptualization between people. This method can be used by people who teach and consult in business/IT alignment. It shows how to analyze different viewpoints and selecting an innovative solution based on thus structured information. The originality lies in the explicit representation of viewpoints, and heuristics on how to make a trade-off between them. We consider what services provided to a customer or a customer of the customer to make sure that the designed solution ensures a long-term survival of the company. We underline the importance of business/IT alignment as a way of ensuring the alignment of organizational and technological change.

Annex 1

Interview Transcript: Sébastien Chevallaz, SFD President

Sébastien Chevallaz, President, March 5 20XX, Lausanne

Alain	You asked me to do an on-line database for your society, the Society of Family Doctor. Can you tell me a bit more?
Sébastien	Yes, SFD advises about internships to medical students. We need a database of internships that will be available to all our advisors so that we can improve the advice we give.
Alain	So, the database should contain information about internships?
Sébastien	Yes.
Alain	And internships are 6 months long positions offered by hospitals that medical students take to be certified as medical doctors?
Sébastien	Yes, exactly, only the internships our students take are specified by FMD and should lead them to be certified as family doctors.
Alain	Do all advisors do the same job?
Sébastien	Not really. Curriculum advisors are the first point of contact for a medical student. They follow the student all along his or her studies and make sure they take the internships specified by FMD. Regional advisors help find the recommended internship in the hospitals in their region. They advise students on the internships they should take to be able to open a practice in their region.
Q	So how does it work?
A	The medical student calls a curriculum advisor who meets them regularly and can send them to meet with a regional advisor if needed. The goal is to help complete their post-graduate training and to help understand how to open their practice in their region of interest.
Alain	So, I suppose that the advisors are not all located in the same office?
Sébastien	Well, they work out of different places, yes. We have regional advisors in the main city if of each region: for example, Sion for Valais or Lausanne for Vaud. We manage five regions: Valais, Fribourg, Genève, Neuchâtel, Jura, Valais, and Vaud (all part of the

Suisse Romande). The curriculum advisors are in Lausanne (in canton de Vaud), the headquarter of SFD.

Alain So, they need to all see the same internships through the on-line database?
Sébastien Yes, that is it. That is why I need you.
Alain And it should be online so that the advisors can access it from anywhere they are?
Sébastien Yes.
Alain What do they use now?
Sébastien They each have their stuff. Excel, paper, e-mail, whatever.

Interview Transcript: Claire Simmens, SFD Secretary

Claire, Secretary, March 12 20XX, Lausanne

Alain Hello, I am Alain. I was sent by Sébastien to better understand your work with SFD and the internships.
Claire Hello. I am Claire. Pleased to meet you.
Alain Pleased to meet you. I was wondering whether you could tell me more about the way you manage internships.
Claire Sure. It is very complicated. I try to figure out which internships are available in hospitals. It is difficult.
Alain Why is it so difficult?
Claire Because I cannot call the hospitals. I have to ask the advisors.
Alain Why so?
Claire Because I do not have contact in hospitals. The advisors do. They are doctors.
Alain So how does it work? You call an advisor, and?
Claire And I ask them to tell me which internships are available in which hospital in their region.
Alain Ah, so you are talking to regional advisors?
Claire Yes. Well, they are all regional advisors, as you call them.
Alain So they give you this information?
Claire Well, not easily. I guess even for them it is difficult to know which internship is available because it changes all the time. A student takes the last internship in a pediatry and suddenly they are not available.
Alain So what do you do?
Claire I do my best. I write down whatever information they give me. Available, not available, no information.
Alain And where do you write it?
Claire In my internship binder.
Alain Can you show it to me?
Claire Sure. It is there, on the shelf. You can pick it up for me?
Alain Yup, here it is. Ah, I see you a table with hospitals, internships, status, etc. Can I take a picture and show it to Sébastien?
Claire Of course.
Alain Oh, I see there are two sections here. What is the other one that says Students?
Claire That one is where I put the information about the internships that the students have taken. There is a sheet for each student.
Alain Interesting. Where do you get this information from? From the advisors?

Claire	No, I regularly call the students and ask them where they are.
Alain	Nice. Can I take a picture of this one too?
Claire	Yes, but be careful, it has the names of students on it. Here, put this post-it over the name so it does not show.
Alain	Thanks a lot. Just one more question. This binder is here in your office. How do the advisors look at it?
Claire	Philippe is here in Lausanne, so he sometimes comes in and looks at it. The others, like Philippe, sometimes come here, less often though. And once every while they call me.
Alain	Great. Thanks again. I will share this with Sébastien if you agree.
Claire	Sure. I was happy to help.
Alain	May be a last request, would you mind to help me write a typical and concrete scenario on how SFD provides advice to the MD in training? If you can talk of a case of someone you personally know. This scenario will help me for understanding how things are done concretely.
Claire	I know an FD that just set up a practice. Her name is Carmen Barras. She came to see us at the end of her training as an FD. I know her as we come from the same village, called Randogne, located above Sierre, in Valais. It is closed to the Crans-Montana ski resort. Carmen did discover SFD via our website, 2 years back. She called us and I did set an appointment with Dr. Sébastien Chevallaz, our president, in Lausanne. It was in the conference room next door. I remember it lasted quite a while. They met and Dr. Chevallaz asked a lot of feedback on how her work was, he then checked that what was done was compliant with the FMD requirements. Last he gave some recommendations for the remaining internships.
Alain	Did he provide actual internship info?
Claire	May be but I doubt. Usually, he recommends the disciplines in which the internships should be done. The actual internships are usually recommended by our contact in the canton. In this case: Dr. Franck de Kalbermatten.
Alain	Do you know how this went.
Claire	Yes as she called me afterward. Her meeting was very useful. It did happen in Sion. She told me that Franck helped her to find internships that were very useful for an FD in Randogne.
Alain	Can you explain more?
Claire	In Winter, the FD in Randogne has to care about ski injuries. So she did her internship in traumatology in Sion.
Alain	And what is Carmen doing now:
Claire	I called her recently. She will open a group practice in Randogne with another FD coming from Geneva. Her practice will allow the current FD in Randogne to retire and his patients will be taken care of by these new doctors.
Alain	Let me recap who is who in this story. We have:

- Claire Barras, the FD in training.
- Phillipe Chevallaz, as curriculum advisor located in Lausanne.
- Franck de Kalbermatten, as regional advisor located in Sion.

– Christian Aymon, the doctor who did retire.
– And yourself, Claire located in Lausanne.

Is this correct?

Claire   Yes.
Alain   Obviously, what SFD did for Claire was very useful. Do you do an evaluation of your
          services with the MD in training? Did Claire suggest some improvements?
Claire   Now that you mentioned it, yes indeed.
Alain   Great story, can I use it in my models? Do you think Claire would agree? It would allow us
          to get a much better understanding of how AFS is working.
Claire   I am sure she will agree. I call her and let you know if she has a problem with you using
          her story. She is really enthusiastic about what SFD did for her.

Annex 2

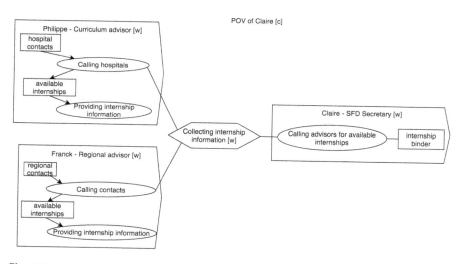

Fig. 6 Point of view of the SFD secretary

References

Beyer, H. R., & Holtzblatt, K. (1995). Apprenticing with the customer. *Communications of the ACM, 38*, 45–52.

Lakoff, G., & Johnson, M. (1980). *Metaphors we live by*. Chicago: University of Chicago.

Regev, G., & Wegmann, A. (2011). Revisiting goal-oriented requirements engineering with a regulation view. In *International symposium on business modeling and software design* (pp. 56–69). Springer.

Regev, G., Hayard, O., & Wegmann, A. (2011). Service systems and value modeling from an appreciative system perspective. In: *International conference on exploring services science* (pp. 146–157). Springer.

Regev, G., Hayard, O., & Wegmann, A. (2012). What we can learn about business modeling from homeostasis. In: *International symposium on business modeling and software design* (pp. 1–15). Springer.

Regev, G., Bajic-Bizumic, B., Golnam, A., Popescu, G., Tapandjieva, G., Saxena, A.B., & Wegmann, A. (2013). A philosophical foundation for business and IT alignment in enterprise architecture with the example of SEAM. In *Proceedings of the third international symposium on business modeling and software design* (pp. 131–139). SCITEPRESS-Science and Technology.

Rosenhead, J. (2013). Problem structuring methods. In S. I. Gass & M. C. Fu (Eds.), *Encyclopedia of operations research and management science*. Boston: Springer.

Rosenhead, J., & Mingers, J. (Eds.). (2001). *Rational analysis for a problematic world revisited*. Chichester: Wiley.

Rychkova, I., Regev, G., & Wegmann, A. (2008). Using declarative specifications in business process design. *IJCSA, 5*, 45–68.

Solé, M., Muntés-Mulero, V., Rana, A.I., & Estrada, G. (2017). Survey on models and techniques for root-cause analysis. *arXiv*, preprint arXiv:1701.08546.

Wade, M., & Marchant, D. (2014). *Are you prepared for your digital transformation? Understanding the power of technology AMPS in organizational change. Tomorrow's challenges*. IMD Lausanne, Switzerland.

Wegmann, A., Regev, G., Rychkova, I., Lê, L. -S., Cruz, J., & Julia, P. (2007). Business and IT alignment with SEAM for enterprise architecture.

Tatiana Porté is a Research Assistant in the Laboratory of Systemic Modeling in the School of Computer and Communication Sciences of Ecole Polytechnique Fédérale de Lausanne (EPFL) where she works on developing methods for analysis and design of business and IT services and applying them in IT strategy and business/IT alignment projects.

Gil Regev is a Senior Researcher at the School of Computer and Communication Sciences of the Ecole Polytechnique Fédérale de Lausanne (EPFL) since 1997, and Knowledge Manager at Itecor since 2008. Prior to joining EPFL, Gil worked for Logitech in Switzerland and California from 1988 to 1997. He is Vice President of the Swiss Knowledge Management Forum.

Alain Wegmann worked for 15 years at Logitech in development (Switzerland, USA, and Taiwan), manufacturing (Taiwan), and marketing (USA). In 1997, he became a professor at EPFL. He heads a laboratory that develops the SEAM method; a method designed to work on the business and IT alignment. SEAM is applied to define business and technical strategies, as well as business and IT services (ITIL compatible). SEAM is applied for teaching and consulting.

Part IV

Digital Transformation

Systematic Review of the Literature on SME Digitalization: Multi-sided Pressure on Existing SMEs

Andrea Meier

1 Introduction

An accelerated competition across a broad range of industries as an effect of increasing globalization, internationalization, urbanization, demographic change, and market demands has caused a huge pressure on enterprises. Aiming to adapt to these challenges small- and medium-sized enterprises (SMEs) are particularly suffering from lacking resources and capacities. Digitalization has been increasingly playing a central role in the scientific, managerial, and political discussion about how to face and overcome emerging challenges (European Commission 2018; Kagermann et al. 2016). Digital transformed products and services as well as value chains are highlighted as a vital solution approach for achieving a sustainable development and a means for realizing competitive advantages.

Literature offers insights into the affordances of digitalization mainly for large companies. Studies dealing with digital impacts with an explicit view on SMEs have been rather scarce up to now (Birkel et al. 2019; Chan et al. 2019). Thus, there is a need for more deep insights into the potential transformational ways of SMEs as into how to engage with digitalization or how to adapt structures and processes (Coreynen et al. 2017). A considerable number of research contributions from various disciplinary fields has provided evidence of how enterprises deal with digitalization and how this could be related to performance. A core theme of efforts is related to the identification of enabling, determining, or hampering factors also referred to as assets, variables, and influencers. However, similarly to the names of these factors, there are several factors displayed relating to different terms covering different topics. This in turn has led to a high inconsistency and often lacking understanding of potential enablers or obstacles to transformational efforts of SMEs. Scholars tackled this issue by exploring and synthesizing previous literature

A. Meier (✉)
University of Innsbruck, Innsbruck, Austria
e-mail: andrea.meier@student.uibk.ac.at

© The Author(s), under exclusive license to Springer Nature Switzerland AG 2021
D. R. A. Schallmo, J. Tidd (eds.), *Digitalization*, Management for Professionals,
https://doi.org/10.1007/978-3-030-69380-0_14

(Dam et al. 2019; Imgrund et al. 2018; Sommer 2015; Tarutė and Gatautis 2014). Acknowledging the academic contribution of these efforts, nevertheless, it has to be stated that they either have used very small sample sizes with a restricted focus on industry and time or have acquired the data in a non-transparent way. Moreover, digitalization in most SME studies is not defined explicitly or applied as a general term for engaging either with a single digital technology, like big data or social media, or a bundle of technologies, which often is referred to as Industry 4.0 (Birkel et al. 2019).

To address these gaps this study aims to

- Clarify the understanding and scope of digitalization by identifying technological foci of previous research.
- Synthesize the heterogenous enablers and obstacles of SME digitalization resulting from the review analysis into a comprehensive framework.

Thus, the chapter at hand is concerned with an enhanced comprehension of SME digitalization and pre-conditions rendering digital transformation to be successful by merging these in a conceptual framework. For this chapter, digitalization is equally used to digital transformation on the one hand, and enablers will be used synonymously with determining factors, assets, pre-conditions, and (influencing) variables.

This effort is structured the following way: The subsequent Sect. 2 depicts the research methodology applied. Thereafter, the presentation of the findings from the analysis and synthesis (Sect. 3) is followed up by a discussion of the findings, theoretical and managerial implications, and a derivation of potential further research avenues (Sect. 4).

2   Review Methodology

An extensive search process was conducted comprising peer-reviewed, scholarly journal contributions from the last two decades. According to Denyer and Tranfield (2009) and Moher et al. (2009) this review followed a pre-defined stage-oriented process, which comprises (1) search string definition, (2) database and (3) article selection, (4) article classification, and (5) article analysis (see Fig. 1). The search string "digital AND (SME* OR small and medium sized enterprise*)" was applied to attain a comprehensive and profound data sample. Several databases, e.g. SCOPUS, Web of Science, Wiley Online Library, were utilized to mitigate potential biases. This retrieval ended up in 538 results. After removing duplicates and applying a pre-defined list of inclusion and exclusion criteria to the abstracts (available from the author upon request) such as commercial focus, time span from the beginning of 2000 to mid of 2019, and organizational level of analysis the sample finally consists of 77 articles. Thereafter, a narrative analysis of the full texts was conducted to identify themes across the diversity of contributions from different theoretical orientations, applying different methods and foci.

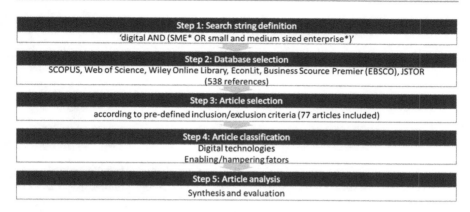

| Step 1: Search string definition |
| 'digital AND (SME* OR small and medium sized enterprise*)' |

| Step 2: Database selection |
| SCOPUS, Web of Science, Wiley Online Library, EconLit, Business Scource Premier (EBSCO), JSTOR (538 references) |

| Step 3: Article selection |
| according to pre-defined inclusion/exclusion criteria (77 articles included) |

| Step 4: Article classification |
| Digital technologies
Enabling/hampering fators |

| Step 5: Article analysis |
| Synthesis and evaluation |

Fig. 1 Review and analysis process (according to Tranfield et al. 2003; Moher et al. 2009)

3   Analysis and Synthesis Results

The analysis of factors enabling SME digitalization and the different foci on technologies uncovered an inconsistent body of knowledge and understanding of the topic under investigation.

Technological Foci of Previous Research

Most contributions analyzed, lack an underlying definition of digitalization for their investigations. As far as definitions, in general, are provided, studies refer to digitalization mostly to leveraging digital resources and technologies to internal and external value creation processes and models (Neirotti and Raguseo 2017; Romanelli 2018). Within SME related research authors mostly implicitly refer digitalization to either a mere techno-centric understanding (Cenamor et al. 2019) or a strategic topic (L. Li et al. 2018; Ukko et al. 2019).

In terms of technological foci extant research relate their investigations to several classes of technologies (see Fig. 2). Early studies concentrated their view on the impacts of e-commerce (e.g. Feindt et al. 2002), followed by investigations into the utilization of websites and adopting e-business, i.e. IT assistance of information exchange processes along digital networks (e.g. Sebora et al. 2009). Next, the rapid emergence of the internet and mobile technologies was reflected by studies from 2010 onwards (e.g., Harrigan et al. 2010; Stankovska et al. 2016). This technological focus was succeeded by research more recently focusing on digital platform (Jin and Hurd 2018), social media (Birkel et al. 2019), big data (Dam et al. 2019), and data cloud (Gupta et al. 2013) technologies.

Authors of the contributing articles display diversity in their perspectives on technology that range from approaching digital impacts from one single technology across a bundle of technologies towards digital technologies in general.

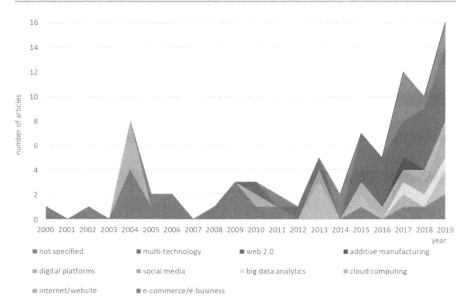

Fig. 2 Digital technologies focused on in previous research

Conceptual Framework of Enabling and Hampering Factors (THIOMC)

Drawing from the analysis results a categorical conceptualization was derived. This was supplemented by insights from interviews, that the author is currently conducting to extend knowledge about SME's social media utilization as a special class of digital technologies. The author followed the suggestions for exploring technological change by Sharif (1999) as an outline for categorization. Sharif identified four main categories to be vital for businesses in general to successfully master and exploit technological change comprised by the THIO approach: These are Technoware, Humanware, Inforware, and Orgaware. The framework has already guided previous studies on other specific topics of interests in innovation and technology management research (e.g., Kilubi 2015). During analyzing the data sample, the author recognized two more categories emerging that are considered relevant to the topic under investigation, namely these are Manageware and Contextware. Thus, the dimensions for anchoring the synthesis results were extended to the THIOMC framework. As displayed in Fig. 3 most of the previous contributions dealt with Orgaware and Contextware (each 22%), followed by Manageware (19%), Technoware (13%), and Humanware lying equal with Inforware (each 12%).

Subsequently, the results of analyzing the SME digitalization enablers and obstacles are to be presented more explicitly in terms of the main THIOMC categories (see Table 1).

Fig. 3 The THIOMC framework—enablers for SME digitalization (based on Sharif 1999)

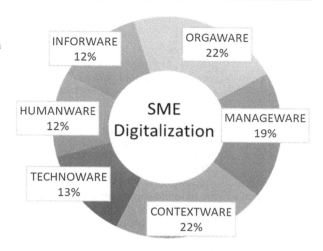

Technoware: This dimension encompasses physical capacities and technical assets aiming to intensify human power for value generation. It may originate from within or beyond an enterprise (Sharif 1999). Extant research most frequently mentioned access to a firm's internal and external technical infrastructure, compatibility, uncertainty, complexity, situatedness, and relative advantages respectively costs of digital technologies.

Humanware: This category relates to the incorporated tacit human capabilities (Sharif 1999). Evidence of significant impacts within this category mainly is stated for employees' knowledge and skills. Other enabling factors revealed by this review are related to the subdimensions of human resource allocation within powerful teams, employees' involvement and commitment, as well as employees' age.

Inforware: This cluster refers to documented and recorded knowledge and facts and is considered to speed up learning and to decrease the need for resources (Sharif 1999). Significant enablers mentioned mostly are forth and foremost data security and perceived outcome respectively lacking performance measurements, followed by data quality, open communication, and data management.

Orgaware: This category refers to organizational characteristics and incorporated schemes, processes, and structures as a base for coordinating and performing value generation activities (Sharif 1999). The reviewed studies suggested most evidence for agility and adaptivity, firm size, financial resources, operational capability, culture, and firm age lying equal with product and services.

Manageware: Owner–manager behavior, attitudes, and profile are captured by this category, since managerial support and commitment have a domino effect on shaping, providing, and allocating resources and capabilities (Saunila et al. 2019). In this vein, assets mostly mentioned are owner–manager's commitment and openness, strategic orientation, managerial knowledge and experience (digital literacy and entrepreneurial skills), innovativeness and agility, age and gender, as well as leader's time resources.

Table 1 SME digitalization enablers emphasized in literature

Technoware	References	Frequency	Percentage [%]
Access to technical infrastructure	Birkel et al. (2019); Chen et al. 2016; Dam et al. (2019); Hagsten and Kotnik (2017); Harrigan et al. (2010); Horváth and Szerb (2018); Jones et al. (2014); Kiselicki et al. (2015); Lee et al. (2009); Osterwalder (2004); Philip and Williams (2019); Piscitello and Sgobbi (2004); Scuotto et al. (2017a); Wong and Sloan (2006), Zhu et al. (2004); Stockdale and Standing (2006)	16	20.8
Compatibility and integrability	Alshamaila et al. (2013); Birkel et al. (2019); Bracht and Masurat (2005); Cenamor et al. (2019); Dini et al. (2008); Engels (2017); Harrigan et al. (2010); Molero et al. (2019); Scuotto et al. (2017a)	9	11.7
Complexity and ease of use	Alshamaila et al. (2013); Birkel et al. (2019); Cenamor et al. (2019); Sebora et al. (2009) Shaltoni et al. (2018); Traşca et al. (2019); van der Loo et al. (2015); Gupta et al. (2013)	8	10.4
Relative advantage/costs	Alshamaila et al. (2013); Lucchetti and Sterlacchini (2004)	2	2.5
Situatedness	Morgan-Thomas (2016); Scuotto et al. (2017c)	2	2.5
Uncertainty	Alshamaila et al. (2013); Birkel et al. (2019); Bouwman et al. (2018); Coreynen et al. (2017); Dam et al. (2019); Engels (2017); Eriksson and Hultman (2005); Gagliardi (2013); Morgan-Thomas (2016)	9	11.6
Humanware	References	Frequency	Percentage [%]
Age of employees	Meyer (2011)	1	1.3
Allocation / powerful teams	Acar et al. (2005); Li et al. (2018); Meyer (2011); Robu (2013); Sommer (2015); Hagsten and Kotnik (2017); Jin and Hurd (2018)	7	9.1
Employee involvement	Birkel et al. (2019); Foroudi et al. (2017); Stockdale and Standing (2006); Velu et al. (2019)	4	5.2
Knowledge/ skills	Acar et al. (2005); Alford and Page (2015); Alshamaila et al. (2013); Annosi et al. (2019); Birkel et al. (2019); Bouwman et al. (2018); Coreynen et al. (2017); Dholakia and Kshetri (2004); Elia et al. (2019); Engels (2017); Feindt et al. (2002); Foroudi et al. (2017); Gagliardi (2013); Hagsten and Kotnik (2017); Harrigan et al. (2010); Houari and Medjedel (2009); Jin and Hurd (2018); Jones et al. (2014); Koenig and Wigand (2004); Lee et al. (2009); Mack et al. (2017); Mazzarol (2015); Osterwalder	30	39

(continued)

Table 1 (continued)

Technoware	References	Frequency	Percentage [%]
	(2004); Pergelova et al. (2019); Piscitello and Sgobbi (2004); Saunila et al. (2019); Scuotto et al. (2017a); Sommer (2015); Wielicki and Arendt (2010); Li et al. (2016)		
Inforware	References	Frequency	Percentage [%]
Data management	Bracht and Masurat (2005); Dam et al. (2019)	2	2.6
Data quality	Begg and Caira (2012); Bracht and Masurat (2005); Dam et al. (2019)	3	3.9
Data security	Begg and Caira (2012); Birkel et al. (2019); Bracht and Masurat (2005); Dholakia and Kshetri (2004); Dini et al. (2008); Engels (2017); Foroudi et al. (2017); Gagliardi (2013); Gandia and Parmentier (2017); Gupta et al. (2013); Houari and Medjedel (2009); Koenig and Wigand (2004); Levstek et al. (2018); Mazzarol (2015); Quinton et al. (2017); Sommer (2015); Stockdale and Standing (2006); Tsatsou et al. (2010); Wong and Sloan (2006)	19	25.7
Open communication	Bracht and Masurat (2005); Chen et al. (2016); Coreynen et al. (2017)	3	3.9
Perceived outcome	Alford and Page (2015); Annosi et al. (2019); Dinca et al. (2019); Eriksson and Hultman (2005); Gagliardi (2013); Gupta et al. (2013); Ibrahim et al. (2018); Mogoş (2015); Mazzarol (2015); Osterwalder (2004); Quinton et al. (2017); Shaltoni et al. (2018); Sommer (2015); Stockdale and Standing (2006); Vidhyalakshmi and Kumar (2016); Wong and Sloan (2006)	16	20.8
Orgaware	References	Frequency	Percentage [%]
Agility/ organizational structures	Annosi et al. (2019); Barroso et al. (2019); Birkel et al. (2019); Bracht and Masurat (2005); Chan et al. (2019); Coreynen et al. (2017); Dam et al. (2019); Engels (2017); Feindt et al. (2002); Harrigan et al. (2010); Joensuu-Salo et al. (2018); Koenig and Wigand (2004); Levstek et al. (2018); Li et al. (2016); Prindible and Petrick (2015); Robu (2013); Quinton et al. (2017); Saunila et al. (2019); Velu et al. (2019); Wynarczyk (2000); Zhu et al. (2004)	21	27.3
Culture	Dam et al. (2019); Levstek et al. (2018); Li et al. (2018); Quinton et al. (2017); Ukko et al. (2019); Velu et al. (2019); Wong and Sloan (2006)	7	9.1

(continued)

Table 1 (continued)

Technoware	References	Frequency	Percentage [%]
Financial resources	Bracht and Masurat (2005); Elia et al. (2019); Engels (2017); Gagliardi (2013); Kiselicki et al. (2015); Lucchetti and Sterlacchini (2004); Osterwalder (2004); Piscitello and Sgobbi (2004); Sommer (2015); Wielicki and Arendt (2010); Zhu et al. (2004)	11	15.3
Firm age	Dholakia and Kshetri (2004); Harrigan et al. (2010); Mack et al. (2017); Meyer (2011); Hagsten and Kotnik (2017)	5	6.5
Firm size	Acar et al. 2005); Alshamaila et al. (2013); Alshamaila et al. (2013); Chan et al. (2019); Dholakia and Kshetri (2004); Dini et al. (2008); Hagsten and Kotnik (2017); Harrigan et al. (2010); Ibrahim et al. (2018); Levstek et al. (2018); Lucchetti and Sterlacchini (2004); Robu (2013); Sommer (2015); Zhu et al. (2004)	14	18.2
Operational capability	Barroso et al. (2019); Bracht and Masurat (2005); Coreynen et al. (2017); Feindt et al. (2002); Lee et al. (2009); Molero et al. (2019); Quinton et al. (2017); Scuotto et al. (2017c); Ukko et al. (2019); Wielicki and Arendt (2010);	10	13.0
Product and services	Barroso et al. (2019); Elia et al. (2019); Houari and Medjedel (2009); Morgan-Thomas (2016); Philip and Williams (2019); Piscitello and Sgobbi (2004)	6	7.8
Manageware	References	Frequency	Percentage [%]
Innovativeness	Alshamaila et al. (2013); Birkel et al. (2019); Bouwman et al. (2018); Chan et al. (2019); Dam et al. (2019); Toanca (2016); Ukko et al. (2019)	7	9.1
Managerial knowledge/ experience	Annosi et al. (2019); Dam et al. (2019); Dinca et al. (2019); Mack et al. (2017); Vidhyalakshmi and Kumar (2016); Lee et al. (2009); Li et al. (2018); Omiunu (2019); Quinton et al. (2017); Wynarczyk (2000)	10	13.0
Owner/manager characteristics	Gagliardi (2013); Ibrahim et al. (2018); Levstek et al. (2018); Middleton and Byus (2011); Pergelova et al. (2019)	5	6.5
Openness/ commitment	Alshamaila et al. (2013); Annosi et al. (2019); Barroso et al. (2019); Chan et al. (2019); Coreynen et al. (2017); Dam et al. (2019); Feindt et al. (2002); Foroudi et al. (2017); Gandia and Parmentier (2017); Houari and Medjedel (2009); Li et al. (2016, 2018); Mack et al. (2017); Mazzarol (2015); Piscitello and Sgobbi (2004); Quinton et al. (2017); Saunila	21	27.3

(continued)

Table 1 (continued)

Technoware	References	Frequency	Percentage [%]
	et al. (2019); Sebora et al. (2009); Stockdale and Standing (2006); Vatuiu et al. (2014); Wynarczyk (2000)		
Strategic orientation	Bouwman et al. (2018); Cenamor et al. 2019; Chan et al. (2019); Coreynen et al. (2017); Dam et al. (2019); Jones et al. (2014); Levstek et al. (2018); Li et al. (2016, 2018); Mazzarol (2015); Osterwalder (2004); Prindible and Petrick (2015); Saunila et al. (2019); Ukko et al. (2019); Vatuiu et al. (2014); Velu et al. (2019); Wielicki and Arendt (2010)	17	22.1
Time resources	Gagliardi (2013); Mazzarol (2015); Stockdale and Standing 2006); Jones et al. (2014)	4	5.2
Contextware	References	Frequency	Percentage [%]
Collaboration/ open innovation	Chan et al. 2019; Engels (2017); Feindt et al. (2002); Foroudi et al. (2017); Gagliardi (2013); Houari and Medjedel (2009); Lucchetti and Sterlacchini (2004); Scuotto et al. (2017c); Toanca (2016); Velu et al. (2019)	10	13
Competitive pressure	Barroso et al. (2019); Birkel et al. (2019); Bouwman et al. (2018); Dholakia and Kshetri (2004); Eriksson and Hultman (2005); Koenig and Wigand (2004); Morgan-Thomas (2016); Piscitello and Sgobbi (2004); Robu (2013); Sebora et al. (2009)	10	13.0
Customer demands	Barroso et al. (2019); Birkel et al. (2019); Coreynen et al. (2017); Feindt et al. (2002); Foroudi et al. (2017); Eriksson and Hultman 2005; Houari and Medjedel (2009); Jones et al. (2014); Khan et al. (2019); Li et al. (2018); Meyer (2011); Osterwalder (2004); Piscitello and Sgobbi (2004); Quinton et al. (2017); Robu (2013); Saunila et al. (2019); Scuotto et al. (2017b); Shaltoni et al. (2018); Stockdale and Standing (2006); Wynarczyk (2000)	20	26.0
Ecological/ social environment	Acar et al. (2005) Birkel et al. (2019); Ukko et al. (2019);	3	3.9
External providers	Birkel et al. (2019); Chen et al. (2016); Jones et al. (2014); Koenig and Wigand (2004); Mack et al. (2017); Vidhyalakshmi and Kumar (2016)	6	7.8
Government support	Dini et al. (2008); Sommer (2015)	2	2.6
Industry	Alshamaila et al. (2013); Horváth and Szerb (2018); Levstek et al. (2018); Lucchetti and Sterlacchini (2004); Morgan-Thomas (2016); Hagsten and Kotnik (2017)	6	7.8

(continued)

Table 1 (continued)

Technoware	References	Frequency	Percentage [%]
Legal infrastructure	Birkel et al. (2019); Dini et al. (2008); Elia et al. (2019); Engels (2017); Foroudi et al. (2017); Houari and Medjedel (2009); Lucchetti and Sterlacchini (2004); Mack et al. (2017); Quinton et al. (2017); Robu (2013); Tsatsou et al. (2010); Velu et al. (2019); Zhu et al. (2004)	13	16.9
Market scope	Alshamaila et al. (2013); Joensuu-Salo et al. (2018); Koenig and Wigand (2004); Lucchetti and Sterlacchini (2004); Osterwalder (2004); Stockdale and Standing (2006); Zhu et al. (2004)	7	9.1
Interdependence	Birkel et al. (2019); Bouwman et al. (2018); Bracht and Masurat (2005); Gandia and Parmentier (2017); Molero et al. (2019); Osterwalder (2004); Quinton et al. (2017); Stockdale and Standing (2006)	8	10.4

Contextware: This dimension relates to capacities and resources originating from beyond the enterprise's border to leverage digital affordances for SMEs (Birkel et al. 2019; Osterwalder 2004; Ukko et al. 2019). Within this perspective previous research mainly emphasized enabling respectively hampering effects in terms of customer demands, legal infrastructure, competitive pressure, collaboration, and open innovation, interdependence and power balance within value chains and networks, market scope, industry, ecological, social, and geographical context, as well as governmental and political support.

4 Discussion and Conclusion

This review may contribute to extending and synthesizing knowledge by analyzing 77 articles from a broad range of business and management literature. Over the last two decades, the field of SME digitalization has increasingly attracted research interest. Nevertheless, according to previous insights into the field under investigation (e.g. Levstek et al. 2018), the review results confirm that the knowledge in the field is still scattered and immature.

Theoretical Contributions and Further Research Potential

Exploring the technological foci of extant studies uncovered a burgeoning attention towards and importance of sophisticated innovative technologies, such as social media or big data. Nevertheless, there is a need for profound studies in the incorporation of digital affordances by SME beyond the currently prevailing restricted views on business processes like marketing and consumer relationship management (Chen et al. 2016). Future research also should shed light on the potential downsides of digitalization, as contributions so far explored mainly positive potentials for value creation and business models. Therefore, calls for critical appraisals of digital adaptation have been released recently (e.g. Welter et al. 2017). Moreover, a comparison of the various technologies in their need of financial, human, and infrastructural resources could be an interesting field for future investigations. Also, the question of how to combine and embrace the different technologies could open further research avenues. Early insights in this vein are provided for the installation of a website with comparison to an e-commerce application by Dholakia and Kshetri (2004).

In terms of factors determining the intensity, pace, and success of SMEs' digital transformation this study reveals that sustaining and generating value through digital transformation is not dependent on exclusive factors but is dependent on a mix of various assets. The optimal course of action depends on both business internal and external factors. The THIOMC approach inspired from the work by Sharif (1999) provides a model that seeks to create a recognition and alignment of its six major components. Each of these components interacts with another. The dimensions and subdimensions reflected on are dynamically interrelated and refer to various business functions, value processes, and business settings.

Insights from this research suggest that SMEs may not be considered as a homogenous group of organizations, but rather are composed of firms with a broad range of heterogeneity. Indeed, businesses of all sizes have had to face challenges emerging from accelerated digitalization and to learn how to deal with the increasingly revolving environment. Nevertheless, in terms of small- and mid-sized firms particular the characteristics of SME start-ups are completely different in the way how they approach the challenges of digitalization (Birkel et al. 2019). In contrast to traditional existing SMEs, start-ups are mostly characterized by young leaders with high digital literacy, highly motivated and appropriately educated employees as well as agile structures and processes. They are increasingly present in knowledge-based intense sectors and often display business models relying on the affordances of digital technologies. Moreover, new firms may benefit from financial funding since this often relates to the first time after business inception (Metzger 2020). Thus, start-up SMEs meet a considerable share of the requirements and pre-conditions as suggested for enabling successful digitalization by the literature and accordingly outlined in the findings section of this review. In contrast, traditional firms mostly originating from the pre-digital era are forced to adapt their business models towards digitalization in order to stay competitive especially towards their larger counterparts. Concurrently, they lack appropriate time as well as financial, human, and technical resources and are increasingly under pressure due to their lower bargaining power (Birkel et al. 2019). Indeed, traditional small- and mid-sized businesses are thought of as late adopters of digital technologies in view of their resource limitations (O'Connor and Kelly 2017). Therefore, traditionally established SMEs are increasingly threatened from both sides, large, global acting enterprises as well as the entry of new, small competitors. Future research should contribute knowledge to this issue by investigating the impediments and accelerators to digital transformation for different classes of SMEs particularly in terms of size, age, and industry in more detail.

Managerial Implications

In practical terms, the conceptualized and extended THIOMC framework could serve as a reference point from which digital transformational decisions can start and be sorted. Enterprises should consider that the different challenges from digitalization are rooted in different enabler categories. Although firms are acting in different contexts with varying resources available, an organization hardly may neglect any dimension of potential impediments to face the challenges caused by digitalization. Depending on the sophistication of each of the components and their potential combination, a bundle of factor sets is available. Nevertheless, one should be aware of the extent of how far these factors might be controlled by an enterprise. Nevertheless, this framework is hoped to assist SMEs in navigating through a phased approach to digitalization.

Concluding Remarks

As every research study, this contribution comes not without limitations. These refer to the determining factors included. The analysis showed how frequently they are mentioned in the literature in terms of playing a significant role in SMEs digital transformation. The results do not provide evidence of the intensity and direction of impacts on the outcome of digitalization. Moreover, they do not offer evidence about the impacts of a specific (sub-)enabler on respective outcome dimensions or performance measures of successful digitalization. Also, this study offers no insights regarding the complex interrelationships among the factors within the THIOMC categories. These shortcomings merit further research attention.

Appendix: SME Digitalization Enablers Classified According to the THIOMC Framework

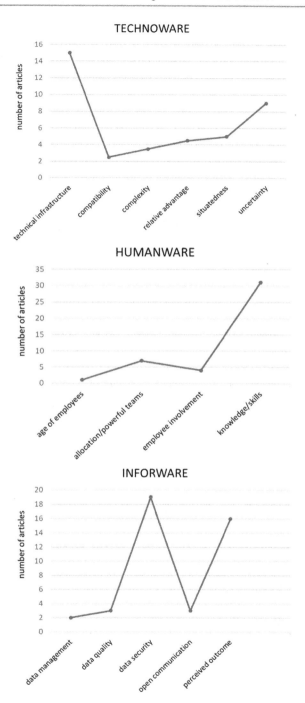

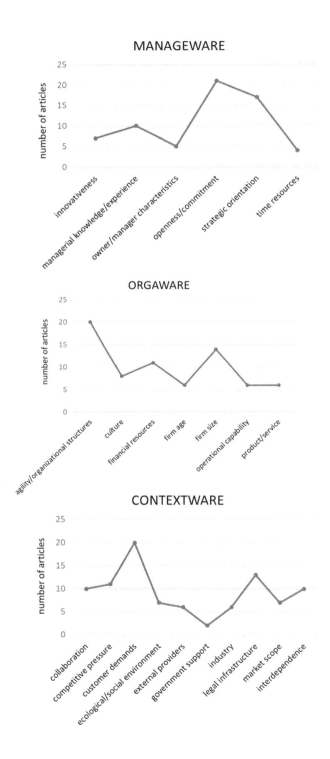

References

Acar, E., Koçak, I., Sey, Y., & Arditi, D. (2005). Use of information and communication technologies by small and medium-sized enterprises (SMEs) in building construction. *Construction Management and Economics, 23*(7), 713–722. https://doi.org/10.1080/01446190500127112.

Alford, P., & Page, S. J. (2015). Marketing technology for adoption by small business. *Service Industries Journal, 35*(11–12), 655–669. https://doi.org/10.1080/02642069.2015.1062884.

Alshamaila, Y., Papagiannidis, S., & Li, F. (2013). Cloud computing adoption by SMEs in the north east of England—A multi-perspective framework. *Journal of Enterprise Information Management, 26*(3), 250–275. https://doi.org/10.1108/17410391311325225.

Annosi, M. C., Brunetta, F., Monti, A., & Nat, F. (2019). Is the trend your friend? An analysis of technology 4.0 investment decisions in agricultural SMEs. *Computers in Industry, 109*, 59–71. https://doi.org/10.1016/j.compind.2019.04.003.

Barroso, R. M. R., Ferreira, F. A. F., Meidutė-Avaliauskienė, I., Banaitienė, N., Falcão, P. F., & Rosa, Á. A. (2019). Analyzing the determinants of e-commerce in small and medium-sized enterprises: a cognition-driven framework. *Technological & Economic Development of Economy, 25*(3), 496–518. Retrieved from https://doi.org/10.3846/tede.2019.9386

Begg, C., & Caira, T. (2012). Exploring the SME quandary: Data governance in practise in the small to medium-sized enterprise sector. *Electronic Journal of Information Systems Evaluation, 15*(1), 3–13. Retrieved from https://search.ebscohost.com/login.aspx?direct=true&db=buh&AN=87403044&site=ehost-live.

Birkel, H. S., Veile, J. W., Müller, J. M., Hartmann, E., & Voigt, K.-I. (2019). Development of a risk framework for Industry 4.0 in the context of sustainability for established manufacturers. *Sustainability (Switzerland), 11*(2). https://doi.org/10.3390/su11020384

Bouwman, H., Nikou, S., Molina-Castillo, F. J., & de Reuver, M. (2018). The impact of digitalization on business models. *Digital Policy, Regulation and Governance, 20*(2), 105–124. Retrieved from http://www.emeraldinsight.com/loi/dprg.

Bracht, U., & Masurat, T. (2005). The digital factory between vision and reality. *Computers in Industry, 56*(4), 325–333. Retrieved from https://doi.org/10.1016/j.compind.2005.01.008

Cenamor, J., Parida, V., & Wincent, J. (2019). How entrepreneurial SMEs compete through digital platforms: The roles of digital platform capability, network capability and ambidexterity. *Journal of Business Research, 100*, 196–206. https://doi.org/10.1016/j.jbusres.2019.03.035.

Chan, C. M. L., Teoh, S. Y., Yeow, A., & Pan, G. (2019). Agility in responding to disruptive digital innovation: Case study of an SME. *Information Systems Journal, 29*(2), 436–455. Retrieved from https://doi.org/10.1111/isj.12215

Chen, Y.-Y. K., Jaw, Y.-L., & Wu, B.-L. (2016). Effect of digital transformation on organisational performance of SMEs. *Internet Research, 26*(1), 186–212. https://doi.org/10.1108/IntR-12-2013-0265.

Coreynen, W., Matthyssens, P., & Van Bockhaven, W. (2017). Boosting servitization through digitization: Pathways and dynamic resource configurations for manufacturers. *Industrial Marketing Management, 60*, 42–53. https://doi.org/10.1016/j.indmarman.2016.04.012.

Dam, N. A. K., Le Dinh, T., & Menvielle, W. (2019). A systematic literature review of big data adoption in internationalization. *Journal of Marketing Analytics, 7*(3), 182–195. https://doi.org/10.1057/s41270-019-00054-7.

Denyer, D., & Tranfield, D. (2009). Producing a systematic review. *The SAGE Handbook of Organizational Research Methods.* https://doi.org/10.1080/03634528709378635.

Dholakia, R. R., & Kshetri, N. (2004). Factors impacting the adoption of the internet among SMEs. *Small Business Economics, 23*(4), 311–322.

Dinca, V., Dima, A. M., Rozsa, Z. Z., Dincă, V. M., Dima, A. M., Rozsa, Z. Z., et al. (2019). Determinants of cloud computing adoption by Romanian SMEs in the digital economy. *Journal of Business Economics and Management, 20*(4), 798–820. https://doi.org/10.3846/jbem.2019.9856.

Dini, P., et al. (2008). Beyond interoperability to digital ecosystems: Regional innovation and socio-economic development led by SMEs. *International Journal of Technological Learning, Innovation and Development, 1*(3), 410–426. https://doi.org/10.1504/IJTLID.2008.019981.

Elia, S., Giuffrida, M., & Piscitello, L. (2019). Does. *Informacion Comercial Espanola Revista de Economia,* (909), 61–73. Retrieved from https://search.ebscohost.com/login.aspx?direct=true& db=buh&AN=138527868&site=ehost-live

Engels, B. (2017). Detours on the path to a European big data economy. *Intereconomics/Review of European Economic Policy, 52*(4), 213–216. Retrieved from https://link.springer.com/journal/volumesAndIssues/10272.

Eriksson, L. T., & Hultman, J. (2005). One digital leap or a step-by-step approach? An empirical study of e-commerce development among Swedish SMEs. *International Journal of Electronic Business, 3*(5), 4. Retrieved from https://doi.org/10.1504/IJEB.2005.008519

European Commission. (2018). Digital Economy and Society Index 2018 Report. Retrieved from https://ec.europa.eu/digital-single-market/en/news/digital-economy-and-society-index-2018-report

Feindt, S., Jeffcoate, J., & Chappell, C. (2002). Identifying success factors for rapid growth in SME E-commerce. *Small Business Economics, 19*(1), 51–62. Retrieved from http://www.jstor.org/stable/40229220.

Foroudi, P., Gupta, S., Nazarian, A., & Duda, M. (2017). Digital technology and marketing management capability: achieving growth in SMEs. *Qualitative Market Research: An International Journal, 20*(2), 230–246. https://doi.org/10.1108/QMR-01-2017-0014.

Gagliardi, D. (2013). Next generation entrepreneur: innovation strategy through Web 2.0 technologies in SMEs. *Technology Analysis & Strategic Management, 25*(8), 891–904. Retrieved from https://doi.org/10.1080/09537325.2013.823151

Gandia, R., & Parmentier, G. (2017). Optimizing value creation and value capture with a digital multi-sided business model. *Strategic Change, 26*(4), 323–331. https://doi.org/10.1002/jsc.2134.

Gupta, P., Seetharaman, A., & Raj, J. R. (2013). The usage and adoption of cloud computing by small and medium businesses. *International Journal of Information Management, 33*(5), 861–874. https://doi.org/10.1016/j.ijinfomgt.2013.07.001.

Hagsten, E., & Kotnik, P. (2017). ICT as facilitator of internationalisation in small- and medium-sized firms. *Small Business Economics, 48*(2), 431–446. https://doi.org/10.1007/s11187-016-9781-2.

Harrigan, P., Schroeder, A., Qureshi, I., Fang, Y., Ibbotson, P., Ramsey, E., & Meister, D. (2010). Internet technologies, ECRM capabilities, and performance benefits for SMEs: An exploratory study. *International Journal of Electronic Commerce, 15*(2), 7–45. Retrieved from http://www.jstor.org/stable/27919911.

Horváth, K., & Szerb, L. (2018). Managerial practices and the productivity of knowledge-intensive service businesses: An analysis of digital/IT and cash management practices. *Strategic Change, 27*(2), 161–172. https://doi.org/10.1002/jsc.2191.

Houari, M., & Medjedel, A. (2009). The perception and attitudes of SMEs managers towards E-commerce in southern algeria: With special reference to the Ghardaia County. *Les Cahiers Du CREAD, 90*, 79–105. Retrieved from https://search.ebscohost.com/login.aspx?direct=true& db=ecn&AN=1112813&site=ehost-live.

Ibrahim, A. M., Hassan, S., & Gusau, A. L. (2018). Factors influencing acceptance and use of ICT innovations by agribusinesses. *Journal of Global Information Management, 26*(4), 113–134. Retrieved from https://doi.org/10.4018/978-1-5525-2107-5

Imgrund, F., Fischer, M., Janiesch, C., & Winkelmann, A. (2018, March). Approaching digitalization with business process management approaching digitalization with business process management as technological advancements have made the Internet ubiquitously available.

Jin, H., & Hurd, F. (2018). Exploring the impact of digital platforms on SME internationalization: New Zealand SMEs use of the Alibaba platform for Chinese market entry. *Journal of Asia-*

Pacific Business, 19(2), 72–95. Retrieved from https://search.ebscohost.com/login.aspx? direct=true&db=buh&AN=129059007&site=ehost-live.

Joensuu-Salo, S., Sorama, K., Viljamaa, A., & Varamäki, E. (2018). Firm performance among internationalized SMEs: The interplay of market orientation, marketing capability and digitalization. *Administrative Sciences, 8*(3), 31. https://doi.org/10.3390/admsci8030031.

Jones, P., Simmons, G., Packham, G., Beynon-Davies, P., & Pickernell, D. (2014). An exploration of the attitudes and strategic responses of sole-proprietor micro-enterprises in adopting information and communication technology. *International Small Business Journal.* https://doi.org/ 10.1177/0266242612461802.

Kagermann, H., Anderl, R., Gausemeier, J., & Schuh, G. (2016). *Industrie 4.0 in a global context: Strategies for cooperating with international partners (acatech St).* Munich: Herbert Utz.

Khan, A. A., Wang, M. Z., Ehsan, S., Nurunnabi, M., & Hashmi, M. H. (2019). Linking sustainability-oriented marketing to social media and web atmospheric cues. *Sustainability, 11*(9). https://doi.org/10.3390/su11092663.

Kilubi, I. (2015). Strategic technology partnering: A framework extension. *Journal of High Technology Management Research, 26*(1), 27–37. https://doi.org/10.1016/j.hitech.2015.04.003.

Kiselicki, M., Josimovski, S., & Joncheski, L. (2015). Implementation of internet technologies in the supply chain of SEMs in macedonia. *Journal of Sustainable Development, 5*(13), 69–87.

Koenig, W., & Wigand, R. T. (2004). Globalization and E-commerce: Diffusion and impacts of the internet and E-commerce in Germany. *I-WAYS, Digest of Electronic Commerce Policy and Regulations, 27*(3/4), 197–227. Retrieved from https://search.ebscohost.com/login.aspx? direct=true&db=buh&AN=16012283&site=ehost-live.

Lee, S. M., Kim, J., Choi, Y., & Lee, S.-G. (2009). Effects of it knowledge and media selection on operational performance of small firms. *Small Business Economics, 32*(3), 241–257. Retrieved from http://www.jstor.org/stable/40344549.

Levstek, A., Hovelja, T., & Pucihar, A. (2018). IT governance mechanisms and contingency factors: Towards an adaptive IT governance model. *Organizacija, 51*(4), 286–310.. Retrieved from https://doi.org/10.2478/orga-2018-0024

Li, W., Liu, K., Belitski, M., Ghobadian, A., & O'Regan, N. (2016). e-Leadership through strategic alignment: an empirical study of small- and medium-sized enterprises in the digital age. *Journal of Information Technology (Palgrave Macmillan), 31*(2), 185–206. https://doi.org/10.1057/jit. 2016.10.

Li, L., Su, F., Zhang, W., & Mao, J.-Y. (2018). Digital transformation by SME entrepreneurs: A capability perspective. *Information Systems Journal, 28*(6), 1129–1157. https://doi.org/10. 1111/isj.12153.

Lucchetti, R., & Sterlacchini, A. (2004). The adoption of ICT among SMEs: Evidence from an Italian survey. *Small Business Economics, 23*(2), 151–168. Retrieved from http://www.jstor. org/stable/40229352.

Mack, E. A., Marie-Pierre, L., & Redican, K. (2017). Entrepreneurs' use of internet and social media applications. *Telecommunications Policy, 41*(2), 120–139. Retrieved from https://doi. org/10.1016/j.telpol.2016.12.001

Mazzarol, T. (2015). SMEs engagement with e-commerce, e-business and e-marketing. *Small Enterprise Research, 22*(1), 79–90. Retrieved from https://search.ebscohost.com/login.aspx? direct=true&db=buh&AN=110167085&site=ehost-live.

Metzger, G. (2020). KfW start-up report 2019—Number of start-ups in Germany continues to grow.

Meyer, J. (2011). Workforce age and technology adoption in small and medium-sized service firms. *Small Business Economics, 37*(3), 305–324. Retrieved from http://www.jstor.org/stable/ 41486135.

Middleton, K. L., & Byus, K. (2011). Information and communications technology adoption and use in small and medium businesses. *Management Research Review, 34*(1), 98–110. https://doi. org/10.1108/01409171111096496.

Mogoş, R. I. (2015). Digital marketing for identifying customers' preferences—A solution for SMEs in obtaining competitive advantages. *International Journal of Economic Practices &*

Theories, 5(3), 240–247. Retrieved from https://search.ebscohost.com/login.aspx?direct=true&db=buh&AN=113828794&site=ehost-live.

Moher, D., Liberati, A., Tetzlaff, J., & Altman, D. G. (2009). Preferred reporting items for systematic reviews and meta-analyses: The PRISMA statement. *BMJ (Online), 339*(7716), 332–336. https://doi.org/10.1136/bmj.b2535.

Molero, G. D., Santarremigia, F. E., Poveda-Reyes, S., Mayrhofer, M., Awad-Núñez, S., & Kassabji, A. (2019). Key factors for the implementation and integration of innovative ICT solutions in SMEs and large companies involved in the multimodal transport of dangerous goods. *European Transport Research Review, 11*(1) https://doi.org/10.1186/s12544-019-0362-8.

Morgan-Thomas, A. (2016). Rethinking technology in the SME context: Affordances, practices and ICTs. *International Small Business Journal: Researching Entrepreneurship.* https://doi.org/10.1177/0266242615613839.

Neirotti, P., & Raguseo, E. (2017). On the contingent value of IT-based capabilities for the competitive advantage of SMEs: Mechanisms and empirical evidence. *Information and Management.* https://doi.org/10.1016/j.im.2016.05.004

O'Connor, C., & Kelly, S. (2017). Facilitating knowledge management through filtered big data: SME competitiveness in an agri-food sector. *Journal of Knowledge Management, 21,* 156–179.

Omiunu, O. G. (2019). E-literacy-adoption model and performance of women-owned SMEs in Southwestern Nigeria. *Journal of Global Entrepreneurship Research, 9*(1), 1. Retrieved from https://doi.org/10.1186/s40497-019-0149-3

Osterwalder, A. (2004). Understanding ICT-based business models in developing countries. *International Journal of Information Technology & Management, 3*(2–4), 1. Retrieved from https://doi.org/10.1504/IJITM.2004.005042

Pergelova, A., Manolova, T., Simeonova-Ganeva, R., & Yordanova, D. (2019). Democratizing entrepreneurship? Digital technologies and the internationalization of female-led SMEs. *Journal of Small Business Management, 57*(1), 14–39. https://doi.org/10.1111/jsbm.12494.

Philip, L., & Williams, F. (2019). Remote rural home based businesses and digital inequalities: Understanding needs and expectations in a digitally underserved community. *Journal of Rural Studies, 68*(September), 306–318. https://doi.org/10.1016/j.jrurstud.2018.09.011.

Piscitello, L., & Sgobbi, F. (2004). Globalisation, E-business and SMEs: evidence from the Italian District of Prato. *Small Business Economics, 22*(5), 333–347. Retrieved from http://www.jstor.org/stable/40229331.

Prindible, M., & Petrick, I. (2015). Learning the building blocks of service innovation from SMEs. *Research Technology Management, 58*(5), 61–63. Retrieved from http://10.0.21.61/08956308X5805008.

Quinton, S., Canhoto, A., Molinillo, S., Pera, R., & Budhathoki, T. (2017). Conceptualising a digital orientation: antecedents of supporting SME performance in the digital economy. *Journal of Strategic Marketing, 26*(5), 427–439. Retrieved from https://doi.org/10.1080/0965254X.2016.1258004

Robu, M. (2013). A new classification of SMEs in the digital economy context. *Cross-Cultural Management Journal, 15*(1), 150–155. Retrieved from http://cmj.bxb.ro.

Romanelli, M. (2018). Towards sustainable ecosystems. *Systems Research and Behavioral Science, 35*(4), 417–426. https://doi.org/10.1002/sres.2541.

Saunila, M., Ukko, J., & Rantala, T. (2019). Value co-creation through digital service capabilities: the role of human factors. *Information Technology and People, 32*(3), 627–645. https://doi.org/10.1108/ITP-10-2016-0224.

Scuotto, V., Caputo, F., Villasalero, M., & Del Giudice, M. (2017a). A multiple buyer – supplier relationship in the context of SMEs' digital supply chain management. *Production Planning & Control, 28*(16), 1378–1388. Retrieved from https://search.ebscohost.com/login.aspx?direct=true&db=buh&AN=125602845&site=ehost-live.

Scuotto, V., Del Giudice, M., & Carayannis, E. G. (2017b). The effect of social networking sites and absorptive capacity on SMES' innovation performance. *Journal of Technology Transfer, 42*(2), 409–424. Retrieved from https://link.springer.com/journal/volumesAndIssues/10961.

Scuotto, V., Santoro, G., Bresciani, S., & Del Giudice, M. (2017c). Shifting intra- and inter-organizational innovation processes towards digital business: An empirical analysis of SMEs. *Creativity & Innovation Management, 26*(3), 247–255. Retrieved from https://doi.org/10.1111/caim.12221

Sebora, T. C., Lee, S. M., & Sukasame, N. (2009). Critical success factors for E-commerce entrepreneurship: An empirical study of Thailand. *Small Business Economics, 32*(3), 303–316. Retrieved from http://www.jstor.org/stable/40344553.

Shaltoni, A. M., West, D., Alnawas, I., & Shatnawi, T. (2018). Electronic marketing orientation in the small and medium-sized enterprises context. *European Business Review, 30*(3), 272–284. https://doi.org/10.1108/EBR-02-2017-0034.

Sharif, N. (1999). Strategic role of technological self-reliance in development management. *Technological Forecasting and Social Change, 62*(3), 219–238. https://doi.org/10.1016/S0040-1625 (99)00040-2.

Sommer, L. (2015). Industrial revolution—Industry 4.0: Are German manufacturing SMEs the first victims of this revolution? *Journal of Industrial Engineering and Management, 8*(5), 1512–1532. https://doi.org/10.3926/jiem.1470.

Stankovska, I., Josimovski, S., & Edwards, C. (2016). Digital channels diminish SME barriers: the case of the UK. *Economic Research-Ekonomska Istrazivanja, 29*(1), 217–232. Retrieved from https://doi.org/10.1080/1331677X.2016.1164926

Stockdale, R., & Standing, C. (2006). A classification model to support SME e-commerce adoption initiatives. *Journal of Small Business and Enterprise Development, 13*(3), 381–394. https://doi.org/10.1108/14626000610680262.

Tarutė, A., & Gatautis, R. (2014). ICT impact on SMEs performance. *Procedia—Social and Behavioral Sciences, 110*, 1218–1225. https://doi.org/10.1016/j.sbspro.2013.12.968.

Toanca, L. (2016). Empirical research regarding the importance of digital transformation for Romanian SMEs. *Management and Economics Review, 1*(2), 92–108. Retrieved from https://search.ebscohost.com/login.aspx?direct=true&db=ecn&AN=1698959&site=ehost-live.

Tranfield, D., Denyer, D., & Smart, P. (2003). Towards a methodology for developing evidence-informed management knowledge by means of systematic review. *British Journal of Management, 14*, 207–222. https://doi.org/10.1111/1467-8551.00375.

Traşca, D. L., Ştefan, G. M., Sahlian, D. N., Hoinaru, R., & Şerban-Oprescu, G. L. (2019). Digitalization and business activity. The struggle to catch up in CEE countries. *Sustainability (Switzerland), 11*(8) https://doi.org/10.3390/su11082204.

Tsatsou, P., Elaluf-Calderwood, S., & Liebenau, J. (2010). Towards a taxonomy for regulatory issues in a digital business ecosystem in the EU. *Journal of Information Technology (Palgrave Macmillan), 25*(3), 288–307. Retrieved from https://doi.org/10.1057/jit.2009.22

Ukko, J., Nasiri, M., Saunila, M., & Rantala, T. (2019). Sustainability strategy as a moderator in the relationship between digital business strategy and financial performance. *Journal of Cleaner Production, 236*, N.PAG-N.PAG. Retrieved from https://search.ebscohost.com/login.aspx?direct=true&db=buh&AN=138100797&site=ehost-live

van der Loo, S., Chen, L., Edwards, P., Holden, J. A., Karamperidis, S., Kollingbaum, M. J., et al. (2015). Development of a digital tool to overcome the challenges of rural food SMEs. *Scottish Geographical Journal, 131*(3–4), 212–219. https://doi.org/10.1080/14702541.2014.994673.

Vatuiu, T., Vaduva, F., & Udrica, M. (2014). Improving the management of Romanian SMEs through the use of informatic systems. *Journal of Knowledge Management, Economics and Information Technology, 4*(3), 1–13. Retrieved from http://www.scientificpapers.org.

Velu, S. R., Al Mamun, A., Kanesan, T., Hayat, N., & Gopinathan, S. (2019). Effect of information system artifacts on organizational resilience: A study among Malaysian SMEs. *Sustainability (Switzerland), 11*(11), 1–23. https://doi.org/10.3390/su11113177.

Vidhyalakshmi, R., & Kumar, V. (2016). Determinants of cloud computing adoption by SMEs. *International Journal of Business Information Systems, 22*(3), 375–395. https://doi.org/10.1504/IJBIS.2016.076878.

Welter, F., Baker, T., Audretsch, D. B., & Gartner, W. B. (2017). Everyday entrepreneurship—A call for entrepreneurship research to embrace entrepreneurial diversity. *Entrepreneurship: Theory and Practice, 41*(3), 311–321. https://doi.org/10.1111/etap.12258.

Wielicki, T., & Arendt, L. (2010). A knowledge-driven shift in perception of ICT implementation barriers: Comparative study of US and European SMEs. *Journal of Information Science, 36*(2), 162–174. Retrieved from https://search.ebscohost.com/login.aspx?direct=true&db=buh&AN=48945341&site=ehost-live.

Wong, C. H., & Sloan, B. (2006). An emprical survey of the UK construction SMEs' E-procurement readiness from the E-legal aspects. *Journal of Construction Research, 7*(1/2), 81–97. Retrieved from https://search.ebscohost.com/login.aspx?direct=true&db=buh&AN=24943284&site=ehost-live.

Wynarczyk, P. (2000). The role of digital networks in supply chain development. *New Technology, Work & Employment, 15*(2), 123. https://doi.org/10.1111/1468-005X.00069.

Zhu, K., Kraemer, K. L., Xu, S., & Dedrick, J. (2004). Information technology payoff in E-business environments: An International perspective on value creation of E-business in the financial services industry. *Journal of Management Information Systems, 21*(1), 17–54. Retrieved from http://www.jstor.org/stable/40398783.

Andrea Meier is a PhD candidate at the Department of Strategic Management, Marketing and Tourism, Faculty of Business and Management, University of Innsbruck in Austria. She received her Diploma degree in Business Administration and Management from the Ludwig-Maximilians-Universität, Munich. Afterwards she worked for several years in the field of research, technology, and innovation for the Bavarian Ministry of Economic Affairs. Her research interests include SME digital transformation, SME, value chain management, and quality management. As a visiting scholar, she has collected experience at various management schools, namely University of Applied Sciences, Munich, University of Applied Sciences, Ravensburg-Weingarten, and Hochschule Fresenius, Munich.

Identifying Barriers for Digital Transformation in the Public Sector

Linn Slettum Bjerke-Busch and Arild Aspelund

1 Introduction

The adoption of new technology has always brought organizational changes. However, the last decade has brought an acceleration in the number of these changes because digital tools that solve administrative and commercial functions are becoming ubiquitous and available at reasonable cost. In the private sector, digital transformation is viewed as a source of competitive advantage and an enabler for creating more efficient business models and enabling adaptive, flexible and customized mass production capabilities (El Sawy et al. 2016). In the public sector, digital technology can be used to improve client experiences, streamlining processes and transform operations or the operating model. This is often referred to as e-government, e-governance or digital government/governance (West 2005).

Despite the promises, we do not observe a rapid digital transformation of the public sector. Research suggests that the economic and cognitive path dependencies brought about by legacy systems, global operations, work silos and organizational politics make public institutions more reluctant to transform their physical models into digital models (Weill and Woerner 2013). Economic research on innovation focuses predominantly on competitive market factors as the main driver for digital transformation (Christensen and Raynor 2003). In the public sector, where competitive forces are weaker or even absent, we need a greater understanding of the driver and barriers that are limiting digital transformation (Meijer 2015). This study aims to contribute to increase that understanding by studying the barriers for digital transformation in a typical public organization where there are promising potentials for both increased service quality and higher efficiency by adoption of new digital technologies.

L. S. Bjerke-Busch (✉) · A. Aspelund
Department of Industrial Economics & Technology Management, Norwegian University of Science and Technology (NTNU), Trondheim, Norway
e-mail: linn.s.bjerke@ntnu.no; arild.aspelund@ntnu.no

2   Theoretical Background

As digital transformation in the public sector differs to such an extent from the private, there has been some debate on how it should be defined. Based on expert interviews with 40 experts on digital transformation and public service in 12 different countries, Mergel et al. (2019) defined digital transformation in public sector as:

> A holistic effort to revise core processes and services of government beyond the traditional digitization efforts. It evolves along a continuum of transition from analog to digital to a full stack review of policies, current processes, and user needs and results in a complete revision of the existing and the creation of new digital services. The outcome of digital transformation efforts focuses among others on the satisfaction of user needs, new forms of service delivery, and the expansion of the user base. (p.11)

According to this definition, digital transformation in the public sector is not merely transforming analog and manual tools to digital tools, but a broad organizational transition towards new tools, policies, work processes and operations. We will adopt this definition for this study as it fits both the case and the research question.

One way of studying digital transformation in public sector is by the use of an institutional lens (Dimaggio and Powell 1983). From an institutional viewpoint, adoption of new technology is constrained by institutional norms, arrangements, rules and operating modes. However, the adoption of new technologies will also in return influence the organizations (Fountain 2001). Hence, barriers will to a large extent be defined by the technological solutions and work processes that the organization is using at any point in time.

Another view is to look at technology adoption from a change management perspective. From this view the political context of democracy and the juridical context of legislation, rules and bureaucracy is likely to influence the digital transformation process (Kuipers et al. 2014). The context of public sector is therefore relevant when considering barriers to the digital transformation process. The process stages are relevant in considering the events involved in the transformation (Pettigrew 1987). Meijer (2015) defined the different stages of the innovation process as (1) idea generation, (2) idea selection, (3) idea testing and (4) idea promotion. It is reasonable to assume that different public sector context factors will influence the transformation process to varying effects at the different stages in the innovation process.

When studying the public sector, it is important to note that the various public organizations serve interdependently from other public institutions in the sense that they are all supposed to cooperate to create efficient and reliable services to the public. This interdependency of public organizations is very different from what we observe in the private sector where organizations predominantly operate independently in competition with others. For example, in this paper we uncover how the Norwegian Court Administration is integrated in a system of lawmakers, regulators, law enforcers, prosecutors and lawyers, and how they depend on them to efficiently run daily operations.

Hence, digital transformation in public sector affects the whole sector and thus, change will take place at the societal, governmental, organizational and actor levels simultaneously (Hartley et al. 2002). Pettigrew et al. (2001) named these different orders of change. The first order is the subsystem change, the second order is the organizational change and the third order refers to sector change. For the purpose of this study, we find it useful to integrate the perspectives of innovation stages and orders of change in the research framework to identify barriers for digital transformation in the public sector.

Studies of barriers to innovation in general and digital transformation, in particular, have been widely studied in the private sector. The studies on the public sector have been few and far apart. Meijer (2015) defines a barrier as "characteristics, either real or perceived, of legal, social, technological or institutional context which work against digital transformation because they constrain efforts to reconfigure access to information, people and services in ways enabled by ICTs". In this study, we will focus on both internal and external barriers.

Considering previous research on barriers to digital transformation in the public sector we observe that at the sector level research points to political system characteristics, socioeconomic forces, elite decision-making and administrative system characteristics as barriers for change (Pollitt and Bouckaert 2004). As mentioned above, the inherited nature that public organizations have a multitude of stakeholders may make digitalization more complex (Perrott 2009).

At the organizational level, Kane et al. (2019b) detected both behavioural and structural barriers that are driven by the mindsets of the organization and manifested in the organizations' systems. According to institutional theory (Dimaggio and Powell 1983), there is a reason to believe that this may be even more evident in public organizations as both systems and mindsets are institutionalized. In addition, research shows that organizations find it hard to combine innovation and daily operations within the same organizational structure (Helfat et al. 2007). Strategy is found to be an important driver for transformation in private sector. In the public sector, strategy is often formed at the government level and this may be a challenge for the public organization that has to implement the strategy they have not created internally (Kane et al. 2015).

Finally, on the individual level we have evidence that different types of leadership affect digital transformation (Kane et al. 2019a). This is especially the case in the collaboration between strategic top-level management and IT (Hsu et al. 2018; Li et al. 2019; Weill and Woerner 2013). In public organizations, it is common to differ between administrative leadership and political leadership, and due to this dual nature it may complicate the relationship to IT further, but little research has been done in this area (Kuipers et al. 2014).

3 Research Question

Due to the lack of research and the need for a better understanding of digital transformation of the public sector, we formulate the following research question:

What are the main barriers for digital transformation in public institutions?

4   Research Design

This study seeks to contribute to the knowledge base on digitalization of the public sector by identifying barriers for digital transformation. It seeks to do so by investigating the Norwegian Court Administration and their digitalization project "Digital Courts". As we are seeking a deep understanding of processes that constitutes barriers to change, a case study approach is appropriate (Yin 2014). The study adopts a constructivist grounded approach and a qualitative research method to gain sufficient depth in the data on the actors' experience of the process (Anderson 2010). We interviewed all six members of the top management group. That includes the top manager, two members of the project management group, two IT leaders and one senior advisor. The respondents were selected by a method of purposive sampling (Silverman 2014).

The interviews were retrospective and designed to provide in-depth objective facts about the historical events, strategic processes and decisions, and relations to stakeholders. The interviews were also aimed at gaining subjective insight on the managers' perceptions on the actions and behaviours surrounding the events and took place in May, June and August 2019. All interviews were carried out in the Norwegian language and were audio recorded and transcribed. As part of the analysis, 11 documents from the project organization were included to illuminate the case.

The data was coded by using a thematic analysis. The thematic pattern was driven by the research question and coded in an inductive way. The data was presented to the participants in order for them to adjust or correct misunderstandings. Further, the data was compared to emergent theories and recoded into a set of main categories (Eisenhardt et al. 2016). NVivo was used as a tool in the coding process.

The study is based on a single-case study and hence has limitations in generalizing the findings to the general population (Anderson 2010). However, findings can be transferable to other public organizations where the context is similar. Ethics approval, in this case, was administered through an agreement with, and informed consent, from participants in the study.

5   Findings

The Norwegian Court Administration (NCA) oversees and supports the ordinary courts and the land consolidation courts in Norway. These add up to 104 independent courts—that is, 63 district courts, 34 land consolidation courts, 6 courts of appeal and the supreme court. NCA serves these courts by providing economic budgeting and controlling function, organization and competence development, communication and ICT infrastructure.

Table 1 Timeline of the digital transformation process at the Norwegian Court Administration

Stage	Year	Important events
Idea generation	2007–2008	Development of an ICT strategy
	2009–2012	Digitalization becomes part of the main strategy
	2011	The Actor Portal is launched
	2011	"Project digital collaboration" is established and an intranet for the judicional sector is developed
Idea selection	2013	Start up for a governmental project proposal and financing plan (Norwegian: satsingsforslag)
	2017	The project proposal and financing plan is accepted
Idea testing	2017	Start up for the project "Digital Courts"
	2019	A new court strategy "Courts 2025" is launched
Idea promotion	2019	The Court Administration reorganizes. The project is merged with the main organization Start up project for reorganizing the courts

The study identifies barriers that are specific to the public sector that contribute to the understanding of why public sectors are more resistant to digital transformation. To structure the presentation of the findings, we will first present the case timeline and then use the framework developed above that uses the innovation stages from Meijer (2015) and structuring barriers according to Pettigrew et al. (2001). First, we present the timeline of the transformation according to innovation stages (see Table 1). The timeline provides an understanding of the main events during the process.

The process represents a timeline from 2007 where the organization started the process of developing an ICT strategy. This also marks the start of the idea generation phase where digitalization becomes integrated into the overall strategy and the first actions are initiated to involve internal and external actors in idea generation. NCA begins the application process for state funding of the digitalization project in 2013 and proceeds to develop ideas and solutions, until 2017 when the proposal and financing plan is finally accepted and the project "Digital Courts" is launched. In 2019, the new court strategy "Courts 2025" is released and reorganization to integrate the digitalization project with the rest of the organization is commenced. The timeline shows that this has been a long and slow process spanning 12 years. However, it has also been successful. And even though the digital transformation phase is still ongoing, digitalization in NCA is now fully integrated into the overall strategy and all development processes.

We proceed to present barriers according to the combined Meijer (2015) and Pettigrew et al. (2001) framework. Since digital transformation is defined as an ongoing process and digitalization at NCA ultimately became integrated in the main strategy and therefore all major innovation processes, we have added a stage at the end that addresses this issue. We start with the external barriers—referred to as third-order changes by Pettigrew et al. (2001).

External Barriers

Findings suggest that the external barriers are most common in the stages of idea generation and selection. These barriers are linked to regulations, financial models, lack of system integration and lack of technical standardization. The external barriers are less evident in the test stage and the promotion stage, but more apparent after the organization has matured digitally and digitalization becomes the norm. Some of the identified external barriers are likely to be similar in any organization in digital transformation. However, there are some that are distinctively related to the public sector. In particular, barriers identified in the early stages highlight the interdependency that is particular to the public sector. For example, the court administration does not make their own money in that same way as private entities and large-scale development projects are dependent on funding priorities from the government. Moreover, operations depend on coordinated efforts from a range of other independent actors and the process of arriving at similar technical standards is challenging as there is a clear division of roles, but no hierarchy. These barriers provide insight into why the initial phases of this public digital transformation are so slow (Table 2).

Respondents in the study express a need for a change in governmental models, especially on the financial side, to be able to keep up with the speed of digital transformation in the rest of the society. The administrative director illustrates:

> Project funding is only temporarily, but now we <the NCA> have new needs and new opportunities, so we also have a need for money to keep doing interesting things and continue to innovate.

Internal Barriers: Organizational Level

As we move on to the second-order barriers, we observe that they predominantly occur in later stages and particularly during idea testing and promotion. Once again, we observe that funding and resource allocation remains a problem also at the organizational level. However, here we also observe another factor that is particular to the public sector. An organization like NCA is a typical professional public organization in the sense that it is designed to fulfil a specific public need, and hence, constitutes predominantly of professionals within that area of expertise—in this case, competence in law. This amplifies coordination barriers across silos and in particular between managers, IT staff and the workforce (Table 3).

The organizational barriers are most evident at the test phase. At this stage, new ideas and ways of working meet with established routines. At this stage there are both structural and cultural barriers:

> A lot of terms and conditions were absent when the project started. Everything from policies, strategies, platforms and technologies, architectural choices—that all the time led to new barriers. We didn't succeed in getting the resources we wanted, so we had to put an effort into changing our operational processes

Table 2 External barriers found at different stages of the transformation process

Idea generation	Idea selection	Idea testing	Idea promotion	Continuous innovation
• Regulations • Lack of financial cross-funding • Dependancy on the members in the value chain. Different levels of digital maturity • Lack of digital competence and mindset at politician level and department level • Formal and slow processes for financing • Project funding • Letter of allocation focuses on efficiency and savings, not innovation	• Must prove that innovation leads to more efficiency • Project funding • The Judicial system is autonomous and independent from government, but dependent on governmental funding for innovation. Creates a system where the fox guides the henhouse • Formal and rigid communication structures. Requests are overlooked or ignored or do not receive attention • Large power distance between administrative leadership and politician leadership • Lack of arenas for informal collaboration	• Changes in the role from administrator to service deliverer • Lack of technological standardization and system integration in the sector • Lack of flexibility (e.g. for changing rules and regulations) • Differences in decision-making structures across organizations in the value network		• The biggest challenge is the norm and cultural understanding of the way the public financing system is working • Responsibility for lifespan of services across sectorial org, but without funding • The organizations need to fund their own innovations by digitalizing (at the end it ends)

Several participants mention resource allocation as an important barrier. Important resources are defined by the participants as a digitally skilled workforce, a workforce with a digital mindset and a workforce with an entrepreneurial mindset. In terms of professional culture, this barrier became visible at first through differences in conceptual languages, which was a hinder for collaboration across disciplines and for the ability to adopt new ideas into the organization. Both are critical for digital development:

> What I experience as most challenging is that there is a lot of confusion surrounding concepts. Digitalization is being characterized as a goal instead of a mean to achieve goals and visions. This easily leads to discussions that are, - not confusing, but there are different perspectives

Table 3 Internal organizational barriers found at different stages of the transformation process

Idea generation	Idea selection	Idea testing	Idea promotion	Continuous innovation
Institutionalized culture	• Division of labour. Silo structures • Hierarchical leadership structure • Institutionalized roles and behaviours	• Resource allocation is difficult. In relation to finding the right skills, the right amount or reallocating workforce to new tasks • Differences in work processes across silos • Lack of flexibility. Fixed roles and behaviours • Lack of system integration and standardization across different courts • Lack of ability and mindset to finance our own innovations and developments. Budget is fixed on daily operations • Looks at innovation as something separate from daily operations • Differences in conceptual language between IT, managers and workforce • Changing roles	• Volunteer use of digital tools vs. obligatory use • Lack of experienced need for change amongst users • Resistance amongst users. Autonomy issues due to standardization • Resistance to changing roles and work tasks	

Professional employees are autonomous in the execution of their professions to a large degree. A successful digital transformation is dependent on the involvement of professional employees, and at the same time automation will to some degree remove or change some of their work tasks, eventually altering and changing their professional work identity. In the test phase the participants reported that their colleagues did not see a need for the change, but other resistance responses to change were not detected. The lack of urgency was visible through difficulties in involving employees in the beginning of the development process, and when the employees could choose to adopt digital tools that altered their work tasks or continue work as usual, the latter was preferred:

> We had already developed several solutions, but few of them had been extensively used in the Courts

Internal Barriers: Management Level

In terms of the first-order barriers, we observe a range of barriers until innovations are internalized and move into a continuous innovation phase. The latter might be explained by the fact that professional service organizations, such as the courts, are generally associated with proficiency in driving incremental improvements as long as professional boundaries and work processes are not challenged (Table 4).

Some of the first-order barriers are general factors that are likely to be present in any organization—public or private. However, there are also other barriers that are likely to be specific to the public sector. These barriers are often derived from second-order barriers. For example, strategic decisions are made on the governmental level and communicated to NCA through bureaucratic procedures. Coordinated changes are generally slow and time consuming.

> They (the Justice Department) receive too many written requests. We can use a lot of resources in writing a hearing, and they won't even notice.

The same barrier applies to funding and this creates a challenging task for the leader. Another barrier that is derived from the second order is the relationship with the external stakeholders. Digital transformation of the courts is dependent on coordinated innovation and development processes across a range of other public and private entities, but the legitimacy for orchestrating the transformation process in an ecosystem of all the stakeholders is limited.

Another barrier that was apparent in our study was the role of the top management. In the public sector, managers are often viewed as administrators rather than leaders. Moreover, top managers in professional public organizations are often promoted, and draw legitimacy from, professional merits more than leadership skills. This can lead to direct challenges for leaders of digital transformation in the public sector as the process will depend on influence from other disciplines, e.g. digitally skilled personal, than those that currently dominate the organization. This was also observed in the present case study.

Specifically, in the first stage of idea generation the participants experience the behaviour of the managers in line with an institutional norm of administrative managers in public sector. The IT director reports difficulties in communicating

Table 4 Internal managerial barriers found at different stages of the transformation process

Idea generation	Idea selection	Idea testing	Idea promotion	Continuous innovation
• Traditional governmental administrator management role. Managers role is regulated by rules, institutional norms and "letter of allocation" • Communication with users is "inside-out" • Lack of strategy. Strategy is regulated by "letter of allocation" • Lack of interest and understanding for technology • Lack of cross-competence, especially in between digital technology and strategic leadership • IT is viewed as an efficiency tool, not a mean for creating value • Lack of collaboration and strategic decision-making processes	• Prioritizing process improvement • Lack of trust in the leadership group • Lack of decision-making processes and facilitation of dialogue in the leadership group • Lack of user inquiry and insight • Lack of systematic collaboration with other stakeholders externally and internally	• Public management traditional role and mindset as administrator (as opposed to a leader) • Differences in power relationships • Realization that this is an ongoing project. New priorities. Tech over people • Professional leader hierarchy (not according to line, but profession)	• Power and legitimacy by profession, not by formal position • Leaders are not recruited on leader competence, but professional competence • Lack of competence in change management • Fear of losing influence • Leaders are not recruited on leader competence • Users gain more power in organizational developmental processes	

technological strategic possibilities to the leadership group and to the board members. Similar challenges are also confirmed by other managers. The implications are also apparent in the discourse within the leadership group. Participants report that they were mainly concerned with proceedings within their own field and the distribution of resources between the different departments. They reported difficulties in coordinating strategic discussions and deciding on innovative projects that involved a collaborative effort. A digital transformation may slow down or halt at an early stage, if managers are not able to balance discussions about proceedings and resources with strategy and coordinated decision making.

The first ICT strategy communicated a need to renew the Courts in line with the development in society. They <the managers> had never heard that before. I had to say it three times. And they wondered what that really meant. It sounded very scary to them.

All the participants mention the recruitment of a new administrative director as a trigger for speeding up the digitalization of the courts in NCA. The director's effect on the process, through challenging the norms in public sector, stands out as a testament to the role of leadership in the digital transformation of a public organization. Particularly in the first two stages of the innovation process:

One important thing was (the director's) personal courage. To put it that way... he was so lucid. And showed such a strong leadership. That had never happened before in the judicial sector... We were suddenly in charge of our own digital renewal.

6 Practical Implications

This study has contributed to our understanding of barriers to digital transformation in the public sector. We have identified barriers on all three levels of management and throughout the whole transformation process that are specific to the public sector. The most important of these barriers are:

- Dependency on bureaucratic structures and financial models.
- Interdependency on public and private external stakeholders.
- Professional culture.
- Lack of a need for change.
- Institutionalized management practices and understanding.

From these findings and our study of the Norwegian Court Administration, we deduct three specific implications for managers of public organizations that seek to successfully lead their organization through digital transformation.

Digital Transformation in Public Organizations Requires a Sector-Wide Transformation: Form a Peloton!

The findings show that the digital transformation of the Norwegian Courts is dependent on a simultaneous and coordinated transformation of the whole sector. It makes little sense to digitally transform the courts unless it is coordinated with similar transformations in related public and private institutions such as the police, prosecutors, lawmakers and lawyers. Enabling actors to cross-collaborate may work as a driver for digitalization in the public sector according to the argument of institutional isomorphism as argued by DiMaggio and Powell (1983). Public managers should therefore seek to form a peloton—a pack of riders—that together seek to transform the sector through an ecosystem. Such coordinated efforts might help overcome the funding barriers and identify technical solutions that contribute to efficient and high-quality services from all parties.

Barriers of the Organization: Work with the Norms and Culture!

Public organizations have stronger norms than private sector linked to the understanding of their professional behaviour (Dimaggio and Powell 1983). This study has shown that the focus on profession acts like a barrier to digital transformation and if the public professional organization wants to successfully transform, they need to change their understanding of their role as administrators of a profession to a professional service deliverer.

Management as a Key Factor: Work on Strategy!

The findings suggest that managers in public sector are more likely to succeed with a digital agenda if they challenge the administrative norm of a public manager. Managers that are able to strategically redefine the boundaries to their external stakeholders, and their employees, are more likely to succeed in orchestrating a digital transformation. This requires a close collaboration with public and private stakeholders, a facilitation of multiple perspectives in coordinated strategic discussions, building and involving a digitally skilled workforce in developing new services, and challenging the political agenda. Findings also suggest that the public leadership model needs to be revised to include a more collaborative model of distributed influence.

7   Contribution

Most of the research in economic studies focuses on market barriers. This study suggests that there are some specific barriers for public sector that challenges both the structure and the culture of the government model and the role of public organizations. Further research should look more closely at how public institutions can collaborate to transform together. Research should especially look closer at how managerial capabilities can be developed and used to enable and drive change.

References

Anderson, C. (2010). Presenting and evaluating qualitative research. *American Journal of Pharmaceutical Education, 74*, 141.

Christensen, C., & Raynor, M. (2003). *The innovator's solution. Creating and sustaining successful growth*. Boston: Harvard Business School Publishing.

Dimaggio, P. J., & Powell, W. W. (1983). The iron cage revisited: institutional isomorphism and collective rationality in organizational fields. *American Sociological Review, 48*, 147–160.

Eisenhardt, K. M., Graebner, M. E., & Sonenshein, S. (2016). Grand challenges and inductive methods: Rigor without Rigor Mortis. *Academy of Management Journal, 59*, 1113–1123.

El Sawy, O. A., Kraemmergaard, P., Amsinck, H., & Vinther, A. L. (2016). How LEGO built the foundations and enterprise capabilities for digital leadership. *MIS Quarterly Executive, 15*, 141–166.

Fountain, J. E. (2001). *Building the virtual state*. Cambridge, MA: Brookings Institution Press.

Hartley, J., Butler, M. J., & Benington, J. (2002). Local government modernization: UK and comparative analysis from an organizational perspective. *Public Management Review, 4*(3), 387–404.

Helfat, C., Finkelstein, S., Mitchell, W., Peteraf, M. A., Singh, H., & Winter, S. G. (2007). *Dynamic capabilities: Understanding strategic change in organizations*. Oxford, UK: Blackwell.

Hsu, C. C., Tsaih, R. H., & Yen, D. C. (2018). The evolving role of IT departments in digital transformation. *Sustainability, 10*.

Kane, G. C., Palmer, D., Phillips, A. N., Kiron, D., & Buckley, N. (2015). Strategy, not technology, drives digital transformation. *MIT Sloan Management Review, 14*, 1–25.

Kane, G. C., Phillips, A. N., Copulsky, J. & Andrus, G. (2019a). How digital leadership is(n't) different. *MIT Sloan Management Review, 60*, 34–39.

Kane, G. C., Phillips, A. N., Copulsky, J. & Andrus, G. (2019b). *The technology fallacy. How people are the real key to digital transformation*. Cambridge, MA: MIT Press.

Kuipers, B. S., Higgs, M., Kickert, W., Tummers, L., Grandia, J., & Van Der Voet, J. (2014). The management of change in public organizations: A literature review. *Public Administration, 92*, 1–20.

Li, C., Han, S. H., Kumar, S., & Feng, W. X. (2019). The influence of senior executive support informatization on radical innovation performance. *Industrial Management & Data Systems, 119*, 821–839.

Meijer, A. (2015). E-governance innovation: Barriers and strategies. *Government Information Quarterly, 32*, 198–206.

Mergel, I., Edelmann, N., & Haug, N. (2019). Defining digital transformation: Results from expert interviews. *Government Information Quarterly, 36*.

Perrott, B. E. (2009). *Managing public sector organizations in environmental turbulence*. New York: Routledge.

Pettigrew, A. M. (1987). Context and action in the transformation of the firm. *Journal of Management Studies, 24*(6), 649–670.

Pettigrew, A. M., Woodman, R. W., & Cameron, K. S. (2001). Studying organizational change and development: Challenges for future research. *Academy of Management Journal, 44*, 697–713.

Pollitt, C., & Bouckaert, G. (2004). *Public management reform. A comparative analysis*. New York: Oxford University Press.

Silverman, D. (2014). *Interpreting qualitative data*. London: Sage.

Weill, P., & Woerner, S. L. (2013). The future of the CIO in a digital economy. *MIS Quarterly Executive, 12*, 65–75.

West, D. (2005). *Digital government. Technology and public sector performance*. Princeton, NJ: Princeton University Press.

Yin, R. K. (2014). *Case study research: Design and methods*. Los Angeles: Sage.

Linn Slettum Bjerke-Busch is an industrial PhD candidate at the Department of Industrial Economics and Technology Management, Norwegian University of Science and Technology (NTNU). The working title of her PhD thesis is "Leading Digital Transformations". She is employed as a consultant at Østlyng & Bjerke where her primary fields are leadership development and organizational development. Specifically, her interests and objectives are to contribute to a more sustainable development of organizations, using digital technology.

Arild Aspelund is a Professor at the Department for Industrial Economics and Technology Management, Norwegian University of Science and Technology (NTNU) and Director of the executive programme Master of Technology Management (MTM). His primary academic interests lie in the intersection between innovation, digitalization and sustainability. More specifically, his research seek to address how digital innovations can contribute to a sustainable, but prosperous business future.

Crisis-Driven Digital Transformation: Examining the Online University Triggered by COVID-19

Christian Ravn Haslam, Sabine Madsen, and Jeppe Agger Nielsen

1 Introduction

In both research and practice, digital transformation is receiving much attention and has been coined as the most relevant technology-oriented phenomenon of our times (Wessel et al. 2021). However, a transformation process *"that engenders a qualitatively different organization"* (Besson and Rowe 2012, p. 103) is typically difficult, time-consuming, and incremental. Yet, the COVID-19 pandemic is currently causing many organizations to undergo unexpected, accelerated digital transformation to manage the crisis and be able to maintain their activities. This is especially true of the university sector where many universities have digitalized all their teaching activities to cope with the situation.

In Denmark, the societal measures implemented to curb the spread of COVID-19, including the temporary lockdown of physical public sector facilities—starting medio March 2020—have forced university managers, professors, IT staff, and students to skip the expected gradual transformation process and make all teaching activities 100% digital. This extraordinary situation means that resistance to change and discussions about complicated matters have for a moment vanished in favor of a trial-and-error approach to online teaching. Using the Faculty of Social Sciences at a Danish university as a case, we focus on accelerated digital transformation of core organizational activities. The selected faculty was, literally overnight, totally digitized in the wake of the COVID-19 situation. It, therefore, provides a unique opportunity to study accelerated digital transformation and organizational responsiveness (Madsen et al. 2020), where carefully planned digital transformation strategies and processes were replaced with immediate action and emergent organizing. Hence, we address the following research question: *How can*

C. R. Haslam · S. Madsen (✉) · J. A. Nielsen
Centre for IS Management, Department of Politics and Society, Aalborg University, Aalborg, Denmark
e-mail: haslam@dps.aau.dk; sam@dps.aau.dk; agger@dps.aau.dk

organizations successfully cope with crisis-driven accelerated digital transformation?

Accelerated digital transformation of university-level teaching as a crisis management response to the COVID-19 pandemic constitutes an *"extreme case"* (Flyvbjerg 2006). By studying digital transformation in an extreme situation, we contribute to extant research with new empirical insights as well as theorizing about "accelerated digital transformation" of core organizational activities. For organizations, accelerated digital transformation may become increasingly relevant in a more and more volatile world. Moreover, insight into the practicalities of handling accelerating digital transformation is relevant across sectors and industries as a means of stimulating digital innovation in organizations. As a theoretical concept, accelerated digital transformation refers to the ability of actors at all organizational levels to respond to change and crisis rapidly, collaboratively, and individually by performing the management activities that relate to their organizational roles.

2   Background

Digital transformation is about major changes (Liu et al. 2011; Besson and Rowe 2012) to business models, activities, and competencies to exploit the opportunities offered by digital technology in a strategic way (Kaltum et al. 2016; Vial 2019). Extant literature has focused on maturity models and stages of digital transformation (Valdez-de-Leon 2016), strategies and strategic options for digital transformation (Bharadwaj et al. 2013; Hess et al. 2016), organizational capabilities (Orlandi 2016), CIO roles and leadership competencies (Weill and Woerner 2013a, b; Singh and Hess 2017), how traditional firms navigate digital transformation (Sebastian et al. 2017), and how digital transformation change culture (Karimi and Walter 2015), and organizational identity (Wessel et al. 2021). Svahn et al. (2017) suggest that successful digital transformation requires fundamentally rethinking the organization, while also keeping the core business functioning efficiently.

A commonality in most existing studies is that digital transformation is viewed as a challenging organizational change process loaded with tensions (Baiyere et al. 2020) that unfold in certain stages (Valdez-de-Leon 2016), is likely to meet high-degree of employee resistance, and often takes long time. While appreciating these insights as foundational for understanding digital transformation, the current research is designed to contribute new insight on crisis-driven digital transformation as an accelerated change process, which seems to short-circuit existing ways of understanding digital transformation as long-term development consisting of certain prerequisite steps or stages.

To inform our framing of the new phenomenon of crisis-driven accelerated digital transformation, we turn to the field of crisis management research. The argument for this is twofold. First, the need for accelerated digital transformation arose due to a crisis situation, namely the COVID-19 lockdown, which caused a major breakdown in established physical ways of working, not just in this case but in organizations around the world. Second, the literature on crisis management offers valuable insight into how organizations can handle situations that require immediate organizational response—something which the literature on digital transformation does not focus on to the same extent, as mentioned above.

In general, organizational crises are described as low-probability, high-consequence events, characterized by ambiguity with regard to cause, effect and resolution as well as by a need for swift decisions and actions that mitigate the crisis (Pearson and Clair 1998). Organizational response to crisis is considered successful when the organization is able to maintain or regain the momentum of core activities, the losses of internal and external stakeholders are minimized and organizational learning occurs so that lessons are transferred to future incidents (ibid). While the list of potential organizational crisis is virtually unending (Mitroff et al. 1987), we concentrate on externally triggered accidents, as in the case of COVID-19.

Crisis management scholars have identified five phases—or core activities—for managing an organizational crisis: (a) signal detection which requires managers to sense early warnings that announce the possibility of a crisis, (b) preparation and prevention means that managers are expected to avert crises and prepare, should the crisis occur, (c) damage control, or coping, where managers take action to handle the immediate impact and stop the crisis from expanding to other areas of the organization or its environment, (d) recovery, where managers are responsible for designing and implementing short- and long-term plans to help resume organizational operations, and (e) learning where managers encourage examination of the critical lessons from the crisis (Coombs 1999; Mitroff and Pearson 1993; Pheng et al. 1999; Wooten and James 2008).

Since this study concentrates on accelerated digital transformation as the response for dealing with the occurrence of the COVID-19 crisis, it covers the abovementioned phase c and d. As such, we are particularly interested in the literature's recommendations for damage control, coping strategies, and short-term plans. To this end, the literature emphasizes that managers need to focus on the following: (1) swift decision-making and the ability to see the crisis not only as a threat but also as an opportunity (Brockner and James 2008), (2) communication to shape stakeholders perceptions (Coombs 1995; James and Wooten 2006; Seeger et al. 2003), including attempt to restore calm, inspire confidence, and show empathy in their messaging, and (3) adequate risk-taking, by avoiding unnecessary risk, while ensuring creative thinking and innovation that can help the organization strategize novel ways for overcoming the crisis (Wooten and James 2008).

In summary, organizational crisis requires fast response and several nontrivial activities to deal with unusual circumstances. We use these insights as a starting point to inspire our empirical case study design, particularly with regard to focus areas and vocabulary, and based on our empirical results we develop a conceptual model that delineates defining elements of crisis-driven accelerated digital transformation.

3   Research Method

To explore accelerated digital transformation triggered by the COVID-19 pandemic, we conducted an explorative case study (Yin 2014) at a social science faculty at a Danish university. Aalborg University (AAU) is a public university founded in 1974 with its main campus located in the city of Aalborg in the northern part of Denmark. The university has five faculties covering a wide range of subjects within engineering, medicine, information technology, design, humanities, and social sciences. The university awards bachelor's degrees, master's degrees, and PhD degrees and has more than 23,000 students.

In this research study, we focus on the Faculty of Social Sciences that made all teaching activities 100% online by medio March 2020 and the rest of the semester caused by the COVID-19 situation. Management of the Faculty of Social Sciences consists of the dean, the associate dean for research, the associate dean for education and the heads of the four departments at the faculty; (1) Department of Sociology and Social Work, (2) Department of Politics and Society, (3) Department of Business and Management, and (4) Department of Law. To focus our investigation, we concentrate on the two former departments, which are similar in budget and size with approx. 100 scholars at each department.

During the past 5 years, digitalization of teaching activities has become increasingly important at the Faculty of Social Sciences. In the wake of Aalborg University's overall digitalization strategy (2016–2021), a range of initiatives have been taking at the Faculty of Social Sciences, including employment of a digitalization consultant in 2019, and launching a process toward development of a digital transformation strategy for the faculty. The Dean explained how this process moved slowly forward, loaded with intense discussions and resistance to change among some employee groups. He further explained how the unexpected COVID-19 situation forced a digital transformation of teaching activities, which surpassed his *"wildest imaginations."* As such, the Faculty of Social Sciences provides a unique context for examining accelerated digital transformation.

Data Collection

We follow the recommendation from Yin (2014) to include multiple sources of data in our case study, as summarized in Tables 1 and 2. First, we conducted 28 semistructured interviews (Kvale 2008) with managers, professors, digitalization staff, and students distributed equally across the two departments. All interviews took place during the first 4 weeks of the COVID-19 response period—medio March to medio April 2020. In this way, our data covers a "real time" investigation of the early stage of how the Social Science Faculty coped with accelerated digitalization in a crisis. We held all interviews online (Lo Iacono et al. 2016) using Microsoft Teams or Skype for Business. Interviews lasted one hour on average. The interview guide was adapted to the four stakeholder groups, but all guides covered three broad questions concerning how the faculty coped with accelerated digital transformation:

Table 1 Data sources—interviews

Actor group	#	Description	Application
Managers	Dean (1) Associate Dean (1) Head of Depart. (2) Vice Head of Depart. (2)	Entire top management team	Establishing rich insight into how management responded to the crisis and how they communicated to professors and students
Professors	Full Professors (2) Associate Professors (5) Assistant Professors (3)	Professors with online teaching during COVID-19 period. Equally divided across the two departments. Five females and five males	Acquiring detailed information about online teaching activities during COVID-19. Its benefits, disadvantages, and consequences
Digitization Staff	Digitalization consultant (1) Head IT service (1)	Key digitalization staff at the faculty of social sciences	Triangulation of insights obtained from managers, professors, and students. Adding new insights on the technical aspect of online teaching in crisis
Students	Bachelor level (6) Master level (4)	Equally divided across the two departments. Five females and five males	Detailed information about how online teaching is experienced from a student perspective

Table 2 Data sources—documents

Type	Description	Application
E-mail communication Digitalization strategies PowerPoint presentations Meeting minutes Student evaluations	122 e-mails with COVID-19 communication to professors and students from managers (11th March to 20th April 2020) 23 documents (423 pages)	Background information on digitalization strategy prior to COVID-19 as well as insight into the details of the communicative response to the crisis

(a) which online teaching activities have been initiated during the COVID-19 period and why? (b) how do key organizational actors experience online teaching—its suddenness, benefits, disadvantages, and unintended consequences? (c) how is the rapid transformation of university teaching supported by the management team? All interviews were recorded and subsequently transcribed verbatim by a group of student assistants using online transcription software from Konch's Speech-to-Text platform. All interviews were conducted, and subsequent recordings and transcriptions, stored in compliance with GDPR standards.

Second, we included a range of documents. Due to the extreme situation, the management team at the university produced several formal announcements, procedure descriptions, and guidelines on online teaching for employees and students readily available for analysis. All documents were archived and stored in accordance with GDPR regulations.

Data Analysis

We applied Braun and Clarke's (2006) phases of thematic analysis to move from raw data to theoretical insight. The approach was used to code the text without using an initial a priori coding template, because the purpose of this study is to open-mindedly explore accelerated digital transformation rather than testing a certain theoretical point of view. Firstly, we read the transcribed interviews and available documents and noted down ideas of how the Faculty of Social Sciences was coping with crisis-driven and accelerated digital transformation in a process of getting familiar with the overall dataset. Secondly, we conducted open coding to generate the initial codes. Next, the whole data set was grouped together under similar codes and then sorted into three overall themes. We then reviewed, refined, and defined the themes. In the third stage, we visualized the themes in a model that captures key concepts of relevance for how organizations successfully can cope with accelerated digital transformation. To ensure the quality of the data analysis, we independently analyzed the data then discussed and corroborating our findings and used "member checking" with our key contacts at the faculty.

4   Findings

On Wednesday, the March 11th, 2020, in the evening, the Danish government announced that all noncritical public sector institutions, such as universities, would be locked down to stop the spread of the coronavirus. This created a sharp *before* and *after* in the social science faculty's approach to teaching, as all teaching activities were digitalized with immediate effect. In this section, we present three salient themes that help us understand how it was possible for the social science faculty to become an online university so rapidly. The themes are: (1) leveraging existing resources, (2) intensified communication, and (3) re-organizing core activities.

Leveraging Existing Resources

The social science faculty was able to shift from physical to online teaching over night by leveraging existing digital technologies and knowledge resources. The university had already invested in several technologies that either were explicitly aimed at or had the potential to support online teaching, such as the organization's learning management system Moodle, skype-for-business, MS Teams, and Panopto.

However, before the COVID-19 lockdown period, these technologies were primarily used to support physical teaching, which in turn meant that only basic functionality (e.g., course lists, calendar, and file sharing in Moodle), were used. Yet, a **digital infrastructure** was in place (including support websites, instruction videos, and online tutorials) and immediately, after the lockdown period started, the professors began to explore and use the functionality of these technologies to a much larger extent, i.e., for livestreaming of lectures, video-recorded lectures, PowerPoint slides with voice-over, online chat-sessions between professors and students, for project supervision meetings as well as quizzes, tests, and online oral examinations, including PhD defenses. Paramount for enabling full digitalization of all teaching activities was also that the students could be counted on to have their own computers as well as good Internet connections, thereby creating a strong infrastructure on both the university and the student side.

In addition to the digital infrastructure, all organizational actors, from managers to students, had a high level of **digital maturity** that could be leveraged for online teaching and learning. However, the interviewees report that they did not necessarily realize this before the COVID-19 period, because their digital skills stemmed from other areas. For example, many researchers, particularly the more senior researchers, have experience using digital technologies to collaborate with and maintain relations with international and/or distributed research groups. Most were able to take advantage of this experience for delivering digital teaching and, particularly, for online student supervision. In addition, most junior researchers have (recently) participated in mandatory university pedagogy courses of which at least one focuses on applying digital technologies in education. Our interviewees describe that they did not feel they had reason to apply these technologies prior to COVID-19, because physical teaching was the primary and culturally most valued means of delivery at the social science faculty. However, they were grateful that they had been introduced to and had some hands-on experience with the organization's portfolio of educational platforms and tools during the pedagogical course. The junior researchers state that knowing that they had some skill with digital teaching removed much of the trepidation they would otherwise feel having to adopt unfamiliar technologies very rapidly. Similarly, the students have digital skills from many areas of life, including experience with having to navigate numerous administrative and educational systems and platforms in relation to their university program.

Intensified Communication

Already Wednesday the March 11th, 2020, in the evening after the Danish government's announcement, managers and professors started to communicate with and to each other about what had just happened and how to respond to the situation. Over the next weeks, there was an unprecedented amount of **information dissemination** at and between all organizational levels. This included email communication from deans, study leaders, study boards, etc. with guidelines and rules for how to deal with the new reality.

Our document study shows that the communication was frequent with several emails each day, in an attempt to inform about changes in the Danish governmental announcements, organizationally available digital technologies and support resources as well as managerial decisions, e.g., about preferred modes of teaching (i.e., synchronous or asynchronous), how to conduct online examinations. Moreover, several existing ideas and ideals concerning digitalization of university teaching were reiterated across the faculty. In addition, several managers at faculty and department levels were already involved in digitalization work groups and were quick to push existing ideas and information to staff and students. In addition, emergency response teams were established, with daily/frequent meetings among IT staff and managers as well as involvement of students and student surveys for identifying emerging challenges and informing about how to deal with them.

Some of the emerging challenges that had to be managed concerned: (1) the students' access to empirical data and secure GDPR compliant data collection via digital platforms during the COVID-19 lockdown, (2) rules and regulations for ensuring valid virtual examinations with regard to both the students' legal certainty but also to avoid examination fraud as well as (3) how to help both employees and students cope with anxiety and loneliness due to working/studying from home (Haslam et al. 2021). Managers were highly aware of the latter aspect and aimed to communicate their understanding for the staffs' and students' different life situations and resulting variation in time and ability to adopt to digital teaching as well as the challenging aspects of social distancing.

Supplementing the frequent dissemination of formal information, there was much informal **knowledge sharing** of tips and tricks about "the do's and don'ts" of digital teaching among colleagues via emails, rapidly created Moodle-sites or Teams in MS Teams. In general, the willingness to share knowledge and help colleagues that felt uncertain on how to get started with digital teaching or how do a specific thing was enormous. As one of the informant's state: *"the most important thing has actually been the sharing and help from colleagues."*

The knowledge sharing also covered a hyper awareness of material, for example, from social media channels, that might be relevant for oneself, one's colleagues and/or students. An example of this was a list of references about methods for and advantages and disadvantages of online data collection, which was posted on LinkedIn by a UK researcher and subsequently picked up and shared among the professors and students that participated in our study.

Re-organizing Core Activities

Immediately after the COVID-19 lockdown, it was decided at faculty level to avoid disrupting teaching schedules by immediately digitalizing all teaching activities. Faculty and department managers report being apprehensive about this decision as, prior to the COVID-19 situation, initiatives toward increased digital teaching had been met with significant resistance, leading to a voluntary strategy for adoption to avoid a push back from teaching staff. The resistance toward digital teaching, at the university in general including the Social Science Faculty, stems from a culture where problem-based learning and dialogue with the students are highly valued and constitutive of the organizational identity; resulting in the common assumption that mediated interaction with students is pedagogically and didactically inferior to face-to-face interaction. However, as a response to the COVID-19 crisis, management chose to push for rapid digitalization, supporting this decision with the intensified communication described above. Mainly, by making it clear that **experimentation** was encouraged and that it was acceptable that some experiments would be less successful than others. To the managers relief—and surprise—this strategy worked well. Almost all professors began using available digital technologies immediately and many have spent a great deal of time and effort repeatedly experimenting with these technologies and sharing experiences with each other. Apparently shedding previous inhibitions or reservations.

Initially, most professors approached the new situation by trying to emulate their existing practices on digital platforms. Almost all reported that this was generally a lot easier than they had expected and, therefore, their focus quickly shifted toward translation rather than simple emulation encompassing digital didactics as well as the digital platforms themselves. This is illustrated through the following observations:

1. Initially, professors spent a great deal of time experimenting on a lecture-to-lecture basis, trying new platforms and approaches successively with nothing taken for granted. Although students have been extremely patient and understanding, they report that the main (negative) impact for them had little to do with the digitalization of the lectures and more to do with the lack of stability and predictability surrounding the practicalities of their courses. For example, which platforms would be used, when materials would be available, and how to prepare for a lecture.

2. Technical normalcy arrived much sooner than most had expected. The mechanics of using digital tools have been less of an issue than most dared hope for. It has also become clear that complicated and advanced technical solutions do not necessarily lead to better teaching, learning experiences, and outcomes. Consequently, we now see an emergent tendency for professors to settle on simpler technical solutions (i.e., the simplest solution available that works) and focus more on didactical experimentation within the boundaries these solutions provide. All professors in our study expressed an interest in increased knowledge sharing about digital didactics. Both formally, in the form of best practices gathered and put forward by management, and informally among colleagues.

3. Didactically, there are many contextual factors that must suddenly be considered during lockdown. The type and availability of physical workspaces, access to high-quality IT equipment, high-speed Internet connections, IT-Support, and not least personal and family considerations such as having to home school children affect professors and students alike and have a significant impact on productivity. Therefore, empathic understanding for everyone's specific situation becomes vital when choosing between asynchronous and synchronous forms of teaching, assignment deadlines, group tasks, and so on.

Experimentation has far from subsided and there are still lively discussions and knowledge sharing concerning the practicalities of various tools and platforms. This **continuous reflection** is contributing to a gradual shift in focus from technically driven emulation of existing practices toward translation of practice from an analog to a digital context. The shift toward digital didactics is not unexpected, however, the speed with which it seems to be occurring stands in stark contrast to the more moderate pace of previous digitalization initiatives, indicating that a relatively small amount of motivated collective experience could be enough to overcome initial trepidation.

5   Concluding Remarks

In this research-in-progress chapter, we have examined accelerated digital transformation. Empirically, we have shown how it was possible for the Social Science Faculty at a Danish university to undergo accelerated digital transformation, which shifted the method of delivery from primarily physical to 100% online teaching, essentially within a 24-hour time period—something which all organizational members considered impossible just a few days before it became reality. Figure 1 summarizes the three empirically identified themes, and associated sub-themes, for answering the question of how the organization successfully coped with crisis-driven accelerated digital transformation.

Three key insights for understanding what accelerated digital transformation entails and requires to stand out in this study. First of all, the organization already possessed a high level of organizational readiness for digital teaching, because a digital infrastructure with relevant technologies and support material was in place and because managers, professors, and students had experience with these, and/or similar, technologies, and therefore had enough familiarity and digital maturity for using the technologies for teaching purposes. Yet, in this case, the high level of organizational readiness was unrecognized by all actors prior to the COVID-19 lockdown, among other things, due to a planned longer strategic process and the

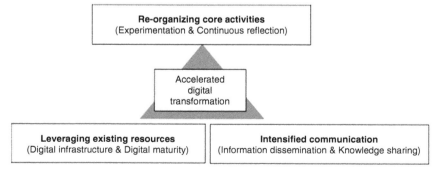

Fig. 1 Empirical themes defining the concept of accelerated digital transformation

expected need to overcome resistance to change. However, when an immediate crisis-response became necessary the existing, slowly accumulated digital and knowledge resources were ready to be leveraged for accelerated transformation.

Secondly, a key finding is that the accelerated digital transformation was possible because actors at all organizational levels actively participated in the transformation process by performing crisis management activities relating to their organizational roles, i.e., in collective crisis management. Managers and emergency response team members partook in ongoing issues identification, decision-making, and information dissemination, while other actors, such as professors and students, went out of their way to experiment with different digital teaching formats, with unusual patience and emphatic understanding for each other's situations, as well as a willingness to share experiences, improvement suggestions, and tips and tricks with each other.

Thirdly, the organizational learning about digital teaching was enormous, because all actors, from managers to students, were engaged in the same types of collective experimentation and with much more frequent feedback loops than usual. The Social Science Faculty is typically characterized by numerous actors participating in many different unrelated research projects and teaching activities, thereby creating less than optimal conditions for alignment of activities and shared learning. However, in this case, the COVID-19 crisis put everybody on the same path, thereby making information dissemination, knowledge sharing, and individual and organizational learning both necessary and possible.

References

Baiyere, A., Salmela, H., & Tapanainen, T. (2020). Digital transformation and the new logics of business process management. *European Journal of Information Systems, 29*(3), 238–259.

Besson, P., & Rowe, F. (2012). Strategizing information systems-enabled organizational transformation: A transdisciplinary review and new directions. *The Journal of Strategic Information Systems, 21*(2), 103–124.

Bharadwaj, A., El Sawy, O. A., Pavlou, P. A., & Venkatraman, N. (2013). Digital Business Strategy: Toward a Next Generation of Insights. *MIS Quarterly, 37*(2), 471–482.

Braun, V., & Clarke, V. (2006). Using thematic analysis in psychology. *Qualitative Research in Psychology, 3*(2), 77–101.

Brockner, J. B., & James, E. H. (2008). Toward an understanding of when executives see opportunity in crisis. *Journal of Applied Behavioral Science, 44*(7), 94–115.

Coombs, W. T. (1995). Choosing the right words: The development of guidelines for the selection of the "appropriate" crisis response strategies. *Management Communication Quarterly, 8*, 447–476.

Coombs, W. (1999). *Ongoing crisis communication: Planning, managing and responding.* Thousand Oaks, CA: Sage.

Flyvbjerg, B. (2006). Five misunderstandings about case-study research. *Qualitative Inquiry, 12*(2), 219–245.

Haslam, C. R., Madsen, S., & Nielsen, J. A. (2021). Problem based learning during the COVID 19 pandemic. Can project groups save the day? *Communications of the Association for Information Systems, 48*.

Hess, T., Matt, C., Benlian, A., & Wiesböck, F. (2016). Options for formulating a digital transformation strategy. *MIS Quarterly Executive, 15*(2), 123–139.

James, E. H., & Wooten, L. P. (2006). Diversity crises: How firms manage discrimination lawsuits. *Academy of Management Journal, 49*(6), 1103–1118.

Kaltum, U., Widodo, A., & Yanuardi, A. W. (2016). Local TV goes global market through digital transformation. *Academy of Strategic Management Journal, 15.*

Karimi, J., & Walter, Z. (2015). The role of dynamic capabilities in responding to digital disruption: a factor-based study of the newspaper industry. *Journal of Management Information Systems, 32*(1), 39–81.

Kvale, S. (2008). *Doing interviews.* Thousand Oaks, CA: Sage.

Liu, D. Y., Chen, S. W., & Chou, T. C. (2011). Resource fit in digital transformation: Lessons learned from the CBC Bank Global e-Banking Project. *Management Decision, 49*(10), 1728–1742.

Lo Iacono, V., Symonds, P., & Brown, D. H. (2016). Skype as a tool for qualitative research interviews. *Sociological Research Online, 21*(2), 1–15.

Madsen, S., Haslam, C. R., & Nielsen, J. A. (2020). Accelerated digital transformation: The case of the online University caused by Covid-19. Selected Papers of the IRIS, Issue Nr 11 (2020). 2.

Mitroff, I., & Pearson, C. M. (1993). *Crisis management: A diagnostic guide for improving your organization's crisis-preparedness.* San Francisco: Jossey-Bass.

Mitroff, I. I., Shrivastava, P., & Udwadia, F. E. (1987). Effective crisis management. *Academy of Management Perspectives, 1*(4), 283–292.

Orlandi, L. B. (2016). Organizational capabilities in the digital era: Reframing strategic orientation. *Journal of Innovation & Knowledge, 1*(3), 156–161.

Pearson, C. M., & Clair, J. A. (1998). Reframing crisis management. *Academy of Management Review, 23*(1), 59–76.

Pheng, L., Ho, D., & Ann, Y. (1999). Crisis management: A survey of property development firms. *Property Management, 17*(3), 231–251.

Sebastian, I. M., Moloney, K. G., Ross, J. W., Fonstad, N. O., Beath, C., & Mocker, M. (2017). How big old companies navigate digital transformation. *MIS Quarterly Executive, 16*(3), 197–213.

Seeger, M., Sellnow, T., & Ulmer, R. (2003). *Communication and organizational crisis.* Westport, CT: Praeger.

Singh, A., & Hess, T. (2017). How chief digital officers promote the digital transformation of their companies. *MIS Quarterly Executive, 16*(1), 1–17.

Svahn, F., Mathiassen, L., & Lindgren, R. (2017). Embracing digital innovation in incumbent firms: How Volvo Cars managed competing concerns. *MIS Quarterly, 41*(1), 239–253.

Valdez-de-Leon, O. (2016). A digital maturity model for telecommunications service providers. *Technology Innovation Management Review, 6*(8), 19–32.

Vial, G. (2019). Understanding digital transformation: A review and a research agenda. *Journal of Strategic Information Systems, 28*, 118–144.

Weill, P., & Woerner, S. L. (2013a). Optimizing your digital business model. *MIT Sloan Management Review, 54*(3).

Weill, P., & Woerner, S. L. (2013b). The future of the CIO in a digital economy. *MIS Quarterly Executive, 12*(2), 65–75.

Wessel, L., Baiyere, A., Ologeanu-Taddei, R., Cha, J., & Jensen, T. (2021). Unpacking the difference between digital transformation and IT-enabled organizational transformation. *Journal of Association of Information Systems, 22*(1), 6.

Wooten, L. P., & James, E. H. (2008). Linking crisis management and leadership competencies: The role of human resource development. *Advances in Developing Human Resources, 10*(3), 352–379.

Yin, R. K. (2014). *Case study research: Design and methods* (5th ed.). Thousand Oaks, CA: Sage.

Christian Ravn Haslam is a Teaching Associate Professor at the Department of Politics & Society, Aalborg University, Denmark. He has over 15 years of professional IT experience in international private and public sector organizations and holds a PhD in strategic digital innovation. He is a researcher at the Centre for IS Management (CIM) and is currently focused on the organizational implications of accelerated digital transformation.

Sabine Madsen is an Associate Professor at the Department of Politics & Society, Aalborg University, Denmark. She is affiliated with the Centre for IS Management (CIM). Sabine Madsen's research covers empirical studies of large-scale organizational change processes, such as agile implementation and digital transformation, which she studies from a sensemaking perspective. She has published in leading IS journals and has also recently published a book on *Theorizing in Organization Studies*.

Jeppe Agger Nielsen is a Professor at the Department of Politics & Society, Aalborg University, Denmark. He is head of research at the Centre for IS Management (CIM). Jeppe Agger Nielsen's research focuses on digital transformation and digital innovation from an institutional theory perspective. His research is published in leading journals such as *MIS Quarterly* and *International Journal of Management Reviews*.

Selecting, Combining, and Cultivating Digital Ecosystems in a Digital Ecosphere

Claus A. Foss Rosenstand

1   Private–Public Partnership and Digital Ecosystems

Nearly all governments have a focus on digitalization; this is also the case for Denmark. To this end, the private–public partnership Digital Hub Denmark was launched in 2018. The vision is to become a digital frontrunner in Europe by 2023. From the beginning of 2019, I got a special research-based innovation management obligation regarding this vision; to help businesses' exponential growth leveraging digital disruptive technologies. In practice, I have helped digital businesses and entrepreneurs with this since 1999 as a board member, supervisor, consultant, or co-founder. However, I cannot help a whole nation through this relatively individual and random approach. Thus, my focus is on nationwide ecosystems in the digital disruptive domain in which Denmark has a global niche foothold.

Ecosystems in the digital domain are often termed digital ecosystems; however, this is typically used according to the digital platform industry, where a combination of AI, big data, and IoT is leveraged. My focus is to bring exponential growth to digital businesses; and to this end, a regional ecosystem should benefit multiple businesses. Therefore, I take my point of departure in Adner's perspective on ecosystems (Adner 2012) where they basically are value-networks, as opposed to simpler value-chains. A sustainable ecosystem is constituted by different stakeholders including customers coupled in a value-system, where each participant gains more value than any of the participants would be able to do without the system (synergy). Ecosystems can be reconfigured for success through separating, combining, relocating, adding, and subtracting ecosystem elements (Adner 2012, pp. 190–191). It can be argued that due to the digital disruptive elements of democratization, demonetize, and dematerialize (Ismail 2014) the barriers for reconfiguration of ecosystems are lower than ever before.

C. A. F. Rosenstand (✉)
Aalborg University, Aalborg, Denmark
e-mail: cr@hum.aau.dk

© The Author(s), under exclusive license to Springer Nature Switzerland AG 2021
D. R. A. Schallmo, J. Tidd (eds.), *Digitalization*, Management for Professionals,
https://doi.org/10.1007/978-3-030-69380-0_17

It can be argued that digital ecosystems are market-driven bottom-up phenomena, as opposed to cluster organizations that are politically implemented top-down systems. Therefore, private market actors should be highly included in governmental support of ecosystems, and to this end, private–public partnerships with private and public key partners are the most inclusive solution. As an example, the founding partners of Digital Hub Denmark are on the private side Confederation of Danish Industry, The Danish Chamber of Commerce, Finance Denmark, and The Danish Industry Foundation, and on the public side Ministry of Industry, Business and Financial Affairs, Ministry of Foreign Affairs, and Ministry of Higher Education and Science (Digital Hub Denmark 2020). The chairman of the board is partner-independent and recruited from the private sector, and the vice-chairman is the permanent secretary of the Ministry of Industry, Business and Financial Affairs.

Existing research using the Business Model Canvas (Osterwalder and Pigneur 2010), contributes with a model of individual digital ecosystems (León et al. 2016). And on a general level, the characteristics for "digital business ecosystems" are well described for a fully decentralized architecture: "No single point of failure or control;... should not be dependent upon any single instance or actor; equal opportunities for access for all; [and (ed.)] scalability and robustness" (Nachira et al. 2007, p. 12). Following this, digital ecosystems cannot be created top-down, they can only be identified and then selected for support—e.g., formally through a national cluster organization representing a politically selected national stronghold. To this practical end, there seems to be a research gap for a canvas model to select, combine, and cultivate multiple digital ecosystems in a private–public partnership with a practical focus on how to orchestrate the digital ecosystem's innovation managers. Following this, the reserach question is:

How to support exponential growth leveraged by digital disruptive technologies through selecting, combining, and cultivating digital ecosystems within the digital disruptive domain? And more practical, how to orchestrate the innovation managers of these ecosystems?

2   Digital Ecosphere for Digital Ecosystems

This work addresses the very early discovery phase, where the approach is explorative and experimental. Thus, the work reflects the first iterations of an action research process, where I am highly driven by (and reflect on) the rationalities that drive practice (Mathiassen 1997). To do this, Digital Hub Denmark hosts a national network for digital ecosystems. Documentations are agendas, minutes, e-mails, and presentations made by members and guests.

Due 2019 and 2020, I identified and selected the digital ecosystems to support. The point of departure was a Startup Genome report funded by Digital Hub Denmark which identified five digital ecosystems, where Denmark has a stronghold; fin-tech, health-tech, robotics, agro-tech, and ed-tech (Gauthier 2019). During 2019, actors from creative industries of gaming, animation, XR, and movies formed a crea-tech ecosystem, and during 2020 actors from the property industry of construction, real

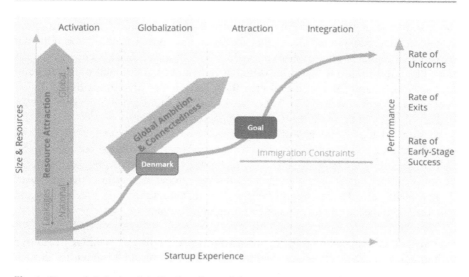

Fig. 1 Denmark is in the globalization phase of the startup ecosystem lifecycle

estate, and mortgage formed a prop-tech ecosystem. Both digital ecosystems are considered national strongholds. Together these seven ecosystems form what I term a "digital ecosphere." These digital ecosystems are identified as a function of ecosystem size, turnover, and investments. However, for selection, three extra criteria have been used; firstly an ecosystem should be formally organized as a nationwide not-for-profit association; secondly, these organizations should be represented by an innovation manager in the position of e.g., cluster director or CEO; and thirdly, the innovation managers must have a global, open, and integrative mindset, where all national businesses are considered as potential ecosystem participants rather than competitors.

One important finding of the Startup Genome report is that Denmark is positioned as a Globalizer in the global startup ecosystem lifecycle (Ibid.). This is illustrated in Fig. 1, where Denmark's position in the globalization phase is in the yellow box. The position measured as startup experience is based on the rate of unicorns, exits, early-stage success. The important insight from the StartUp Genome report is the clear correlation between the size and resources of an ecosystem and the position in the global eco-system lifecycle (left *y*-axis) because this means Denmark has to scale the digital ecosystem to reach the goal of positioning Denmark in the attraction phase (green box). The core difference between the globalization and attraction phase is whether digital talent, startups, and investments are primarily, respectively, detracted or attracted to the ecosystems. Examples of digital ecosystems in the attraction phase are based in Tel Aviv, London, and Stockholm (early stage). Silicon Valley is the core example of a digital ecosystem in the integration phase, integrating startups all over the world. A recent report shows that Denmark since 2014 has attracted more digital talent than it has detracted (HBS 2020), thus the green box is placed in the middle of the Globalization phase. However, more digital startups are needed to move to the attraction phase. An estimate given to Digital Hub Denmark from the selected digital ecosystems shows that Denmark has approximately 1000 potential exponential digital startups, where more than 70% of the revenue is generated from sales of digital solutions that offer different domain-specific digital transformation (not sales of hours). The indicated growth in the number of startups in the digital ecosphere is approximately 20 % per year, and the indicated job growth is even higher. So a doubling in the next 4–5 years is not unlikely.

Startups in the digital ecosphere have a shared agenda regarding exponential growth, leveraged by digital disruptive technologies and thus digital business development regarding strategy, organization, technology, sales, marketing, partnerships, business models, need for capital, networking, processes, agility, management, digital talents, etc. To this significant end, it is meaningful to select, combine, and cultivate digital ecosystems in a coherent digital ecosphere.

The vision is, as formulated with my special research obligation, to help business' exponential growth leveraging digital disruptive technologies. Digital disruptive technologies can be defined as disruptive technology on an exponential growth trajectory regarding price-performance (Lundgaard and Rosenstand 2019; Rosenstand et al. 2018). The core digital disruptive technology is computer power (digital calculations) where the price-performance has been doubling annually since 1890 until today, and it continues due to the exponentially growing number of transistors in an integrated circuit every 18 months known as Moore's law, increase clock frequency, and market forces (Kurzwiel 2005). To this end, I focus on businesses leveraging exponential price-performance of digital disruptive technologies in exponential business models. The idea is to enter the digital age by taking significant more global market shares in the industries represented by the selected ecosystems than the size of Denmark (5.8 million inhabitants) justifies with a linear growth perspective from the industrial age. One important aspect is reducing the limitations for new growth regarding the size of the national talent mass, as it is well known that the growth of an exponential business is far from 1:1 with the number of employees (digital talents). Two other important aspects are; access to customers and investors.

The mission is to move Denmark to the attraction phase, and the strategy is to "hack" the leap between the yellow and green position in Fig. 1 by selecting, combining, and cultivating national digital ecosystems, where Denmark has a global stronghold. Until now digital ecosystems in Denmark have been detached and limited around cities. For a small country like Denmark, with a geographical size comparable to Greater Boston this is simply inefficient in a globally competitive world. To this end, the Danish law of business promotion from 2018, is a strong incentive for national syndication of ecosystems because only one national position in each stronghold is funded as national cluster organizations. National cluster organizations were politically appointed in August 2020, and the industries represented by the seven ecosystems except ed-tech are included or strongly related to different new domain-specific cluster organizations. The ecosystems have remained their geographical epicenters, e.g., is the epicenter of robotics in Odense, but talent, investors, and startups will be included from other parts of Denmark. In practice, this is done by syndicating key ecosystem players—e.g., from 2020, Odense Robotics is a new formal national association.

A coherent digital ecosphere constituted by seven digital ecosystems on a trajectory toward the attraction phase in Fig. 1 is the purpose of the national network for digital ecosystems. Digital Hub Denmark hosts meetings, where an innovation manager from each ecosystem participates together with the CEO of Digital Hub Denmark and me; moreover, special guests are invited.

3   Digital Ecosphere Canvas

In general, an ecosphere is an "open/closed system" for multiple ecosystems. Digital ecosystems are social systems and can thus be understood with system theory (Luhmann 1984). A digital ecosphere is closed to its surroundings because it is self-organized and -structured; however, it is communicative open to its surroundings: In the same way, as a biological ecosphere like the earth is open to energy from sun waves resulting in multiple ecosystems with evolutionary growth, the Danish digital ecosphere is open to energy through talents, customers, and investors resulting in (for now) seven digital ecosystems with exponential growth. With a metaphor, I understand my role as a "gardener" gently and patiently cultivating the ecosphere, so it is ready for exponential growth when it rains. In a way, this is the opposite metaphor of a "rainmaker," which is often used for business development. Metaphorical speaking, I believe we both need gardeners and rainmakers to help businesses succeed.

Both biological and social systems normally consist of multiple differentiated sub-systems communicating more or less effectively with each other. In the digital ecosphere, the seven selected ecosystems are such differentiated sub-systems. Elaborating the system theory is outside the scope of this chapter; however, the point here is that it is a relevant tool for the understanding of a digital ecosphere.

To support exponential growth leveraged by digital disruptive technologies through selecting, combining, and cultivating digital ecosystems within the digital disruptive domain, I have created a canvas for a digital ecosphere. In an iterative action research process, I have shared, discussed, and developed the canvas with the ecosystem innovation managers, with good coworkers in Digital Hub Denmark, and with other innovation researchers. To this end, it is a highly dynamic canvas supporting the co-creation process of forming the digital ecosphere. The last version from November 2020 is illustrated in Fig. 2 and has in earlier versions been presented to Digital Hub Denmarks's board illuminating the private–public partnership. One earlier version of the canvas has also been published, presented, and discussed at the International Society for Professional Innovation Management (Rosenstand 2020).

The canvas is constituted by intertwined market verticals and horizontals. The selected digital ecosystems constitute the market verticals where the ecosphere owners have identified ecosystems representing industries with strongholds in the form of global value propositions—"bundle of products and services that create

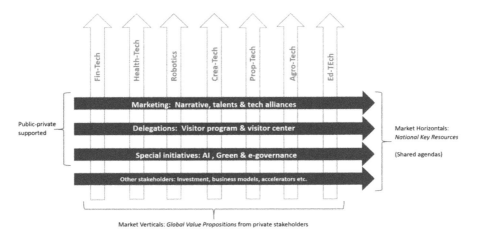

Fig. 2 Digital ecosphere canvas exemplified with Digital Hub Denmark

value for a specific customer segment" (Osterwalder and Pigneur 2010 p. 22). The common denominator for the value propositions across the ecosystems is digital transformations; however, each ecosystem has specialized its digital transformation towards different significant domains. For example, is fin-tech specialized in the digital transformation of the financial sector, both nationally and globally.

A market horizontal should meet a need for a wide range of businesses across different industries. Thus, there must be shared agendas across the selected ecosystems cultivating and combining them. The public supported initiatives in Fig. 2 are aligned with Digital Hub Denmarks's private–public owners' decision on the annual goals within marketing, delegations, and special initiatives. The canvas is open to other horizontal players regarding investment, business models, accelerators, etc. To this end, the market horizontals can be considered national key resources to the ecosphere "... describing the most important assets required to make a business model [of ecosystems (ed.)] work (Osterwalder and Pigneur 2010, p. 34)." The goal with the key resources in the ecosphere is what I term ecosystem efficiency. Examples from Digital Hub Denmark of key resources in market horizontals are campaigns to attract digital talents, tech-alliances through (virtual) delegations to attract customers, and a mapping of the digital ecosphere of approximately 1000 best exponential startups to attract investors. Moreover, foreign talent pools are identified with pull and push factors for future talent attraction. Digital talents such as data scientists can contribute to the whole digital deep-tech ecosphere, and because talent attracts talent it is important to illuminate the size of the whole ecosphere instead of a single ecosystem. A practical implication is a new design of Digital Hub Denmark's homepage as a portal illuminating the ecosphere and its ecosystems starting with a specific focus on talent attraction. This is planned to be expanded with a focus on customers and investors.

The canvas illuminates where the public supported initiatives make a difference to the individual ecosystems. An example was a tech-alliance with outreach to Tokyo, where it was decided to bring 10–20 fin-tech and 5–10 robotics business; however, due to the Corona situation, the outreach was virtual. One important agenda was to support a potential interdisciplinary corporation between fin-tech and robotics—e.g., converging drones and insurance solutions. To this end, the ecosphere canvas also supports the orchestrating of the ecosystem's innovation managers.

4   Conclusion

The digital ecosphere canvas support exponential growth leveraged by digital disruptive technologies as a tool for selecting, combining, and cultivating digital ecosystems within the digital disruptive domain. And more practical it can help to orchestrate innovations managers of the selected ecosystems.

The canvas might also be applied to other ecospheres in other industries and non-digital sectors? However, as stated, reconfiguration of ecosystems is more efficient when they are (potential) digitally connected. For example, physical distance is a much lesser obstacle. The canvas might also be useful on other levels like EU or regional. The canvas needs to be applied to other types of ecospheres to test this.

Acknowledgments Thank for the valuable feedback to:

- CEO Camilla Rygaard-Hjalsted, Digital Hub Denmark
- CEO Thomas Krogh Jensen, Copenhagen Fintech (fin-tech)
- CEO Jesper Grønbæk, Health Tech Hub Copenhagen (health-tech)
- Cluster Director Mikkel Christoffersen, Odense Robotics (robotics)
- CEO Jan Neiiendam, Vision Denmark (crea-tech)
- Hub Director Jakob Stoumann, Proptech Denmark (prop-tech)
- CEO Anne-Marie Hansen, Agro Food Park (agro-tech)
- CEO Thor Ellegaard, EdTech Denmark (ed-tech)
- Former Head of PR & Communication Dorte Egelund, Digital Hub Denmark
- Master student Leyli Iranpour, Entrepreneurial Engineering, Aalborg University
- The International Society for Professional Innovation Management (ISPIM)

References

Adner, R. (2012). *The wide lens—A new strategy for innovation*. London: Portfolio/Penguin.
Christensen, C. M., Raynor, M. E., & McDonald, R. (2015). *What is disruptive innovation?* Boston: Harvard Business Review Press.
Digital Hub Denmark. (2020). www.digitalhubdenmark.dk. Accessed 1 Nov 2020
Gauthier, J. F. (2019) *Accelerating the success of the copenhagen startup ecosystem & accelerating the success of the Western Denmark Startup Ecosystem*. https://drive.google.com/file/d/1CDTn5UDeiIml_eXGy21zbG_CJsR-ssxE/view. Accessed 1 Nov 2020.

HBS. (2020) *Digitale talenter og muligheder for at tiltrække mere talent til Danmark [Digital talents and options for attracting moretalent to Denmark].* https://www.dropbox.com/sh/hd1xvooxjdqr4iz/AAA2-sfaJDDkfcEDYfs-MRsga/Survey%20%26%20English%20summary?dl=0&subfolder_nav_tracking=1. Accessed 1 Nov 2020. Link includes English Summary: https://www.dropbox.com/sh/hd1xvooxjdqr4iz/AAA2-sfaJDDkfcEDYfs-MRsga/Survey%20%26%20English%20summary?dl=0&preview=Digital+talents+-+english+summary.pdf&subfolder_nav_tracking=1. Accessed 1 Nov 2020.

Ismail, S. (2014). *Exponential Organizations – Why new organizations are ten times better, faster, and cheaper than yours (and what to do about it).* A Singulartiy University Book, Diverson Books.

Kurzweil, R. (2005) *The singularity is near—when humans transcend biology.* Viking.. http://stargate.inf.elte.hu/~seci/fun/Kurzweil,%20Ray%20-%20Singularity%20Is%20Near,%20The%20%28hardback%20ed%29%20%5Bv1.3%5D.pdf. Accessed 1 Nov 2020.

León, M. C., et al. (2016) Designing a model of a digital ecosystem for healthcare and wellness using the business model canvas. *Journal of Medical Systems, 40,* Article 144. Springer Link.

Luhmann, N. (1984). *Soziale Systeme—Grundrisz einer allgemeinen Theorie.* Suhrkamp Taschenbuch.

Lundgaard, S. S., & Rosenstand, C. A. F. (2019). *Investigating disruption—A litterature review on core concepts of disruptive innovation theory.* Aalborg University Press.

Mathiassen, L. (1997). *Reflective systems development.* Doctoral thesis. Aalborg University, Department of Computer Science.

Nachira, F., Dini, P., & Nicolai, A. (2007). *A network of digital business ecosystems for Europe: Roots, processes and perspectives.* Bruxelles: European Commission. https://www.semanticscholar.org/paper/A-Network-of-Digital-Business-Ecosystems-for-Europe-Nachira-Dini/8932731c1827c45a5c43ff21b809cc125eda99ec. Accessed 1 Nov 2020.

Osterwalder, A., & Pigneur, Y. (2010). *Business model generation: A handbook for visionaries, game changers, and challengers.* New York: Wiley.

Rosenstand, C. A. F. (2020, June 7–10). Selecting, combining, and cultivating digital deep-tech ecosystems. In *The ISPIM innovation conference—Innovating in times of crisis, virtual.*

Rosenstand, C. A. F., Gertsen, F., & Vesti, H. (2018, June 17–20). A definition and a conceptual framework of digital disruption. In *The ISPIM innovation conference—Innovation, the name of the game Stockholm, Sweden.*

Claus A. Foss Rosenstand is Digital Hub Denmark Professor at Aalborg University, Denmark. The professorship is a cooperative agreement between Digital Hub Denmark and Aalborg University; helping organizations to exponential growth by leveraging digital disruptive technologies. To this end, he has taken initiative to the Danish Digital Ecosphere, which includes seven digital ecosystems: Fin-tech, Health-tech, Robotics, Crea-tech, Prop-tech, Agro-tech, and Ed-tech (www.digitalhubdenmark.dk).

His roles as researcher, co-founder, entrepreneur, disseminator, and board member are a cohesive, interdisciplinary work within the digital disruptive domain.

Since 1999, he has co-founded or joined more than ten digital startups. Recent examples are www.askcody.com, www.ambolt.io, and www.reflevel.com.

The Pro-Poor Digitalisation Canvas: Shaping Innovation Towards SDGs 1 and 10

Malte Jütting, Franka Blumrich, and Svenja Lemke

1 Introduction

Digital technologies have taken the world by storm. Between 2005 and 2015 alone, the number of people with access to the Internet has more than tripled (World Bank 2016, p. 2). Within the last 5 years, more than one billion users have joined the community of the 'connected', gaining access to a good that today is recognised as a basic need (ITU 2019). Its transboundary nature is a core feature of the digital revolution: With technology access expanding to some of the most remote areas of Asia, Africa and Latin America, more developing country households today have a mobile phone than access to electricity or clean water (Deichmann and Mishra 2019, p. 22). Still, the fact that an ever-growing community of 4.1 billion 'connected' today stands against around 3.5 billion 'unconnected' is an important reminder of the remaining fault lines (ITU 2019). And with 90% of those currently barred from digitalisation and its prospects residing in the developing world, their coordinates appear all too familiar (Pepper and Jackman 2019, p. 31). Yet, the connectivity gap spanning between Global North and Global South is only one among numerous digital divides. Even within national societies, a lack of infrastructure, affordable mobile and data tariffs, access to basic education and digital literacy and the persistence of cultural norms undermining equal opportunity in the digital sphere and beyond may lead to a substantial number of people being sidelined in a world that, allegedly, is growing closer together by the minute (Deichmann und Mishra 2019; Krone and Dannenberg 2019; Roberts and Hernandez 2019; Unwin 2019). Against this backdrop, politicians, international donors as well as the private sector—including both big players, such as Facebook and Google, as well as small

M. Jütting (✉) · F. Blumrich · S. Lemke
Fraunhofer IAO, Fraunhofer Institute for Industrial Engineering, Center for Responsible Research and Innovation (CeRRI), Berlin, Germany
e-mail: malte.juetting@iao.fraunhofer.de

© The Author(s), under exclusive license to Springer Nature Switzerland AG 2021
D. R. A. Schallmo, J. Tidd (eds.), *Digitalization*, Management for Professionals,
https://doi.org/10.1007/978-3-030-69380-0_18

313

(social) start-ups—continue to increase their efforts and fund a myriad of new initiatives aiming to close the 'digital divide'.

Despite these efforts, a scientifically sound concept on how to translate SDGs 1 ('no poverty') and 10 ('reduced inequality') into innovation management practices is still lacking. Consequently, Roberts and Hernandez (2019, p. 2) point to the lack of structured, holistic approaches that would allow for the evaluation of digital technologies' pro-poor potential. Closing this knowledge gap is critically important to enable a more careful assessment of digital innovations' impact in developmental settings and design policies to bridge rather than deepen existing inequalities.

This chapter aims to contribute to the debate by introducing a profound conceptual understanding of the linkage between digital innovations and different facets of both poverty and inequality. To allow for the identification of those dimensions critical for distinguishing pro-poor from non-pro-poor digital innovations, the chapter through a review of scholarly literature and a focus group discussion on the one and the screening of grey literature and expert interviews on the other hand considers both academic as well as practitioners' perspectives on the issue at stake.

Hereupon, the Pro-Poor Digitalisation Canvas is introduced as a scientifically sound, practice-oriented tool for evaluating digital innovations' pro-poor potential in a structured manner. To this end, the chapter is guided by the following research questions:

- *How can existing strands of research as well as practitioners' insights be integrated into a holistic framework for assessing the developmental potential of digital innovation in light of SDGs 1 ('no poverty') and 10 ('reduced inequality')?*
- *How can the conceptual framework be translated into a hands-on tool, guiding innovation practitioners in the assessment and (further) development of digital solutions?*

To answer these questions, the remainder of this contribution is structured as follows: The next section describes the methodological approach of both underlying research as well as tool development. While the third section lays out the conceptual framework, the subsequent section displays the Pro-Poor Digitalisation Canvas based on a said theoretical foundation. Before concluding, section five discusses the chapter's contribution, reflects upon its limitations as well as prospects for further research.

2   Methods

In accordance with the research interest outlined above, the development of the Pro-Poor Digitalisation Canvas proceeded in three steps: exploration, development and piloting (see Fig. 1). While the exploration phase aimed at equipping the tool with a sound scientific foundation, the development phase was meant to transform the resulting conceptual framework into a hands-on tool for practitioners.

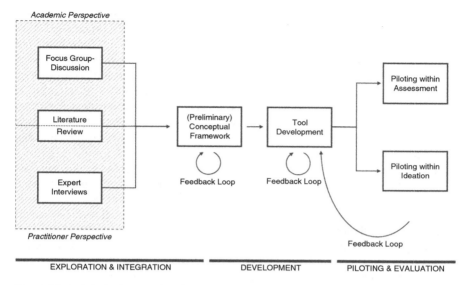

Fig. 1 Methodological approach and development process (Authors' Illustration)

Throughout the on-going piloting phase, the tool's usability is tested across different application settings. Various feedback loops within and across the phases illustrate the process's iterative approach.

Exploration and Integration

As different strands of previous academic research and practical work were known to have already grappled with some partial aspects of the research question, an integrative approach was adopted to translate previous work into a holistic framework. Considering that 'often, practice information is ahead of the academic literature and may contain valuable insights for research' (Konietzko et al. 2020, p. 7), academic perspectives (review of academic literature + focus group discussion among researchers) were supplemented with those of practitioners (review of grey literature + qualitative expert interviews). In concrete terms, the analysis proceeded in the following three steps:

1. *A thorough review of existing academic and non-academic literature.* Reflecting the research's integrative aim, a narrative literature review encompassing academic and grey literature was conducted (Jones 2004). Following this review approach, texts are not accumulated to an all-encompassing stock of literature but purposefully chosen with regard to their contribution to the specific research question (Cooper 1988, p. 110; Baumeister and Leary 1997, p. 318). The literature analysis started by engaging with the discourse around the 'multi-dimensionality of poverty' (OPHI 2015) as well as extreme inequalities (Doyle and Stiglitz

2014) and included the 'Capabilities Approach' (Sen 1999), its operationalisation (Nussbaum 2003) and application within the field of ICT4D (Andersson et al. 2012). Subsequently, conceptualisations of 'innovation at the Bottom of the Pyramid' (Gobble 2017), 'inclusive innovation' (Chataway et al. 2014; Foster and Heeks 2013; George et al. 2012) as well as recent investigations into various aspects of digital development (Foster et al. 2018; Graham 2019; Pickren 2018) were reviewed. As grey literature is 'by its nature, often more inclusionary than standard, peer-reviewed and commercially published work' (Jones 2004, p. 99), it was deemed highly relevant to this chapter's specific research interest. For this reason, 28 non-academic sources were reviewed.

2. *A structured focus group discussion.* Aiming to further broaden the range of perspectives and identify additional relevant dimensions to the framework, a structured focus group discussion complemented the literature review (Stewart et al. 2007). Ten researchers from Fraunhofer and TU Berlin, all with substantial experience in the field of responsible research and innovation, thereby forming a homogenous group of experts (Lamnek and Krell 2016, p. 407), were selected for this purpose. The 1.5 h-long session was guided by a semi-structured question-naire and facilitated by two moderators. Drawing on a number of reference projects focusing on women, refugees, people with disabilities and the urban–rural divide, for example technological innovations' ability to address the needs of specific (potentially marginalised) societal groups was explored. Making use of not only the explorative, but also the creative power of focus group settings (Stewart et al. 2007), the second half of the discussion aimed at developing a first set of criteria determining a digital innovation's inclusiveness. Discussion minutes, as well as photographic documentation, were used to record workshop results for further processing.

3. *Qualitative semi-structured expert interviews.* Seeking to integrate practitioners' perspectives into framework and ultimately tool development, five qualitative, semi-structured expert interviews were conducted. Drawing on Gläser and Laudel (2009), experts were defined as people who hold specialist knowledge with regard to the issue at stake. Selection of experts followed a purposeful and criteria-based sampling approach (Westle 2009, p. 170). Based on a preliminary shortlist of the most relevant organisations within the field of digital development, the following five were selected to cover both national and multinational agencies as well as non-governmental actors: Department for International Development (DfiD), Deutsche Gesellschaft für Internationale Zusammenarbeit (GIZ), United States Agency for International Development (USAID), World Food Programme (WFP), World Wide Web Foundation. Individual interviewees were nominated by their respective organisations. Aiming to both validate scientific concepts and integrate new insights, Witzel's (2000) problem-centred approach was applied throughout the interviews (Lamnek and Krell 2016, p. 348). A semi-structured guide, focusing on the three thematic complexes, including the respective organisation's digitalisation approach, its perception of the link between digitalisation, poverty and inequality as well as factors determining the success of pro-poor digitalisation efforts, was used to organise the interviews, which

lasted between 30 and 45 min. Interview minutes were processed following the concept of 'thematic analysis', prioritising the summary of argumentation structure and content over exact transcription (Froschauer and Lueger 2003, p. 158).

Development

Making scientific findings—such as the results of the exploration phase—and underlying theoretical considerations accessible and most importantly useable for practitioners is far from trivial. In order to allow for informed decision-making among innovators, policymakers, and development actors, complexity must be reduced while preserving accuracy. For this purpose, an interdisciplinary approach, bringing expertise from social sciences, business and economics, human–machine interaction as well as design research to the table, was applied. Design-based perspectives were considered particularly important as they 'can provide a range of practical tools for participatory processes', hereby facilitating 'shared insights into technological developments' (Heidingsfelder et al. 2015, p. 293).

Against the backdrop of the popularity of (Social) Business Model Canvases in entrepreneurship and innovation management (e.g. Osterwalder and Pigneur 2010; Joyce and Paquin 2016), a similar canvas approach was chosen to make the complexity of pro-poor digital development accessible to innovation management practice. 'Providing accessible, visual representation' (Joyce and Paquin 2016, p. 3) of a digital innovation and its potential impacts on SDGs 1 and 10, such a canvas-based approach does not only allow for status quo assessments but also facilitates the creative (further) development of digital solutions. Especially if implemented in cross-functional, interdisciplinary and international teams—as typically found in international development cooperation—canvases have proven effective for communicating ideas among different stakeholders and screening them for strengths, weaknesses and hitherto neglected blind spots. Over the course of the development process, practitioners' feedback was iteratively integrated throughout two feedback loops.

Piloting and Evaluation

The third—ongoing—phase aims at piloting the Pro-Poor Digitalisation Canvas and testing its functionality within different application contexts. As the Canvas is meant to perform not one but two different functions—pro-poor assessment of digital innovations and their (further) development—its utility must consequently be evaluated for both settings separately. While the application of the Canvas for innovation development remains yet to be piloted, its usability for assessment purposes has already been tested.

In order to evaluate the tool's utility for the pro-poor assessment of digital innovations, a comprehensive overview of 30 technological approaches currently implemented or tested for application in development settings was compiled based on the analysis of 16 key foresight studies and reports (e.g. IDS 2016; UN 2018;

WEF 2019). For five of said technological approaches, exemplary solutions were selected and made subject to an in-depth analysis guided by the Pro-Poor Digitalisation Canvas. Drawing on the guiding questions as laid out in the Canvas and its supplementing User Manual, the pro-poor impact of each solution was assessed. In doing so, strengths, weaknesses and blind spots of the tool itself were identified and documented.

For the purpose of testing the Pro-Poor Digitalisation Canvas in creative ideation settings, different preliminary workshop concepts were designed around the tool. However, their implementation and evaluation respectively are still pending.

3   Towards an Integrated Framework

The debate on (digital) innovations' potential for sustainable development is by no means a novel one. Consequently, today's field of research appears scattered and highly fragmented. Similarly, a brief analysis of different policies reveals a variety of different understandings of and approaches to the issue at stake. Seeking to integrate different strands of research, the three most important, often conflicting discourses on the role of innovation for sustainable development are briefly outlined below:

Grounded on Schumpeter's (1934) understanding of innovation as the road to economic prosperity, the first line of thought investigates the former's role in creating economic value and upgrading domestic production activities. In line with Schumpeter's argument, a lack of innovation and entrepreneurial activity is believed to be one of the most important impediments to economic development (Becker et al. 2012, p. 918). Taking on a bottom-up perspective, a second strand of research seeks to identify the 'appropriate technology' (Schumacher 1973) by focusing on concepts such as 'grassroots' or 'frugal innovation' (Knorringa et al. 2016; Leliveld and Knorringa 2018). 'Bottom of the pyramid' approaches (Gobble 2017) on the other hand often take on a firm perspective, asking what an innovation must look like to serve 'the bottom billion'. A third strand of research turns to innovations' ability to tackle societal challenges and in turn promote human development by asking how it may contribute to resolving longstanding socioeconomic issues such as hunger and disease (Klochikhin 2012, p. 44). Ultimately, Jiménez (2016, p. 3) points to the need for integrating the above-mentioned perspectives by focusing on the question 'who is innovating, for whom and what, and under what circumstances'.

Emerging against the background of the debate on 'innovation for development' briefly outlined above, today's digital development discourse plays out along largely similar lines: Focusing on digital tools' impact on dynamics of economic development, authors such as Foster et al. (2018), Graham (2019), Mann (2018), Murphy et al. (2014) and Pickren (2018) consider the role of digital entrepreneurship and big data in processes of economic value creation. Building on investigations into the appropriateness of different innovations for development contexts, Roberts and Hernandez (2019) research those aspects that need to be considered to ensure access on a large scale, ranging from infrastructure over costs and skills. Lastly, authors such as Aker and Mbiti (2010) as well as Heeks and Molla (2009) analyse the

Table 1 Summary of research strands (Authors' Illustration)

	Research Strand #1	Research Strand #2	Research Strand #3
General Innovation and Development Discourse	(Local) innovation as a means to upgrade along global value chains and to drive economic development (Schumpeter 1934; Becker et al. 2012)	(Appropriate) innovation as a means to include the excluded (Knorringa et al. 2016; Leliveld and Knorringa 2018; Schumacher 1973)	Innovation as a means to tackle longstanding socioeconomic challenges (Klochikhin 2012)
Digital Development Discourse (often ICT4D)	Digital innovation must allow for local value-creation and upgrading along the value chain (Graham 2019; Murphy et al. 2014; Pickren 2018)	Digital innovation must be appropriate, accessible and usable for all (Roberts and Hernandez 2019)	Digital innovation can unfold its impact along several dimensions (Aker and Mbiti 2010; Heeks and Molla 2009)
Practitioner perspective	Promoting (digital) entrepreneurship and local innovation (e.g. GIZ Make-IT)	Ensuring access to (digital) innovation on different levels (e.g. World Bank Moonshot Initiative; G20 #eskills4girls initiative)	Introducing (digital) innovation to address particular socioeconomic challenges (e.g. WFP Innovation Accelerator)
Focus question	How is (digital) innovation produced and delivered?	How is (digital) innovation accessed and used?	How does (digital) innovation tackle socioeconomic challenges?
Blind Spot	What is (digital) innovations' broader impact on people and planet?	Who is developing (digital) innovation? On what terms?	Who might be excluded from production and use of (digital) innovation?

mechanisms by which digital technologies contribute to solving socioeconomic challenges.

Insights gained throughout the analysis of grey literature and expert interviews show real-life programmes and policies to be largely structured around the same triad: While some initiatives focus on the promotion of local digital entrepreneurship (see, e.g. GIZ Make-IT), others seek to implement digital tools in the pursuit of rather narrowly defined goals, such as food security (see, e.g. WFP). Still, others are invested in the promotion of connectivity and digital literacy, moving from a single-issue focus on connectivity towards more comprehensive approaches within recent years.

Systemising existing strands of research and pairing them with practitioners' insights, the analysis illustrates that focusing on single issues, such as (physical) access, is insufficient for digital technologies to significantly contribute to SDGs 1 and 10. Acknowledging deficiencies in existing conceptual approaches (see Table 1), Fig. 2 as well as the following paragraphs lay out the foundations of a new, integrated framework accounting for three equally valid dimensions: The first

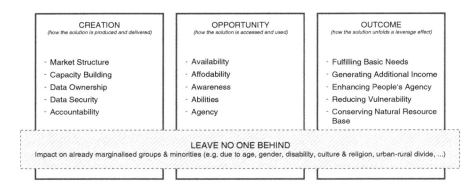

Fig. 2 Conceptual framework (Authors' Illustration)

dimension focuses on how a given solution is produced and delivered, seeking to identify those that allow for local value creation and upgrading of economic activities. The second dimension addresses issues of technology appropriateness and accessibility by asking how solutions are accessed and used by target populations. Lastly, the third dimension lays out five ways for digital innovation to deliver developmental impact.

Creation

The first dimension addresses the question of *how a digital solution is produced and delivered*. Acknowledging that these processes make for an important source of potential inequalities, five sub-dimensions are of particular relevance:

- *Market Structure*: Digital innovation tends to concentrate market power among a handful of platform providers, thereby exacerbating not only economic but also political imbalances (Leliveld and Knorringa 2018, p. 11).
- *Capacity Building*: Reducing existing inequalities requires opportunities for an 'upgrading' of economic activities (Murphy et al. 2014). Building domestic capital to enable 'higher value-adding activities'—such as processing and analysing data generated through digital business models (Mann 2018)—depicts an essential lever in the creation of digital innovations.
- *Data Ownership*: Recognising data as the key economic resource of the twenty-first century, having control over (and the ability to potentially monetise) one's data is a source of political, social and economic power (Foster et al. 2018; Graham 2019a; Pickren 2018).
- *Data Security:* As the 'poorest and most marginalised are also more likely to suffer disproportionally from some of the darker aspects' (Unwin 2019, p. 45) of digitalisation (e.g. cybercrime and online sexual harassment), data security must not merely be understood as an add-on to pro-poor digital solutions but an integral component of them.

- *Accountability*: While digital solutions have the potential to include and grant agency to marginalised groups, they often risk side-lining them even further. Hence, providers of digital solutions should be transparent and accountable to local politics and civil society.

Opportunity

Moving along the value chain, the second dimension seeks to answer the question of *how a given solution is accessed and used*. In order to assess the divergence in opportunities determining access and use of digital innovations, the Canvas draws upon the comprehensive concept of 'access' as introduced by Roberts and Hernandez (2019), distinguishing the following five sub-dimensions (also referred to as access barriers):

- *Availability:* Availability refers to the presence of indispensable physical infra-structure, e.g. digital devices, mobile network coverage or broadband access (also referred to as connectivity). However, availability must not be understood in binary terms (connected vs. unconnected) but conveys more detailed gradations (e.g. with a view to stability of connectivity and data rates).
- *Affordability:* Even with the necessary physical infrastructure available, restrained financial resources might prevent some social groups from continuous and unrestricted use (e.g. cost of hardware and electricity, mobile and data tariffs). As is the case with availability, affordability is not binary with different levels of connectivity being reflected in their respective prices.
- *Awareness:* Even if digital solutions are physically available and affordable, a lack of awareness regarding their existence, functions and relevance among the target group must be considered as a third potential access barrier.
- *Abilities:* Effectively using digital innovations might presuppose a set of physical (e.g. being able to see or to hear) and cognitive (e.g. some level of (digital) literacy) abilities, resulting in unequal access based on the availability, respectively, unavailability of abilities and skills (Deichmann and Mishra 2019, pp. 22–23).
- *Agency:* Being an active agent of change rather than a passive recipient of external support is central to people's empowerment and thus an integral part of pro-poor development (Sen 1999). To exercise agency, people must be endowed with both freedom and opportunity to make informed choices about the use or non-use of digital solutions.

Outcome

Acknowledging that different types of innovation yield different societal and economic impacts, the third dimension investigates whether and—if so—*how a given solution unfolds its leverage effect*. Incorporating ideas from the basic needs (Javed

Burki and Ul Haq 1981), the capability (Sen 1999) and the sustainable livelihoods (Scoones 1998) approach as three of the most common theoretical foundations of pro-poor development, digital innovations' leverage effects are conceptualised in reference to the following five impact mechanisms:

- *Fulfilling Basic Needs:* Digital innovations have the potential to contribute to the satisfaction of some of the most basic needs, including food, water, education, health care and nowadays access to the Internet itself.
- *Generating Additional Income:* Furthermore, digital innovations can open up hitherto inexistent business and entrepreneurship opportunities, thereby generating additional income and/or creating jobs (Aker and Mbiti 2010; Krone and Dannenberg 2019, p. 81; Pepper and Jackman 2019, p. 29). The establishment of new distribution channels through e-commerce platforms or micro-work in the gig economy are only some examples in this regard.
- *Enhancing People's Agency:* Sen's (1999) idea of 'development as freedom' suggests moving beyond a merely materialistic view of development. Against this background, a digital solution can be assessed based on its ability to enhance people's agency and facilitate their political and social inclusion.
- *Reducing Vulnerability:* Daily life in developing countries is often inherently risky for the poor (e.g. crop failures, natural disasters, epidemics, conflict). Digital solutions can not only provide information about potential shocks and facilitate traditional ways of reducing risk through kinship networks but also enable new ways of safeguarding, e.g. through micro-insurances (Aker and Mbiti 2010, pp. 219–220).
- *Conserving the Natural Resource Base:* Acknowledging the poor's reliance on the natural resource base of their immediate environment (especially in rural areas), a digital innovation's ability to reduce environmental burdens and conserve rather than deplete resources makes for a fifth impact mechanism.

Leave No One Behind (LNOB)

The pledge to 'leave no one behind' lies at the heart of the Agenda 2030, obligating a multitude of actors to join forces in an effort to reduce poverty and inequality around the globe. Shining a light on some of the hitherto most marginalised groups of society, the LNOB principle constitutes a cross-cutting issue and needs to be considered at every stage of the digital innovation value chain. With its three dimensions and 15 sub-dimensions, the framework outlined above offers detailed guidance for assessing any digital solution's impact on marginalised communities separately—whether their discrimination is based on age, gender, disability, culture and religion or the urban–rural divide—and innovating on their behalf. Doing so, for example implies ensuring the highest degree of data security when dealing with personal information of people at risk of (political) persecution, reconsidering a solution's cognitive prerequisites in a context where literacy cannot be presumed and reflecting upon the perils of an agency-enhancing digital tool giving an (additional) voice to men rather than serving under-represented women.

4 Putting It to Use: The Pro-Poor Digitalisation Canvas

Accounting for the complexity of not only issues of poverty and inequality in themselves but their reciprocal interaction with digital tools and technologies is key for shaping digitalisation for a pro-poor purpose. Thus, it is critically important to not merely focus on technical prerequisites for implementation but rather assess both the conditions under which digital solutions are developed, the nature and scope of opportunities they provide to target populations as well as the type of impact they ultimately bring about.

Pro-Poor Digitalisation Canvas and User Manual

In order to break down the conceptual framework outlined in the previous section and make it accessible and most importantly useable for practitioners, the centrepiece of the Pro-Poor Digitalisation Canvas is a single-sided template (=the actual canvas, see Fig. 3), guiding the assessment process. The Canvas itself is designed in a relatively lean way, laying out only one guiding question per dimension. However, a complementing 'User Manual' provides additional guidance (see Fig. 4 for exemplary page). To this end, the User Manual outlines each dimension's underlying rationale and auxiliary sub-questions, further operationalising the guiding question, and refers readers to additional resources. With the help of the assessment section, any digital solution's pro-poor impact can be evaluated along the 15 sub-dimensions. Generally, the application of the Pro-Poor Digitalisation Canvas follows a three-step process as described below:

1. *Reflecting upon the underlying need.* As 'starting with the people—not the technology' is one of the most important rules in designing human-centred digital solutions, the Pro-Poor Digitalisation Canvas internalises this principle. The three questions in the template's first section encourage reflection upon the envisioned group of beneficiaries, their needs and the means by which the solution aims to serve those needs.
2. *Assessing 'Creation—Opportunity—Outcome'.* Step 2 makes up the core of the Canvas, operationalising the conceptual framework as outlined in the previous chapter. Along with a total number of 15 questions, an existing or to be developed digital innovation is scrutinised in reference to the three dimensions creation (*how the solution is produced and delivered*), opportunity (*how the solution is accessed and used*) and outcome (*how the solution unfolds a leverage effect*). The User Manual provides additional guidance and context throughout the evaluation process with the radar chart allowing to quickly visualise results. Whereas for 'Creation' and 'Opportunity' all sub-dimensions are equally important and must

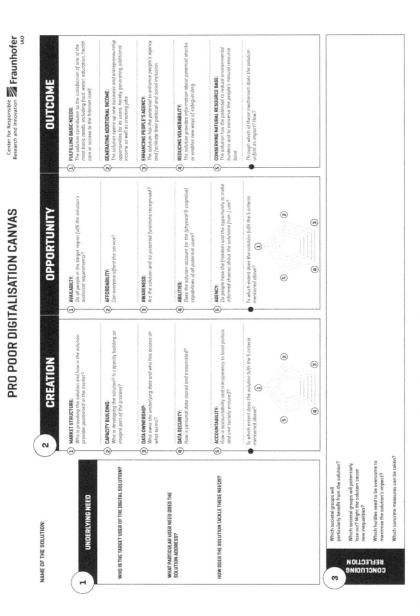

Fig. 3 Pro-Poor Digitalisation Canvas (Design: Lynn Harles, Fraunhofer IAO, CeRRI)

CREATION | DATA SECURITY

Rationale:	As the *"poorest and most marginalised are also more likely to suffer disproportionally from some of the darker aspects"* (Unwin 2019, p. 45) of digitalisation (e.g. cybercrime, online sexual harassment, etc.), data security is not an add-on to pro-poor digital solutions but must be an integral component of them.
Guiding Question:	*How is personal data stored and transmitted?*
Auxiliary Sub-Question(s):	• Does the solution follow the principles of data minimisation (= adequate, relevant, limited to what is necessary)? • Has a risk analysis regarding data security been carried out? • Does a data management plan exist? • Which safeguard mechanisms are in place? • Are the measures in place appropriate given the level of the users' vulnerability?
Assessment: (0-5 points)	*To what extent does the solution take matters of data security into account and deploy pre-emptive measures?* (1) Data security measures do not exist or show substantial gaps. (2) Data security measures are fragmentary, but collection and processing of personal data are kept to a minimum. (3) Data security measures are adequate (reflecting users' vulnerability) and based on an initial risk assessment and data management plan. (4) Data security measures are fully GDPR (or equivalent) compliant. (5) Data security measures go beyond what is required by GDPR (or equivalent) standards.
Additional Resources:	• GDPR Checklist: (https://gdpr.eu/checklist/) • GIZ (2018): Responsible Data Guidelines. (https://mia.giz.de/qlink/ID=245420000) • GIZ (2018): Responsible Data Guidelines – Toolbox. (https://mia.giz.de/qlink/ID=245422000) • ICRC (2017): Handbook on Data Protection in Humanitarian Action. (https://www.icrc.org/en/publication/handbook-data-protection-humanitarian-action) • Open Data Institute (2019): Data Ethics Canvas (https://theodi.org/article/data-ethics-canvas/) • UN OCHA (2019): Data Responsibility Guidelines. (https://centre.humdata.org/wp-content/uploads/2019/03/OCHA-DR-Guidelines-working-draft-032019.pdf)

Fig. 4 'User Manual', Exemplary Page (Fraunhofer IAO, CeRRI)

be considered simultaneously, it is sufficient to follow only one of the 'Outcome' dimension's five impact mechanisms.

3. *Thinking ahead.* Having analysed a given solution and its potential for pro-poor impact along the three dimensions, step 3 provides room for some overarching questions. It encourages reflection upon potentially negative impacts and helps to dissect (structural) barriers standing in the way of the solution's successful implementation, pointing out measures for further improvement.

Application Setting

The Pro-Poor Digitalisation Canvas lends itself to application in a number of different settings. The two most important ones shall be discussed in the following:

Firstly, it may serve as a tool for assessing already existing solutions with a view to their pro-poor potential. Through its structured, step-by-step analysis, it allows for the identification of strengths and weaknesses and may thus help policymakers and development actors to prioritise different technology-based solutions in line with country-specific policy goals and decide upon appropriate settings for introducing such novel tools. Beyond that, it may provide guidance to innovators and entrepreneurs seeking to adapt any given solution for a pro-poor purpose.

Secondly, the Pro-Poor Digitalisation Canvas is equally viable for supporting processes of solution co-creation among the above-mentioned group of actors. Over the last years, hitherto unattended formats such as hackathons, ideation challenges and long-term accelerator programmes have increasingly gained popularity in the development community. Throughout such formats, the Canvas may serve as a key reference for creating a shared vision among a multitude of actors and supporting the iterative nature of innovation processes.

5   Discussion

Theoretical Contribution

The chapter improves the current understanding of the conceptual linkage between digital innovation and SDGs 1 and 10—in other words pro-poor development—by (a) systemising existing research strands, (b) enriching them through practitioners' insights and (c) integrating the different perspectives as well as insights from adjoining fields of research into a holistic picture. The analysis illustrates that focusing on single aspects, such as (physical) access to digital technologies, is not enough to progress significantly towards SDGs 1 and 10—if there is a positive contribution at all. The chapter equips the innovation management community with a more holistic understanding of the linkage between digital innovation, poverty and inequality, contributing to the operationalisation of SDGs 1 and 10 within the context of (digital) innovation management.

Accounting for the non-binary and multidimensional nature of digital inclusion, the chapter addresses each of the three knowledge gaps identified by Roberts and Hernandez (2019, p. 2). By embracing the authors' criticism of the binary distinction between 'the connected' and 'the unconnected', this chapter highlights the multifaceted nature of digital in- respectively exclusion. Drawing on Roberts and Hernandez (2019) five dimensions of access, it takes matters one step further by additionally considering issues of creation and outcome. Secondly, treating the works of said authors as a gold standard in this regard, the chapter acknowledges the imperative of including non-user perspectives for understanding the diversity of access barriers. Lastly, the Pro-Poor Digitalisation Canvas as introduced as part of this contribution may be understood as a direct response to the lack of structured approaches for evaluation digital technologies' developmental impact articulated by the authors.

Practical Contribution

Theoretically conceptualising the linkage between digital innovation and pro-poor development, the presented framework enables practitioners, such as politicians, development agency staffers and innovators within (social) start-ups, to carefully assess and ultimately shape digital innovations' developmental impact. To this end, the 'Pro-Poor Digitalisation Canvas' was developed. Across different applicatory settings, the Canvas and its theoretical underpinnings yield three important practical contributions: Firstly, its holistic perspective allows for the development of policy recommendations to shape digitalisation for a pro-poor purpose on a structural level. A comprehensive list of such recommendations pertaining to both concrete technologies as well as the more general agenda of pro-poor digitalisation has been compiled as part of the broader research project underlying this contribution. Secondly, the Canvas enables innovation practitioners and other stakeholders alike to evaluate digital solutions' pro-poor potential in a structured manner prior to piloting them on the ground. Lastly, it is equally suitable for purposes of ideation and solution development. While it can serve as a quick-check tool as part of shorter workshop formats, it may as well provide the basis for more sophisticated Pro-Poor Accelerator Programmes spanning across several weeks. Corresponding concepts were already drafted and are currently awaiting implementation. Adding to the list of canvas-based approaches in innovation management, the Pro-Poor Digitalisation Canvas distinguishes itself through its deliberate digital and pro-poor focus. While other tools such as the Social or the Triple Business Model Canvas disregard the particularities of situations of extreme poverty, they may provide fruitful in the design of business models suitable for pro-poor digital solutions.

Limitations and Further Research

One potential limitation of the research presented throughout this chapter pertains to its generalisability. Notwithstanding its holistic approach, the Pro-Poor Digitalisation Canvas—as any other framework—is meant to reduce complexity. Specifically tailored to the development context, the presented framework may benefit from some strategic, context-specific adaptions. For example, in some circumstances, it may appear beneficial or even necessary to prioritise some aspects of the Canvas over others. What is more, pre-deployment assessment of canvas dimensions may prove difficult for some solutions, presupposing an in-depth understanding of solutions' social, political, economic and environmental implementation contexts. While recognising the difficulty of performing such an assessment for practitioners, failing to do so risks further exacerbating existing inequalities through the implementation of digital tools.

With the introduction of the Pro-Poor Digitalisation Canvas as a tool for the structured assessment of digital technologies' developmental potential as requested by Roberts and Hernandez (2019), new questions arise on the research agenda. Among other issues, the tool's application over the course of ideation processes in different developmental contexts provides a promising case for further inquiry. Beyond its envisioned scope, it seems worth considering what the tool-based approach and its grounding principles might have to offer for guiding digitalisation processes in the Global North as well. Far from being an exclusive problem of the Global South, digitalisation is posing far-reaching questions, pertaining to its economic, environmental, social and political consequences, to industrialised nations as well.

6   Conclusion

This chapter contributes to the existing research on pro-poor digital development by introducing the Pro-Poor Digitalisation Canvas as an analytical framework for evaluating digital solutions' developmental potential in a structured and holistic fashion. By considering not only matters of digital solution's adoption but paying close attention to their terms of production and developmental impact, the three-tiered framework adds to and moves beyond access-focused models of digital inclusion. The expanded canvas model—spanning across the three dimensions of creation, opportunity and outcome—pays tribute to the multifaceted nature of poverty and inequality and its interplay with digital technologies, thereby supporting policymakers, development agencies and innovators themselves in their pursuit of digitalisation that leaves no one behind.

Acknowledgements The project team sincerely thanks all project partners and experts, who shared their knowledge and experience with us by participating in interviews or the focus group discussion. This chapter was developed within the context of a project funded by the Deutsche Gesellschaft für Internationale Zusammenarbeit (GIZ) GmbH and the German Federal Ministry for

Economic Cooperation and Development (BMZ). The views and conclusions contained herein are those of the authors and should not be interpreted as necessarily representing official policies or endorsements, neither expressed nor implied.

References

Aker, J. C., & Mbiti, I. M. (2010). Mobile phones and economic development in Africa. *Journal of Economic Perspectives, 24*(3), 207–232.

Andersson, A., Grönlund, A., & Wicander, G. (2012). Development as freedom – How the capability approach can be used in ICT4D research and practice. *Information Technology for Development, 18*(1), 1–4.

Baumeister, R. F., & Leary, M. R. (1997). Writing narrative literature reviews. *Review of General Psychology, 1*(3), 311–320.

Becker, M., Knudsen, T., & Swedberg, R. (2012). Schumpeter's theory of economic development. 100 years of development. *Journal of Evolutionary Economics, 22*(5), 917–933.

Chataway, J., Hanlin, R., & Kaplinsky, R. (2014). Inclusive innovation. An architecture for policy development. *Innovation and Development, 4*(1), 33–54.

Cooper, H. M. (1988). Organizing knowledge syntheses. A taxonomy of literature reviews. *Knowledge in Society, 1*(1), 104–126.

Deichmann, U., & Mishra, D. (2019). Marginal benefits at the global margins. The unfulfilled potential of digital technologies. In M. Graham (Ed.), *Digital economies at global margins* (pp. 21–24). Cambridge: MIT.

Doyle, M. W., & Stiglitz, J. E. (2014). Eliminating extreme inequality. A sustainable development goal, 2015–2030. *Ethics & International Affairs, 28*(1), 5–13.

Foster, C., & Heeks, R. (2013). Conceptualising inclusive innovation. Modifying systems of innovation frameworks to understand diffusion of new technology to low-income consumers. *European Journal of Development Research, 25*(3), 333–355.

Foster, C., Graham, M., Mann, L., Waema, T., & Friederici, N. (2018). Digital control in value chains. Challenges of connectivity for east African firms. *Economic Geography, 94*(1), 68–86.

Froschauer, U., & Lueger, M. (2003). *Das qualitative interview. Zur praxis Interpretativer analyse Sozialer Systeme*. Wien: WUV-Universitätsverlag.

George, G., Mcgahan, A. M., & Prabhu, J. (2012). Innovation for inclusive growth. Towards a theoretical framework and a research agenda. *Journal of Management Studies, 49*(4), 661–683.

Gläser, J., & Laudel, G. (2009). *Experteninterviews und Qualitative Inhaltsanalyse als Instrumente Rekonstruierender Untersuchungen*. Wiesbaden: VS Verlag für Sozialwissenschaften.

Gobble, M. A. (2017). Innovation at the bottom of the pyramid. *Research-Technology Management, 60*(3), 62–67.

Graham, M. (Ed.). (2019). *Digital economies at global margins*. Cambridge: MIT.

Graham, M. (2019a). Changing connectivity and digital economies at global margins. In M. Graham (Ed.), *Digital economies at global margins* (pp. 1–18). Cambridge: MIT.

Heeks, R., & Molla, A. (2009). *Impact assessment of ICT-for-development projects. A compendium of approaches*. Retrieved January 24, 2020, from http://hummedia.manchester.ac.uk/institutes/gdi/publications/workingpapers/di/di_wp36.pdf

Heidingsfelder, M., Kimpel, K., Best, K., & Schraudner, M. (2015). Shaping future. Adapting design know-how to reorient innovation towards public preferences. *Technological Forecasting & Social Change, 101*, 291–298.

IDS. (2016). *Ten frontier technologies for international development*. Retrieved March 15, 2020, from https://opendocs.ids.ac.uk/opendocs/bitstream/handle/20.500.12413/12637/Main_Report_2016_Ten_Frontier_Tecnologies_for_International_Development.pdf?sequence=2&isAllowed=y

ITU. (2019). *Measuring digital development*. Retrieved March 15, 2020, from https://t.co/2CfDfRTXct

Javed Burki, S., & Ul Haq, M. (1981). Meeting basic needs. An overview. *World Development, 9* (2), 167–182.

Jiménez, A. (2016). *A capabilities approach to innovation. A case study of a technology and innovation hub in Zambia.* Retrieved May 01, 2020, from https://aisel.aisnet.org/cgi/viewcontent.cgi?article=1075&context=ecis2016_rp

Jones, K. (2004). Mission drift in qualitative research, or moving toward a systematic review of qualitative studies, moving back to a more systematic narrative review. *The Qualitative Report, 9*(1), 95–112.

Joyce, A., & Paquin, R. L. (2016). The triple-layered business model canvas. A tool to design more sustainable business models. *Journal of Cleaner Production, 135*, 1474–1486.

Klochikhin, E. (2012). Linking development and innovation. What does technological change bring to the society? *The European Journal of Development Research, 24*(1), 41–55.

Knorringa, P., Peša, I., Leliveld, A., & van Beers, C. (2016). Frugal innovation and development. Aides or adversaries? *The European Journal of Development Research, 28*(2), 143–153.

Konietzko, J., Bocken, N., & Hultink, E. J. (2020). A tool to analyze, ideate and develop circular innovation ecosystems. *Sustainability, 12*(417).

Krone, M., & Dannenberg, P. (2019). Development or divide? Information and communication technologies in commercial small-scale farming in East Africa. In M. Graham (Ed.), *Digital economies at global margins* (pp. 79–101). Cambridge: MIT.

Lamnek, S., & Krell, C. (2016). *Qualitative Sozialforschung.* Weinheim: Beltz Verlag.

Leliveld, A., & Knorringa, P. (2018). Frugal innovation and development research. *European Journal of Development Research, 30*(1), 1–16.

Mann, L. (2018). Left to other peoples' devices? A political economy perspective on the big data revolution in development. *Development and Change, 49*(1), 3–36.

Murphy, J. T., Carmody, P., & Surborg, B. (2014). Industrial transformation or business as usual? Information and communication technologies and Africa's place in the global economy. *Review of African Political Economy, 41*(140), 264–283.

Nussbaum, M. (2003). Capabilities as fundamental entitlements. Sen and social justice. *Feminist Economics, 9*(2–3), 33–59.

OPHI. (2015). *Measuring multidimensional poverty. Insights from around the world.* Retrieved March 15, 2020, from http://www.ophi.org.uk/wp-content/uploads/Measuring-Multidimensional-Poverty-Insights-from-Around-the-World.pdf

Osterwalder, A., & Pigneur, Y. (2010). *Business model generation. A handbook for visionaries, game changers, and challengers.* Hoboken, NJ: Wiley.

Pepper, R., & Jackman, M. (2019). A data-driven approach to closing the internet inclusion gap. In M. Graham (Ed.), *Digital economies at global margins* (pp. 29–32). Cambridge: MIT.

Pickren, G. (2018). The global assemblage of digital flow. Critical data studies and the infrastructures of computing. *Progress in Human Geography, 42*(2), 225–243.

Roberts, T., & Hernandez, K. (2019). Digital access is not binary. The 5'A's of technology access in the Philippines. *The Electronic Journal of Information Systems in Developing Countries, 85*(4), 1–14.

Schumacher, E. F. (1973). *Small is beautiful. A study of economics as if people mattered.* London: Blond & Briggs.

Schumpeter, J. A. (1934). *The theory of economic development. An inquiry into profits, capital, credit, interest, and the business cycle.* Cambridge: Harvard University Press.

Scoones, I. (1998). *Sustainable rural livelihoods. A framework for analysis.* Retrieved February 15, 2020, from https://www.ids.ac.uk/publications/sustainable-rural-livelihoods-a-framework-for-analysis/

Sen, A. (1999). *Development as freedom.* Oxford: Oxford University Press.

Stewart, D. W., Shamdasani, P. N., & Rook, D. W. (2007). *Focus groups. Theory and practice.* Thousand Oaks: Sage.

UN Department of Economic and Social Affairs. (2018). *World Economic and Social Survey 2018. Frontier Technologies for Sustainable Development.* Retrieved February 13, 2020, from https://

www.un.org/development/desa/dpad/wp-content/uploads/sites/45/publication/WESS2018_full_web.pdf

Unwin, T. (2019). Digital economies at global margins. A warning from the dark side. In M. Graham (Ed.), *Digital economies at global margins* (pp. 43–46). Cambridge: MIT.

WEF. (2019). *Top 10 emerging technologies 2019*. Retrieved March 15, 2020, from https://www.weforum.org/agenda/2019/07/these-are-the-top-10-emerging-technologies-of-2019

Westle, B. (2009). Auswahlverfahren. In B. Westle (Ed.), *Methoden der Politikwissenschaft* (pp. 157–176). Baden-Baden: Nomos.

Witzel, A. (2000). Das Problemzentrierte Interview. *Forum Qualitative Sozialforschung – Theories, Methods, Applications, 1*(1), 1–9.

World Bank. (2016). *World Development Report 2016. Digital Dividends*. Retrieved February 15, 2020, from https://www.worldbank.org/en/publication/wdr2016

Malte Jütting is a senior expert at the Center for Responsible Research and Innovation (CeRRI) at Fraunhofer IAO, where he supports public and private sector clients in designing collaborative innovation processes and making innovation work for sustainable development. Prior to that, he gained additional experience at the Federal Ministry for Economic Cooperation and Development (BMZ), the Deutsche Gesellschaft für Internationale Zusammenarbeit (GIZ) GmbH as well as in the private sector. Malte studied Political Science and Economics (BA) and holds a master's degree in Development Studies from the London School of Economics and Political Science (LSE).

Franka Blumrich studied Psychology, Human Factors and Design Thinking at FSU Jena, Technical University Berlin and HPI d-school in Potsdam. She has a special interest in responsible and sustainable technology design and innovation. Previously research assistant at the Center for Responsible Research and Innovation (CeRRI) at Fraunhofer IAO, she currently works as project manager for social innovation at Social Impact.

Svenja Lemke is a research assistant at the Center for Responsible Research and Innovation (CeRRI) at Fraunhofer IAO. She studied Political Science, Economics and International Relations at Freie Universität Berlin, Tel Aviv University and the Lebanese American University, Beirut. Her work focuses on the role of innovation for sustainable development and in the context of forced migration in particular.

Part V

Digital Implementation

Digital Needs Diversity: Innovation and Digital Leadership from a Female Managers' Perspective

Anne E. Gfrerer, Lars Rademacher, and Stefan Dobler

1 Problem

Accelerating innovation cycles are transforming the business landscape at an unprecedented rate, putting pressure on established business models and corporate firms. Organizations are facing times of high uncertainty and constantly changing customer needs due to new disruptive technologies. They have to exploit current product and service advantages while simultaneously exploring new potential businesses (O'Reilly and Tushman 2011). These requirements make new leadership competencies necessary for managers to guide a firm through digital transformation times (Kane et al. 2019). Consequently, a new form of leadership, which can be called digital leadership, is arising (Kane et al. 2019). Although theoretically compelling and practically increasingly popular, research on digital leadership is still at an early stage. Existing research provides a first overview on challenges that digital leaders face. However, they lack in-depth explorations of digital leadership characteristics. Moreover, a commonly agreed definition of digital leadership is still missing.

At the same time, research shows that apart from new leadership competencies, gender diversity within the management team is a key factor for innovation and digital transformation success (Østergaard et al. 2011). But it is only rarely in place. In the light of the importance of gender diversity to succeed within the digital

A. E. Gfrerer (✉)
University of Innsbruck, Innsbruck, Austria
e-mail: anneliese.gfrerer@student.uibk.ac.at

L. Rademacher
Darmstadt University of Applied Sciences, Darmstadt, Germany
e-mail: lars.rademacher@h-da.de

S. Dobler
Ludwigshafen University of Business and Society, Ludwigshafen, Germany
e-mail: stefan.dobler@lb.hwg-lu

© The Author(s), under exclusive license to Springer Nature Switzerland AG 2021
D. R. A. Schallmo, J. Tidd (eds.), *Digitalization*, Management for Professionals,
https://doi.org/10.1007/978-3-030-69380-0_19

transformation and innovation context, the question raises, what female managers expect digital leadership to be and what challenges they face from a corporate view. We are not aware of any study that explores the concept of digital leadership from the viewpoint of female managers. Even though literature suggests that gender diversity in the management team is relevant for corporates' performance and business success (Campbell and Mínguez-Vera 2007). Thus, the main focus of our research lies in exploring the concept of digital leadership from a female managers' perspective.

2 Current Understanding

Looking at the phenomenon of digital leadership through the lens of innovation management perspective can explain why gender diversity matters for innovation and digital transformation in incumbent firms. Our study is based on what we already know from literature about the concept of digital leadership, and on innovation theories and its findings on diversity. In our empirical study, we explore the factors and components that digital leadership requires from a female managers' perspective. The theoretical background of this chapter is divided into two sections. In the first section, we elaborate on the current understanding of the concept of digital leadership, and in the second, we focus on the role of diversity in the light of innovation theories.

Digital Leadership in an Ambidextrous World

The ability to exploit existing business and explore new business ideas at the same time is known as ambidexterity, a term that has become more polar over time (Zhang et al. 2019). Studies show that ambidexterity is positively related to the innovative performance of an organization (Rosing and Zacher 2017). One key feature mentioned with regard to managers' abilities in the context of ambidexterity and digital transformation is the necessity of new leadership competencies (O'Reilly and Tushman 2011).

Digital Transformation and the Necessity for new Competencies

Digital transformation is strongly related to innovation. Innovation within incumbent firms is mostly driven by new technological possibilities and digital transformation overall (Hinings et al. 2018). Moreover, innovation processes themselves are subject to digitalization (Hinings et al. 2018).

At the same time, digital transformation is a major challenge for incumbent firms. Digital transformation can be defined as a process of reinventing a business to digitize operations and becoming digitally ready (Schallmo et al. 2017). Becoming a digital leader and guiding a company through the bumpy times of digitalization, also within recurring crises modes, is still perceived as difficult by managers of corporate organizations (Berghaus and Back 2016). This might also be due to the variety of new competencies that are needed for digital transformation success. Ferrari (2013) elaborated five areas that should be taken into account when determining one's digital competence: (1) information management, (2) communication, (3) content creation, (4) safety, and (5) problem solving. These competencies are relevant for all members of incumbent firms, whether managers or employees.

The Concept of Digital Leadership

Leadership is an important quality in organizations, and it is necessary for introducing change and innovation (Holt and Vardaman 2013). The literature differentiates between leadership and management. Whereas leadership can be defined as "doing the right thing" for the success of an organization, management can be referred to as "doing the thing right" (Bennis and Townsend 1989). As the most powerful actors in a company, managers play an important role in the digital transformation process. They function as role models (Fuchs 2011) who have to lead the organization through the necessary change processes. Moreover, as role models they need to gain and maintain the trust of the employees in the manager's ability to become a digital leader and to successfully implement the desired transformation.

Guiding a company successfully through the necessary digital transformation, therefore, affects and changes the work design and leadership of organizations massively (Schwarzmüller et al. 2018). Working in network structures rather than hierarchical systems represents an immersive change in working methods and requirements for managers and employees in contrast to doing "more of the same" within their firms' more homogeneous internal environments. These aspects make the concept of digital leadership even more important.

As a term, the concept of digital leadership has so far mainly been used by consultants and lacks a clear definition, as literature shows (Bersin 2016; Kane et al. 2019). Mostly it is defined as leadership in the digital age overall and in phases of transformation into digitalization especially (Wilson 2004). From a corporate view, the concept of digital leadership matters for both the organizational level—concerning management support and the necessary firm capabilities, for example—and the individual level—regarding individual beliefs and competencies, for instance (Holt and Vardaman 2013). In their case study, focusing on the organizational level, El Sawy et al. (2016) define digital leadership as "doing the right things for the strategic success of digitalization for the enterprise and its business ecosystem" (El Sawy et al. 2016, p. 142).

At the individual level—on which our research is based—the concept of digital leadership refers to individuals within organizations—in our case, managers. Existing research results claim that the fundaments of good leadership are also valuable in the face of digital change. Based on the study results of Kane et al. (2019), skills that managers need and that remain the same can be seen in articulating the value change will bring, owning the transformation as an executive, and equipping employees to fulfil the digital transformation tasks successfully. At the same time, research provides a first overview of possible challenges that make digital leadership so special: the increased pace of doing business, the shift in organizational culture and working in network structures, the corresponding tension between changemakers and employees with a more traditional mindset, and the greater expectations of productivity (Kane et al. 2019). However, existing research lacks explanations and further suggestions as to how the concept of digital leadership should be defined and what components it contains.

Diversity as a Prerequisite for Digital Leadership and Innovation

What makes digital leadership so complex for managers of companies are the organizational and individual factors on which successful digital transformation depends. Literature suggests that next to the new competencies mentioned above, moreover, a broad set of factors are relevant for the digital transformation of incumbent firms. These are innovation, creativity, flexibility, an open organizational culture, change readiness, open and transparent communication, development of employees, and corresponding talent pools (Ferrari 2013; Holt and Vardaman 2013; Kane et al. 2015).

Diversity in the Light of Innovation Theories

Diversity—especially gender diversity and cognitive diversity—provides exactly the assets that are needed to succeed along a value-based and impactful innovation and digitalization process. Innovation theories and research studies show that diversity does make a positive difference with regard to innovation and digital transformation success (Østergaard et al. 2011; Yang and Konrad 2011; Zhan et al. 2015). There is consensus among scientists that diversity acts as an important source of innovation (Hewlett et al. 2013; Van der Vegt and Janssen 2003). This includes diversity in the management team. Studies have found significant evidence of a positive relationship between gender diversity on boards and marketing innovation, for example (Galia and Zenou 2012). At the same time, diversity of teams and heterogeneity—understood as the quality or state of being diverse in character or content—are often one of the major challenges faced by firms when seeking to digitally compete (Bassett-Jones 2005). Literature shows that major challenges can be seen precisely in this need for collaboration of diverse teams (Weiblen and Chesbrough 2015). Key factors in this respect are the culture clash and differences of participants per se. This illustrates the fact that diversity covers challenges and opportunities for managers of incumbent firms along with their innovation and digital transformation processes and on their way to digital leadership.

Gender Diversity and Cognitive Diversity

Different approaches can be distinguished in diverse literature. Two important streams can be found in gender diversity and cognitive diversity approaches. Previous research findings have confirmed that gender diversity in the management team positively influences firm performance (Marinova et al. 2015). At the same time, the proportion of female managers in corporate organizations is still low across all industries, as the following figures reveal (Deloitte 2019):

- Proportion of female board members in the 30 largest companies: 28% in the USA, compared to 15% in Germany.
- 9.3% female board members in German companies overall.
- An analysis of more than 8600 companies in 49 countries showed that women held 16.9% of all global board seats in 2018, up from 15.0% in 2016.
- Only 5.3% of board chair positions in 49 countries were held by women in 2018.

Other studies have found that cognitive diversity in the management team also matters for firm performance (Kilduff et al. 2000). Cognitive diversity is the inclusion of people who have different ways of thinking, different viewpoints, and different skill sets in a team or business group (Kilduff et al. 2000). Studies have identified four main types of personality and workstyle: pioneers, drivers, integrators, and guardians (Johnson Vickberg and Christfort 2017):

- Pioneers value possibilities, and spark energy and imagination. They believe risks are worth taking and focus on the big picture. They are drawn to bold new ideas and creative approaches.
- Drivers value challenge and winning. They generate momentum, tackle problems, use data, employ logic, and view issues as black and white.
- Integrators value connection and draw team members together. They are diplomatic and focused on consensus. They believe relationships on the team and responsibilities to the team are paramount.
- Guardians value stability, order, and rigor. They are pragmatic and risk-adverse. They believe that facts, history, and details are baseline requirements for decision-making and action.

There is evidence that perceptions between diverse internal target groups of a firm vary. This includes the fact that perceptions of male and female managers with regard to leadership can differ (Alimo-Metcalfe 1995; Muchiri et al. 2011; Wille et al. 2018). We, therefore, assume that differences in perceptions between male and female managers do also exist concerning the concept of digital leadership.

Extending diversity, especially gender diversity, is perceived as a key problem that managers are still struggling with along the digital transformation journey of corporate organizations. Companies are putting massive efforts in trying to attract female managers to their firms. Therefore, deeper insights are necessary into what digital leadership includes in the view of female managers.

As shown above, there is a need for digital leadership in an ambidextrous world, where digital transformation and the value of innovative power are predominant. At the same time, diversity—including the important management team—is relevant in order to foster innovation and transformation. Even though its relevance is growing, scholars agree that there is a need for more clarity on what is meant by digital leadership and its different aspects (El Sawy et al. 2016). Added to this, we have little knowledge about how the concept of digital leadership is perceived from a female managers' view.

3   Research Question

As illustrated above, in spite of increasing research on innovation management and digital transformation, little is known about the components and challenges of digital leadership from a female managers' view. We suggest that the perspective of female managers with regard to digital leadership is relevant for executives and innovation professionals from organizations across all industries. To ensure future business, the importance of female managers arises as actors in incumbent firms. Corporations are still struggling to increase the number of females at all management levels and are debating the right measures to take to increase the proportion of female managers in top, middle, and lower management positions.

In this discussion, the question arises as to what the perspective of female managers looks like with regard to digital leadership. It is important for firm executives to be aware of this perspective in order to be able to attract females to corporate management positions in digital transformation times more easily. This presupposes knowing what female managers expect digital leadership to be, what kind of organizational culture and context factors they perceive as relevant, and what challenges they see to achieve digital leadership. Therefore, based on the theoretical foundation of innovation theories and its findings regarding the relevance of diversity, our research question is formulated as follows: what are the characteristics of digital leadership and what are the competencies needed for digital leadership from the perspective of female managers?

4   Research Design and Sample

Grounded on a thorough literature review and the illustrated theoretical background on digital leadership and diversity within innovation theories, the methodology of this research is based on a mixed methods approach. In the prestudy, we conducted semistructured, qualitative interviews. This allowed us to obtain in-depth insights to elaborate on the constructs for the subsequent quantitative main study. The goal of the prestudy was to explore items that were mentioned by the interviewees concerning the construct of digital leadership and to explore participants' perceptions of diversity and leadership overall. We approached field actors directly in accordance with Giddens' (1984) structuration approach: we argue that in this fairly new market development structural elements do not exist per se but are shaped and altered by activities of the same market actors (Giddens 1984). Therefore, we assume that it is vital to understand the rules and resources which work as a shared actor- and situation-transcending knowledge. We address the actors from the research field as "knowledgeable agents" (Giddens 1984) who provide insights that we used to validate categories and generate items for the subsequent quantitative main study. To ensure extensive insights, we included different industries. The sample consisted of five female managers as agents who are experts in change initiatives within corporations from four industry sectors. The industry sectors that were selected are leaders in innovation and digital transformation and are therefore acting as first movers in this respect:

- Information technology: Hewlett Packard and Fujitsu
- Media: Sky
- Strategic consulting: Deloitte
- Telecommunications: Telekom

The interviews lasted 30–45 min, and were recorded and then transcribed. After the data collection, two researchers coded and analyzed the dataset independently. Each code was related to a category when the term, synonym, or description was stated by the participants interviewed (Mayring 2014). In order to ensure inter-rater reliability, the meanings of the categories were continuously negotiated.

The explorative main study referred to in our chapter uses a quantitative online survey as a research strategy. A questionnaire was developed using an in-depth analysis of the academic literature and the prestudy results. The survey consisted of 14 questions on digital transformation, digital leadership, and diversity (gender and cognitive diversity). We developed the constructs and items based on the prestudy and literature results. We ranked the items of the construct of digital leadership on a continuum from self-related to externally related items (illustrated in Table 1), which was adapted from the differentiation of personality characteristics as suggested by Wille et al. (2018). The survey questionnaire also included a set of questions with the possibility to add open answers. Concerning the construct of digital leadership, we asked respondents to optionally add their own understanding of related skills and characteristics. Respondents were offered eight alternative items and were asked to choose the three most important appropriate ones in their view. In order to improve the reliability and validity of the study, we analyzed the additional qualitative answers from the main study to enrich the interpretation of quantitative analysis results.

We conducted the survey online. Ninety female managers from the DACH region took part. Of this sample, around one-third of the female managers surveyed come from top management, about 38% from middle management, and 28% from the lower management level. The study covers 14 different industry sectors, whereby manufacturing and the provision of other economic services dominate with a share of 21.1% each, followed by information and communication with 16.7%. The age of the respondents can be regarded as normally distributed. Participants come from

Table 1 Items related to skills and characteristics of the construct of digital leadership

Items	Agreement (%)	Reliance	Item source
Self-reliance			
Own expertise and willingness for life-long learning about digital technologies	38.9	8	Expert-based (prestudy); Ferrari (2013)
Curiosity and interest in technological innovations	70.0	7	Expert-based (prestudy)
Active role in shaping and owning the digital change within the company	66.7	6	Expert-based (prestudy); Kane et al. (2019)
Role model for a positive error culture	12.2	5	Expert-based (prestudy); Fuchs (2011)
Open knowledge and information handling	30.0	4	Expert-based (prestudy)
Openness to new working time models such as trust working time, home office	12.2	3	Expert-based (prestudy); Schwarzmüller et al. (2018)
Communicate at eye level in network structures and moderate team processes	17.8	2	Expert-based (prestudy); Schwarzmüller et al. (2018)
Empathy and social skills to articulate value change will bring to employees	51.1	1	Expert-based (prestudy); Kane et al. (2019)
External reliance			

different company departments, including human resources, sales and marketing, the CEO office, production, and research and development.

The two types of data sources accompanied by the literature enabled us to develop a comprehensive understanding of the phenomenon.

5   Findings

Qualitative Prestudy

The qualitative prestudy showed that the respondents expect a further rise in dynamics within the scope of digitalization. In some cases, this means having to rebuild well-functioning business processes quickly in order to keep pace with the change, develop new business ideas and keep other processes constant at the same time (ambidexterity). The study also revealed that the interviewees believe that leadership by female managers is perceived differently from that of male managers. In the perception of the participants, this is due to the fact that women are attested to other leadership qualities that they have acquired in their respective personal socialization processes. In the view of the interviewees, women also embody these qualities in a different manner.

Diversity is an important aspect when it comes to management and leadership. The female managers surveyed see this by far not only reduced to gender or quota. In their view, the focus is also on the question of personality, on what the respondents described in part with what theory calls cognitive diversity. In the participants' view, the right mix of personality types is important for digital transformation success.

Concerning digital leadership, interviewees define it overall as leadership in times of digital transformation. They agree that giving employees orientation and clarity in times of uncertainty and fostering diversity to enable innovation are important goals in this respect. The following skills and characteristics were mentioned by the experts as relevant with regard to digital leadership. Great relevance is seen in improving skills in communicating at eye level in network structures and in moderating team processes, as well as in the empathy necessary to articulate the value that change will bring to employees. Curiosity and interest in technological innovations together with the willingness to embrace lifelong learning with regard to digital technologies are also mentioned as success factors. Participants perceive women to be much more eager to experiment and to be open to making mistakes in the sense of an open error culture, which they claim to be an important value as well. According to the participants, women's more open error culture helps companies in a dynamic environment when working with agile planning, for example. They perceive fast trial and error with a high level of error-friendliness as being important, so that trying something out is rewarded positively. In addition, playing an active role in shaping and owning the digital change within the company, handling knowledge, and information openly, and openness to new working time models, such as trust-based working hours and home office, were also mentioned as important characteristics for digital leadership. Overall, they state that creating diversity is one of the most important prerequisites for future business success.

Quantitative Study

These results were integrated into the main study, in which we explored the research question concerning the components and challenges of digital leadership in a broader empirical approach.

First of all, concerning digital transformation, almost 90% of the female managers surveyed expect digital transformation to change the processes or even the entire business model of their company. At the same time, nearly half of the female managers surveyed perceive their companies as not ready and still in the discovery phase regarding a digital strategy. Moreover, 45% of participants state that there is a lack of female role models concerning digital transformation topics within their firms. In this context, with 87.8%, the digital transformation is clearly rated as a cultural challenge rather than a technological one (4.4%), with 7.8% of participants claiming other corporate challenges to be relevant. From the point of view of the respondents, digital transformation is a process that should be carried out by both managers and employees (78.9%). It is perceived as a comprehensive process. Therefore, in the view of the female managers surveyed, leaving sole responsibility to the level of top management or appointing a chief digital officer, for example, will not lead to innovation or digital leadership.

The respondents associate digital leadership with the following skills and characteristics (participants were asked to select the three most important items). Curiosity and interest in technological innovations are perceived as most relevant (70.0%), followed by playing an active role in shaping and owning digital change (66.7%), and the empathy and social skills required to articulate the value that the change will bring to employees (51.1%). Having expertise and the willingness to embrace life-long learning with regard to technologies as well as handling knowledge and information openly are relevant to 38.9% and 30.0%, respectively. The aspects of communication at eye level in network structures and of moderating team processes, together with being a role model for a positive error culture and openness to new working time models are rated less important, with the results for each being under 20%. These results clearly reveal the important characteristics and skills of digital leadership in the perception of the female managers surveyed: they underline the relevance of managers' own digital competencies and the associated willingness to embrace lifelong learning, together with the ability of being an active role model for change, and of motivating and convincing employees of the necessary change that the digital transformation brings along.

Concerning cognitive diversity, 37.8% of participants perceive themselves as drivers who value challenge and winning, want to see their ideas realized, and can inspire team members to do so. 36.7% rate themselves as integrators who draw teams together. Guardians, who value stability, and pioneers, who take more risks, are only represented by 13.3% and 12.2%, respectively. Looking at cognitive diversity split within this result on the concept of digital leadership reveals that 50% of the respondents who rate themselves as drivers perceive their own expertise and willingness to learn about digitalization as being particularly important, for example. Guardians value communication at eye level in network structures and moderating team processes (41.7%), and also the handling of knowledge and information openly (41.7%). 60% of integrators rate empathy and social skills required to lead employees to change as relevant, and 81.8% of pioneers regard openness to new technological developments as an important aspect (see Fig. 1).

Moreover, there are significant differences between cognitive diversity types, which become apparent when the corresponding items are created on a continuum between strong self-reliance and strong external reliance (Table 1). The skills and characteristics associated with a digital leader split into types of cognitive diversity are significant in a pooled t-test ($p = 0.0366*$). The extreme poles in the area of self-reliance are dominated by drivers, and in the area of external reliance by integrators.

The discussion of the empirical findings shows that from the perspective of the female managers in this study, the skills and characteristics needed for digital leadership are very much change-related and refer to change and digital readiness of managers and organizations.

First of all, concerning self-reliance and external reliance items, the characteristics of digital leadership mentioned refer to both: managers' own

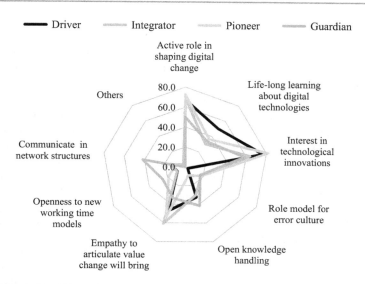

Fig. 1 Descriptive: Skills and characteristics associated with a digital leader split into types of cognitive diversity ($n = 90$)

competencies that are needed for digitalization of a firm as well as the ability to inspire and lead others—in this case, employees—through the massive change processes that digital transformation brings with it.

Second, a look at the individual items shows that the three highest rated characteristics refer to two main aspects. On the one hand, the expansion of the managers' own knowledge and skills is relevant. Referring to their competencies, it is perceived as important for the managers to have their own interest in technological innovations and the ability to embrace lifelong learning with regard to digital technologies, and to safeguard their own expertise instead of simply relying on digital officers or experts at the firm. On the other hand, employees' perceptions of change also have to be managed. The outcomes of the study show that digital leaders need the ability to act as role models, play an active role and own the change processes of the firm, and that they need to convince employees of the value that change will bring, manage their perceptions and motivate them to follow them on their path to digital leadership.

Third, looking at the different personality types of managers, the study results revealed that differences in perceptions of digital leadership do exist. Whereas self-reliance characteristics are significantly more relevant to drivers than to other types, integrators, especially refer to external reliance characteristics that involve others as being extremely important.

6   Contribution

Our study aimed to gain deeper insights into the concept of digital leadership. We contribute to the digital leadership and innovation literature by expanding our knowledge about perceptions of the concept of digital leadership that are relevant within the context of the innovation and digital transformation of incumbent firms. Our results shed light on the components of digital leadership and the challenges managers should focus on and overcome. With regard to the concept of digital leadership, we add the perspective of a target group that is still underrepresented in incumbent firms: female managers. This perspective is highly relevant on the innovation journey in times of digital transformation. We contribute to the literature in two ways: first, our findings help us to expand our knowledge about the concept of digital leadership and explore it from the perspective of female managers by using their perspectives as "knowledgeable agents" (Giddens 1984). Relevant characteristics and skills are evaluated. The outcome of our study confirms parts of the study on digital leadership conducted by Kane et al. (2019), in the respect that articulating the value that change will bring for employees and owning the transformation as an executive are important aspects for successfully fulfilling the digital transformation tasks and becoming a digital leader. At the same time, our study adds new relevant items concerning managers' self-reliance and external reliance characteristics on topics like role model function and lifelong learning. Second, we identify connections between different types of cognitive diversity and the characteristics of digital leadership on the continuum between self-reliance and external reliance factors. Concerning limitations, future research should explore the perspectives of male managers and other target groups within the innovation ecosystem, apart from gender diversity—cultural diversity and age diversity, for example—to gain a holistic perspective of digital leadership components and challenges from the viewpoint of different stakeholders.

7   Practical Implications

The challenges for companies trying to enhance digital leadership clearly show that organizations and their leaders are still struggling to adapt to the requirements of digital leadership and to embrace diversity to ensure future success. The characteristics of digital leadership explored illustrate—and may help practitioners to evaluate—the main aspects that managers should strive for with regard to their own competencies as well as their ability to encourage employees to follow them. Based on the results of the study, we suggest implications in two areas: (1) managers should be aware of the characteristics and success factors of digital leadership and the differences in perception that may exist, and (2) female managers need to expand their individual skills and digital readiness in order to act as role models for young female talents to follow their path. Overall, as illustrated, our study shows that digital leadership includes many new opportunities for female managers in the digital age.

References

Alimo-Metcalfe, B. (1995). An investigation of female and male constructs of leadership and empowerment. *Women in Management Review, 10*(2), 3–8.

Bassett-Jones, N. (2005). The paradox of diversity management, creativity and innovation. *Creativity and Innovation Management, 14*(2), 169–175.

Bennis, W. G., & Townsend, R. (1989). *On becoming a leader*. Boston, MA: Addison-Wesley.

Berghaus, S., & Back, A. (2016). Stages in digital business transformation: Results of an empirical maturity study. In *Proceedings of the Mediterranean Conference on Information Systems*, MCIS 22, Paphos, Cyprus (pp. 1–17).

Bersin, J. (2016, December 1). *Digital leadership is not an optional part of being a CEO*. Harvard Business Review. Retrieved April 2020, from https://hbr.org/2016/12/digital-leadership-is-not-an-optional-part-of-being-a-ceo

Campbell, K., & Mínguez-Vera, A. (2007). Gender diversity in the boardroom and firm financial performance. *Journal of Business Ethics, 83*(3), 435–451.

Deloitte Global Center for Corporate Governance. (2019). *Women in the Boardroom: A Global Perspective. Deloitte Report*. Deloitte Company website. Retrieved April 2020, from https://www2.deloitte.com/global/en/pages/risk/articles/women-in-the-boardroom-global-perspective.html

El Sawy, O. A., Kræmmergaard, P., Amsinck, H., & Vinther, A. L. (2016). How LEGO built the foundations and enterprise capabilities for digital leadership. *MIS Quarterly Executive, 15*(2), 141–166.

Ferrari, A. (2013). DIGCOMP: A framework for developing and understanding digital competence in Europe. In Y. Punie & B. N. Brecko (Eds.), *JRC scientific and policy reports*. Luxembourg: Publications Office of the European Union.

Fuchs, S. (2011). The impact of manager and top management identification on the relationship between perceived organizational justice and change-oriented behavior. *Leadership and Organization Development Journal, 32*(6), 555–583.

Galia, F., & Zenou, E. (2012). Board composition and forms of innovation: Does diversity make a difference? *European Journal of International Management, 6*(6), 630–650.

Giddens, A. (1984). *The constitution of society. Outline of the theory of structuration*. Glasgow: Bell and Bain Limited.

Hewlett, S. A., Marshall, M., & Sherbin, L. (2013). How diversity can drive innovation. *Harvard Business Review, 91*(12), 30–31.

Hinings, B., Gegenhuber, T., & Greenwood, R. (2018). Digital innovation and transformation: An institutional perspective. *Information and Organization, 28*(1), 52–61.

Holt, D. T., & Vardaman, J. M. (2013). Toward a comprehensive understanding of readiness for change: The case for an expanded conceptualization. *Journal of Change Management, 13*(1), 9–18.

Johnson Vickberg, S. M., & Christfort, K. (2017). Pioneers, drivers, integrators, and guardians. *Harvard Business Review, 95*(2), 50–57.

Kane, G. C., Palmer, D., Phillips, A. N., Kiron, D., & Buckley, N. (2015). Strategy, not technology, drives digital transformation. *MIT Sloan Management Review and Deloitte University Press, 14*, 1–25.

Kane, G. C., Phillips, A. N., Copulsky, J., & Andrus, G. (2019). How digital leadership is(n't) different. *MIT Sloan Management Review, 60*(3), 34–39.

Kilduff, M., Angelmar, R., & Mehra, A. (2000). Top management-team diversity and firm performance: Examining the role of cognitions. *Organization Science, 11*(1), 21–34.

Marinova, J., Plantenga, J., & Remery, C. (2015). Gender diversity and firm performance: Evidence from Dutch and Danish boardrooms. *The International Journal of Human Resource Management, 27*(15), 1777–1790.

Mayring, P. (2014). *Qualitative content analysis: Theoretical foundation, basic procedures and software solution*. Klagenfurt: SSOAR.

Muchiri, M. K., Cooksey, R. W., Di Milia, L. V., & Walumbwa, F. O. (2011). Gender and managerial level differences in perceptions of effective leadership. *Leadership & Organization Development Journal, 32*(5), 462–492.

O'Reilly, C. A., & Tushman, M. L. (2011). Organizational ambidexterity in action: How managers explore and exploit. *California Management Review, 53*(4), 5–22.

Østergaard, C. R., Timmermans, B., & Kristinsson, K. (April 2011). Does a different view create something new? The effect of employee diversity on innovation. *Research Policy, 40*(3), 500–509.

Rosing, K., & Zacher, H. (October 2017). Individual ambidexterity: The duality of exploration and exploitation and its relationship with innovative performance. *European Journal of Work and Organizational Psychology, 26*(5), 694–709.

Schallmo, D., Williams, C. A., & Boardman, L. (2017). Digital transformation of business models – Best practice, enablers, and roadmap. *International Journal of Innovation Management, 21*(8), 1–17.

Schwarzmüller, T., Brosi, P., Duman, D., & Welpe, I. M. (2018). How does the digital transformation affect organizations? Key themes of change in work design and leadership. *Management Review, 29*(2), 114–138.

Van der Vegt, G. S., & Janssen, O. (2003). Joint impact of interdependence and group diversity on innovation. *Journal of Management, 29*(5), 729–751.

Weiblen, T., & Chesbrough, H. W. (2015). Engaging with startups to enhance corporate innovation. *California Management Review, 57*(2), 66–90.

Wille, B., Wiernik, B. M., Vergauwe, J., Vrijdags, A., & Trbovic, N. (2018). Personality characteristics of male and female executives: Distinct pathways to success? *Journal of Vocational Behavior, 106*, 220–235.

Wilson, E. J. (2004). Leadership in the digital age. In G. R. Goethals, G. Sorenson, & J. M. Burns (Eds.), *The encyclopedia of leadership*. Thousand Oaks, CA: Sage.

Yang, Y., & Konrad, A. M. (2011). Diversity and organizational innovation: The role of employee involvement. *Journal of Organizational Behavior, 32*(8), 1062–1083.

Zhan, S., Bendapudi, N., & Hong, Y.-Y. (October 2015). Re-examining diversity as a double-edged sword for innovation process. *Journal of Organizational Behavior, 36*(7), 1026–1049.

Zhang, Y., Wei, F., & Van Horne, C. (2019). Individual ambidexterity and antecedents in a changing context. *International Journal of Innovation Management, 23*(3), 1–25.

Anne Gfrerer is a PhD student at the University of Innsbruck, Chair of Innovation and Entrepreneurship, Strategic Management. Prior to her PhD studies, Anne Gfrerer was head of communication and innovation management for HypoVereinsbank/ UniCredit, since 2009. She combines the research perspective as well as the professional experience as a top manager of a corporate bank. In line with her research focus on innovation and digital leadership, she regularly gives guest lectures about organizational change culture and innovation leadership. Before her professional career, she had started her academic career at the Ludwig-Maximilians-University, Munich in the fields of Internet and innovation.

Lars Rademacher, MA, PhD, is a professor for Public Relations at Darmstadt University of Applied Sciences and adjunct lecturer and researcher at Cork Institute of Technology (CIT), Ireland. He serves as a director at the Institute of Communication and Media and heads the international master program Media, Technology and Society (MSc). Before joining academia, Lars spent more than 15 years as a communication consultant, account executive, media relations manager, and executive coach working for a number of national and multinational companies including BASF and Volkswagen. His research interests cover public legitimacy, PR ethics, digital leadership, executive communication, CSR, and compliance communication.

Stefan Dobler (born 1980) has been teaching at numerous universities and academies for almost 15 years. His focus is on scientific work, statistics, economics, media, and communication. In the last few years, he has dealt specifically with entrepreneurship and corporate management. After 6 years as a project manager in a market research and consulting institute, he founded his own research and consulting company. He studied political science in his first degree and in his second degree in economics for a diploma.

Developing Creative Leaders: Learner's Reflections on Methodology and Pedagogy

Detlef Reis and Brian Hunt

1 Introduction: The Call for Creative and Effective Creative Leader Development Programs

Research Background and Relevance

With the new millennium, many business thinkers suggest that humanity has reached a new stage of economic development, the innovation economy (e.g., Canton 2007) or creative economy (Howkins 2001). At the same time, Canton (2007) suggests that in the early twenty-first century, many business trends are driven by speed, exponential change, complexity, risks, and surprises. Von Stamm (2017) noted the importance of creativity and innovation to respond with new solutions to the challenges of the modern VUCA world (volatility, uncertainty, complexity, ambiguity).

Against this background, it is unsurprising that in practitioners' surveys (e.g., IBM 2010; World Economic Forum 2015), business leaders emphasize the crucial importance of creativity as a dominant leadership trait to maneuver a highly dynamic business environment, and the need for organizations to develop more top talents and executives into creative leaders.

An IBM (2011) study reported that two out of three Chief Human Resources Officers of the world's leading organizations were at a loss where to begin their CEO-directed initiatives to develop more creative leaders. Why? The study authors suggested that organizations seem to fail at developing creative leaders as they rely on traditional leadership development programs that use conventional methodological and pedagogical formats that are not particularly creative. The authors stress that

D. Reis (✉) · B. Hunt
Thinkergy Limited, Kowloon, Hong Kong

Thinkergy Limited, Bangkok, Thailand
e-mail: dr.d@thinkergy.com

© The Author(s), under exclusive license to Springer Nature Switzerland AG 2021
D. R. A. Schallmo, J. Tidd (eds.), *Digitalization*, Management for Professionals,
https://doi.org/10.1007/978-3-030-69380-0_20

to develop creative leaders effectively, the training programs employed to do so must use a creative methodology and pedagogy, and not a traditional, long-established one.

Research Subject, Problem, and Objectives

In response to the call above for new training formats for creative leadership development, the first author of this chapter purpose-designed a new creative leader development method named Genius Journey (Reis 2015). This program sets out to enable learners to acquire the creative success mindsets (attitudes and action routines) of outstanding creative leaders and to gradually expand their creative confidence, competence, and consciousness levels (Reis 2015, 2020, 2022). The program employs a journey metaphor as an experiential pedagogical format to teach candidates the said mindsets both effectively and creatively (Reis 2015, 2022).

Our present chapter is part of an ongoing research program that we designed to investigate the effectiveness and creativeness of this comparatively new creative leader development program. In this research program, we (a) introduce the Genius Journey program, (b) assess if learners rate the chosen approach to be both creative and effective, and (c) seek deeper level insights from learners of how they experience the program and perceive the value, creativity, and effectiveness of its methodology and pedagogy on a personal level. This chapter has the following research antecedents (see also Fig. 1):

- Reis (2015) introduces the methodology used by the Genius Journey program, and outlines to what extent it builds upon—and differs from—earlier approaches to enhance individual creativity and develop creative leaders.
- A second conceptual paper (Reis and Hunt 2017) describes in detail the experiential pedagogy (structure, contents, and activities) employed in this new creative leader development program.
- In an empirical paper, Reis et al. (2018) asked learners to rate the methodology and pedagogy of the Genius Journey program in quantitative terms, thereby confirming the efficacy and creativity of the chosen approach in general terms.
- In a second empirical paper, Reis et al. (2020) investigated how learners experience their inner heroes' journeys while undergoing the program. The results offered deeper level insights on what excursions, exercises, and activities of the Genius Journey program resonate and add value to individual learners on a personal level.

With our new paper, we want to widen these insights as to why the Genius Journey approach works. Thereby, we set out to investigate why learners deem the chosen methodology and pedagogy to be valuable, creative, and effective. We also explore which of a myriad of pedagogical tools used in the program appeal most with learners, and why.

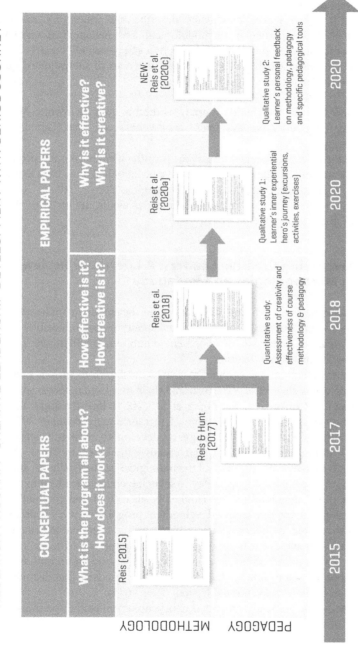

Fig. 1 Overview of the pedagogical tools used in the Genius Journey program

Research-Guiding Questions

This empirical paper investigates the overarching research question:

How did creative leader candidates describe and exemplify ex-post their perceptions of those particular methodological and pedagogical elements that make the Genius Journey program both effective and genuinely creative?

We explored this research-guiding question with a set of subordinated questions: How do creative leader candidates . . .

1. Define and describe the Genius Journey method in their own words?
2. Exemplify the effectiveness and creativeness of the Genius Journey methodology?
3. Evaluate the effectiveness and creativeness of the Genius Journey pedagogy?
4. Assess the personal value of various creative pedagogical tools used in the Genius Journey program of creative leadership development?
5. Express their overall sentiments and main takeaways from "traveling the Genius Journey" at the end of the program?

2   Developing Creative Leaders: A Literature Review on Methodologies and Pedagogy

Creative leadership is an evolving domain within management studies at the intersection of the domains of leadership, individual creativity, and innovation. The niche domain of creative leadership development combines the literature on creative leadership with educational theories.

The pertinent literature approaches creative leadership from various perspectives. For example, van Velsor et al. (2010) frame their discussions more on traditional leadership styles. Conversely, Sternberg et al. (2004) link the topic to different strategic action programs. Another strand of literature (e.g., Basadur 2004; Puccio et al. 2011; Williams and Foti 2011) suggests developing creative leaders by using classic innovation process methods and creative thinking strategies. Antes and Schuelke (2011) advocate the use of technological tools (such as simulations, e-mentoring, and social media) as a way to leverage creative leadership capacity.

In contrast, and as advocated by Hughes et al. (2018), the first author of this chapter developed a creative leader development program (Genius Journey) with a novel, well-structured methodology (Reis 2015), and an experiential pedagogy (Reis 2017) that aims to achieve a lasting creative metamorphosis of leaders' mindsets. The Genius Journey method proposes ten creativity-enhancing mindsets (attitudes and action routines) alongside ten creativity-limiting mindsets that distinguish creative leaders from more conventional leaders (Reis 2015).

The method is theoretically grounded in psychological studies on traits of genius (e.g., Feist 1999; Sternberg 1999), biographies of creative leaders (e.g., Branson 1998; Isaacson 2007, 2011), semi-biographical training programs on creative leaders (e.g., Gelb 1998; Gelb and Miller Caldicott 2007), and training programs to enhance individual creativity (e.g., Ray and Myers 1986; Cameron 1992), among others. In his Genius Journey model (Reis 2015, 2020), the first author proposes that prospective creative leaders ought to acquire the conducive mindsets in a specific sequential order based on a hierarchy of expanding consciousness levels. The Genius Journey method also employs a journey metaphor to teach the creative success mindsets of creative leaders to candidates in a genuinely creative format. To pedagogically animate the method, the first author developed an experiential creative leadership development program aligned with Kolb's (1984, 2015) experiential learning cycle theory.

In our current qualitative research, we report how creative leader candidates describe and exemplify their subjective perceptions of what methodological and pedagogical elements make the Genius Journey program both effective and genuinely creative. As outlined above, in Sect. 1, this chapter is a further pillar in our ongoing research program on creative leadership development.

3   Research Design and Methodology

Research Design

Using a social constructionist perspective, we have applied Reis' (2015) Genius Journey model of creative leadership and Kolb's (1984) experiential learning cycle theory as theoretical frameworks to determine how and to what extent the Genius Journey supports creative mindset transformations in prospective creative leaders.

Methodology

This empirical study follows a qualitative research design. Between 2012 and 2015, we collected data from five cohorts of learners at the end of a 12-week long development program in creative leadership. This training was offered as an elective as part of a master's in management program at a university in Bangkok, Thailand. The learners were mainly business professionals in the age range 25–35 years from Thailand (55%) and a variety of ten other, mostly European, countries (45%). We collected qualitative data from 35 participants about their personal experience of undergoing the Genius Journey program of creative leadership development.

We collected data by asking learners after the end of the program to write a reflective essay of 6–8 pages. We used a set of open-ended guiding questions that probed how the learners experienced their transformational journey through the Genius Journey program of creative leader development; we reported these findings in earlier research (Reis et al. 2020). Interestingly, and unprompted, many learners chose to also comment on the methodology and pedagogy used in the program, as well as on the value of different creative pedagogical tools. Due to the richness of these data, we feel also compelled to report this feedback because it exemplifies the learners' responses (to the methodological and pedagogical value of the program) in more personal terms. In exploring the proffered data, we followed the flow of the subordinated research-guiding questions.

4   Findings

We present our findings on how the creative leader candidates reflected on the course methodology and pedagogy of the Genius Journey method of creative leadership in the order of the research-guiding questions.

Creative Leader Candidates' Definitions

We observed that many prospective creative leaders chose not to merely repeat the given definition of the creative leadership course program. Intriguingly, they developed their own interpretative—and even metaphorical—definitions of what the Genius Journey program aspires to do. Collectively, these informal, personal descriptions of the learners recast an abstract, theoretical definition into a more profound, more practical, and more applied format. Here is an example of how one learner personalized and "translated" the given definition of the course methodology for herself:

> After the first class I went home, and I started typing on my computer "genius journey" because I was eager to know what it was about and this is the definition that I found on the thinkergy website: 'Genius Journey is: An experiential, action-oriented creative leadership development program that enables you to reconnect with your creativity and your inner genius.' On a theoretical level, this is what the genius journey is about, but on a practical level, it is a lot more: it has been a journey around Bangkok, around the college, and, most importantly, inside myself. It has been a journey in which all the stops were just as important as the final destination, and every week I have discovered more and more things about myself.—ITALIAN FEMALE 1

Another prospective creative leader shared the following definition:

> According to its formal definition, the genius journey is 'an experiential, action-oriented individual creativity training program that enables you to reconnect with your creativity and your inner genius by providing you with creative mindsets and cognitive skills of genius thinkers and creative business leaders in order to transform into an authentic, creative leader in the innovation economy.' In my personal opinion, the Genius Journey has been much more than that. It has been an on-going challenge with myself, an introspective itinerary where I had the possibility to face both my strong points and my limits, and of course, a path during which I learned a significant amount of new concepts and gained many relevant insights.—ITALIAN FEMALE 2

Other prospective creative leaders defined the Genius Journey method as "a combination between theory, principle, philosophy and relaxation" (THAI MALE 8) that jointly bring out the creative personality of a learner, or described the method metaphorically as "a mirror and reflect myself back by telling me who I am, what I really love to do and what aspects should be improved" (THAI FEMALE 1) to transform into a creative leader.

Creative Leader Candidates' Views on the Methodology

In an earlier study (Reis et al. 2018), we provide quantitative evidence of both the efficacy and the creativity of the Genius Journey method of creative leader development. In this current qualitative study, creative leader candidates offer in-depth explanations of why this is the case.

Many learners highlighted the effectiveness of the Genius Journey model with its ten destination stops (and related creativity-limiting Stop- and creativity empowering Start-mindsets). For example, one learner expressed this notion as follows: "Overall, I think the Genius Journey Method is great. The concept of Stops/Starts clearly explains the growth of creative leadership in everyone and shortcut the learning process." (THAI FEMALE 3).

Some creative leader candidates also grasped the interconnectedness and imminent sequence and hierarchy of the ten destination stops of the Genius Journey model:

> The fact that reflecting on one stop just made me jumping back to another stop reveals the—in my eyes—most important thing about the journey in order to fully understand its meaning: It is not just a journey during which you pass through the first stop, then the second, then the third and so on until you reach your last and final destination where the journey is over. In my eyes, the opposite is the case. All stops interact with each other. Some are prerequisites of others. Starting with stop number 1 doesn't mean that you will never come back to it at a later point in time. It is therefore not a journey that is traveled within 12 weeks, it is a life-long journey which has just started.—GERMAN MALE 3

Several learners also commented on the importance of the BE-DO-HAVE-WOW-principle (that links to Zen Buddhist teachings), which underlies the flow of mindsets taught at the ten "destination stops" in the Genius Journey model. One learner stated that "The Genius Journey Stops are well structured to teach us the fundamental concept to the advanced level such as Genius Journey Formula BE > DO > HAVE > WOW." (THAI MALE 6) Another learner elaborated on this point in greater detail:

> Another great component of the Genius Journey is its formula BE-DO-HAVE-WOW! This approach uncovered insights into my personality. I used to be more the guy who was acting the other way around: HAVE-DO-BE. I was more concerned about where I will end up and how I have to adjust my behavior for achieving my goals. This creates risk that you wear a mask instead of being yourself. But the BE-DO-HAVE approach goes the other way around. I have to focus on my personality and my abilities first and then apply them the best way I can in order to come up with outcomes that I am satisfied with. It is a very essential approach, which I took away from the Genius Journey.—GERMAN MALE 3

Creative Leader Candidates' Views on the Pedagogy

The creative leader candidates also shared their opinions on the overall effectiveness and creativity of the pedagogy used in the Genius Journey program that aligns with Kolb's experiential learning cycle. One learner commented on how this pedagogical approach supports gradual creative mindset transformation:

> A big reason is the experiential approach. We focused more on cognitive thinking and mindsets of proven creative leaders (books and articles about them, their inventions, quotes), which was complemented by scientific material from Creative Leadership research. This mixture didn't only increase my knowledge, but it changed my way of thinking. The Genius Journey content not only touched my surface, but also bored through it. Plain material only from scientific books may vanish pretty fast after the exam. But my learning outcomes from the Genius Journey will stay with me longer. If I follow my goal, seeing the Genius Journey as a long life travel that has just started, they may accompany me through my whole life.— GERMAN MALE 3

Other creative leader candidates highlighted how the Genius Journey pedagogy animates the four phases of Kolb's learning cycle (do and experience; reflect on the experience; conceptualize the learnings; apply the learnings). For example, one learner stated that "You have practice how to learn. Learn how to fail, learn how to win, learn how to pause, learn how to start, learn how to be a success. Everything evolves with the learning." (THAI MALE 9). Another learner commented that "During all the weeks I enjoyed most to reflect myself and to learn more about me. I really appreciate these kinds of training because they help me become a more reflecting, open-minded, and creative person." (GERMAN FEMALE 1). Yet another learner commented on the effect of this pedagogical approach in greater detail:

> On a more general level I have really enjoyed the genius journey; I have to be honest and admit that at the beginning I was a bit unsure about the outcome of the class and I didn't really know if becoming more creative was just a utopia or something feasible but class after class I kept being more and more fascinated by the topic. Also, the Genius Journey notebook with the exercises really helped me. I had to write down things I have never thought about, and it is very hard. I also enjoyed the Genius Journey on a scholastic level. In a certain way, it has been one of the hardest courses that I have ever done: it is much easier to write papers about a specific topic because it is all about having good references, but in this specific case I was my only reference, and I had to investigate myself in order to do the exercises.— ITALIAN FEMALE 1

The same learner also highlighted the importance of experiencing this pedagogy both individually and as a member of a learning cohort, and also showed an intuitive sensitivity to Kolb's experiential learning cycle:

> Therefore, the journey had two perspectives: the internal and individual one and the collective one. The former concerned the exercises in the Genius Journey notebook and the practice in my everyday life of what I learned during the class: it was sort of the interior dimension of the itinerary. The latter concerned the classes and the trips outside that we have done together and also the fact of sharing personal experiences and thoughts.—ITALIAN FEMALE 1

Creative Leader Candidates' Views on the Various Pedagogical Tools

In the present study, we also investigated prospective creative leaders' in-depth views on the usefulness of different pedagogical tools used in the Genius Journey program. This qualitative feedback ties into the respective quantitative feedback in an earlier study (Reis et al. 2018). Figure 2 provides an overview of the key pedagogical tools of the Genius Journey program, and where they feature in the program schedule.

Check in Audit/Check out Audit Tool

At the start of the program, prospective creative leaders fill out a survey that raises their awareness on their limiting mindsets. A roadmap visualizes the results of this Genius Journey Check-In Audit and flags up critical destination stops where learners have to overcome limiting mindsets and routines that currently prevent them from reconnecting to their inner creativity. One learner described the value of this tool as follows:

> To learn more about myself, I enjoyed filling out the "Check-In Audit" of the Genius Journey. The result of the questionnaire is charted in the "Genius Journey Focus Map" At every stop, there is a gap between my current and desired state. The largest gaps between my current and desired state can be observed in stop two and nine of the genius journey.— GERMAN MALE 1

Post-program, the creative leader candidates repeat the audit exercise to track and map out their progress in a check-out survey. All learners reported that their creative leader potential increased (range of 30–100% with an average value of 70%). Interestingly, more reflective creative candidates tended to rate their progress more conservatively (after all, rating one's creative leadership potential is relative, and depends whether you compare yourself with your study peers and fellows at work or with a Leonardo da Vinci):

> I know that I haven't closed all of my gaps, which I initially identified during the Check-in Audit at the beginning, substantially. Some of them decreased already (e.g. my ego and being critical), but for most of the gaps I realized during the last 12 weeks how big they really are. Today, I rather shift the scale of my gap-analysis than seeing gaps as closed.— GERMAN MALE 3

Creative Leader Self-Study and Portraits

In parallel to the first nine-course sessions of the Genius Journey program, each learner needs to study the life of one admired creative leader. Later on, they need to sum up their learnings in a report and a pitch presentation for the entire learning cohort. The diversity of creative leaders selected includes business leaders and innovators (such as Thomas Edison, Steve Jobs, and Richard Branson), universal or scientific geniuses (like Albert Einstein, Leonardo da Vinci, Johann Wolfgang von Goethe, Isaac Newton, and Benjamin Franklin), spiritual leaders (such as Jesus of Nazareth, Gautama Buddha, and Lao Tze), political leaders (like Abraham

GJ Pedagogical Tool	Perceived VALUE * (mean out of 7; n=41)	Perceived ENJOYMENT * (mean out of 7; n=41)	CHECK-IN	Start of a session	In-class [Lecture] & Activities	Out-of-class [Trips] & Activities	Homework [Genius Exercises]	CHECK-OUT	Sample comments on tool by selected learners
Check-in Audit & Focus Map	5.71	5.17	♦						"To learn more about myself, I enjoyed filling out the "Check-in Audit" of the Genius Journey. The result of the questionnaire is charted in the "Genius Journey Focus Map." At every stop, there is a gap between my current and desired state. The largest gaps between my current and desired state can be observed in stop two and nine of the genius journey." — GERMAN MALE 1
Dare to Share [Peer-to-Peer-Sharing]	N/A	N/A		♦					"Dare to Share is one of the most important activity that can make our course more easy to understanding. I think this kind of activity create two way communication environment and I have shared together with create some question during the class." — THAI MALE 5
In-Class Lectures & Activities	6.39	6.05			♦		◇		"My most interesting experience was the week that we do absolute relaxation activities in the class, and I also cleared up my mind by doing meditation after I got home, before going to sleep. I felt calm and absolutely relaxed. The next morning, I felt fresher and more focused on my work. I came up with a couple of good ideas within little time." — THAI FEMALE 5
Field Trips & Outdoor Activities	6.05	6.44			♦		◇		"The most interesting experience on my Genius Journey was when I visit Benjakiti Park. At first, I was surprised that the teacher was running and got sweat. It was interesting since we had a class in a park and I felt like I had a field trip liked when I was young with my school. The activities that we did in the park were unusual things that I never did before or used to do a long time ago." — THAI FEMALE 7
Genius Exercises	5.83	4.15			◇	◇	◇		"My life is 1-99 was a really interesting exercise to do. It forced me to think into details about what I already accomplish in my life and what I would like to accomplish in the future! It is a way to see who you really are and where you really want to go." — DUTCH FEMALE 1
Genius Notebook	N/A	N/A			♦	♦	◇		"One key thing I will take from this course is also that I enjoy to have a notebook to write down my thoughts. For me it doesn't necessarily have to be on paper, it can also be on the computer though. I find the idea of writing down all my thoughts in itself very intriguing and am certain that this will help me grow substantially." — SYRIAN MALE 1
Creative Puzzles	5.56	5.51			♦	♦			"The creative puzzles are one of the best tools that encourage me to think outside the box. They help me to realize that if I keep doing things in the same way or the same as the others, I will get the same result, no improvement. Hence, I need to step outside my comfort zone, my cozy box, and look at the things at the different perspectives so that I can gain creative solutions." — THAI FEMALE 9
Buddy Coaching	4.90	4.63				◇			"I have known more than 20 new friends from more than 5 countries, which I am not sure I can find this kind of connection from anywhere. During the Genius Trips, we can have more time to get to know each other better and better." — THAI FEMALE 1
Genius Leader Self-Study	6.27	6.12							"What has also been extremely helpful to learn the importance of believing is analyzing the journey of my creative leader, Coco Chanel, and listening my classmates' leaders journeys." — ITALIAN FEMALE 5
Genius Portraits [Pitch & Reports]	6.37	5.98			♦				"I highly enjoyed preparing the presentation on Salvador Dali. Seeing how he faced different challenges in life, how he harvested his creativity, lived with his ego, etc. gave me a lot of insights into how I can become a better leader and what things I will have to focus on in the future." — SYRIAN MALE 1
Final Review Session	6.34	6.02			♦				"I enjoyed most the last class exercise when we went again through all Genius Journey stops to review key learnings." — THAI MALE 4
Check-out Audit & Progress Map	N/A	N/A						♦	"I know that I haven't closed all of my gaps, which I initially identified during the Check-in Audit at the beginning, substantially. Some of them decreased already (e.g. my ego and being critical), but for most of the gaps I realized during the last 12 weeks how big they really are. Today, I rather shift the scale of my gap-analysis than seeing gaps as closed." — GERMAN MALE 3
Genius Journey Review Toys	5.76	5.88			♦			♦	"Another WOW tool for me to make me continue is… WOW balls in the last class. When I folded it into the ball and different angles having different Genius Journey, it was the very great tool to remind me about my Journey." — THAI MALE 6
Visual Presentation Slides	6.27	5.88			♦				"I love slides of presentation every class. Not difficult to remember, visually stimulating and inspiring." — THAI FEMALE 5
Course Handout [Booklet]	6.05	5.24					◇		"The handout and the exercise pack was attractive and very useful. Most of them are very nice, I really want it." — THAI FEMALE 10

GENIUS JOURNEY PROGRAM

* Quantitative results as reported in Reis et al. (2018)

♦ Action [Activities & Lectures]   ◇ Reflection [Introspection & Self-study]

Fig. 2 Overview of the pedagogical tools used in the Genius Journey program

Lincoln and Nelson Mandela), sports leaders, top achievers, and kinaesthetic geniuses (including Bruce Lee and Mohammad Ali), and artistic geniuses in the creative arts in the broadest sense (such as Pablo Picasso, Salvatore Dali, Mark Twain, Wolfgang Amadeus Mozart, and Ludwig van Beethoven).

Most learners provided accounts of how useful this biographical exercise is in animating the contents of the Genius Journey methodology by linking it to the lives and mindsets, challenges, and achievements of their favorite creative leader. Here are some sample comments:

> The most valuable homework for me was the creative leader report. I have to analyse my creative leader with the Genius Journey. It can help me fully understand about the concept and how all ten stops apply to people in real life. Also, it shows the result of lacking any stops as well. For example, if Jimi Hendrix can balance himself and be creative without using drug and alcohol, all of his outcome may be much better than what he had done so far.—THAI MALE 7

> I highly enjoyed the preparing the presentation on Salvador Dali. Since a long time I enjoy his art and actually have several of his paintings in my room in Germany. I also visited his museum and his house in Spain, which both gave me good insights into his person. By doing this project however I was able to view him from an entirely different angle than I had viewed him before, learn several new things about him, and see how he and I can relate to one another. Seeing how he faced different challenges in life, how he harvested his creativity, lived with his ego, etc. gave me a lot of insights in how I can become a better leader and what things I will have to focus on in the future.—SYRIAN MALE 1

> The assignment to study biography of Creative person and analyses his action. It make me surprise very much of what my favorite leadership being, thinking and doing. I can learn many things in that exercise and it is a good lesson for me to use in my life.—THAI MALE 9

> One of the most value exercises is the learning about creative leaders. One of the best ways of learning is to learn from the experts, this course provides a very good opportunity for us to learn about great people in the world/country. Their biographies, characteristics and wow moments are a good content that inspire us to believe about human energy and potential that each individual has. The real examples are good tools and powerful guidance that we can apply and take it as lesson- learned.—THAI FEMALE 1

> Asking us to talk about our creative leader was a relevant idea. For my part, it made me realize that even the biggest and most powerful leaders went through darker moments before accomplishing outstanding achievements. If I take the example of Yves Saint Laurent, he managed to be one of the most influent fashion designer of the 20th century despite several faults such as the lack of self confidence and shyness. That's why we have to keep dreaming and believe in our future.—BELGIAN FEMALE 1

> Another best idea from the course is the assignment about favorite leadership. This assignment teaches me to find some a model and study about his biography then you will so surprise that how he can does while normal people cannot do or not thinking about it. My favorite leadership is Benjamin Franklin. After I study his biography, I got many ideas to use in my life. That inspire me to study other Creative person to see how they work, how they think and how they act to be the lessons to use in my life—THAI MALE 9

Another thing I have learned so much during the course is when I studied about my Creative Role Model; Blake Mycoskie. His passionate, creative ideas, and courageous to take a step and think big at the beginning, until his success in both donating and business are really realistic and practical in my view. His business start with less than US$3,000 and his knowledge on shoes business is limited but he believes in himself and do it. It makes me realize to let go of all limited points that I used to block myself from what I want to do. To see how much my role model and other who involve both givers and receivers can gain their happiness in life is amazing and truly motivating.—THAI FEMALE 4

The value of this pedagogical tool is twofold: studying one's favored leader, and learning from the presentations of other learners portraying their favorite leader:

I really appreciate to assist at the different presentation for creative leader. It is very interesting to understand how well known people succeed in their life. I also discover new people such as Jack Ma that has a very interesting profile, starting from nothing and becoming this successful businessman following his own ideas, it was a great example of creative leader. I remember the video that we see about him when he was talking about the different step of the life, what you should do at what age, it learnt a lot from this and I think that I will take it in consideration.—FRENCH MALE 1

What has also been extremely helpful to learn the importance of believing is analyzing the journey of my creative leader, Coco Chanel, and listening my classmates' leaders journeys.—ITALIAN FEMALE 2

The exercise also raised the awareness level of learners who studied and portrayed spiritual creative leaders that the essential contents of the Genius Journey method align with universal tenets of world religions and spiritual schools of thought ("Especially the Leader Role Model, I have studied and compared Genius Journey and Buddha's ways which are in line together."—THAI MALE 5

Genius Notebook

Earlier programs to develop one's genius potential and personal creativity (such as those of Cameron (1992) and Gelb (1998)) suggest learners maintain a personal notebook during a creative leader development program. The Genius Journey program has adopted this practice and asked creative leader candidates to capture their thoughts, ideas, and insights about themselves and the program in their "Genius notebook." Many creative leader candidates expressed their appreciation for this pedagogical tool, as the following two accounts exemplify:

One key thing I will take from this course is also that I enjoy to have a notebook to write down my thoughts. For me it doesn't necessarily have to be on paper, it can also be on the computer though. I find the idea of writing down all my thoughts in itself very intriguing and am certain that this will help me grow substantially.—SYRIAN MALE 1

In the future I will occupy my mind with new ideas and write them down. I did that during the Genius Journey, but also in my spare time to reflect on feelings, situations and ideas that I considered to be worth to rethink again. For me writing down is a strong exercise to really deal with issues and I noticed, once I have written things down for myself, I have a clearer picture about the issue and myself. It made it really easy to open up to other people and talk and discuss about it. Since I recapped situations for myself I felt a strong connection to the truth and strengthen the feeling, who I really am and what is important to me. In that way I feel comfortable in my talks and discussions with other people and it is even easier to explain my thoughts and ideas, without being misunderstood or scrutinized negatively.—GERMAN MALE 2

Peer-to-Peer Experience Sharing

At the beginning of each class session, learners got the opportunity to share how they have applied the genius mindset taught in the previous class and the related home-work from the Genius Exercises at work and in their everyday life (thus completing the previous session's learning cycle of Kolb's (2015) experiential learning model). Overall, most creative leader candidates appreciated the peer-to-peer experience sharing exercise (called "Dare to Share") at the beginning of each session. For example, one learner commented:

> Dare to Share is one of the most important activity that can make our course more easy to understanding. I think this kind of activity create two-way communication environment and I have shared together with create some question during the class."—THAI MALE 5

Apart from learning how different learners have applied the concepts in their environment, "Dare to Share" also allowed to get to know other learners on a deeper, more personal level, as one learner highlighted:

> In terms of interesting experience, the Genius Journey had greatly contributed to get to know other people. Even though I have already had the opportunity to meet those people in other courses, this one helped us to break through social and language barriers. I truly believe that this course helped us to go beyond superficial relationships. The experience-sharing exercises were helpful to go more in-depth in our relationships. I think that sharing personal anecdotes every week enabled us to get a better idea of whom each of us really was. Besides, it gave us an authentic and true preview of each personality. Also, I have learned that I can sometimes be too judgmental as I have become friends with people I didn't expect.—BELGIAN FEMALE 1

Interestingly, some creative leader candidates suggested ideas on how to amplify the relevance of the exercise, for example, by "pushing" more learners to share their experiences:

> Every class had a dare 2 share, which was very good. This concept could be extended by having people speak about certain exercises and what they experienced. Speaking about things, rather than only writing them down, often makes us understand them better. It also takes courage to share personal experiences, meaning that everybody would automatically improve at several fronts (courage and topic he is speaking about). For example students could have shown their power move and explained why it's their power move.—SYRIAN MALE 1

In this context, one learner confides why some learners dared to share more experiences than others, as the exercise forces learners to leave their comfort zone:

> Concerning the most challenging part of the Genius Journey, I felt quite embarrassed to share my experiences and personal histories in front of people I barely knew at the beginning

of the course. In this sense, presenting and defending who was my creative leader was a little bit stressful and challenging for me. I was scared that people didn't care or understand what I wanted to explain. Everything went well in the end and that has confirmed that I could make it despite the doubts I could feel. It has helped me to overcome the fear of speaking in front of a group. I feel now more comfortable when I have to share or defend my ideas.—BELGIAN FEMALE 1

Creative Puzzles

In most sessions, a creative puzzle was given out to the creative leader candidates. While most creative puzzles found in books and magazines have only one or a few fixed solutions, the first author designed these open-ended creative puzzles to invite greater creativity levels by allowing for multiple or even an unlimited number of solutions. Then, the learners had time until the next session to work out their proposed solution, which they had to pitch to the course instructor. One learner commented on the creativity-building value of this approach as follows:

> The creative puzzles are one the best tools that encourage me to think outside the box. They help me to realize that if I keep doing things as the same way or same as the others, I will get the same result, no improvement. Hence, I need to step outside my comfort zone, my cozy box and look at the things at the different perspectives so that I can gain the creative solutions.—THAI FEMALE 9

Buddy Coaching

In our earlier quantitative study (Reis et al. 2018), we found that peer-to-peer coaching and feedback worked well for some but not all of the creative leader candidates. Successful "buddy pairs" seemed to have compatible personalities, learning ambitions, and interests that allowed them to build up the level of trust needed to confide more personal information. For example, one learner shares how well it can work overall:

> The Genius Journey reminds me that we are all human with different tastes and personalities. I will now keep in mind that I can get on well with people who first seem different or even strange to me. A striking example was the exchange of the notebook with my buddy. At the beginning of the course, I directly knew that I would undoubtedly get on well with her. Nevertheless, doing this activity with her strengthen our friendship as we mutually learned funny but also most serious stories about each other. That's why sharing experiences and getting to know people was the most interesting part of the Genius Journey for me.—BELGIAN FEMALE 1

Another learner also emphasized the friendship-building nature of the course program:

> I have known more than 20 new friend from more than 5 country which I am not sure I can find this kind of connection from anywhere. During Genius trip we can have more time to get to know each other better and better.—THAI MALE 5

Stream-of-Consciousness Writing

Cameron (1992) recommended in her individual creativity development program to write "morning pages," which is a stream-of-consciousness writing exercise that helps offload non-conducive thoughts, express feelings of gratitude, and state goals and planned actions for the day, among others. Interestingly, none of the creative leader candidates mentioned this tool, indicated that although the course instructor sees value in the tool, it was not much practiced and liked by the learners. Time limitations are the most likely explanation for this result, as most learners prioritized the weekly homework assignments (Genius Exercises) that led to more direct learnings and concrete applications of the course contents.

Creative Leader Candidates' Personal Takeaways

In our earlier paper (Reis et al. 2020) describing the inner hero's journey of creative leader candidates, we cited vivid examples of the "ultimate boon" (the "reward stage" in Campbell's (1949) monomyth model) that prospective creative leaders received while going through the Genius Journey program in creative leadership. Among others, learners reported the following specific significant takeaways: acquiring knowledge of advanced creative thinking strategies; using the "body-mind" connection to change emotional states; inducing states of flow; and in a few cases, even experiencing a moment of personal breakthrough creativity. In the present study, we present more general comments on the impact of the Genius Journey program on learners.

Some prospective creative leaders commented that the program "has been extremely touching and it had a strong impact on my life" (ITALIAN FEMALE 2), "helped me find out who I really am, what I really want to do and what I want to be in my life which other business courses can't give me" (THAI FEMALE 10), "helped to fight a few demons and to feel better, stronger, and more open—to feel more creative and self-confident." (FRENCH FEMALE 1), and made them do "many things that I have never thought that I will be able to do it." (THAI FEMALE 1) One learner commented on the impact as follows:

> I thoroughly enjoyed the Genius Journey. Knowledge gained from the Genius Journey was beyond expectation. It is much more than learning something for career growth. It was about being able to live a happy life. The dynamics of the Genius Journey are vast, covering and touching on much at all levels (body, mind & soul).—THAI MALE 4

Another learner described her learnings from the Genius Journey program:

> I strongly think that the content of the course is very valuable. It is like a journey that takes me through dreams and treasures I seek elsewhere and then find on my doorstep. I can be a genius, and I can be a creative leader. What I have learned is the essential wisdom of listening to my heart and, above all, following my dreams.—THAI FEMALE 9

Some creative leader candidates rightly perceived that the end of the course program is the beginning of their "real" personal Genius Journey and that they need to continue with their efforts to cultivate the mindsets of creative leaders beyond the program:

In this course, I have learned a lot! During the 12 sessions and the eight weeks of this course, I almost constantly think about the Genius Journey Stops, the exercises, and what we discussed in class. Because to me, this course is not only about "course material"; it is about a way of living your life.—DUTCH FEMALE 1

In the past, I used to think about myself how closed I am, and I do not like this side of my personality. I thought that it is something I cannot change. However, the Genius Journey has proven that what I thought was wrong, and I can actually change myself and my behaviors to be a better person and finally be a creative leader. Nonetheless, this is not the end for me, and I will move forward all the time following the Genius Journey path.—THAI FEMALE 4

5 Discussion, Conclusion, and Future Research Perspectives

Discussion

This study provides practitioners and educators in the domains of innovation, creativity, and leadership development with deeper-level insights into elements of a transformational course methodology and pedagogy needed to develop creative leaders successfully. It casts some light upon why creative leader candidates rated the effectiveness and creativity of both the Genius Journey methodology and the pedagogy as very high in an earlier study (Reis et al. 2018).

In particular, our current study findings:

1. Demonstrate the importance of the different elements of both the course methodology and the pedagogy, which integrate into a "Gestalt" that jointly induce a transformational effect on a prospective creative leader as the course program unfolds over a couple of months.
2. Confirm the effectiveness of many pedagogical tools used by the Genius Journey program to develop creative leaders (creative leader study and portraits, notebook, in-class and homework exercises, open-ended creative puzzles, check-in and -out audits, review toy), and a potential to further evolve others (buddy coaching, open peer-to-peer experience sharing).
3. Indicate that learners make sense of formal definitions and theoretical constructs by personalizing these into more practical interpretations.
4. Suggest that Reis' (2015) Genius Journey model and Kolb's (2008) experiential learning cycle pedagogically align both on a macro-level (overall program) and on a micro-level (session introducing 1–2 destination stops of the Genius Journey).

Conclusion and Implications

This study confirms the findings of our earlier studies (Reis et al. 2018, 2020) that creative leaders can be developed effectively and creatively with a training program that blends a literature-based methodology with an experiential pedagogy that unites to form a Gestalt, a well-designed whole that adds more value than the sum of its parts.

We envision our research to have implications for three groups of stakeholders:

- Innovation educators can gain a more in-depth understanding of how their chosen methodological and pedagogical approaches need to integrate to make a creative leader development program creative, effective, and ultimately transformational. Also, educators can obtain ideas on what other creative pedagogical tools they may add to the general methodological activities of their course programs to augment learning and support the acquisition of creative leader mindsets.
- Human capital development officers will gain a deeper understanding of methodological and pedagogical elements of a creative leader development program from a learner's perspective. This awareness can help separate the wheat from the chaff when selecting both the right creative leadership development program and a competent delivery partner.
- Innovation researchers may gain novel inspirations for future research projects in the niche domains of creative leadership development and innovation education and training.

References

Antes, A. L., & Schuelke, M. J. (2011). Leveraging technology to develop creative leadership capacity. *Advances in Developing Human Resources, 13*, 318–365.

Basadur, M. (2004). Leading others to think innovatively together: Creative leadership. *The Leadership Quarterly, 15*, 103–121.

Branson, R. (1998). *Losing my virginity. The autobiography*. London: Virgin Books.

Cameron, J. (1992). *The Artist's way. A spiritual path to higher creativity*. New York: Penguin Putnam.

Campbell, J. (1949). *The Hero with a thousand faces*. New York: Pantheon Books.

Canton, J. (2007). *The extreme future. The top trends that will reshape the world in the next 20 years*. New York: Plume – Penguin Group.

Feist, G. J. (1999). The influence of personality on artistic and scientific creativity. In R. J. Sternberg (Ed.), *Handbook of creativity*. New York: Cambridge University Press.

Gelb, M. J. (1998). *How to think like Leonardo da Vinci*. New York: Dell Publishing.

Gelb, M. J., & Miller Caldicott, S. (2007). *Innovate like Edison*. New York: Penguin.

Howkins, J. (2001). *The creative economy. How people make money from ideas*. London: Penguin.

Hughes, D. J., et al. (2018). *Leadership, creativity, and innovation: A critical review and practical recommendations*. The Leadership Quarterly.

IBM. (2010). *Capitalizing on complexity. The Global CEO Study 2010*.

IBM. (2011). *Working beyond Borders. The Global Chief Human Resource Officer Study 2011*.

Isaacson, W. (2007). *Albert Einstein: His life and universe*. London: Simon & Schuster.

Isaacson, W. (2011). *Steve jobs: A biography*. New York: Simon & Schuster.

Kolb, D. A. (Ed.). (1984). *Experiential learning: Experience as the source of learning and development*. Prentice-Hall: Englewood Cliffs, NJ.

Kolb, D. A. (2015). *Experiential learning: Experience as the source of learning and development* (2nd ed.). Pearson Education: Hoboken, NJ.

Kolb, A. Y., & Kolb, D. A. (2008). Experiential learning theory: A dynamic, holistic approach to management learning, education and development. In S. J. Armstrong & V. Fukamia (Eds.), *Management learning, education and development* (pp. 41–62). London: Sage.

Puccio, G. G., et al. (2011). *Creative leadership. Skills that drive change.* Thousand Oaks, CA: Sage.

Ray, M., & Myers, R. (1986). *Creativity in business.* New York: Broadway Books.

Reis, D. (2015) *Genius journey: Developing genuine creative leaders for the innovation economy.* XXVI ISPIM innovation conference. Budapest, Hungary, 14–17 June, 2015.

Reis, D. (2017). *Creatively teaching creative leadership: Course design, methodology, and pedagogy.* 2017 ISPIM innovation forum. Toronto.

Reis, D. (2020). *The Executive's guide to innovation.* Highlands Ranch, CO: Authors' Place Press.

Reis, D. (2022, forthcoming). *Genius journey: Developing authentic creative leaders for the innovation economy.* Parts 1-2. Highlands Ranch, CO: Authors' Place Press.

Reis, D., & Hunt, B. (2017). *Training businesspeople in structured innovation: Tracking down long-term impacts.* XXVIII ISPIM Innovation Conference. Vienna, Austria.

Reis, D., Hunt, B., & Parisot, X. (2018). *Creatively developing creative leaders: Learner's feedback on methodology and pedagogy.* XXIX ISPIM Innovation Conference. Stockholm.

Reis, D., Hunt, B., & Parisot, X. (2020). *Creatively developing creative leaders: Revealing the inner Hero's journey.* ISPIM connects Bangkok innovation conference. Bangkok.

Sternberg, R. J. (Ed.). (1999). *Handbook of creativity.* New York: Cambridge University Press.

Sternberg, R. J., Kaufman, J. C., & Pretz, J. E. (2004). A propulsion model of creative leadership. *Creativity and Innovation Management, 13*, 145–153.

Van Velsor, E., Mccauley, C. D., & Ruderman, M. M. (Eds.). (2010). *The center for creative leadership development handbook of leadership development.* San Francisco: Wiley.

Von Stamm, B. (2017). Innovation: A necessity, not nicety. In R. Elkington (Ed.), *Visionary leadership in a turbulent world: Thriving in the new VUCA context.* Bingley: Emerald.

Williams, F., & Foti, R. J. (2011). Formally developing creative leadership as a driver of organizational innovation. *Advances in Developing Human Resources, 13*, 279–296.

World Economic Forum. (2015). *The global competitiveness report 2015–2016.* Geneva: World Economic Forum.

Detlef Reis is the Founder and Chief Ideator of the innovation know-how company Thinkergy (www.thinkergy.com). He is the creator of four proprietary innovation methods marketed by Thinkergy: The innovation process method and toolbox X-IDEA; the innovation people profiling method TIPS; the innovation culture transformation method CooL—Creativity UnLimited; and the creative leadership development method Genius Journey. Dr. Reis is also an Adjunct Associate Professor at Hong Kong Baptist University and served as a faculty at two universities in Thailand (The Institute for Knowledge and Innovation, South-East Asia, Bangkok University, and the College of Management, Mahidol University).

Brian Hunt In an academic career spanning more than three decades in several continents and cultures, Dr. Brian Hunt has worked in multinational corporations (MNCs) and academic institutions of international repute. Now retired, Brian devotes part of his time to academic research. His areas of enquiry include processes of teaching and learning in the fields of creativity, education theory and practice, and strategies for organizational development. Brian has published books and academic journal articles on business and management topics, and presented at international conferences.

An Integrated Approach to Digital Implementation: TOSC-Model and DPSEC-Circle

Daniel R. A. Schallmo and Christopher A. Williams

1 Introduction

Nowadays, digital strategy development is similar to the digital transformation of business models, an integral part of a company's activities. Although digital strategies and digitally transformed business models exist, some companies still face the challenge of executing them systematically.

A study published in Forbes found that 70% of all digital implementation initiatives will fail to reach their goals (Zobell 2018). Reasons for these failures include lacking a clear digital strategy, not integrating employees, failing to include customer orientation, not considering employees' concerns, lacking a suitable culture, maintaining inefficient system records, and having inadequate capabilities (see: Rossello-Mora and Sutcliffe 2019; Sun 2019; Zobell 2018; Tabrizi et al. 2019). Companies also seldom have clarity on how to prioritize running and planned digital initiatives.

We conducted a literature review of existing theoretical approaches. The main findings reveal that the existing theories on digital implementation are insufficient, and, to the best of our knowledge, an integrative digital implementation approach does not exist in the current literature. Within our contribution, we will develop an integrated approach to digital implementation.

D. R. A. Schallmo (✉) · C. A. Williams
Neu-Ulm University of Applied Sciences, Neu-Ulm, Germany
e-mail: daniel.schallmo@hnu.de

2   Theoretical Background

Based on existing approaches, we place digital implementation along with the
following essential aspects of strategic-level digitalization: digital strategy and
digital transformation of business models and the environment in the digital context.
This classification is shown in Fig. 1.

The term "digital strategy" is defined as follows:

> ...the strategic form of digitization intentions of companies. The short- and mid-term
> objectives are to create new or to maintain competitive advantages. Within the digital
> strategy, digital technologies and methods are applied to products, services, processes, and
> business models. To develop a digital strategy, the company and its environment have to be
> analyzed as a basis for several future scenarios. The digital strategy consists of a vision,
> mission, strategic objectives, strategic success factors, values, and measures (Schallmo et al.
> 2019; see also: Bharadwaj et al. 2013; Fraunhofer IAO 2016; Hille et al. 2016; Rauser 2016).

We use Schallmo et al. (2017) definition for digital transformation of business
models as:

> [concerning] itself with individual business model elements, the entire business model, value
> chains, and the networking of different actors in a value network. The digital transformation
> serves to more clearly define the digital strategy within business models. It is based on an
> approach with a sequence of tasks and decisions that are logically and temporally related to
> each other (2017; see also: Bowersox et al. 2005; Westerman et al. 2012; Mazzone 2014;
> PwC 2013; Bouee and Schaible 2015).

Digital implementation realizes a company's digital strategy and supports the
digital transformation of one or several business models. The following areas are
relevant for digital implementation (Schallmo et al. 2019): technology, organization,
skills, and culture.

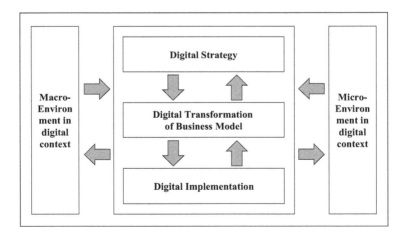

Fig. 1 Classification in the context of Digitization (Schallmo 2019)

The environment in the digital context is oriented toward the macro- and micro-environment of companies. The macro-environment includes the following dimensions: political, economic, sociocultural, technological, ecological, and legal. The micro-environment includes the following dimensions: potential new entrants, rivalry among competitors, substitution of products and services, bargaining power of customers, and bargaining power of suppliers. Naturally, the general business environment plays a role in strategic analysis and business model innovation. However, the "environment" in a digital context considers the influence of the respective dimensions from the perspective of digitization (Schallmo et al. 2019).

3   Research Questions and Research Design

Research Questions

Several existing approaches have advanced our knowledge of digital strategy and transformation. However, they do not address digital implementation as a logical consequence and do not include an integrated approach.

Based on the problem described and our current understanding, we will answer the following main research questions:

- Which theoretical approaches exist for digital implementation?
- What is the main content of digital implementation, and what are the most important dimensions?
- What does an integrated approach to digital implementation look like?

Research Design

We conducted a literature review to gain insight into existing approaches for the development of digital implementation practices. Within this literature review, we analyzed the Leavitt's System Model (1965) as a basis for organizational change. We also analyzed five approaches of a digital strategy that include a step for the implementation of the digital strategy. Based on this, we developed an integrated approach to digital implementation.

4   Literature Review on Existing Approaches

The digital implementation has a significant relationship to the change of organizations; therefore, we considered Leavitt's System Model that is also known as Leavitt's diamond model (Leavitt 1965). It is seen as an integrated model to organizational change management. According to Leavitt, a change in any component of a system (=organization), the impact on other components should be evaluated and the proper balance should be found.

The four main components of an organization are:

- Structure: Grouping of individuals and teams in and organization—hierarchical structure, relationships, communication patterns, and coordination.
- Technology: Tools that are applied to fulfill the tasks.
- People: Skills, attitudes, and behaviors in the workforce.
- Tasks: Individuals and teams fulfill tasks.

Kraewing's (2017) digital strategy approach targeted internationally active executives in medium-sized companies with an increased interest in digital transformation. The last step of Kraewing's approach is the implementation of the strategy with an individual implementation of the strategic objectives and continuous improvement. He also considers relevant phases of transformation within a change-management model. In the implementation phase, the following three methods are considered: (1) scrum as an agile project management method with fixed cycles (sprints), (2) digital value creation with an overview of the value-added potential of the digital as a product, and (3) A checklist of all major actions and issues for the implementation of digital strategy.

Greiner et al. (2017) developed an approach for digital strategy (here also digitization strategy) that is based on theoretical findings and consulting experiences. The last step of his is the action plan for digital actions, which includes options for concrete measures through a prioritization process. The approach includes two methods in this phase: (1) Balanced Scorecard and (2) economic efficiency calculation with the comparison of expenses and income of the strategic measure.

Rauser (2016) designed his approach to the digital strategy based on experiences from consulting several companies. He considers the implementation in achievable steps as the last phase of his approach. The following methods and characteristics are mentioned: (1) agile project management, (2) iterative process, (3) UX process for obtaining user experience feedback, (4) KPI map as a representation of individual digital activities and their influence on defined corporate goals, and (5) lead nurturing funnel as an overview of the different sales initiatives of the request to purchase decision.

Petry (2016) formulated an approach that is aimed at executives who want to explore the implications of digitization in the context of business and people leadership. He considers the strategy implementation as the last step and includes the following methods: (1) Lean-Startup, (2) Scrum, and (3) participatory workshops and two speed IT as a modular and flexible IT architecture.

The basis of Cordon's et al. (2016) approach is a theoretical research based on existing models (classical and more modern strategic approaches), augmented by studies and practical examples. Digital strategy (here also digital strategy) focuses on the use of Big data and in the last phase, the implementation of the strategy or business model is conducted with the Lean Startup method.

As the review illustrates, the existing approaches address single methods and characteristics for the digital implementation. An integrative digital implementation approach does not exist.

5   Integrated Approach to Digital Implementation

Based on our research, including the review of existing approaches, we now present an integrated approach to digital implementation. The approach consists of four main dimensions that are represented in our TOSC-Model and in our DPSEC-Circle with five phases.

TOSC-Model

The TOSC-Model represents the most relevant dimensions of the digital implementation (Schallmo et al. 2019):

- Technology: For example, use of sensors, creation of databases, networking of components.
- Organization: For example, definition of structures and responsibilities, establishment of departments, definition of processes.
- Skills: For example, IT know-how (hardware, software application/development, etc.), use of collaboration tools, development of leadership and collaboration skills, acquisition of methods.
- Culture: For example, cultural anchoring in the company, sensitization of employees, communication within the company.

These dimensions interact with each other, are dependent and therefore influence each other. They support the achievement of the digital strategies goals and contribute to the operational excellence, customer experience, and digital excellence as shown in Fig. 2.

DPSEC-Circle

The integrated approach for the digital implementation is also based on a procedure model with the following five phases that are iterative and shown in Fig. 3.

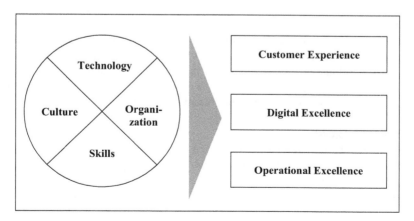

Fig. 2 TOSC Model and Influence

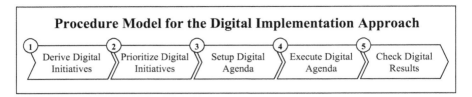

Fig. 3 Procedure model for the digital implementation approach

The five phases of the procedure model will be explained in the following section.

Derive Digital Initiatives
Within this phase, digital initiatives are derived, mainly based on the following sources. The first is the company's analysis (Rauser 2016; Hille et al. 2016; Kraewing 2017; Greiner et al. 2017) across the relevant areas (e.g., organization, processes, IT, infrastructure, systems, technologies, capabilities, and existing initiatives) and digital maturity analysis. Ideally, these analyses are conducted in the context of digital strategy development and the defined digital strategy with projects and measures (Rauser 2016; Peppard and Ward 2016; Petry 2016; Cordon et al. 2016; Kraewing 2017). The second is the digitally transformed business model, which is based on best practices, digital transformation enablers, the digital value network, and digital customer experiences. The derived digital initiatives are assigned to the categories of the TOSC Model with technology, organization, skills, and culture (Schallmo et al. 2019).

Prioritize Digital Initiatives
The derived and categorized digital initiatives are then evaluated in terms of their impact, time, cost, and so on. They are also included in an influential matrix to measure their mutual influence. The result is an active and passive sum of each digital initiative revealing its influence on (active sum) and by other initiatives (passive sum) (Vester and Hesler 1980). Then they are included in a digital initiative matrix with four categories: (1) slow digital initiatives, (2) active digital initiatives with a prime influence, (3) passive digital initiatives, being highly influenced, and (4) critical digital initiatives with. Thus, it is possible to prioritize the derived digital initiatives, and to focus on the most important and immediate.

Setup Digital Agenda
The prioritized digital initiatives are included in a visual tool, the digital agenda. The digital initiatives are accompanied by two important propositions: change and communication management (esp. internal communication), which includes the purpose definition applying the "why, how, what" principle (Sinek 2009; Cameron et al. 2014). In addition, the digital initiatives are described in detail, including

responsibilities, timeframes, key performance indicators, objectives, resources, actions, and a budget.

Execute Digital Agenda

Within this phase, the digital agenda is executed. This means that all the digital initiatives are implemented properly, applying agile methods (e.g., Scrum and Lean). Also, the implementation of digital initiatives is checked and adjusted if necessary. In addition, the influence on customer experiences, operational excellence, and digital excellence is measured. Additionally, the defined digital strategy and the digitally transformed business model should be considered regarding the measurement of the influence.

Check Digital Results

The last phase is to check the digital results within the three main categories customer experience, digital excellence, and operational excellence. Thus, the previously defined objectives of the phase 3 setup digital agenda are relevant. The deviation is identified, and the actions, objectives, and so on are adjusted. The checked/reviewed digital results are executed permanently while still allowing for adjustments throughout the process.

The described phases are iterative and part of the integrated approach and included into the DPSEC-Circle for digital implementation, which is shown in Fig. 4.

6   Contribution

This research summarizes existing approaches to digital implementation. Based on this, we deliver an integrated approach for how to successfully implement a digital strategy and a digitally transformed business model. The integrated approach consists of the TOSC-Model and of the DPSEC-Circle with five phases: derive digital initiatives, prioritize digital initiatives, set up a digital agenda, execute a digital agenda, and check/review digital results. This closes an existing research gap regarding digital implementation.

7   Practical Implications

Senior managers and business developers will gain an integrated approach to digital implementation, digital initiatives from the digital strategy, and the digital transformation of their business model. The integrated approach enables companies to take advantage of implementing their digital strategy; companies can optimize their current business and create a distinct competitive advantage.

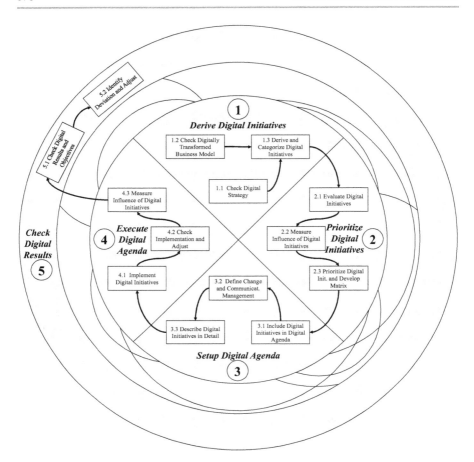

Fig. 4 DPSEC-Circle for digital implementation

---

8   Limitations

The aim of this chapter was to report our research results on existing approaches to digital implementation. The reader should bear in mind that due to theoretical constraints; the results may not be generalizable. Furthermore, some aspects (e.g., validation by practitioners) need to be further investigated. Therefore, conducting further interviews with practitioners, to validate our integrated approach is recommended.

9 Recommendations for Further Research

Further research on the needs of practitioners would be worthwhile. For example, it would be interesting to create a knowledge building community where researchers and practitioners can exchange needs and experiences across several countries and industries. Another possible area of future research would be to test our approach to digital implementation with practitioners and to analyze case studies. Lastly, future studies need to demonstrate quantifiable benefits of digital implementation.

References

Bharadwaj, A., El Sawy, O., Pavlou, P., & Venkatraman, N. (2013). Digital business strategy: Toward a next generation of insights. *MIS Quarterly, 37*, 471–482.

Bouee, C. E., & Schaible, S. (2015). Die Digitale Transformation der Industrie. *Roland Berger Strategy Consultans und Bundesverband der Deutschen Industrie eV, Berlin, 46*, 78.

Bowersox, D. J., Closs, D. J., & Drayer, R. W. (2005). The digital transformation: Technology and beyond. *Supply Chain Management Review, 9*(1), 22–29.

Cameron, K. S., Quinn, R. E., DeGraff, J., & Thakor, A. V. (2014). *Competing values leadership.* Cheltenham: Edward Elgar Publishing.

Cordon, C., Garcia-Milà, P., Ferreiro Vilarino, T., & Caballero, P. (2016). *Strategy is digital: How companies can use big data in the value chain.* Cham: Springer.

Fraunhofer, I. A. O. (2016). *Lightweight robots in manual assembly-best to start simply.* Technical report.

Greiner, O., Riepl, P., & Kittelberger, D. (2017). Die digitale Strategie – der Wegweiser zur systematischen Digitalisierung des Unternehmens. In M. Kieninger (Ed.), Digitalisie-rung der Unternehmenssteuerung: Prozessautomatisierung, Business Analytics, Big Data, SAP S/4HANA, Anwendungsbeispiele (pp. 19–32). Stuttgart: Schäffer-Poeschel.

Hille, M., Janata, S., & Michel, J. (2016). *Digitalisierungsleitfaden: Ein Kompendium für Entscheider im Mittelstand im Auftrag der QSC AG.* Kassel: Compendium.

Kraewing, M. (2017). *Digital Business Strategie für den Mittelstand: Entwicklung und Konzeption mit internationaler Ausrichtung.* Freiburg: Haufe.

Leavitt, H. (1965). Applied organizational change in industry: Structural, technological and humanistic approaches. In J. March (Ed.), *Handbook of organizations* (pp. 1144–1170). Chicago, IL: Rand McNally.

Mazzone, D. M. (2014). *Digital or death: Digital transformation: The only choice for business to survive smash and conquer.* Smashbox Consulting.

Peppard, J., & Ward, J. (2016). *The strategic management of information systems: Building a digital strategy.* New York: Wiley.

Petry, T. (2016). *Digital Leadership: Erfolgreiches Führen in Zeiten der Digital Economy.* München: Haufe.

PwC. (2013). *Digitale Transformation – der größte Wandel seit der industriellen Revolution.* Frankfurt: PwC.

Rauser, A. (2016). *Digital strategy: A guide to digital business transformation.* North Charleston: CreateSpace Independent Publishing Platform.

Rossello-Mora, R., & Sutcliffe, I. C. (2019). *Reflections on the introduction of the digital protologue database – a partial success.*

Schallmo, D. R. (2019). *A. Jetzt digital transformieren* (2nd ed.). Wiesbaden: Springer International.

Schallmo, D. R., Williams, C. A., & Boardman, L. (2017). Digital transformation of business models. *International Journal of Innovation Management, 21*(08).

Schallmo, D. R., Williams, C. A., & Lohse, J. (2019). Digital strategy – Integrated approach and generic options. *International Journal of Innovation Management, 23*(08).

Sinek, S. (2009). *Start with why: How great leaders inspire everyone to take action*. London: Penguin.

Sun, M. (2019). Businesses predict digital transformation to be biggest risk factor in 2019. *Wall Street Journal*.

Tabrizi, B., Lam, E., Girard, K., & Irvin, V. (2019). Digital transformation is not about technology. *Harvard Business Review, 13*.

Vester, F., & Hesler A. (1980). *Sensitivitätsmodell/Sensitivity Model*. Frankfurt am Main: Regionale Planungsgemeinschaft Untermain.

Westerman, G., Tannou, M., Bonnet, D., Ferraris, P., & McAfee, A. (2012). The digital advantage: How digital leaders outperform their peers in every industry. *MIT Sloan Management and Capgemini Consulting, MA, 2*, 2–23.

Zobell, S. (2018). *Why digital transformations fail: Closing the $900 billion hole in Enterprise strategy*.

Daniel R. A. Schallmo is an economist, management consultant, lecturer, and author. He is a professor for digital transformation and entrepreneurship at the Neu-Ulm University of Applied Science, director of the Institute for Entrepreneurship, and member of the Institute for Digital Transformation. His research focuses on digitalization (digital maturity, digital strategy, digital transformation of business models, and digital implementation) and the development and application of methods to the innovation of business models, mainly in business-to-business markets. He is the author of numerous publications (10+ books, 20+ articles) and speaker (100+ speeches; 7000+ participants). He is a member of various research societies and a reviewer.

Christopher A. Williams is a strategic management researcher, consultant, and author. He is currently completing his PhD in the field of Innovation Management at Johannes Kepler University Linz. He holds a BA in Communication, an MBA in General Management, and a MA in Learning, Technology and Education, University of Nottingham. His research focuses on strategic management topics, learning and instruction, human resources management, and corporate communication. He brings this practical experience and hard won insights to bear when consulting companies in the development and implementation of new digital maturity models, corporate communication strategies, and blended learning educational programs.

Challenges, Lessons and Methods for Developing Values-Based Intrapreneurial Culture

Jakub Kruszelnicki and Henning Breuer

1   Introduction

Innovation management is developing from a specialized discipline to an ongoing challenge for organizational development and human resource departments. Instead of pursuing isolated innovations, more and more organizations seek to grow innovators and to establish an innovation culture based on motivating values and entrepreneurial opportunities for employees. Fostering intrapreneurship, i.e. entrepreneurship from within the organization, is one widespread approach to bring about such cultural changes in a bottom-up manner (Ahuja 2019).

Innovators often tend to favour ideas and creativity over systematic management processes but sourcing creativity from inside of the company as a long-term activity requires manageable processes and structures. One way of connecting both perspectives is introducing an incremental investing process, based on different milestones for validating market results and Minimal Viable Product—MVP progress. Here, structured intrapreneurship programmes enhance the innovator experience, foster digital transformation skills and open up organizations to adopt new ideas. This approach allows screening of more potential innovations in a relatively short time using few resources.

Self-efficacy, appreciation of their meaningful work and the "fame" in the company or the image as an innovator-expert are sometimes stronger motivators than a cash reward (Kruszelnicki 2019). As a direct response, the emerging discipline of employer branding applies the reputation of an organization to attract a

J. Kruszelnicki (✉)
Creative Labs sp. z o.o. ul, Cracow, Poland
e-mail: kuba.kruszelnicki@wearecreativelabs.com

H. Breuer
UXBerlin Innovation Consulting and HMKW University of Applied Sciences for Media, Communication and Management, Berlin, Germany
e-mail: h.breuer@hmkw.de

qualified workforce through promotion of trust, inclusiveness and openness for new ideas. Personal values of employees that for long were expected stay "in the parking lot" (Pearce 2019) outside of the company, assume a pivotal role to attract, motivate and engage intrapreneurs, and to drive innovation that matters (Breuer and Lüdeke-Freund 2017). Following the values-based innovation framework (Breuer and Lüdeke-Freund 2017), we assume that successful intrapreneurship programmes should actively work with notions of the desirable (i.e. values) on behalf of different stakeholders (different departments, top management, employees) in the organization. In particular, we attend to the ways that new, intrapreneurship-related values such as mutual trust are introduced by the programme, and how values of employees are systematically taken into account. Finally, we seek to identify some of the challenges that result from the attempts to facilitate intrapreneurship, to overcome organizational inertia, and to deal with potential conflicts (Tiku 2019) once values are released to the stages of innovation.

In this chapter, we explore some examples of challenges, lessons and methods for developing values-based intrapreneurial culture through case studies based on expert interviews. This review of cases and factors of success or failure will be relevant for innovation managers, who want to foster intrapreneurship in their organization or seek ready to implement methodological solutions. It will also provide references for researchers investigating different intrapreneurship approaches. Insights, gained from the literature and expert interviews on inside-out innovation, and a reflection of our own experiences with values-based and employee-led innovation (Birkinshaw and Duke 2013), allow us to identify gaps of knowledge, and to formulate questions for empirical research.

With this review, we help to realign personal values of employees with the overarching normative statements of organizations. We seek new ways to turn breaking boundaries between personal notions of the desirable and corporate practises from a source of conflict into a resource for innovation, redesigning a new landscape of challenges and opportunities together with HR and innovation professionals.

2   A Brief Review of Intrapreneurship and the Adobe Kickbox Approach

Intrapreneurship as a concept was introduced by Gifford Pinchot (Pinchot 1985; Pinchot and Pinchot 1978) in 1978. The intrapreneur takes direct responsibility within a large corporation for turning an idea into a profitable product, service or business model through assertive risk-taking and innovation (Krippendorff 2019).

The popularization of the term was accompanied by several changes in its understanding. In particular, the digitalization of entrepreneurial tools and adoption of the lean start-up approach (Ries 2011) through large organizations have expanded the outreach of intrapreneurial programmes and made them accessible for regular employees. Using both approaches as building blocks, Mark Randall (Randall 2015), Innovation Director at Adobe, has initiated a pan-corporate intrapreneurship movement called Kickbox (Kickbox 2019), which has evolved through the Creative Commons community (Kickbook 2020) and led to different adaptations like Swisscom Kickbook, The Rabobank InnovAid Blackbox (Innovaid 2020) or the Creative Labs STARTBOX (Creative Labs 2020). This intrapreneurship programme in a box has inspired global corporations to experiment with the innovative ideas of their employees and to establish an innovation culture based on trust. The programme offers an individual, gamified entrepreneurship path for any employee that considers oneself entrepreneurial or innovative. In this sense, Kickbox is inclusive and scalable to any number of beneficiaries. It embeds self-directed learning exercises and includes a direct cash budget without the necessity to report any costs or advances. This radically independent and "bottom-up" approach gave the programme very good results in Adobe and created a global benchmark also in terms of values-driven transformation. The main value that has been introduced via this programme is trust in undiscovered skills of all the employees in the company. The unlocking of innovation potential from inside-out has to reflect the start-up reality, where every author of the idea is responsible for managing the budget and learning new skills on his/her way to validate the idea. There is no previous approval of the ideas that come into the pipeline, the verification is done via persistence of the author and market pull of the idea. The hierarchical approach and silos driven corporate structure is disrupted by a trust driven, multidisciplinary approach. This analysis of the expert interviews and case studies will explore lessons learned from this approach.

3　Case Studies

We investigate kickbox-derived intrapreneurship programmes, and explore challenges, factors of success or failures, methodological approaches and experiences in dealing with them based on semi-structured expert interviews at three large corporations. All three have used initial Adobe Kickbox approach and two of them belong to the open-source community kickbox.org. We also draw from our own experiences in the creation, implementation and utilization of self-explanatory facilitation tools to foster values-based intrapreneurship. In this first attempt of case studies, we have interviewed three programme implementation leaders from three different European countries: Sjoerd Peters, Innovation Manager and Moonshot Campaign Manager at Rabobank from the Netherlands, Carlos Alvarez-Iglesias, Founder and CEO of Knowledge Investors that implemented kickbox programme in Abanca from Spain, and David Hengartner, Co-Founder and CEO at GETKICKBOX.COM powered by Swisscom Digital from Switzerland.

4   Abanca: Adobe Kickbox—Implementation by External Consulting Company

The first case is linked to the most classical Adobe Kickbox "ready-to-use" framework implemented in 2018/2019 by external consultants in the Spanish banking sector company Abanca. The collaboration lasted two editions and achieved full knowledge transfer into the company which nowadays implements continuously this programme internally by its Innovation Department. Its ideas pipeline starts with 200 applications, out of which 25 get to the first (ideation and market validation) phase and around two ideas per edition get funded by the company with seed capital. The initial budget of each intrapreneur is only coaching and 500 EUR per idea validation, nevertheless, the programme caused a huge enthusiasm among the participants. The additional novelty in the Abanca approach was opening the programme also for five ideas coming from local university graduates—external input that helped Abanca open a new dialogue with future employees.

The Abanca Innova (Abanca 2020a) programme allowed growth and influence of Innovation Department. The innovation consciousness of the employees allowed more effective work for them as well as sourcing new talent from the baccalaureates of the intrapreneurship programme.

5   Rabobank: InnovAid Campaign—Implementation by Internal Innovation Department

Rabobank—InnovAid training—implementation by the innovation department. Our second case study describes a "tailor-made" approach done by the innovation team, which 5 years ago has adapted the Adobe Kickbox approach and moulded it into an Intrapreneurship training/programme including the InnovAid Blackbox (Innovaid 2020). Since then it evolved into an intrapreneurship acceleration program named Moonshot, from the editions aiming every business possible, to defined scope of employees' ideas related with Rabobank business up to defined scope open for any participant including outside of company ideas by innovators. It consists of the following key components: action-oriented workshops, online learning environment, innovation training and personalized coaching. At the end of every course, a Pitch-day event takes place where all participants pitch their idea and learnings. Apart from the entrepreneur fast track within the organizational structure, the participants of the programme can access quality resources put into their disposition such as free training, toolkit with Lean Startup and Design thinking exercises, innovators mindset 1:1 coaching, time for experiments during the working hours, and 500 euros for experiments, pitching to business unit leads and an Innovators Diploma. The InnovAid training including the Blackbox is also embedded in the Rabobank Moonshot campaign (Rabobank 2020). In this ideation and acceleration programme, Rabobank gives all employees worldwide the opportunity to come up with radical ideas. The 20 best ideas from over the world will follow the InnovAid programme to validate and substantiate the idea based on data. On Pitch Day at HQ in Utrecht, the best ideas will be selected for a customized accelerator programme and try to get to the market. Per edition about 200 qualitative ideas are submitted, a Top20 will follow the InnovAid programme, three to eight ideas will go through the Accelerator programme. Results after 4 editions (2015–2018): 14 ideas and teams were selected for the Accelerator programme. Six of them (43%) reached market fit and are scaling today; two ideas (14%) were adopted by the relevant business line and were further taken up there; one idea (7%) product waits until the right time arrives for Rabobank; two ideas (14%) were successfully invalidated within the Accelerator programme and three ideas (21%) did not make solution or market fit. InnovAid has over 2000 graduates.

6   Swisscom–Kickbook–Kickbox Adaptation that Became a Spin-off

The third case study is showing the highly visible implementation of Adobe Kickbox method in Europe. Initially, the Kickbox Adobe scheme was used in order to pilot and validate this approach in Swisscom environment, however, it have quickly evolved into a tailor-made Kickbook methodology that was adapted to the internal structure of the company and the lessons learnt during this process. This transformation was implemented under the direct supervision of Mark Randall—the original inventor of the box approach at Adobe. It has started in 2015 as a 5 ideas pilot but immediately expanded to 50 ideas. Now, it counts over 500 graduates of the Kickbook intrapreneurship programme. Development of 120 ideas has been funded, and 15 products are currently under development. Via the Kickbox approach, Swisscom have managed to get to a pipeline that constantly grows by incorporating new corporate clients into the portfolio.

One and a half years ago after showing the results on different events, Swisscom started to get questions from external clients asking for support in implementing the Kickbox approach. They started to run pilots with their own versions of the methodology collaborating with five corporate early adopters and creating five running products. Since 2019 Swisscom started to implement and automate the process so it could suit any external client. Now they can say that 70 clients are using the Kickbook intrapreneurship programme. The authors are still hosted by Innovation team in Swisscom but there is a potential for Kickbook to become a spin-out of the mother company.

All three of our case studies are connected with a similar initial approach but very different angles of implementations and versatile outcomes. We can see the variations not only in methodology, which evolves moulding into company necessities and needs, but also the cultural fit of the programme in some it is a first ignition towards innovation, in others it is an additional component of mature innovation department's portfolio. For this reason, we decided to focus our analysis on motivations, key results, organizational influence and innovation values-based cultural transformation.

7   Motivations and the Initial Approach

To look for favourable conditions for initiating intrapreneurship we first focus on the context of the organization. The motivation to engage in intrapreneurship often stems from radical changes in the overall sector and the possible threats to the company and its business model. In the first two cases of Abanca and Rabobank, the wider context of banking sector is key. The constant disruption of the traditional services by fintech trends and start-up community forces banks to reinvent themselves and respond to this potential threat. The following popular quote reflects the state of the art in this sector:

> Clients do not need banks anymore; they need banking solutions (S. Peters, reference in personal communication, March 3, 2020).

A request emerged from the Board of Directors, concretely from the Head of Innovation Department with strong support of the Human Resources Department. The reason was to strengthen the personal development path of Abanca employees and at the same time source new business ideas from within the company. At the same time, the company decided to prepare and launch the external accelerator programme for Start-Ups. The Intrapreneurship perspective seemed to be the right approach to complete this vision from inside of the organization.

Just as with other banks, innovation is high on the agenda at Rabobank since the traditional revenue model is under pressure. At the same time, customer service must be improved since bank customers get used to advanced customer experience of companies such as Coolblue and Uber and expect similar experiences from their bank. Finally, banks seek sustainable business models, because new parties (e.g. FinTech start-ups like Revolut) add pressure to the market shares and revenue models of traditional banks. One way to foster innovation is to enable employees with the support of the Moonshot and InnovAid programmes. In the case of Rabobank, the aim was to introduce the innovation culture to the company on wide level offering participation to employees from all the locations and disrupting the departments' usual scope of work by creating interdisciplinary teams enabling cross-polinization of organization as a whole.

Swisscom is a different case from the telecommunications sector, in which competition has been driven by innovation for several years already. Swisscom's intrapreneurship approach emerges from Corporate Venturing activities and is focused on open innovation ecosystem building. Initially, Kickbox was a one-man experiment testing internally its radical bottom-up approach. It suited perfectly Swisscom's data-driven mindset derived from telecom industry open for market validations via experiments online. Nevertheless, after first implementation the programme discovered good projects with market potential and achieved cultural transformation. Those two factors opened a fast track for this approach and helped to acquire a bigger budget and team expansion. Since it became an official innovation department task, Swisscom started to professionalize this process and made its own version. The major milestone was a software that helped to run this Kickbox and to make it an automatized service for all employees. In this case, we see the Kickbox expansion as a natural bottom-up process, which seems to be the first intrapreneurial project itself. This proves the maturity of the company in the sense of innovation values that embed it. The philosophy and the mindset promoted by the programme had to be put in practice from the bottom-up perspective of one employee initiative. Key, values-based directives driving the programme are expressed by key sentences of the campaign like:

- "Stop playing HIPPO"—detaching from the Highest Paid Person in Organisation opinion and stick to data-driven validation.
- "No BLA, just do!"—practice-oriented self-education.
- "I'm the CEO of my idea"—the openness of the company for new ideas and the flexibility to validate them.
- "Life's a Pitch"—constant communication about the idea and the constant validation.
- "Better ask for forgiveness than to ask for permission"—showing the goal-oriented mentality disrupting the corporate frameworks and rules.

Therefore, the strategic fit of the programme should be aligned with the initial strategy of the company and aim to key areas (markets, technologies and business models) to create synergies. Here, intrapreneurship creates inclusive collaboration with all the business units.

8 Intrapreneurs Success Stories

Generally, not more than 10% of the participants of intrapreneurship programme make it to the end and get funded by the company. The number can be increased by direct involvement of the Board of Directors as supporting profiles, negotiating with supervisors or managers of the participants and the flexibility of the entire company. Without "top-down" communication and approval, there is no possibility of creating a company-wide intrapreneurship movement. It is also important to keep motivating the authors of the ideas to work proactively without fear of losing their initial position or being moved lower if the innovative idea fails the final tests. The entire company has to accept and adopt the rules of the programme. Incorporating flexibility in corporate structures where hierarchical interdependencies are not static and the margin to reinvent their own scope of work is foreseen as something natural. Nevertheless, it is important to emphasize the fruitful implementations of the whole value chain.

> We are enablers but the more independent approach of intrapreneurs the better. We never overcoach, we intervene only when its needed (D. Hengartner personal communication, March 30, 2020).

In Rabobank, apart from the Innovation Department, Innovation Factory all the company needs to be aligned with the goals of the programme and support its implementation from different department's points of view. It is important to launch the call via direct messages from the CEO and other Board Members and to disseminate it by all internal channels. This demonstrates the innovation-oriented company motivation during the intrapreneurship experiment and shows its importance. Previous intrapreneurs should encourage new candidates with new ideas to join the programme by showing their success stories. Essential component of this goal is promoting the outcomes of the previous Moonshot editions. Among others that build the company intrapreneurs portfolio, we can find such cases as MOOVEMENT (Moovement 2020), an app that monitors cattle, PEAKS (Peaks 2020)—an investing bot assistant for smartphones and SUREPAY (Surepay 2020)—which secures payments. Each physical location of the office needs an ambassador of the programme who would encourage local colleagues to join. Each business line manager has to define the scope of ideas that might be suitable for their business unit development (in line with "innovation thesis" areas). The dissemination of the best practices through all the company serves to break the silos management structure and make all the workers aware of the challenges that the company is facing in terms of innovation. It also promotes the intrapreneur role models that characterize work colleagues that were able to go out of their comfort zones and think wider than their everyday competence-based tasks.

We need entrepreneurs to dive into the unknown (S. Peters, personal communication, March 3, 2020).

In Abanca, the travel insurance service (Abanca 2020b) exemplifies the new services created, tested and scaled during Kickbox programme that have managed to successfully integrate as a new product in the Abanca portfolio.

It is a way to reinvent yourself as an employee, by waking the restlessness in creating something new. It's a new canal to generate this restlessness to influence radical change in corporate structure (C. Alvarez-Iglesias, personal communication, March 25, 2020).

In Swisscom, the intrapreneurial value chain filters the ideas and the innovators' motivations via Kickbook programme as initial validation phase. The Kickbook exercise filters the wide batch of ideas into market validated business model assumptions worth pursuing. The six-stage lean ideation and validation process verifies not only ideas but also the overall entrepreneurship capacity of their authors. The real green light starts in the next stage—Bluebox, where the idea gets first internal funding for Minimal Viable Product. The initial investment and the official entrepreneurship action start in the Golden box phase, where the innovator becomes an internal Startuper. Such scenarios can be shown, for example by 2 spin-offs and 2 internal innovative products that have emerged from the intrapreneurship programme. Solutions like Thingdust (Thingdust 2020)—plug and play workspace analytics or Noow.art (Noow.art 2020)—platform to buy, sell and display digital artworks have successful spun-off from the mother company. The entrepreneurial spirit can also be seen in internal products portfolio expansion, like, for example Asport (Swisscom 2020a)—a fully automated video production system for popular sports or Drone recognition and defence services (Swisscom 2020b).

Even if we are looking here on those gems of intrapreneurial programme we should not forget that it is all about the critical mass of the innovativeness in the ecosystem. It is about revealing unexplored skills and making them useful. It is a way of unlocking new staff profiles, scanning the managerial talent and possible new sources of future directives. The single successful start-up initiatives are not the only equivalent of the programme success.

9   Breaking the Corporate Silos Structures and Synchronizing Participants

Entrepreneurial skills and talent are valuable assets for companies to identify, pursue and open new business lines. However, they need to create trust around uncertain projects and normalize them in the company over time to increase innovation maturity and to keep up related activities. The initial approach of intrapreneurship in all three cases came as Innovation department initiative that in the first place had to introduce this approach to higher management, often finding a key alliance with colleagues from HR.

In Abanca, we have experienced a kind of competition between HR and Innovation departments, both had to cooperate competing for the Board of Directors visibility. In Kickbox approach HR appreciates the identification of new talent discovery. From this perspective, the programme becomes also an opportunity for Human Resources to attract the students and young people showing the banking sector as an attractive employer.

> You should make a lot of noise around this programme—change the company way of thinking—use the HR department as your amplifier! (C. Alvarez-Iglesias, personal communication, March 25, 2020).

In the Swisscom case, the HR department got strongly interested in the transformational side of the Kickbox programme. The cultural transformation of the company and self-education of our employees has become a driver for HR–Innovation alliance. It is clearly seen from day one, when you open the box and you see the personal letter from the Head of HR Department to supervisors of the participants, encouraging them to give more time and flexibility to participating employees. This programme also raised the retention of employees and created competitive employer branding satisfying the crucial needs of the HR staff. In the later stages of the first pilot, the Business Units were also involved to screen the output of the programme. They could identify interesting initiatives during the Demo Days, which could work to their benefit. Once spill over effects have reached the Board of Middle Managers, the Kickbox approach becomes present in company general culture, involving and influencing everyday approaches to new and non-standard ideas. The proactive and innovation-oriented attitude of the employees can then be introduced to a controlled process of iterative validation filtering the ideas worth pursuing. Additionally, Kickbook collaborates with the Sustainability Department which is looking for projects that would reflect the corporate responsibility of the company by assembling tailor-made assessments. This means that the bottom-up impulses from the employees are evaluated not only from business opportunity point of view but also from the values that the company would like to communicate. This exercise connects the top-down Corporate Social Responsibility programme with employee initiatives putting it into practice.

> The core team is internal innovation department, with special unit devoted to intrapreneurship. They lead the process. However, there are some key alliances needed for full blossom of the programme. You need a spill over effect throughout all the company (D. Hengartner personal communication, March 30, 2020).

In Rabobank, the InnovAid intrapreneurship and Moonshot programme idea and its design come from the Innovation Department; however, the scoping campaign is aligned with every business line and nowadays corresponding to the challenges marked by their "innovation thesis" and Value Pockets (values-driven innovation priority areas of the company development) that are matching with the innovation strategy. The call for innovators is launched directly by Chief Executive Officer (CEO) and other Board members in a brief video and involves past intrapreneurs encouraging employees to join, the message is boosted by local ambassadors assigned in each location of the offices, the campaign involves also the Chief Digital Transition Officer who sends the activating e-mail to all the company. In exchange, apart from Innovation Department, all the company needs to be aligned with the goals of the programme. The message from the CEO and other Board members needs to be disseminated by all internal channels of internal communication.

The side effect of the Kickbox approach is building bridges not only between the innovation-oriented employees but also on management levels. If properly aligned, this may create the spill over effect that will involve areas of the company that until now have never cross-pollinized.

10   Cultural Transformation Through Entrepreneurial Values

After describing and analyzing the essential and short-term effects of the programme, looking at the intrapreneurs' ideas and their business potential that may be unlocked through Kickbox approach, we focus on the impact of this programme on company's culture. We notice a transformational capacity of this process enabling the entire structure, motivations and growth dynamics to adopt an innovation mindset.

The case of Abanca exemplifies how the programme influences the innovation culture in the company and allows more and more people to talk openly about their ideas. Kickbox programme introduces a new way of thinking to Abanca. Changing the model of the corporate framework by engaging new, internal, public to interact and co-create around new business models. According to the interview with Carlos Alvarez, several values-driven outcomes have been noticed after the second edition of the programme in Abanca. The Kickbox approach influenced the critical mass of the innovativeness in the company ecosystem by creating an entrepreneurial space in the traditional company where employees could play with inventing new business models. This led to a novel way of evaluating the staff, considering their unexplored skills and making them useful. Aligning it with Human Resources policies it created a new way of unlocking new staff profiles, scanning the managerial talent and possible new source of future directives in the company enabling tailor-made career paths. Additionally, the motivational effect has been noticed among long-term staff. In this group, Kickbox was also an opportunity for employees to introduce their personal project into professional life, showing the motivations that drive them outside of office environment. This connection often activated the people who did not usually overperform. The positive effect has been emphasized by this group who were surprised by the fact that traditional company has opened up for novel ideas, which in the past tended to be blocked and removed from the system. Kickbox in Abanca introduces a way to reinvent yourself as an employee, by waking the restlessness in creating something new. It is a new canal to generate this persuasiveness through radical change in corporate structure.

> First focus on the introduction of innovation culture and create a movement, a dynamic that generates talent from one edition to another. Only after few years we can become picky about the ideas (C. Alvarez-Iglesias, personal communication, March 25, 2020).

Rabobank statements also confirm the fact that intrapreneurship is only possible if the culture of the organization and its employees allow this. If the company seeks to transform its culture towards more innovation driven, it should start by reviewing and establishing new values to which the employees (including management) and the organizational structure would adapt. The Moonshot and InnovAid programmes effectively contribute to the required cultural change. Those programmes not only filter, validate and scale innovative ideas of the employees but create a space in the company where the creativity is encouraged, embraced and effectively supported. The intrapreneurs are becoming visible role models that communicate this change towards the organization. Their success stories showcase new values that are introduced by the company and motivate others to follow the innovation movement. Rabobank case shows clearly the snowball effect of this cultural change on 5 years' timeline.

Swisscom has benefitted in different ways but mainly from the new projects coming from within the company, new multidisciplinary teams that have emerged during the intrapreneurship programme, the creation of spin-off companies that are exploring new markets, and constant flow of innovative business ideas to be validated. Additionally, Swisscom's HR Department emphasizes the non-direct transformational impact of self-education programme, as well as employer branding and innovative brand attached to it which builds an image of the company that attracts talent. Via Kickbook programme, Swisscom shows the trust to its employees, gives them green light for their initiatives and visibility on the management. The company also enables its employees to create internal teams, create their new jobs in Swisscom, like the Kickbook team itself. After few editions, different company building blueprints have been tested, so employees can fit into any start-up strategy without the need of leaving their job. Since the intrapreneurship programme is in the portfolio Swisscom added to the job description the important statement: "You are actively building Swisscom". Any employee is asked to reinvent himself and the sector using the Kickbox approach.

The cases reviewed in this chapter demonstrate the introduction and co-creation of a renewed innovation culture through implementation of the Kickbox approach. In the original Adobe Kickbox implementation as well as in three cases reviewed, we can see how companies work with values to facilitate and foster intrapreneurship. Companies considering an introduction of such intrapreneurship activity should acknowledge the role of and work with the intrapreneurial values being involved.

Transformation of the corporate culture may start with detaching from the hierarchical approach in decision-making where the opinion of the Highest Paid Person in Organisation (HiPPO) opinion is not as determining as the outcomes of data-driven validations. This means that general strategy of the company can be influenced by radically "bottom-up" approach based only on internal and external market inputs. Reconfiguring the established decision-making processes and positions will be an initial hurdle to overcome.

Independence and self-reliance are the qualities searched and filtered by intrapreneurship programmes. Their discovery relies on openness of the company for new ideas and the flexibility to adopt them based on a traceable validation. A trust-based relationship should grant intrapreneurs access to resources of the company in exchange for their contributions and willingness to share risks.

Another shift is expected from Human Resources, which must embrace practice-oriented self-education of the employees. Pre-determined training modules as the regular stimulation becomes less important than entrepreneurial approach towards professional growth. Self-determination of personal assets at work starts to shift the career planning programmes giving employees more space to influence their future in the company. The skills of future management and directive profiles should consider entrepreneurial skills based on trust and access to company resources. The profiles that make the most out of the company environment qualify as future leaders.

Similar to entrepreneurship, intrapreneurship is not for all the employees, not everyone is willing to take the associated risks and to invest the time and personal resources required. The route designed for the participants of kickbox programme is testing and validating not only the initial ideas but the overall skill set of their authors. That is why during the interviews we often heard that Kickbox programme is not about creating innovative ideas, but about creation of serial innovators and the according mindset within the company.

Constant problem solving and adaptation to market reality require a proactive attitude, not only within the programme framework but also outside of it. The intrapreneurs themselves can be seen as goal-oriented scouts that are testing the company's flexibility and ability to evolve towards an innovation-driven culture, getting out of the comfort zone. This means that intrapreneurs should "better ask for forgiveness than for permission" showing the goal-oriented mentality that may be disrupting the corporate frameworks and rules. This should be a conscious choice of both sides—the company and the innovator itself should expect to be in certain way a troublemaker.

Intrapreneurs will need to constantly communicate about the idea and to validate the innovation-related hypothesis. Intrapreneurship is not only about convincing others about the idea but also to be open to pivot depending on feedback, resembling the lean start-up mindset operating in a more controlled environment.

This matchmaking between the company values including those that facilitate and foster intrapreneurship, and individual values of intrapreneurs should be the foundation that delivers the key impact for kickbox activities. Such an approach can be enhanced if values-based innovation management methods (Breuer and Lüdeke-Freund 2017) are systematically integrated into the six levels or steps of the process, e.g. through an initial values-based challenge framing and sourcing, using values as a heuristic for ideation, or values-based business modelling (Breuer and Lüdeke-Freund 2018). Such a values-based extension allows not only fostering intrapreneurship and cultural change, but also sensitizes employees for the normative guidelines of the organization and helps them to generate ideas that (might not yet fit from an operational perspective, but) fit in a strategic prospect. The awareness and right implementation intrapreneurship programme allow companies to enhance their innovation culture by tackling relevant challenges. Is the current pandemic is one of the challenges that pull companies out of the comfort zone and into experimenting with new business models, markets and technologies? This process can be digitized, and ideas may emerge straight from employees' homes through intrapreneurship programmes. Shipping kickboxes directly to potential intrapreneurs' homes would invite them to co-create the future of their companies.

References

Abanca. (2020a). *Acceleradora fintech en Galicia 2019, Abanca Innova*. Retrieved April 22, 2020, from http://abancainnova.com/es/

Abanca. (2020b). *Seguro viaje Abanca. Asistencia al viajero | Abanca*. Retrieved April 22, 2020, from https://www.abanca.com/es/seguros/seguro-viaje/

Ahuja, S. B. (2019). *Why innovation Labs fail*. HBR. https://hbr.org/2019/07/why-innovation-labs-fail-and-how-to-ensure-yours-doesnt?

Birkinshaw, J., & Duke, L. (2013). Employee-led innovation. *Business Strategy Review, 2*, 46–51.

Breuer, H., & Lüdeke-Freund, F. (2017). *Values-based innovation management. Innovating by what we care about*. Hampshire, GB: Palgrave Macmillan.

Breuer, H., & Lüdeke-Freund, F. (2018). Values-based business model innovation: A toolkit. In L. Moratis, F. Melissen, & S. O. Idowu (Eds.), *Sustainable business models* (pp. 395–416). New York: Springer.

Creative Labs. (2020). *We are creative Labs*. Retrieved April 22, 2020, from www.wearecreativelabs.com

Innovaid. (2020). *Building better intrapreneurs*. Retrieved April 22, 2020, from https://www.innovaidtoolkit.com

Kickbook. (2020). *Kickbook shop*. Retrieved April 22, 2020, from https://kickbook.getkickbox.com

Kickbox. (2019). Swisscom Kickbook – Kickbox Open Source. Retrieved October 18, 2019, from https://kickbox.org/swisscom-kickbook/ Kickbox (2020). Welcome to Kickbox.org. Retrieved April 22, 2020, from www.kickbox.org

Krippendorff, K. (2019). *Driving innovation from within: A guide for internal entrepreneurs.* Columbia University Press.

Kruszelnicki, J. (2019). 10 conditions of an effective program to support intrapreneurship in a large company. https://www.linkedin.com/pulse/10-conditions-effective-program-support-large-company-kruszelnicki/

Moovement. (2020). *GPS ear tags for cattle tracking | mOOvement.* Retrieved April 22, 2020, from https://www.moovement.com.au/

Noow.art. (2020). *The digital art market.* Retrieved April 22, 2020, from https://www.noow.art/

Peaks. (2020). *Invest your spare change – Peaks.* Retrieved April 22, 2020, from https://www.peaks.com

Pearce, N. (2019). *Why people—And companies—Need purpose.* Retrieved April 29, 2020, from https://hbr.org/podcast/2019/04/why-people-and-companies-need-purpose

Pinchot, G. (1985). *Intrapreneuring: Why you don't have to leave the corporation to become an entrepreneur* (2nd ed.). Berrett-Koehler. Retrieved April 29, 2020.

Pinchot, G., & Pinchot, E. S. (1978). *Intra-corporate intrapreneurship.* Retrieved April 22, 2020, from https://drive.google.com/file/d/0B6GgwqtG-DKcSlpsbGRBZkZYSlk/view

Rabobank. (2020). *New Rabobank moonshots and startups present themselves on demo day.* Retrieved April 22, 2020, from https://www.rabobank.com/en/about-rabobank/innovation/innovative-entrepreneurs/articles/20170530-new-rabobank-moonshots-and-startups-present-themselves-on-demo-day.html

Randall, M. (2015). Presentation at TNW conference Europe 2015. Retrieved April 22, 2020, from https://www.youtube.com/watch?reload=9&v=YiQUJ3CX53A

Ries, E. (2011). *The lean startup: How Today's entrepreneurs use continuous innovation to create radically successful businesses.* New York: Crown Business.

Surepay. (2020). *We're here to make online payments safer.* Retrieved April 22, 2020, from https://www.surepay.nl/en/

Swisscom. (2020a). *Asport – Swisscom.* Retrieved April 22, 2020, from https://www.swisscom.ch/en/business/sem/asport.html

Swisscom. (2020b). *Drone recognition and defence.* Retrieved April 22, 2020, from https://www.swisscom.ch/en/business/broadcast/offers/radio-communication/drone-solution.html

Thingdust. (2020). *Thingdust – plug and play workspace analytics.* Retrieved April 22, 2020, from https://thingdust.com/

Tiku, N. (2019). Three Years of Misery Inside Google, the Happiest Company in Tech. Retrieved from https://www.wired.com/story/inside-google-three-years-misery-happiest-company-tech/

Jakub Kruszelnicki is working on innovations since 2007, working in the field of international R&D&I projects management and exploitation. His practical experience ranges from academia (Director of Technology Transfer Centre of the Cracow University of Technology; Universitat Autonoma de Barcelona) via private industrial research and its exploitation (LEITAT Technological Center; Knowledge Innovation Market) through researching European innovation ecosystems (H2020 OaSIS) as well as co-founding accelerator (Creative Labs) and Transfer of Technologies developed via cascade funding sources (Fundingbox). Connecting those fields of expertise Jakub is exploring the technological and business aspects of innovations and developing tailor-made methodologies for the public and private market.

Henning Breuer is a professor for business psychology at the University of Applied Sciences for Media, Communication and Business in Berlin and founder of UXBerlin—Innovation Consulting. Since 2001, he works with large companies, public organizations and start-ups, providing workshops and consulting on innovation management and culture, sustainable business models, future scenarios and ethnographic research. Henning co-authored numerous scientific publications including a book on "Values-Based Innovation Management—Innovating by What We Care About". As visiting professor and researcher he also worked at the University of Chile (Santiago), the University of Applied Sciences in Potsdam and Waseda University (Tokyo).

A Practitioner-Oriented Toolkit to Foster Sustainable Product Innovation

Christoph Haag, Florian Nögel, and Kai Krampe

1 Introduction

The world is facing incrementing problems with human-caused changes for the worse of our ecological system—such as climate change, plastics-polluted oceans, and global deforestation. In this matter the digital transformation of our societies and globalized economies holds both; opportunities to improve the situation by de-materializing economic entities (such as products and processes) and thus making them less resource consuming, but also risks to even worsen the situation by abstracting and estranging resource-consuming economical or societal activities (such as physical logistics processes or global data traffic and storage).

However, in order to de-stress our ecological system, actions will be needed from both sides: top-down, via laws and regulations, and bottom-up, by voluntary actions from private citizens as well as economic players, i.e., manufacturing and service companies (cp. Bungard and Schmidpeter 2017).

For decades companies have learned how to align their development activities with the main concern of market success and profitability. Methods like target costing and design-to-cost, quality function deployment, or design thinking are meant to guide product innovation teams toward customer satisfaction at low cost in order to achieve an utmost level of competitiveness. Now, with the increasing call for more sustainability, companies need additional, normative frameworks, and methods that help to guide development teams toward more sustainable product innovation—without significantly compromising the competitiveness goals. We see three requirements that should be fulfilled by such a method:

1. The objective scope of the method should not be limited to the substantial product itself but cover its entire lifecycle (cp. He et al. 2006). Since the question of

C. Haag (✉) · F. Nögel · K. Krampe
TH Köln, Gummersbach, Germany
e-mail: christoph.haag@th-koeln.de

© The Author(s), under exclusive license to Springer Nature Switzerland AG 2021
D. R. A. Schallmo, J. Tidd (eds.), *Digitalization*, Management for Professionals,
https://doi.org/10.1007/978-3-030-69380-0_23

C. Haag et al.

whether a product is sustainable or not is depending on all lifecycle aspects: what supplied material it is made of, how it is manufactured, the way it is packaged, sold and distributed, how the customer makes use of it, and the manner it is disposed at the end of its useful life.

2. Looking at the targeted dimension of ecological sustainability the method should take an utmost broad scope and aim at completeness. Because otherwise, when having only an eye on one ecological hot spot (such as greenhouse gas (GHG) emissions during manufacturing) while ignoring other critical causes of ecological harm (such as nature incompatible waste disposal), the actions taken might lead to what is called "schlimmbesserung," i.e., improvement for the worse.

3. The method should have contentual substance, i.e., should not be limited to pure procedural instructions. While procedural and methodological knowledge is quite important in the context of innovation and product development, this knowledge only is commonly not sufficient to generate powerful innovative product ideas. Particularly in the critical phase of ideation, more substantial methods help to catalyze and enhance results in a manner consistent with the intended goal.

An example for such a substantial method is the TRIZ contradiction matrix comprising the 40 inventive principles, as described by Altshuller et al. (1997). The 40 inventive principles serve as substantial, context-related impulses for development teams on their search for solving technical contradictions. The important role that TRIZ plays for technical problem solving in the development process (cp. Koltze and Souchkov 2017) is aimed at by the present chapter with regard to environmentally relevant problems.

In the past, view models have been published to give such kind of support to product development teams. These models link sustainability aspects to product lifecycle phases. However, their applicability is versatile, but also very general (cp. Scholz et al. 2018; Spengler and Schröter 2001). Our research-in-progress intents to tackle this lack of contextual, substantial guidance for innovation teams. A toolkit is presented in this chapter to foster sustainability thinking and help ideate sustainable solutions during the development of new products and services. With regard to the lifecycle of consumer goods and services, it holds generic principles to reduce or eliminate the ecological harm that such products potentially cause along their life cycles. The introduced "Design-to-Sustainability Matrix" is constructed in a way that any interdisciplinary development team can reach out to this toolkit with a specific design challenge and come to generic principles for solving this challenge in an ecologically friendly way.

2   Research Design

Our developed toolkit is based on a case study survey examining a set of 196 consumer product innovations (both goods and services) from recent past (2010–2020). The set contains two subsets; a first subset of 98 innovative products which can be considered distinctly environmentally friendly (in comparison to the former product that was intended to be substituted by the innovation), and another subset of 98 innovations that were each recognized as being particularly harmful to the ecological system.

Each such innovation case was examined with regard to two aspects:

1. The product lifecycle phase(s) in which the innovation's beneficial resp. harmful implication for the ecological system takes effect.
2. The field(s) of environmental issues that the innovation affects in a beneficial resp. harmful way.

The following frameworks were applied to operationalize those aspects and provide a structure for classification.

Framework 1: Product Lifecycle Model

In search of a holistic framework that has the potential to capture all thinkable ecological implications that product innovations might have, two different viewpoints were taken into consideration: first, a company-oriented value chain view, as for instance known from the Accounting and Reporting Standard of the Greenhouse Gas Protocol, distinguishing between different company activities, such as direct and indirect, upstream and downstream activities (The Greenhouse Gas Protocol 2020, p. 26), and second, a product-oriented lifecycle view, as known, e.g., from lifecycle analysis (cp. Hendrickson et al. 2006).

Since our framework is intended to capture ecologically relevant consequences implied by singular products (and not by companies as a whole) it was decided for a product lifecycle model. The final model adopts the classification of the Cradle-to-Grave Matrix by Stamm (2008, p. 279) and comprises five phases (Fig. 1).

Fig. 1 Lifecycle phases of products

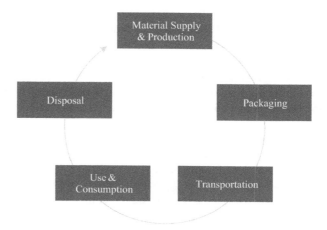

However, in contrast to Stamm's approach, our depicted model explicitly includes the packaging of products as one distinct phase (instead of assigning it to the distribution phase), since packaging in many cases can be a decisive influence factor for a product to be ecologically beneficial or not. Furthermore, our final model does not include the pre-production phase, i.e., the design and engineering phase, because the model should focus on lifecycle phases in which the ecologically beneficial or harmful impact becomes effective, which is seldomly the pre-production phase.

Framework 2: Fields of Environmental Issues

Several approaches were examined and evaluated for applicability as an utmost complete typology of ecological issues potentially affected by new product innovations. The following ones were identified as being most suitable for our purpose:

In its list of environmental standards (GRI 300 series), the Global Reporting Initiative covers seven topics for companies to take up position in their reporting: materials, energy, water and effluents, biodiversity, emissions, waste, and environmental compliance (cp. Global Reporting Initiative 2020).

The German government leans on several standards (among them also the GRI 300 series) to come up with a sustainability strategy that addresses the following environmental fields of interest: resource conservation, climate protection, renewable energies, land use, biological diversity, mobility, agricultural land use, and air pollution (cp. Deutsche Bundesregierung 2012).

The Sustainability Accounting Standards Board (SASB) uses a similar classification to structure those ecologically relevant aspects that publicly owned US companies should report on: climate change risks, environmental accidents and remediation, water use and management, energy management, fuel management and transportation, GHG emissions and air pollution, waste management and effluents, as well as biodiversity impacts (cp. SASB 2013, S. 8).

The Cradle-to-Grave Matrix by Stamm (2008, p. 279) covers eight environmental fields: waste relevance, soil pollution and degradation, water contamination, air contamination, noise, consumption of energy, consumption of natural resources, and effects on ecosystems.

From our research, we identified three main categories of environmental fields of criticalness that all above-mentioned approaches address:

- Climate change
- Resource scarcity
- Environmental pollution

Climate change as one category comprises two essential factors that cause man-made global warming; the GHG generation and the clearing of forests which results in less CO_2 being converted into oxygen.

The category resource scarcity basically describes the usage of critical raw materials. The "criticalness" can be linked to the type of natural resource classified as follows (cp. Mildner 2010, p. 6; Rogal 2008, p. 58):

- Exhaustible, nonrenewable resources (e.g., fossil fuels)
- Exhaustible, nonrenewable but recyclable resources (e.g., metals and minerals)
- Renewable resources with declining reserves (soil, groundwater, trees)
- Renewable resources with unlimited reserves (solar, wind, and geo energy)

Only the usage of latter type of natural resource can be considered uncritical and therefore will not be considered in our later framework.

Environmental pollution as the final category encompasses the contamination of the subsystems of our ecological system (earth, water, and air), noise and light pollution as well as littering as a directly observable phenomenon leading also to contamination effects in the long run.

Data Collection and Quantitative Analysis

After setting up the two classification schemes for both aspects (a) and (b) an interdisciplinary team of 10 test persons (all master students at TH Köln from the fields of economics, technology, and design) evaluated all 196 innovation cases in terms of those aspects. The guiding questions were framed as follows:

1. Having a close look at the examined product innovation (in comparison to the former product that is intended to be substituted by the innovation), in which product lifecycle phase(s) does the innovation's beneficial resp. harmful implication for the ecological system take effect?
2. Which field(s) of environmental issues is/are affected by this implication that the innovation inevitably brings with increasing diffusion (and substitution of the former product)?

In total, a set of 1960 data points was generated in that way, each data point representing a link between an innovation case and its assignment in terms of guiding questions (1) and (2), as assessed by one test person.

3   Research Findings and Toolkit

As an intermediate result, the entire data set was consolidated to an "innovation landscape" (Fig. 2) that shows the percental distribution of those assignments within the applied classification model.

Greener shaded cells show intersections of particularly higher relevance whereas purely white cells indicate that there was no data point, i.e., none of the innovation

| | Global environmental challenges | | | | | | | | |
| | Climate change | | Ressource scarcity | | | Environmental pollution | | | |
	Greenhouse gas emission (CO2, methan etc.)	Disforestation	Consumption of non-renewable, non-recyable resources (energetically used fossile fuels)	Consumption of non-renewable, recyable resources (metals, rare earths, minerals, plastics etc.)	Consumption of renewable, recyable resources with declining supply (water, sand, wood etc.)	Air contamination (fine particles, nitric oxide etc.)	Water and Soil contamination	Light and Noise pollution	Littering
Production	0,9%	5,3%	0,6%	21,1%	13,6%	0,0%	0,4%	0,0%	0,2%
Packaging	0,0%	0,1%	0,0%	4,8%	1,5%	0,0%	0,0%	0,0%	0,2%
Distribution	1,4%	0,0%	0,6%	0,0%	0,1%	1,0%	0,0%	0,3%	0,0%
Use / Consumption	6,0%	1,3%	6,2%	3,7%	5,2%	2,7%	1,6%	2,1%	0,7%
Disposal	0,0%	0,0%	0,2%	1,1%	0,1%	0,0%	0,6%	0,0%	16,4%

Fig. 2 Percental distribution of the 196 innovation cases

cases by none of the test persons, assigned to this intersection. However, most interfaces were assigned by at least a minimum of 20 data points. This threshold was used to decide whether the intersection should be considered in the following.

After assigning the 196 innovations to the intersections of the matrix, the research team revealed for each case the underlying generic principle(s) that cause(s) the distinctly beneficial or harmful ecological impact of the respective product innovation. Afterward the identified principles were clustered and consolidated.

In this way, 40 sustainability principles were defined and allocated to the corresponding intersection(s) of the matrix (Fig. 3). Each principle was formulated as a simple-to-understand, fairly unambiguous, and meaningful instruction. These instructions were correspondingly assigned to the phase of the lifecycle in which they have the strongest impact and to the environmental issue that they are related to.

The body of this 5×9 matrix provides 45 cells which partly contain numbers from 1 to 40. These represent the 40 Sustainable Product Innovation Principles that derived from the qualitative study of the 196 product innovations (Table 1). Similar to the 40 innovative principles of TRIZ these generic principles are intended to serve as impulses and catalysts for brainstorming activities in order to come up with specific, precisely fitting ideas for the product in question.

When looking at the matrix it is noticeable that the quantity of the principles is not evenly distributed to the cells. While some fields contain many principles other fields do not contain any number. This circumstance reflects the percental distribution of innovation cases as shown in Fig. 2 and furthermore allows for identifying the core topics that have to be dealt with along the product development process.

The matrix and its principles can be applied in two ways; to examine and improve existing products, or to generate sustainable features for new products in development. In both use cases, the products can be viewed from a problem perspective and/or a process perspective.

- Problem-oriented view: Here the guiding question should be: "Which ecological aspects are potentially affected critically by our product?" Therefore, the matrix is viewed from top to down, using the fields of environmental harm as starting points for a column-directed examination.
- Process-oriented view: From this viewpoint, the guiding question is: "Which phases of our product's lifecycle are concerned and need special care in order to create an overall ecologically friendly solution?" Here, the matrix is applied from left side, i.e., using the lifecycle phases as starting points for a line-directed investigation.

When using the column-directed examination, specific environmental matters of highest concerns (e.g., global warming) can be tackled by discussing all phases of a product's lifecycle. Using the line-directed approach, a specific lifecycle phase can be focused and improved selectively (i.e., in terms of a single environmental field) or holistically.

	Climate change		Ressource scarcity			Environmental pollution			
	Greenhouse gas emission (CO2, methan etc.)	Disforestation	Consumption of non-renewable, non-recyable resources (energetically used fossie fuels)	Consumption of non-renewable, recyable resources (metals, minerals, plastics etc.)	Consumption of renewable, recyable resources with declining supply (water, sand, wood etc.)	Air contamination (fine particles, nitric oxide etc.)	Water and soil contamination	Light and noise pollution	Littering
Production	8; 11; 13; 14; 15; 17; 22; 23; 26; 27; 28; 29; 30; 31; 35; 38; 40	3; 8; 11; 12; 13; 14; 17; 22; 24; 26; 27; 33; 38; 40; 41	7; 8; 17; 23; 26; 35; 40	7; 10; 11; 13; 14; 15; 17; 20; 22; 23; 24; 26; 27; 29; 30; 40; 31; 32; 33; 34; 35; 39; 41	3; 7; 8; 11; 13; 14; 15; 17; 20; 22; 23; 24; 26; 27; 28; 29; 30; 31; 33; 35; 38; 40; 41	7; 8; 14; 17; 22	8; 11; 13; 15; 17; 22; 23		
Packaging		16; 17; 25; 40		13; 14; 15; 17; 20; 22; 23; 26; 39; 40; 41	14; 16; 17; 23; 25; 26; 27; 34; 40; 41		13; 15		13; 15; 17; 20
Distribution	7; 10; 14; 17; 21; 28; 34; 40		7; 28; 34	11; 15; 17; 40	15; 40	7; 13; 14; 26; 28; 34; 40		7; 14	
Use / Consumption	1; 2; 4; 7; 8; 9; 10; 11; 12; 14; 15; 17; 22; 26; 33; 34; 35; 36; 37; 40	11; 12; 14; 17; 22; 25; 26; 36; 40	1; 2; 4; 7; 8; 9; 10; 11; 12; 15; 27; 29; 33; 34; 35; 35; 37; 40	11; 12; 13; 15; 17; 22; 23; 27; 29; 30; 35; 41	7; 4; 11; 12; 13; 14; 15; 17; 19; 22; 25; 26; 27; 35; 40	5; 7; 8; 10; 11; 26; 33; 40	12; 15; 20; 27; 40	4; 6; 10; 12; 34	11; 13; 14; 15; 17; 22; 26; 27; 40
Disposal			13; 17; 31	23; 33	12; 14; 17; 26; 27	23	15; 17; 20; 22; 26; 27; 39; 40		11; 12; 13; 14; 15; 17; 20; 22; 23; 26; 27; 28; 30; 31; 33; 34; 35; 35; 40; 41

Fig. 3 Design-tosustainability matrix

Table 1 The 40 sustainable product innovation principles

Index	Principles
1	Use excess energy (e.g., thermal losses)
2	Save energy through insulation
3	Use renewable energy from eco-friendly sources
4	Use more efficient energy-saving products
5	Use other sources of energy
6	Reduce noise pollution through new technologies
7	Implement eco-friendly transport and distribution technology
8	Change the production method to reduce emissions
9	Regulate and canalize energy flow
10	Increase the utilization of capacities
11	Minimize the resource consumption of the product in use
12	Change users' behavior in terms of product/service use
13	Eliminate dispensable materials of the product and its packaging
14	Digitize activities or content
15	Change the physical condition of the product to reduce packaging and waste
16	Reduce the amount of shipping-related packaging to a minimum
17	Use universal product components instead of specific ones
18	Implement modular product structures with a high level of exchangeability
19	Reduce water consumption
20	Substitute toxic ingredients with environmentally harmless ones
21	Reduce transportation by using regionally and seasonally available resources
22	Transform disposable products into reusable ones
23	Make disposable products out of biodegradable materials
24	Make single-use product unnecessary
25	Replace single-use products with reusable ones
26	Design reusable products in a valuable, timeless way
27	Substitute nonrenewable materials with renewable ones
28	Establish closed, circular systems to expand life spans of products
29	Strive for the longest possible product life span
30	Design standardized, uniform products for better reusability and reparability
31	Avoid material mixes of products and/or make them easily separable
32	Make use of refillable consumables and operating supplies
33	Create recycled products with continuing recyclability
34	Consider resource wastage and environmental effects in product pricing
35	Design and produce essentially needed products without ethical conflicts
36	Compensate adequately for the consumption of scarce resources
37	Label ecologically friendly products to increase awareness
38	Intense the use of limitlessly available resources and by-products
39	Consider the environmental impact of products in terms of use and disposal
40	Adapt product sizes and amounts depending on demand

4   Conclusion

The presented toolkit can be applied in any development context (new design or re-design). Having the product lifecycle phases as one orientation axis and the ecological challenges as the other, improvement measures can be found selectively and to the point. Thus, the toolkit helps innovation teams from early stages on to ensure ecologically sustainable product innovations and offers a fast and easy-to-apply approach for the creation of ecologically sustainable products.

References

Altshuller, G., Shulyak, L., & Rodman, S. (1997). *40 principles: TRIZ keys to technical innovation.* Technical Innovation Center, Inc.

Bungard, P., & Schmidpeter, R. (2017). *CSR in Nordrhein-Westfalen: Nachhaltigkeits-Transformation in der Wirtschaft, Zivilgesellschaft und Politik.* Berlin: Springer Gabler.

Deutsche Bundesregierung. (2012). *Nationale Nachhaltigkeitsstrategie.* Fortschrittsbericht 2012. Berlin: Bund.

Global Reporting Initiative. (2020). *GRI Environmental Standards 300 Series.* Available online: https://www.globalreporting.org/standards/gri-standards-download-center

Greenhouse Gas Protocol. (2020). *Corporate accounting and reporting standards.* Available online: https://ghgprotocol.org/standards

He, W., Ming, X. G., Ni, Q. F., Lu, W. F., & Lee, B. H. (2006). A unified product structure management for enterprise business process integration throughout the product lifecycle. *International Journal of Production Research, 44*(9), 1757–1776.

Hendrickson, C. T., Lave, L. B., & Matthews, H. S. (2006). *Environmental life cycle assessment of goods and services: An input-output approach.* Washington, DC: Resources for the Future.

Koltze, K., & Souchkov, V. (2017). *Systematische Innovation: TRIZ-Anwendung in der Produkt- und Prozessentwicklung.* München: Hanser.

Mildner, S.-A. (2010). *Konkurrenz um knappe Ressourcen.* Projektpapier, Stiftung Wissenschaft und Politik, Deutsches Institut für Internationale Politik und Sicherheit.

Rogal, H. (2008). *Ökologische Ökonomie* (2., überarbeitete und erweiterte Auflage). Wiesbaden: VS Verlag.

SASB. (2013). *Conceptual framework of the sustainability accounting standards board.* San Francisco: Sustainability Accounting Standards Board.

Scholz, U., Pastoors, S., Becker, J. H., Hofmann, D., & van Dun, R. (2018). *Praxis-handbuch Nachhaltige Produktentwicklung.* Berlin: Springer.

Spengler, T., & Schröter, M. (2001). Einsatz von Operations Research im produkt-bezogenen Umweltschutz – Stand und Perspektiven. *BFuP – Betriebswirtschaftliche Forschung und Praxis, 3*, 227–244.

Stamm, B. v. (2008). *Managing innovation, design and creativity* (2nd ed.). Hoboken: Wiley.

Christoph Haag is a professor for technology management at TH Köln—University of Applied Sciences. For his research and teaching, he draws back on many years of practical experience in the automotive, chemical, and machinery and construction industry—holding positions in procurement, costing, and innovation management. Complementary to his academic position Christoph counsels companies in the fields of sustainable innovation and customer-centered product design.

Florian Nögel completed his bachelor's degree in industrial engineering and management and his master's degree in product design and process development at TH Köln University of Applied Sciences. Simultaneously to his studies, he gained professional experience in production management and worked in a start-up company in Colombia. Today, Florian consults companies in the areas of strategy, project management, and innovation.

Kai Krampe graduated with a bachelor's in industrial engineering and management and a master's in product design and process development at TH Köln University of Applied Sciences. Simultaneously to his studies, he worked as a research assistant at the Institute for Business Administration and Management. Kai gained industrial experience in the areas of product development, automation technology, and renewable drive technologies.

Success Factors when Implementing Innovation Teams

Mikael J. Johnsson, Ewa Svensson, and Kristina Swenningsson

1 Problem

Recently, Johnsson (2017b) developed a methodology for creating high-performing innovation teams, the CIT-process, which aims avoiding group-related problems. The process is demonstrated in the following section. As teams increase job satisfaction, reduce job stress, and time pressure (e.g., Cordero et al. 1998) and reach the market faster (Highsmith 2009), the purpose of the new approach was to diminish well-known issues in the creation of innovation teams, such as conflicts occurring in new groups conduction innovation work (e.g., Kristiansen and Bloch-Poulsen 2010) and group dynamic problems in general (e.g., Wheelan 2013), and to support organizations in matching the ever-increasing speed of new products and services being launched on the market (e.g., Chen et al. 2010).

This chapter is part of a prior study that identified problems in the implementation of high-performing innovation teams (Johnsson et al. 2019), which originate from the need of studying the CIT-process when being used by practitioners, for example, consultants in innovation management, to support organizations in creating innovation teams. For this reason, the current study aims to explore factors that contribute to the success of practitioners using this process.

M. J. Johnsson (✉)
Blekinge Institute of Technology, Karlskrona, Sweden
e-mail: mikael.johnsson@bth.se

E. Svensson · K. Swenningsson
Crearum AB, Linköping, Sweden
e-mail: ewa.svensson@crearum.se; kristina.swenningsson@crearum.se

2   Current Understanding

Processes and knowledge regarding innovation teams have been developed for a long time (Farris 1972; Im et al. 2013; McDonough 2000; McGreevy 2006; Neuman et al. 1999; Pearce and Ensley 2004; West et al. 2004; Zuidema and Kleiner 1994). However, in contrast to prior research regarding the creation of innovation teams, Johnsson provides, through the CIT-process, hands-on advice comprising five steps, summarized in the following.

First, ensure the commitment of top management and team sponsors. Johnsson stresses this step as crucial because management sets the direction of innovation work. With no clear direction based on a company strategy, the innovation work may drift away from the business model.

Second, identify an innovation team convener (convener), who encourages common leadership as a team. Unlike a project manager, a convener encourages common leadership, through which the team members act as one unit. The convener keeps the agenda up to date and acts as the innovation team's communication channel to management and the team sponsor.

Third, introduce the convener to the processes of innovation management and group dynamics. If the convener is unfamiliar with the group development process, structured innovation work or the CIT-process itself, he or she should be introduced to the upcoming work, preferably by an innovation facilitator. This also applies to inexperienced managers and team sponsors. This step is significant because innovation is highly complex work; it spans from the CIT-process to market launch and value creation (Johnsson 2018), meaning that the innovation team is dependent on resources and support through a range of activities and decisions. The group dynamic process is well established (e.g., Tuckmann and Jensen 1977; Wheelan 2013), in which a group develops into a team through several phases, known as "forming-storming-norming-performing." The storming phase is exceptionally difficult because the team members tend to challenge not only the leader but also each other and the project as such, which drains energy and resources. Therefore, it is important to educate the convener and the entire innovation team so as to ease the recognition of potential upcoming problems.

Fourth, the convener gathers, preferable, four to six team members, with a minimum of three and maximum of seven members, of diverse functionalities who are key persons within their area of competence. These individuals should also feel positively toward multifunctional work and be proud of the company/organization they work for, and they should be motivated to contribute to the development of new products/services.

Fifth, the kick-off, the official start of the innovation project, first by establishing the norms of the innovation teams and then by setting the goal of the project. At the kick-off, all prior steps are repeated to align all team members with the same mindset. The CIT-process is conducted by management, the sponsor, and the convener, with the support of an innovation facilitator if the organization is inexperienced in creating innovation teams.

In prior studies of the CIT-process, the focus has been on identifying factors that both enable the innovation team's work (Johnsson 2017a) and are considered most important in ongoing innovation projects (Johnsson 2016a, b). Further, Johnsson (2018) has observed that an innovation facilitator is significant in creating innovation teams if the organization is inexperienced in such work. Despite prior research on the CIT-process, little is known about the success factors of practitioners using this process to support organizations in creating innovation teams. This research aims to explore these factors.

3 Research Question

What success factors, if any, occur when practitioners use the CIT-process to support an organization in creating innovation teams?

4 Research Design

This research was conducted in two steps, spanning from the pre-phase to the first steps in the ideation phase. In the first step, two consultants (practitioners) were identified and educated on the CIT-process at a consultancy firm, to act as innovation facilitators in accordance with Johnsson (2018). The practitioners were chosen because they were innovation management professionals certified by Innovationsledarna, which is associated with the International Society for Professional Innovation Management (ISPIM). In their profession, the practitioners have been involved in developing the innovation management ISO standard, ISO 56002. In the process of evaluating the practitioners' innovation-related skills, experience and knowledge, the practitioners were orally interviewed, and they answered a statement-based questionnaire. The interviews lasted about 40 minutes and were audio recorded. Relevant sections were transcribed. In the interviews, the practitioners answered questions such as the following:

- What experience do you have in advising innovation projects?
- What experience do you have in practical innovation work?
- What experience do you have on the process of innovation and group dynamics?
- Do you understand your role as an innovation facilitator?

The questionnaire consisted of 40 statements, based on Johnsson (2018), through which the practitioners assessed their abilities, for example:

- I have the ability to give concrete advice.
- I have the ability to steer back innovation teams that lose focus.
- I am available for support when the innovation team needs me.
- I assure the innovation team that uncertainty is OK.

- I create confidence in innovation teams to do things that innovation teams do not normally do.
- I challenge the innovation team if necessary.
- I have good coaching skills.
- I encourage the innovation team to push their boundaries.
- I facilitate the innovation team through the convening person.
- I have a good knowledge of the innovation process.

In the second step, with support from the practitioner, three innovation teams (Teams A–C) were created out of six organizations to conduct real innovation projects, that is, no fictive simulations. Team A consisted of four individuals and was created at one of the participating organizations. Team B was based on two organizations and consisted of 14 individuals. Finally, three organizations created one interorganizational innovation team: Team C, consisting of six individuals.

As the practitioners used the CIT-process, data were collected through recurrent reflective conversations with the practitioners and documented as filed notes, focusing on success factors as the work progressed and on whether the practitioners felt that they were in control. Furthermore, data were collected through transcribed, semistructured, in-depth interviews with the practitioners and the conveners from all innovation teams, which were audio recorded, approximately one month into the ongoing innovation projects. In the interviews, which lasted about 40 min, the respondents were explicitly asked, "What success factors have you noticed as the innovation team emerges?" and "Do you see the innovation team as a team?" The interviews also covered the practitioners' work by asking questions such as "Do you feel that the practitioner has control over the situation?" Data regarding success factors were collected through workshops with the practitioners, recalling the different projects and separating out success factors regarding the CIT-process's five steps.

The focus of the interviews was to identify success factors when the practitioners used the CIT-process and to identify potential problems related to group dynamics. The data were analyzed through thematic analysis, by clustering and identifying themes (Boyatzis 1998) and charting these themes based on both the structure of the CIT-process and in the innovation process suggested by Tidd and Bessant (2013). Theories in the group dynamic process, as suggested by Wheelan (2013) were used to identify group-related problems.

5 Findings

The findings from this study are demonstrated in the following (Tables 1, 2, 3, 4, 5 and 6).

Three main themes appeared as key success factors: knowledge adoption, knowledge transition, and knowledge transfer.

The participants' ability to adopt new knowledge (knowledge adoption) and convert it into action (knowledge transition) was identified throughout the use of

Table 1 Ensure management and sponsor commitment (CIT-process step 1)

| What | Success factor by function | | | Effect |
	Management	Convener	Facilitator	
Team A				
Management and facilitator had an established relationship	Facilitator provided freedom based on trust	–	Based on trust by management, the facilitator could work freely	Quick, clear, and swift process
The problem was well known	Management provided a clear task	Confident convener with support from management and facilitator	–	Quick, clear, and swift process
Manager/sponsor had a strong and clear position in the organization	Able to decide and prioritize the project	–	Easy to plan for preparation, efficient work	Calm and confident work
Team B				
–	–	–	–	–
Team C				
Major challenge to work on.	Decision to initiate a project based on identified problem	–	–	Identified problems made decision to start easier
Resolve of massive resistance	Powerful internal work to anchor idea	–	–	Project definition emerged
Support by management	Top management supported work at all times	Calm and confident in work	Calm and confident in work	Feeling of safe work environment

the CIT-process at all levels in the organizations, starting both with the practitioners advising management and sponsors providing distinct directions for the innovation projects and supporting the innovation teams' ongoing work. With clear directions, the conveners in Team A and Team C managed to attract team members with suitable competences, and with the support of the practitioners, they established the innovation teams. On Team B, however, management caused significant problems by ignoring the practitioners' advice, for example, by inviting twice as many team members as recommended to the kick-off and not informing the practitioners about it. However, at the kick-off, the practitioners split Team B into two sub-innovation teams (Team B1 and Team B2), and these new teams were then successfully established, but the process was not as effective as the other teams.

Knowledge transfer was observed through the practitioners' facilitating skills, as they educated and advised all participants on the go, depending on the situation.

Table 2 Identify convener (CIT-process step 2)

What	Success factor by function			Effect
	Management	Convener	Facilitator	
Team A				
Convener identification	The sponsor chose an appropriate convener	Confident in role as convener with support from management and facilitator Competence in communication and design	–	Rapid process to identify convener
Team B				
Meeting to focus on project setting and participants	Discussion on projects setting and participants	–	–	Holistic overview of expectations and a clear deadline go/no go
Team C				
Convener was prepared for project but not about facilitation	Management had pointed out a suitable candidate	Instant project accept	–	Rapid start but need of convener preparation about facilitator function
Support for work by management	Top management supported work at all times	–	–	Feeling of safe environment by convener

Table 3 Introduce convener to process (CIT-process step 3)

What	Success factor by function			Effect
	Management	Convener	Facilitator	
Team A				
Meeting facilitator and convener one on one	–	Interested to learn	–	Well organized preparation. High energy
The sponsor chose a competent convener	–	Good collaboration convener-facilitator. Good interaction and easy to work together, agile work by informal meetings between team meetings		Rapid process. Efficient work due to the convener's competence in communication and design
Team B				
Meeting facilitator and conveners one on one	–	Individuals who were interested and wanted to try	–	Despite unclear directions the facilitators accepted the role
Team C				
Mind-set	–	Open-minded even though not fully understood the project and methodology	Sent information and explained at meetings	Quick understanding

Table 4 Gather team members (CIT-process step 4)

What	Success factor by function			Effect
	Management	Convener	Facilitator	
Team A				
Meeting facilitator and convener one on one	–	Interested to learn	–	Well organized preparation. High energy
The sponsor chose a competent convener	–	Good collaboration convener-facilitator. Good interaction and easy to work together, agile work by informal meetings between team meetings		Rapid process. Efficient work due to the convener's competence in communication and design
Team B				
Meeting facilitator and conveners one on one.	–	Individuals that were interested and wanted to try	–	Despite unclear directions the facilitators accepted the role
Team C				
Mind-set	–	Open-minded even though not fully understood the project and methodology	Sent information and explained at meetings	Quick understanding

Important to highlight is that the innovation teams operated in different business areas. The practitioners, however, managed to adjust their advice according to situation.

None of the innovation teams, despite the problems creating Team B, indicated group dynamic problems. However, Team A and Team C emerged faster than the other innovation teams.

6   Contribution

In this research, practitioners were participating in the role of innovation facilitators. Literature on innovation facilitators within the field of innovation management indicates that this is an important role supporting innovation within organizations. This study contributes to prior research by indicating that innovation facilitators also spur the creation of innovation teams. Additionally, the study contributes to knowledge of the CIT-process by indicating that this process supports the creation of innovation teams if conducted as suggested and if the participating individuals have the ability to adopt new knowledge.

Table 5 Kick off project (CIT-process step 5)

What	Success factor by function				Effect
	Management	Convener	Facilitator	Team	
Team A					
Good plan for kick-off	–	–	Trusted the process	–	Good start
Established norms	–	–	–	Good discussions	Loyal to project
Worked on task	–	–	–	Buy-in, questioned and modified	Motivation and more specific task. Team understood the task but also modify and further develop task in a good way
Team B					
Good kick-off with two teams with two conveners	–	–	–	High level of motivation. Interesting discussions on task	–
Recruitment of members that want to contribute	–	–	–	–	The right people can do almost anything
Team C					
Clear facilitation	–	–	Clear and concise communication	–	Team members quickly realized the basic conditions in the process, which enabled a good continuation
Management support	Top management supported work at all times	–	–	Feeling of safe environment	–
Tools for getting to know each other	–	–	–		Team members got to know each other

Table 6 Quotes regarding success factors in the CIT-process

Role	Quote related to success factors
Manager	"…a general reflection is that is has been very fun to try this way of working. It seems obviously working. In the calendar, the work is spread out, but in terms of investment it is actually very small for how much you get out of it."
Sponsor	"…I think it's **fundamental**"…"I think (the facilitator) has the **experience to actually foresee** how the team is going to behave, how they going to react. And I think it's very good that, (the facilitator) has been working with companies before and (the facilitator) **knows what to expect** and (the facilitator) **knows how to counterattack** somehow. I mean, all of the team members are very result oriented, like engineers work every day delivering, delivering, delivering. Of course, giving them this fluffy task is very hard for them, so, I think (the facilitator) is great at **not only explaining the methodology, leading the team through the different activities, but I think that it's very good that also knowing when to stop them**"…"I think, eeah, (the facilitator) knows to handle the team"…"without **not causing any disturbance** or anything so (the facilitator) just smoothly leads them to something else"…"So, I think (the facilitator) is pretty good at that."
Sponsor	"…Well. **We would never have been able to do this ourselves, for sure. After all, we need the innovation coach,** or (referring to the facilitator) in this case. It is a success factor. I think, even though we had received a book on how it (referring to the CIT-process) works, I do not think we could have succeeded without having that support. **In general, I think the way of working has been good**. Because you take the time to set things properly and document it, you can put it aside and move on, focusing on what you have agreed upon."
Team member	**"I think we are all curious. We want something. We are here of our own free will"…"I think it's great that we have (referring to the facilitator). Someone (referring to the facilitator) who can hold us in the hand and guide us to what we really should do. Otherwise, we just get stuck, or we don't really know what to do."**
Team member	"I think we are quite similar in the group as individuals. **It is not a group of five completely different individuals but five individuals who are fairly similar and have about the same background or similar background.**"
Team member	"…we have very **diverse backgrounds, different ways of thinking about things, and everyone's mind is allowed to take up space**" … "I think that works great because **you get the chance to drift away sometimes, and if you go too far away, you will be nudged back on track (by the facilitator)**. But it's really not are stuck on a straight track; there is space to explore, but you will always go forward."
Team member	"I think it's great that **we have diverse professions and different personalities.**"
Team member	"One success factor is that **we have different backgrounds and that we are in different places in this large organization**. In my daily work, I have a holistic position; another member is working in a completely different department. [name 1] works close to the users at the operational level, and [name 2] has a completely different role."
Team member	"… **This team is a success factor**" … "when one of us had an obstacle, **you were not replaced by someone else. I think this is a success factor, because then you feel safe on this team.** You do not have to start with new views. We are a strong team that meet regularly, which is great" "… It is also good with **obvious things as setting up rules to respect each other's points of view and respect each other's competence.** Unfortunately, we have too often been told what to say, what

(continued)

Table 6 (continued)

Role	Quote related to success factors
	can or cannot be, but here, all that was taboo. And **if anyone ever came near that way of acting, the facilitator stopped it immediately**, which was great. Of course, these things are obvious, but it is not so in reality always. So, I think it is a success factor.". . . "Perhaps this was possible because someone was regulating it from the start. **Here, the facilitator has from the beginning been talking about and making us set rules**. It was a quite soft start but very clear focus on the rules. It is like kindergarten really, but sometimes it is needed.". . ."**We are all here for a reason. Everyone is here because of the person's competence.**"

7   Practical Implications and Future Work

The practical implications from this research mainly concern the implementation of the CIT-process. For example, innovation leaders may benefit from the results when implementing the CIT-process in their own organization, and consultants may use the results when advising or educating clients in the use of the CIT-process. Given the limited number of participating organizations in this research, further studies on the implementation of the CIT-process are suggested to increase understanding and to develop educational tools.

References

Boyatzis, R. E. (1998). *Transforming qualitative information: Thematic analysis and code development*. New York: Sage.

Chen, J., Damanpour, F., & Reilly, R. R. (2010). Understanding antecedents of new product development speed: A meta-analysis. *Journal of Operational Management, 28*, 17–33.

Cordero, R., Farris, G., & DiTomaso, N. (1998). Technical professionals in cross-functional teams: Their quality of work life. *Journal of Product Innovation Management, 15*, 550–563.

Farris, G. F. (1972). The effect of individual roles on performance in innovative groups. *R&D Management, 3*(1), 23–28.

Highsmith, J. (2009). *Agile Project Management: Creating innovative products*. Crawfordsville: Addison-Wesley.

Im, S., Montoya, M. M., & Workman, J. P. (2013). Antecedents and consequences of creativity in product innovation teams. *Journal of Product Innovation Management, 30*(1), 170–185.

Johnsson, M. (2016a). Important innovation enablers for innovation teams. In *The XXVII Innovation Conference – Blending Tomorrow's Innovation Vintage*, Porto.

Johnsson, M. (2016b). The importance of innovation enablers for innovation teams. In *The 23rd EurOMA Conference*, Trondheim, Norway, June 2016.

Johnsson, M. (2017a). Innovation enablers for innovation teams – A review. *Journal of Innovation Management, 5*(3), 75–121.

Johnsson, M. (2017b). Creating high-performing innovation teams. *Journal of Innovation Management, 5*(4), 23–47.

Johnsson, M. (2018). The facilitator, its characteristics and importance for innovation teams. *Journal of Innovation Management, 6*(2), 12–44.

Johnsson, M., Swenningsson, K., & Svensson, E. (2019). Problems when implementing innovation teams. In *The XXX Innovation Conference – Celebrating Innovation: 500 Years Since DaVinci*, Florens, Italy, 16–19 June 2019.

Kristiansen, M., & Bloch-Poulsen, J. (2010). Employee driven innovation in team (EDIT) – Innovative potential, dialogue. *International Journal of Action Research, 6*(2–3), 155–195.

McDonough, E. F., III. (2000). Investigation of factors contributing to the success of cross-functional teams. *Journal of Product Innovation Management, 17*(3), 221–235.

McGreevy, M. (2006). Team working: Part 2 – How are teams chosen and developed. *Industrial and Commercial Training, 38*(7), 365–370.

Neuman, G. A., Wagner, S. H., & Christiansen, N. D. (1999). The relationship between work team personality composition and the job performance of teams. *Group & Organization Management, 24*(1), 28–45.

Pearce, C. L., & Ensley, M. D. (2004). A reciprocal and longitudinal investigation of the innovation process: The central role of shared vision in product and process innovation teams (PPITs). *Journal of Organizational Behavior, 25*(2), 259–278.

Tidd, J., & Bessant, J. (2013). *Managing innovation – Integrating technological, market and organizational change* (5th ed.). West Sussex: Wiley.

Tuckmann, B. W., & Jensen, M. A. C. (1977). Stages of small-group development revisited. *Group and Organization Management, 2*, 419–427.

West, M., Hirst, G., Richter, A., & Shipton, H. (2004). Twelve steps to heaven: Successfully managing change through developing innovative teams. *European Journal of Work and Organizational Psychology, 13*(2), 269–299.

Wheelan, S. A. (2013). *Creating effective teams – A guide for members and leaders*. Lund: Studentlitteratur AB.

Zuidema, K. R., & Kleiner, B. H. (1994). Self-directed work groups gain popularity. *Business Credit, 96*(9), 21–26.

Mikael Johnsson is an assistant Professor at Mälardalen University, Sweden. He earned his PhD at Blekinge Institute of Technology, Sweden, in 2016, where he developed knowledge on high-performing innovation teams and factors enabling their work. During his postdoc period, he continued his research in collaboration with consultancy firms, and wrote a book on how to stepwise create high-performing innovation teams. Currently, as a senior researcher, his research is on global high-performing innovation teams and on Artificial Intelligence's (AI) effect on the research process. Aside from the academic work, Mikael is consulting as an innovation management specialist.

Ewa Svensson is the founder of Crearum and a market economist with a passion for developing people's creativity. She has extensive experience in public and private businesses, where she focuses on innovation work linked to new services, organization, marketing, and processes. Ewa has contributed to the standardization work of innovation management (ISO 56002) and also to the development of the certification process for the role of innovation leaders, and is a skilled trainer and coach for innovation skills and methods.

Kristina Swenningsson has a Master's degree in Applied physics and Electrotechnology. She has long and wide-spread experience from leading positions in mainly technology companies from small startups to companies with several hundred employees with a focus on business development, sales, and marketing in Sweden and internationally. Kristina has extensive experience as a consultant in business development and leadership with a focus on innovation ability and methods for idea development and creativity as a partner in Crearum. Kristina has participated in the work on the standard for innovation management (ISO 56002) and certification of innovation leaders, and is a skilled trainer and coach for innovation skills and methods.

Fly the Flag, How to Innovate Management Practices for the "Best in the World"

Maria Vittoria Colucci and Anna Forciniti

1   Context and Needs

Ferrari is the most famous Italian company in the world, a historic and exceptional brand. In 2020, Ferrari was awarded the second consecutive year the title of the world's strongest brand by Brand Finance, the leading international independent brand valuation and strategy consultancy. With a Brand Strength Index (BSI) score of 94.1 out of 100, Ferrari tops the list of only 12 brands to be awarded the highest AAA rating. Brand Finance measures brand strength based on the efficacy of a brand's performance on intangible measures compared to its competitors.

The "best engineers in the world" work and express their talent here. Managers express a solid technical expertise. However, the business model is changing, and moving toward greater complexity, teams grow and innovation is a constant pressure. The sector is rapidly evolving due to new emission standards, new technologies, the rise of hybrid and electric, and production processes that need to be updated due to the increased transverse nature of components. These essential changes affect the very nature of Ferrari automobiles and demand radical transformation. Internally, the company has experienced a significant change in leadership and experimented with new management approaches. The Technology Department, the beating heart of the company, is most strongly impacted by these changes. The department has also grown in size consistently, which has required a change in management style. Furthermore, managers need to make a radical change of mindset that has never before been faced by this company: their leadership can no longer rely only on technical expertise but must be integrated with the ability to manage teams and their complexity in order to allow their people to best express their talents, improve performance factors, clarify roles and responsibilities within the team and delegate effectively. In particular, it became necessary to shift the focus

M. V. Colucci (✉) · A. Forciniti
Evidentia srl, Milan, Italy
e-mail: mariavittoria.colucci@evidentia.it; anna.forciniti@evidentia.it

© The Author(s), under exclusive license to Springer Nature Switzerland AG 2021   421
D. R. A. Schallmo, J. Tidd (eds.), *Digitalization*, Management for Professionals,
https://doi.org/10.1007/978-3-030-69380-0_25

from operational excellence to innovation excellence, which was already present in the automobiles' development, but that needed to be reinforced department-wide. The legacy management system was no longer helpful, and the company required innovation.

We decided to address this challenge by acting directly on people's daily behaviours and performance factors, creating a management innovation program with a systemic logic and acting at different levels of practices: mindset, processes, day-to-day tools, and reinforcing the practices.

The program was named "Fly the Flag" to represent Ferrari's need to hold high the standard of excellence in management practices and in technological innovation.

This program is characterized by:

Engagement of the "final users" in order to understand their needs; their daily experience with the workplace setting and environment in which they carry out their jobs, performance factors of managerial work, triggers that determine a positive or negative outcome when tackling a problem and the relationships between peers, leaders, and associates. We carried out 33 interviews using the Job To Be Done approach, where internal clients indicated the changes they wanted to make but could not because there are constraints that stop them.

Involvement of all management levels into the program, not just those that were initially considered for the intervention: senior and junior managers but also the Top Management, at different stages of the process. This allowed us to intervene at different levels in the decision-making process and create conditions for true, lasting change.

Online facilitation as due to COVID-19, the last part of the program was 100% online.

2 Topics

The subject of the intervention were daily management practices:

- The scheduling and management of meetings, during which it is important to achieve the appropriate balance of involvement to guarantee the presence of all necessary competencies and promote efficacy.
- The decision-making process, which is affected by factors of complexity, speed, and technical expertise. (Ahmed and Omotunde 2012; Kahneman 2017)
- The delegating process, which requires a balance of hyper-specialization and overall vision of the automobile (including performance, design, and user experience).
- The Innovation of their management practices by finding solutions to the internal customer frictions. (Scharmer and Kaufer 2015).

3   Approach and Methodologies

The management innovation intervention followed the Design Thinking methodology (Panetti 2017). We defined the directions to work based on the needs and frictions collected from those involved and worked on implementing the change program by working on step-by-step adjustments based on feedback (Appelo 2016; Ariely 2016).

The directions identified were methods of collaboration, decision processes, and delegation mechanisms. Starting from the identification of these objectives, we worked on the system of meetings. We began making adjustments to the process based on daily observations of existing habits and the measurement of KPIs.

We began by eliminating redundancy and inefficiency, and used this new and improved system to design a meeting schedule through an iterative process. The autonomous decision-making abilities of individuals and therefore of the system improved in each successive attempt (Bote 2018).

Examples of specific methodologies used:

1. The LEGO® SERIOUS PLAY® Method is a facilitated meeting, communication, and problem-solving process in which participants are led through a series of questions, probing deeper and deeper into the subject. Each participant builds their 3D LEGO® model in response to the facilitator's questions using specially selected LEGO® elements. These 3D models serve as a basis for group discussion, knowledge sharing, problem-solving, and decision-making.
   The LEGO® SERIOUS PLAY® Method improves group problem-solving. By utilizing visual, auditory, and kinesthetic skills, the Method requires participants to learn and listen, and it provides all participants with a voice. The Method serves as a shared language regardless of culture or position.
2. Management Success Cards® is a tool focused on the needs of frantically busy managers and leaders who seek instant extreme focus learning.
   It consists of 65 colour-coded management skill development cards designed to coach managers through professional development. Each card inspires and drives people to think and act confidently, productively, and successfully. We explicitly used this tool to train the skills of delegating and providing feedback.
3. Impro
   We created a safe space for people to thrive, take chances, fail, engage in "Yes, and. . ." types of exercises, and suspend judgment and improve critical thinking.
4. Day by day improvement
   we developed sessions embedded in daily operational work: individual coaching on the job for managers and collaborators, team coaching on real working groups, and short workshops on performance factors issues. (Senge et al. 2010; Kluger and Nir 2010; Ofman 2002; Buckingham and Goodall 2019)
5. KPIs co-design
   we co-designed KPIs to measure the impact of the development program on performance (business) factors.
   Some of the KPIs we applied were:
   - # of person-hours/week planned in meetings
   - # of person-hours/week spent in meetings

- # meetings/week with the same content
- # of personal actions/month delegated based on the outcome of meetings
- Team goals reached/ Individual goals reached
- % of cases tackled using improvement actions determined

6. FORTH Innovation Method (Van Wulfen 2013)

We facilitated four online workshops using virtual boards inspired by the FORTH methodology for nine interfunctional groups in a 6-week process.

All the groups worked on the same management innovation assignment and, based on it, they formulated four innovation opportunities for each group. Then they explored trends and technologies and gathered customer frictions. In the third workshop, they brainstormed to raise ideas, then chose the best ones and transformed them into idea directions and concepts.

We ended with five new managerial solution clusters ready for implementation.

4 Lessons Learned

Identifying *business indicators* as well as objectives from the beginning.

Continuous engagement with daily activities always beginning from the experience of the "end users" and from their frictions, as this can lead to constant discoveries, including that the problems identified by the buyer do not reflect the entire picture, or are just the effect of the frictions experienced by the end-users (Singler 2019; Wiringa 2018).

We showed the value of using specific methodologies in *real workplace situations*, seeing what is happening first hand and understanding the settings in which people work, for example: where do meetings take place, how do people carry out their jobs (e.g. sitting or standing, their workspace setting).

Working in an *agile* manner, by planning interventions based on short phases made up of workshops followed by the observation of practices, to propose adjustments and changes through coaching on the job.

New rules for online facilitation:

- *Have an online mindset as* It is not enough to transfer the activities from offline to online, but It's about understanding and using all the advantages of the online. The most important is to work synchronously and asynchronously, to optimize group interactions and leave time and space for individual work.
- *Less is more*: Be simple (based on the technological skills and habits of your participants), calibrate the use of technology. The possibilities are endless even in simplicity. Of course, do not forget to give small challenges; the participants will learn new tools to give them enthusiasm and motivation.

- *Provide the human touch*: Remember that there are different learning styles, so use a mix of online methods, experiential and theoretical, emotional, and cognitive—and collaborative ways to ensure everyone gets engaged.
- *Manage Time*: Online time is completely different from live time. Always design the session with the *"accordion approach"*: consider in advance what you can jump if you are short of time and what you can add if you have spare time.

References

Ahmed, M. T., & Omotunde, H. (2012). Theories and strategies of good decision making. *International Journal of Scientific & Technology Research*.

Appelo, J. (2016). *Managing for happiness. Games, tool and practices for motivate any team*. Wiley.

Ariely, D. (2016). *Payoff. The Hidden Logic that Shapes Our Motivation*.

Bote, R. M. (2018). *Come prendiamo le decisioni? I meccanismi neurali della scelta*. Neuroscienze & Psicologia.

Buckingham, M., & Goodall, A. (2019). La trappola del feedback. *Harvard Business Review*.

Kahneman, D. (2017). *Thinking, Fast and Slow, McMillian, 2011*

Kluger, A. N, & Nir, D. (2010). The feedforwardinterview. *Human Resource Management Review*.

Ofman, D. (2002). *Core Qualities*. Scriptum.

Panetti, R. (2017). *Theory U, learning organizationse design thinking*. Franco Angeli: Strategie, strumenti e tecniche per l'innovazione profonda.

Scharmer, O., & Kaufer, K. (2015). *Leadership in un futuro che emerge. Da ego-sistema a eco-sistema: nuove economie e nuove società*. FrancoAngeli.

Senge, P. et al. (2010). *The fifth discipline handbook: Strategies and tools for building a learning organization*. London: Nicholas Brealey.

Singler, E. (2019). *Nudge management*. Pearson.

Van Wulfen, G. (2013). *The innovation expedition. A visual toolkit to start innovation*. Amsterdam: BIS Publisher.

Wiringa, A. A. (2018). *Start reverse*. Performance Solutions: Il viaggio.

Maria Vittoria Colucci, A long experience and passion for helping people and organization to evolve and innovate. I am an organizational development expert, innovation facilitator, executive counsellor, and coach. Co-founder of Evidentia (www.evidentia.it). For the past 25 years, I have been working with organizations and people to promote their development and accompany their change. My expertise is on innovation and remote facilitation, cultural and leadership innovation, people wellbeing. Graduated in Economics, Bocconi MBA, FORTH Innovation Master facilitator, Executive counsellor, and Coach. Co-cured the Italian version of the book "The Innovation Expedition" of Gijs van Wulfen. mariavittoria.colucci@evidentia.it; https://www.linkedin.com/in/mariavittoriacolucci/

Anna Forciniti, Evidentia co-founder (www.evidentia.it). Management consultant for 24 years, I like working on innovation facilitation, management, and cultural innovation by building bridges: between people and organizations, between the numbers of business and the embellishments of arts and culture. Graduated in Economics and Sustainable Development, FORTH Innovation Method Master facilitator, Executive coach WABC™. Evidentia is where I can contribute to a culture of sustainability, innovation, and social impact. Co-cured the Italian version of the book "The Innovation Expedition" of Gijs van Wulfen. anna.forciniti@evidentia.it; https://www.linkedin.com/in/annaforciniti/

Lightning Source UK Ltd.
Milton Keynes UK
UKHW020628020622
403888UK00006B/728